Understanding Adolescent Health Behaviour

A Decision Making Perspective

Kanayo Umeh

CAMBRIDGE
UNIVERSITY PRESS

CAMBRIDGE UNIVERSITY PRESS
Cambridge, New York, Melbourne, Madrid, Cape Town, Singapore, São Paulo, Delhi

Cambridge University Press
The Edinburgh Building, Cambridge CB2 8RU, UK

Published in the United States of America by Cambridge University Press, New York

www.cambridge.org
Information on this title: www.cambridge.org/9780521698023

First published 2009

Printed in the United Kingdom at the University Press, Cambridge

A catalogue record for this publication is available from the British Library

Library of Congress Cataloguing in Publication data
Umeh, Kanayo F., 1969–
Understanding adolescent health behaviour : a decision making perspective / by Kanayo F. Umeh.
    p.   cm.
Includes bibliographical references and index.
ISBN 978-0-521-87526-4
1. Risk-taking (Psychology) in adolescence.   2. Behavior disorders in adolescence.   I. Title.
RJ506.R57U64   2009
618.92′89–dc22

                                                              2008049140

ISBN 978-0-521-87526-4 hardback
ISBN 978-0-521-69802-3 paperback

To my wife and son, Oby and Oli

Books are to be returned on or before
the last date below.

Unc

Smo
teen
mak
book
iour
fresh
pow
coun
decis
by a
the t
whos

KAN
of Ps

Contents

List of figures   *page* viii
List of tables   x
List of boxes   xi
Preface   xiii
Acknowledgements   xvi

1 Introduction   1

2 Choice   40

3 Goals   67

4 Fear   94

5 Consistency   120

6 Competence   144

7 Avoidance   181

8 Impulsivity   211

9 Change   238

References   255
Index   290

Figures

1.1	Deciding to smoke	*page* 10
1.2	Prospect theory	16
1.3	The conflict-theory model	19
1.4	Gender differences	33
2.1	How universal is the concept of free will?	48
2.2	Freedom of choice	49
2.3	Free will in context	61
3.1	Goal theory	70
3.2	Priorities for the decision maker	73
3.3	Health as a goal	74
3.4	Gender differences	85
3.5	Feedback and goal attainment	88
4.1	Fear of immediate and remote threats	99
4.2	Social anxiety	100
4.3	A schematic representation of the drive reduction model	102
4.4	Fear and the proverbial anomaly	106
4.5	Impact of phobias	113
5.1	Cognitive dissonance and decision making	122
5.2	Consistency in decision making	123
5.3	Consistency in choice	125
5.4	Adherence to prior behaviour	130
5.5	Going public	133
5.6	Public commitment	135
5.7	Social desirability and consistency	137
6.1	Seeking information	148
6.2	Cognitive deliberations may drive decisions	156
6.3	The theory of compliant detraction	164
6.4	Compliant detraction	166
6.5	Healthy and unhealthy decisions	167
6.6	An illustration of compliant detraction with respect to condom use	168

7.1	Effect of thought suppression	187
7.2	Prevalence of avoidance	193
7.3	Procrastination	204
7.4	Gender differences	205
8.1	Impulsivity	213
8.2	Sensation seeking	219
8.3	A sense of doom	226
8.4	Frantic search	228
8.5	Effect of panic on choice	232
9.1	Group change	242
9.2	Individual change and continuity	244
9.3	Prior experience and resistance to change	251

Tables

1.1 What teenagers consider when deciding whether to use
    condoms during sexual intercourse   *page* 35

3.1 Reasons given by adolescents for selected health behaviours   78

4.1 Teenagers associate different levels of fear with each decision
    option   106

7.1 Some forms of avoidance utilised by teenagers in response to
    health related problems, based on selected studies   185

7.2 Health problems and worst case scenarios that may be used
    to justify inaction   191

Boxes

1.1 Media spotlight: opportunity and adult misconduct *page* 6
1.2 Contextual issues: the Fundamental Attribution Error 8
1.3 Research spotlight: the Myers Briggs Type Indicator 32
2.1 Media spotlight: power/status effects on free will 45
2.2 Media spotlight: free will and economic constraints 51
2.3 Media spotlight: free will in Western culture 55
2.4 Research spotlight: maximising choice 57
2.5 Contextual issues: social constraints on free will 60
3.1 Research spotlight: does feedback facilitate goal attainment? 87
3.2 Contextual issues: intrinsic goals and activity type 90
4.1 Media spotlight: fear references in teenage magazines 97
4.2 Research spotlight: the effect of reassurance 104
4.3 Research spotlight: does fear impair good decision making? 112
4.4 Contextual issues: situational interpretation of fear 116
5.1 Research spotlight: minimising personal control to explain inconsistency 139
6.1 Research spotlight: are competent decision makers more reasonable? 158
7.1 Contextual issues: do family circumstances negate avoidance? 196
7.2 Research spotlight: does avoidance hamper competence? 199
7.3 Media spotlight: ignoring signs of illness 207
8.1 Media spotlight: impulsivity in emergency situations 215
8.2 Media spotlight: panic in response to a traffic incident 223
8.3 Research spotlight: are panic-prone teenagers less sensible? 231
8.4 Media spotlight: when peers provoke impulsive choice 235

Preface

I won't pretend writing this book was easy. It wasn't. Yet, I find the concept behind it even more intriguing now it's finished than when I first started writing.

A few days before submitting an initial draft of the manuscript to my publisher I observed several teenagers climbing precariously over a spiked iron fence just outside my home. The threat of injury was considerable. Yet, these youngsters complacently went about their reckless endeavours, seemingly oblivious to the risks. Scenes like this are common worldwide. They fuel a stereotype of teenagers as thoughtless, impulsive risk takers, and raise numerous questions about the soundness of their decision making. Did they stop to think about potential hazards before acting? Do risks matter? Or is conforming to the peer group activity more important? Even if risks are considered, would this be sufficient to dissuade such unhealthy behaviour? Such scenes provide the impetus for books like this one.

When I began writing this book I was determined that it would not end up being yet another conventional text on adolescent health behaviour, one which merely documents the results of endless health behaviour or lifestyle surveys, often leaving readers rather more bewildered at the end than they were before reading the text. It was not my intention to write a book that merely offers a repackage of familiar products. Similarly, I had no desire to serve up the usual cocktail of explanations for adolescents' behaviours, such as peer pressure, self-centredness, parental influence, self-esteem issues, delinquency, hostility, depression, identity, coping, parent–child conflict, and so on. Books that cover these issues are abundant – almost any academic bookshop will have them – so it would be silly to publish yet another text that simply reinvents the wheel.

The primary focus here is on decision making, whether as a momentary act or as a protracted process, a deliberate manoeuvre or a subconscious event. Human beings, many philosophers argue, exercise free will. They retain freedom of choice irrespective of personal and situational forces acting upon them. Familiar phrases or questions like 'Look before you leap', 'If your friends jumped off a cliff, would you jump with them?' and 'It's a no-brainer' all denote an ingrained belief in Western culture that, whatever the circumstances, a person can choose freely from alternative courses of action. Thus, for example, criminals are berated for making wrong lifestyle choices, often with little regard for any adverse childhood experiences, or current social deprivation.

The method by which people exercise their free will – in other words, how they arrive at decisions – can be crucial in understanding their actions. Thus, for

example, a boy who acts on impulse may be more susceptible to peer pressure than his friend who usually pauses to contemplate his options before acting. Similarly, a girl who habitually puts off difficult decisions may be slower to abandon a risky behaviour than another panic-prone youngster stricken by a perpetual sense of impending doom, and in a hurry to take protective action.

This argument can also be appreciated in the context of a reckless teenage driver with a car loaded with friends. Many factors may affect the driver's performance in manoeuvring the vehicle, including the opinions of the passengers, their relationship with the driver, the driver's self-confidence and mental health, and even physical or climatic factors such as interior temperature, humidity and lighting. But if a behavioural scientist wishes to understand why the car is being driven recklessly, he has two options. He can either study the personal and situational factors acting on the driver, such as peer pressure, or he can scrutinise the driver's decision making. For example, does he appear to think before acting, react impulsively to changing road conditions, and/or deliberately ignore road hazards when deciding how fast to go?

If there is an accident, the police will be particularly interested in the driver's decision making. Although it may turn out that the passengers were goading the driver to speed, the police will want to know why the driver allowed such pressure to affect his judgement, negating considerations of health and safety. Focusing solely on how personal and situational factors such as peer pressure, self-esteem and parental factors influence adolescent health behaviour only provides a partial account of events. It can be argued that these variables are mediated by free will. That is, they can only affect behaviour to the extent that an individual allows them to. A competent decision maker may try to remain careful and objective, irrespective of the circumstances, whereas an incompetent decision maker may allow his thinking to be skewed by outside influences.

This book is targeted mainly at behavioural science academics, scholars and students, although it wouldn't surprise me if the odd teenager finds it interesting. I have tried to eschew psychological jargon, where possible, but ultimately some background in psychology or social science may facilitate understanding. Psychologists have become so engrossed in their own theories and research that they have developed a rather flamboyant language of their own – what many people refer to as 'psychobabble'. This vernacular often makes little sense to anyone except psychologists themselves. However, this situation is by no means peculiar to psychology – medicine for instance is notorious for its 'big' words, as can clearly be heard in medical dramas. Jargon makes simple and interesting phenomena appear abstract and unwieldy to the untrained (and occasionally trained) eye.

By minimising fancy academic lingo, where possible, I believe it is possible to write an interesting textbook that is enjoyable to read. Whether I have achieved this goal is up to the readers to judge. It is fair to say that I have used jargon many times in this book, and unavoidably so, to capture accurately the psychological meaning of many an argument. If there are areas in which this proves an irritation

to the reader, then I apologise in advance, but suggest that the disappointed reader take the philosophical view that breaking the habit of a lifetime is unlikely to be an entirely successful affair. I always prefer reading psychology written in the style of a newspaper article: a succinct heading, simple terms, and a concision and clarity that your average person on the street can understand. Unfortunately this is not the way most psychologists are trained to write. Thus writing a book that attempts to eschew jargon can be a particularly trying affair for many psychologists, myself included.

Initially I had wanted this book to be based almost entirely on scientific evidence and reasoning, particularly evidence derived from traditional randomised scientific experiments (in which control, placebo and treatment groups are compared on some measure) and, to a lesser degree, semi-experimental field studies (no randomisation) and correlational studies (questionnaire surveys). However, any academic who appreciates qualitative research will concede that some of the best scientific data come in the form of personal experience, anecdotes, intuitions and impressions. While this kind of evidence is less reliable, it is typically more realistic, providing a better depiction of everyday life. Thus, many arguments in the book are based on just this type of 'evidence', and I make no apologies. I also read a lot of correspondence sent by adolescents to various Internet websites, and magazines, plus newspaper accounts of teenage activity in my local community here in Liverpool, England, not to mention the odd teenage biography. Traditional scientific evidence on decision making and health behaviour in adolescence is so limited that reliance on other forms of literature is unavoidable.

Finally, this book steers clear of mathematical or economic accounts of decision making. While these perspectives have their academic merits (which are considerable), they are incompatible with the basic theme of this text, which is about behavioural descriptions of decision making, rather than arithmetical permutations. In my view numerical and exact models lack realism. They are just too orderly, precise and predictable to capture adequately the nonsensicality, instability and unpredictability of human decision making. These accounts often denote a kind of 'uncorrupted' and 'mechanical' rationality that simply isn't within the realm of messy real-life human decision making.

I'm sure this view may be controversial with some readers. But such controversy may be a good thing, helping to inform our understanding of teenage health behaviour. All in all, my hope is that this book shows another 'side' to the adolescent decision maker that perhaps was previously hidden from view, or simply ignored, or forgotten. Whether I have achieved this will be up to the readership to judge.

Acknowledgements

This book was largely inspired by my doctoral thesis, written at the University of Leicester, England, during the 1990s, under the supervision of Dr Gillian Penny and Dr Jim Robinson. I wish to extend my profound thanks to almost one thousand teenagers who volunteered as subjects, most of whom will now be in their mid to late twenties, and making decisions in ways that are probably beyond the scope of this book.

Much of my doctoral research was inspired by the pioneering work of Professor Leon Mann, and in particular his colleague, the late Professor Irving Janis. Their writings on human decision making span several decades and, for a starry eyed novice PhD student utterly bewildered by the overly geometric, abstract and often chaotic literature on decision making, provided a much needed breath of fresh air, and a realism, combined with a strong sense of 'hmm, this sounds like how I make decisions' that is rarely found in the literature. I was also enthused by the efforts of Professor Howard Leventhal, who has shed considerable light on the notion of decision making, not just as goal directed behaviour, but also as a dynamic process. Elliot Aronson's writings in social psychology have also been an inspiration. Although he is not a decision theorist specifically, his simple, down to earth and concise way of explaining otherwise complex psychological phenomena made me better appreciate the importance of eschewing unnecessary jargon in academic expression.

I am very much indebted to numerous teenagers for making themselves available for a chat, even though I'm sure they had more exciting things to do with their time. These include Lorraine Omari-Asor, Aishia Mills, Abbi Igwemma, Lindsay Rogers, and many others. Sincere thanks to Cambridge University Press for 'getting' the philosophy behind this book, and supporting it even when I wasn't always entirely sure what specific arguments would evolve, their content, and how long the manuscript would take to complete. In particular, thanks to Andrew Peart and Carrie Cheek for their patience and support.

Finally, a book like this would clearly have been impossible to write without the patient support of my wife Oby. She had to endure almost three years of books, journal articles and other documents littering the house untidily, and my long hours spent locked away in the university library, not to mention regular discussions about teenagers, teenage movies and magazines, and numerous other

subjects pertaining to this special group of humans. Her superbly cooked meals, warmth and understanding spurred me on in a way she may never realise. God bless her. Then there is my little son, Olisa, who is pure entertainment, and a bundle of joy that has changed my life forever. He kept me company for weeks on end, generating continuous laughter, and keeping me awake long enough to type away into the night, until the work was finished.

1 Introduction

Learning outcomes

By the end of this chapter readers should have a better understanding of the following:

1 the meaning and definition of decision making
2 key models used to describe and explain decision making
3 the nature of health behaviour and its various dimensions
4 the definition of adolescence and the unique features that typify adolescent decision making
5 theoretical and empirical arguments for the importance of decision making in understanding adolescents' health behaviour
6 how this book fits in with wider professional psychology.

Chapter summary

This chapter considers the meaning of the term 'decision making', and how this construct can inform our understanding of adolescent health behaviour. Decision making is considered both as an elaborate process, with several stages, and as a single momentary event. The distinction is made between rational or competent choice, and biased or simplistic problem solving strategies. The chapter describes key models of decision making, highlighting the importance of certainty, the probability and value of potential outcomes, and people's preferred decision making styles. The concept of health behaviour is introduced and defined, highlighting the distinction between sick role, illness and health behaviour. Adolescent decision making is described as multifaceted, incorporating both competent and defective strategies, with potentially significant implications for a variety of health behaviours. The chapter concludes with a discussion of the relevance of this book as a supplementary text in professional psychology.

Chapter outline

I begin this chapter by introducing the concept of decision making, with its inherent ambiguities and multidimensionality. Next I discuss some key decision making theories, with particular emphasis on the conflict-theory model. The concept of health behaviour is defined, followed by a definition of adolescence. I look at the nature of decision making in adolescence, reviewing selected studies from the literature. This chapter concludes with some discussion of the relevance of this book to academic subjects in professional psychology.

What is decision making?

A teenage boy finally throws away all his cigarettes and gives up smoking for good, after months of 'trying to quit'. A plump schoolgirl makes a snap decision to go on a diet after being teased by some other girls in her class. An adolescent diagnosed with kidney failure agrees to undergo a kidney transplant after detailed consultations with his parents and doctor.

The notion of decision making is such a familiar and ubiquitous concept to almost anyone with a basic education (and many without), regardless of culture, that its meaning and definition should be fairly obvious. Yet the reality is that, in psychology at least, this is far from the case.

Problematic definition

Like many other psychological phenomena (e.g. personality), there is no universally accepted definition of human decision making to be found in psychology textbooks and journal articles. Some psychologists describe decision making as a process, unfolding gradually over time, through a series of steps (e.g. Janis and Mann, 1977; Prochaska *et al.*, 1994). Others portray it as a single static event, in which various emotions, thoughts, and other personal and situational factors combine simultaneously to determine a person's choice (Rogers, 1975, 1983; Ajzen, 1980, 1991).

Part of the problem in defining human decision making is that it is not solely a psychological phenomenon. For example, a decision to cut down on alcohol consumption can be understood from both psychological and economic perspectives.

A psychologist would view the decision as the outcome of a complex interplay between psychological mechanisms, such as stress, personality, cognitions, emotions and previous behaviour. An economist by contrast is likely to see things in terms of financial cost–benefit considerations.

Thus, even if psychologists could agree on a definition of decision making, this characterisation is likely to be considered narrow and inadequate by economists and professionals from other social sciences.

Another problem encountered in defining decision making is that it is a complex and multifaceted phenomenon that can be difficult to recognise, and may vary across individuals and situations.

For example, two youths might make a decision to quit smoking. Yet, their decisions may vary widely in terms of the number and type of options considered (none, several, thousands), the number of other people consulted for advice (e.g. one, several, thousands), and their relationship to the decision maker (friends, family, doctor), the amount of time it took to arrive at a decision (e.g. several years or a split second), what triggered the decision in the first place (e.g. a threat, a challenge or nothing in particular), and how quickly the decision is implemented (e.g. immediately, several weeks later).

To make matters worse, it may not always be obvious to observers that a decision was made, especially if the commitment wasn't made public. Even the decision maker may not have made a conscious choice to quit smoking, but rather simply 'drifted' into this position with barely any deliberate thought at all.

One decision maker may be driven entirely by emotion while another might base her choice solely on logic, or even arithmetic. Furthermore, the way any one individual makes decisions may vary widely across different scenarios or situations. For example, a boy who is careful and considered when there is a lot at stake (e.g. a serious threat of death or disease) may become impulsive and thoughtless in less urgent situations (e.g. considering what toothpaste to use).

In view of these complexities, several competing accounts of decision making have emerged over the years in psychology. One of the most notable debates concerns whether decision making is a process, unfolding gradually through a series of stages, or merely a single momentary event that occurs at a particular point in time. Another debate concerns whether decisions are inherently rationalistic, biased and/or a matter of simplistic rules of thumb.

Let's consider each of these issues.

Decision making as a process

The idea here is simple. People arrive at decisions through a series of stages or steps, which typically unfold over a discernible period of time (Janis and Mann, 1976, 1977, 1982; Janis, 1983, 1984, 1986; Prochaska and Velicer, 1997; Byrnes, 2002). Failure to progress successfully through all the stages, for example owing to intellectual limitations, stress and other impediments, generally impairs the quality of the final decision.

Proponents of this idea general identify an initial stage when the need for a decision becomes apparent, followed by several stages during which the decision maker clarifies what he or she is trying to achieve (i.e. sets goals), searches for and evaluates the available options, makes a commitment, and then proceeds to implement it.

There appear to be three basic steps, based on existing behavioural science literature (e.g. Janis and Mann, 1976, 1977; Friedman, 1996; Byrnes, 2002): recognising

a problem and setting goals; deliberating about possible solutions; and making a commitment.

Problem recognition and goal setting. The individual becomes aware of a development that necessitates a decision. For example, a teenage smoker may start contemplating giving up cigarettes after developing a respiratory infection. He decides what his priorities or goals are (e.g. protecting his health, looking good, impressing friends), and sets about pursuing them.

Mental deliberation. The decision maker surveys his options and evaluates their various costs and benefits. He may browse the Internet for information, seek advice from significant others, and reflect on previous experiences that may be relevant. The objective here is to identify the best option, the one that stands the best chance of achieving his goal(s).

Commitment and implementation. The person makes his choice, and starts to implement it. He may communicate his decision to significant others, and make tangible preparations to execute his decision. For example, a smoker who has decided to quit may announce his plans to friends, throw away all his cigarettes, and join a local smoking cessation support group.

Implicit in this view of decision making is the notion of rationality (Edwards, 1961), the idea that people weigh up various pros and cons in a logical manner, and then select any option that best maximises their potential gains and/or minimises possible losses.

Decision making as an event

One school of thought views decision making as a single event, occurring at a specific moment. The key distinguishing feature of this approach is the absence of stages or steps of decision making. Essentially, decisions simply occur as in one step. Various models used by health psychologists to explain risk behaviours, such as the health belief model (Rosenstock, 1974), protection motivation theory (Rogers, 1975, 1983) and the theory of planned behaviour (Ajzen, 1980) all epitomise this view of decision making.

These models identify various thoughts, emotions and other psychological conditions that may lead to a healthy or unhealthy choice (e.g. to carry on smoking or quit), with no particular reference to stages of decision making.

For example, widely used frameworks such as the health belief model (Janz and Becker, 1984) and protection motivation theory (Rogers, 1983) propose that beliefs about the seriousness of a threat, one's vulnerability to the threat, and the benefits or efficacy of recommended preventive action, instantaneously affect a person's motivation to adopt health protective behaviours.

Decisions are assumed to 'happen' once various psychological influences have been brought to bear on the individual. So, for example, a person may decide to go on a diet once he develops a favourable attitude towards dieting, or forms an intention to do so (Ajzen, 1991). No protracted time sequence is imposed, or even suggested, by these models.

Casual observation of everyday decision making would lend some credence to this view of decision making. Think about the last few decisions you made this morning. Were they all protracted and deliberative or snap on-the-spot judgements? Chances are that, for most readers, many daily decisions amount to momentary assertions, lasting seconds or just a few minutes.

The concept of rationality

Until very recently human decision making was traditionally viewed as an essentially rationalistic affair. In other words, decisions were based on careful and objective evaluation of the costs and benefits of alternative courses of action. People typically made decisions that offered the maximum benefit and/or entailed the fewest costs, compared with the competing decision alternatives.

This rather self-serving view of humanity became established in the early part of the twentieth century, inspired by the works of social philosophers such as Lewin (1951) and Edwards (1961). Kurt Lewin's influence is especially noteworthy. He developed a theory designed to demonstrate how organisational change occurs. Change according to Lewin occurs in a 'force field' that contains both restraining and facilitating forces.

The restraining factors comprise various barriers that impede change, such as habit, financial expense and various hassles: these are the costs of change. Facilitating forces comprise factors that propel change, such as wage increases, customer satisfaction, and profit: these are the perceived benefits of change.

Restraining and facilitating factors correspond to perceived costs and benefits. In rational decision making the priority is to select the least costly and/or most beneficial option. The decision maker is thoughtful, calm and deliberative, and makes every effort to obtain all the relevant information and advice, before a commitment is made.

It should come as no surprise to many readers that this view of decision making, albeit sensible and applicable in many real-life scenarios, is by no means universally accepted. Critiques raise a number of important concerns, perhaps the most notable of which is deadline pressure (Janis and Mann, 1977). Making decisions in a careful step-by-step manner requires time, and this is often in short supply in many everyday situations.

Consider a teenager who is offered a cigarette by a friend. In reality he has only seconds or minutes to respond before the opportunity is missed or withdrawn (e.g. the cigarette is offered to someone else, or consumed by the friend). A schoolboy trying to cross a busy road has to make his move at some point, or risk getting to school late. A youth with a headache can't delay taking medication for too long otherwise the symptoms may get worse. A pregnant girl in labour who experiences acute foetal distress has to decide quickly whether to have a caesarean section. Similarly the driver of a vehicle faced with a traffic emergency, such as imminent collision, has only seconds to act. In any of these scenarios, prolonged decision making is unrealistic. In all these scenarios a decision is required soon, with little or no time for protracted thinking and information seeking.

Another criticism is that step-by-step accounts of decision making are simply too tidy, too orderly, to reflect accurately the disarray of everyday decision making. In the real world things are often chaotic, haphazard and disorganised, with no readily discernible steps or sequences. For example, one event (e.g. death of a relative) may trigger several different decisions, all of which are processed at the same time. Furthermore, a decision once made may be reversed, altered or abandoned, several times over, in just a few minutes (imagine the decisions made by football players during a fast-moving match).

Even without these limitations, the idea of human rationality is always questionable. Do people really think in a logical and sensible manner, even if they have all the time in the world? Many theorists think not. Distinguished psychologist Jean Piaget pointed out that children do not achieve the ability for rational thought until their early teens, and even then this ability remains underdeveloped for several years (Piaget, 1954, 1956). Adults sometimes require a college or university education in order to understand the basic tenets of rational thought.

Even if people can think rationally they may have no desire to. Stress, laziness, indifference, sentimentality, habit, politics and many other factors may easily discourage a person from thinking logically (Petty and Cacioppo, 1986). For example, if an educated and capable politician believes that a rational decision on some aspect of health care policy is likely to lose her votes at the next election, she is unlikely to make such a decision.

Box 1.1 Media spotlight: opportunity and adult misconduct

Why do teenagers engage in risky health behaviours, for example cigarette smoking? One reason is that they can! In other words, they have the opportunity to indulge in such activity. Thus, teenagers smoke because they have access to cigarettes.

The options available to teenagers during decision making are a major factor in determining how they will behave. Risky behaviours are more likely to occur if these are available as viable options. Furthermore, wider society in general may play a huge part in presenting risky behaviour's viable options.

I came across a newspaper article that highlighted this argument (see *Daily Post*, 30 October 2007). A 15-year-old girl was recruited by local authorities in the north-west of England, to visit up to fourteen shops asking to buy a pack of twenty cigarettes. Until recently it had been illegal for shops to sell cigarettes to anyone aged under 16. A few weeks previously this minimum legal age had been raised to 18.

Nevertheless, despite the legal constraints clearly designed to deny younger teenagers access to cigarettes, eliminating smoking as a practicable option, the vast majority of shops agreed to sell cigarettes to the girl.

By offering to sell her cigarettes these shops had effectively created the opportunity to smoke. Smoking was now a feasible option that the girl, as a decision maker, could weigh against the obvious (and often less attractive) alternative of not smoking.

Bias in decision making

Human beings are subjective. Our thinking, reasoning, feelings and actions are slanted and prejudiced in a variety of ways that reflect our own personal preferences, motives and desires. Thus, it follows that any decision we make would at least in part be skewed by these very biases.

The idea of subjectivity in decision making is not new; even rationalistic accounts of decision making recognise this factor (e.g. Janis and Mann, 1976, 1977). Psychological literature contains numerous references to various biases that could, potentially, influence choice (see reviews by Eiser, 1988; Eagly and Chaiken, 1993).

Bias often occurs in the use of personal 'rules of thumb', better known as heuristics (discussed below). However, two other prominent forms of bias particularly associated with decision making are social desirability (Helmes and Holden, 2003) and defensive avoidance (Krohne, 1993).

Social desirability refers to the tendency most people have to portray themselves in a favourable light, especially in public. Thus, when making a decision, it is often far more important to look good (e.g. cool, intelligent, competent, consistent, tough, insightful, clever, mature, and so on) than to reason objectively. So, for example, teenagers often succumb to peer pressure to smoke cigarettes because it is more important for them to impress peers, rather than protect their health (clearly the more sensible goal).

Defensive avoidance is a highly ubiquitous and endemic form of decision making, whereby the decision maker is more preoccupied with reducing stress, rather than making a good decision. It can take various forms, including avoiding disturbing thoughts or stimuli, underestimating personal susceptibility to risk, and shifting decision making responsibility to others (Shinnerer, 2001; Field *et al.*, 2007; Prosser *et al.*, 2007).

For example, faced with the option of continuing to drink alcohol or quitting, many alcoholics routinely opt to keep drinking, simply because they'd rather avoid the severe withdrawal symptoms associated with giving up their addiction. People regularly delay important decisions, defer responsibility to others or simply make the wrong choice, all in a desperate bid to avoid anxiety. Defensive avoidance is discussed in much greater depth later on in this book.

Can people overcome such subjective influences when making decisions? Casual observation and anecdotal evidence would suggest that, with a sufficient degree of education, and intellectual maturity, it is possible to minimise one's biases, if not eliminate them altogether. However, as will be seen in the final chapter of this book, people in general, and adolescents in particular, rarely change their decision making habits over time. Decision making does seem to improve with age (e.g. Mann *et al.*, 1989; Ormond *et al.*, 1991; Petersen and Leffert, 1995), suggesting that any biases may gradually diminish as adulthood approaches.

Box 1.2 Contextual issues: the Fundamental Attribution Error

In my view one of the most important concepts in psychology is what social psychologists term the Fundamental Attribution Error (FAE) (Brehm *et al.*, 1999). Essentially, this refers to mistakes of underestimating the impact of situational factors in a person's behaviour, and overestimating the role of their personality.

For example, the driver of a speeding car is more likely to be seen as a 'bad' or 'reckless' person, rather than a good driver who may be rushing to hospital to see his dying mother, or a doctor on his way to attend a critically ill patient.

One reason people commit the FAE is that situational factors are rarely obvious to the observer, so it becomes almost instinctive to blame an individual's nature. Regardless, in any discussion of decision making, it is vitally important always to bear in mind that decisions aren't made in a vacuum. There is always a context, notably in terms of social, economic, political, cultural and environmental factors. These variables can have a significant impact on the proceedings. For example, teenagers trying to decide whether or not to become sexually active are often heavily swayed by opinions of other teenagers, particularly their friends.

Assuming decision making is rational, this social context helps define what options and outcomes will be considered. For example, an adolescent whose peer group is entirely sexually active, and proud to be, may anticipate a certain degree of mockery from peers should he choose to abstain from sexual activity. This potential social drawback can be critical in determining what decision will be made.

Let's now consider bias that takes the form of short cuts, or simplistic rules of thumb.

Short cuts

Decision making can be a complex activity. Even the most trivial decisions, such as determining which DVD to rent from a video club, or where to go on holiday, can be difficult to make. There are often numerous options to consider, each with a lengthy list of potential costs and benefits, with varying degrees of certainty.

Typically it isn't entirely clear what the options or potential outcomes are, or where and how to obtain further information and advice (Byrnes, 2002). Thus, even the most intellectually gifted adolescents can find themselves completely flummoxed and bogged down trying to find solutions to seemingly intractable problems. Not surprisingly, therefore, people actively look for ways to simplify decision making, so that it is quick and effortless.

One way they do this is by relying on heuristics, according to renowned psychologists Amos Tversky and Daniel Kahneman. A heuristic is a simplistic rule of thumb that enables a person to come to a swift judgement, especially when faced with a difficult or complicated problem (Kahneman and Tversky, 1973). For

example, a common heuristic many people employ when faced with an emergency situation that requires quick thinking is to simply do what others around them are doing. Another is to act on the basis of 'gut instinct'.

Several commonly used heuristics are:

- representativeness (judging based on comparability, 'like goes with like')
- availability (deciding based on what one can remember easily)
- anchoring (deciding in relation to a reference point, a familiar position)
- effort (doing whatever entails the least/greatest amount of effort)
- familiarity (choosing whatever option is most familiar)
- emotion (doing whatever makes one feel good)
- scarcity (selecting something because it is rare)
- attractiveness (accepting a recommendation if the source is attractive).

The first three heuristics are perhaps the best known. The representativeness heuristic entails making a decision based on similarity. People infer that what applies in one situation necessarily applies in another, simply because the two situations are comparable. Consider a youth who chooses to smoke because previous smoking failed to produce any health problems. He compares current and previous smoking, and reasons that since no health problems emerged previously, nothing bad is likely to emerge now.

Anchoring occurs where decisions are based on a person's initial position or 'anchor': typically the decision is biased towards the anchor. For example, someone who smokes five cigarettes per day may find quitting a more viable option than a person who smokes fifty cigarettes daily. This is because smoking no cigarettes is 'closer' to the first person's initial position. Similarly, a woman will more readily agree to attend a breast cancer screening session at her local hospital if she has a family history of breast cancer than if she does not. Thus, her initial position – having a family history of cancer – is key in determining whether or not she opts to screen, and makes the decision easy to reach.

The availability heuristic refers to the tendency for people to make decisions based on what they can most easily remember or imagine. For example, in deciding whether to have a caesarean section or a 'natural' birth, a woman in labour may promptly opt for the latter because this method more easily comes to mind, based on memories of a previous pregnancy.

Other ways to simplify decisions include going for an option that involves the least amount of effort (e.g. opting to keep drinking alcohol simply because this is much easier than abstaining, regardless of the inherent health risks), makes one feel good (e.g. choosing to eat fatty foods over healthier vegetables because one 'likes' the former) or looks most attractive (e.g. buying an expensive car because it looks good, rather than a more economical but uglier alternative).

Overall heuristics are inescapable realities of everyday decision making. Indeed it can be argued that the majority of our decisions are heuristics based. We

routinely cut corners and ignore relevant details, simply to reach decisions quickly and with minimal effort.

Sometimes there are practical reasons that make reliance on heuristics inevitable. The most notable of these is lack of time (Janis and Mann, 1977). Faced with severe deadline pressure, such as a fast-approaching danger or emergency that needs to be averted quickly (e.g. speeding vehicle, approaching tornado, severe chest pains indicating an imminent heart attack), there simply isn't the time to calmly and thoroughly review all the options, and reach an informed decision.

In such situations, reliance on heuristics may actually help save lives. For example, when someone has been badly injured in a car accident, rushing her to hospital is what immediately comes to mind (the availability heuristic), and is also the most sensible thing to do. Spending valuable time thinking about all the possible alternatives (e.g. staying put, going to hospital or calling a doctor to the scene) could be useful on occasion, but very easily lead to loss of life.

1.1 *Deciding to smoke. This decision may be the end result of hours, weeks, months or even years of careful thought, or the application of a simple rule of thumb, such as 'Do it if it feels good!' (Source: SXC).*

Models of decision making

Textbooks in health psychology are awash with various health behaviour models, theoretic frameworks that purportedly 'explain' people's lifestyle choices (e.g. Ogden, 2000; Marks *et al.*, 2005; Morrison and Bennett, 2006). Typically, these frameworks identify various cost–benefit appraisals that influence people's decisions (e.g. Rosenstock, 1974; Rogers, 1975, 1983; Ajzen, 1991).

However, research has shown that people arrive at decisions in a variety of ways, besides just weighing up pros and cons (e.g. Janis and Mann, 1976, 1977; Friedman *et al.*, 1996; Mann *et al.*, 1997, 1998; Tuinstra *et al.*, 2000). For example, they may act on impulse, panic or shift responsibility to someone else. Thus, health behaviour models are one-dimensional, and hence severely limited, because they assume only one particular decision making strategy, and even then merely list key variables, rather than describe the decision making process. For these reasons such frameworks cannot be considered full-fledged models of decision making.

Traditional decision models at the very least describe decision making, whether as a solely cognitive or rationalistic activity, or as a multidimensional event incorporating several varied decision making styles. These theories can be grouped into mathematical and descriptive models.

I will describe two mathematical models and one descriptive framework that appear to have had considerable influence on our understanding of decision making, especially within a health related context, or at least in situations involving risk. These theories are subjective expected utility theory (Edwards, 1961), prospect theory (Kahneman and Tversky, 1979), and the conflict-theory model and decisional balance (Janis and Mann, 1976, 1977).

Since decision making is about change (i.e. adopting a new course of action) it makes sense also to consider models of behaviour change. One very prominent framework widely applied to health behaviour, and hence worthy of discussion here, is the transtheoretical model of behaviour change (Prochaska and Velicer, 1997).

Subjective expected utility

Imagine a high school student who is faced with a choice between two brands of cigarettes, G and H. Although smoking either brand could result in lung cancer, Brand G has been known to cause a particularly aggressive form of the disease. Furthermore, about 10 per cent of people who smoke this brand get lung cancer, whereas only 3 per cent of Brand H smokers suffer the same fate.

Which brand will she choose? According to subjective expected utility (SEU) theory she will select Brand H. How so? Well, this model posits that people faced with a choice between two options will consider the consequences of each. In particular, they will estimate the importance or value attached to each outcome (e.g. is it something desired or despised?), and its likelihood of occurrence (e.g. is it guaranteed to happen, or merely a remote possibility?).

In essence a decision maker weighs the importance and probabilities of perceived costs and benefits, in determining which option to choose. This is the essence of SEU theory, originally proposed by Leonard Jimmie Savage, in the mid 1950s.

The model can be summarised by the following equation:

$$\sum v(O1), p(O1)$$

where v stands for the value or importance attached to each outcome (O). This value may be negative (i.e. a cost) or positive (i.e. a benefit). Note that the higher or lower the value, the more extreme or intense the value attached; p denotes the probability of each outcome.

The product of values and probabilities for all potential outcomes is summed for each option. The alternative most likely to be chosen is the one that offers the greatest subjective expected utility, that is, the most positive outcomes with the greatest certainty.

It goes without saying that this overly mathematical and predictable view of human decision making is highly questionable. Do people really perform this complex arithmetic (consciously or unconsciously) when making real-life decisions? There is limited evidence that they do.

Studies have shown that SEU and other models based on this formulation (e.g. the health belief model, theory of planned behaviour) account for a very limited percentage of the variance in decision making, sometimes less than a third of the variation (see reviews by Janz and Becker, 1984; Eagly and Chaiken, 1993; Milne *et al.*, 2000).

Most readers, I'm sure, will struggle to recall any recent decisions that entailed this complicated intellectual dance, especially decisions made under stress or severe time constraints, or in the face of various distractions. Yet, there is evidence that SEU theory has some applicability to adolescent health behaviour (e.g. Bauman *et al.*, 1985; Gilbert *et al.*, 1986; Hine *et al.*, 2002; Kuther, 2002).

A study by Hine *et al.* (2002) demonstrated the explanatory value of this framework with respect to teenage smoking. They found that social factors such as smoking by friends and family, as well as current cigarette use, predicted future smoking, but only indirectly, by influencing probability estimates of the emotional benefits of smoking. For example, teenagers who currently smoked, and had friends who smoked, believed that smoking was more likely to help them deal with stress, compared with adolescents who didn't smoke and were less exposed to smokers. In turn, the more probable this emotional benefit was judged to be, the greater the likelihood of future smoking.

Despite evidence like this, some theorists see SEU as a flawed theory. One problem is that it doesn't account for people's attitudes towards certainty and uncertainty. For example, regardless of value, people may prefer certain outcomes over merely probable ones, and will readily shy away from an uncertain gain even if it is high valued (Nau, 2006)! Many adolescents, for instance, aren't impressed by information about the health benefits of not smoking, largely because this

outcome is merely probable, not certain (there is no guarantee that a non-smoker will live significantly longer than a smoker). This type of argument forms the basis for what's known as prospect theory, which is discussed in the next section.

Another problem is that SEU views decision making as a largely intellectual exercise, and makes little reference to emotion[1] (Welch, 2006). Given that adolescence is often typified by strong emotional experiences, in view of the developmental and transitional changes that occur during this period (Petersen and Leffert, 1995), SEU may ultimately have very limited applicability in adolescents' daily decisions.

In recent times there has been a growing acceptance in health psychology that overly rationalistic accounts of decision making do not accurately depict what happens in the real world, especially with regard to children and adolescents, whose intellectual abilities may not be fully developed (Ogden, 2000; Umeh, 2002; Morrison and Bennett, 2006).

Prospect theory

People sometimes make seemingly irrational decisions, for example selecting an option that entails greater risks compared with the alternative. Why do smokers opt to smoke despite recognising the potential health risks? Why would a cancer patient choose a modestly effective treatment procedure over a more potent one?

These seemingly 'stupid' decisions aren't adequately explained by SEU theory. For example, people still opt to smoke despite the increased probability of negative health outcomes. Assuming that all other potential outcomes are equal for both alternatives, deciding to smoke does indeed seem like an unreasonable choice. How can this anomaly be explained?

Developed by Kahneman and Tversky (1979), prospect theory was designed to address the shortcomings of SEU theory. It offers an intriguing account of risky decision making. Central to this formulation is the concept of certainty. People purportedly have different attitudes towards certainty and uncertainty, and this can distort an otherwise rational decision making process.

Decision making purportedly occurs in two phases: framing and evaluation.

Framing

The way options are 'framed' (i.e. are presented or appear to the individual) helps determine which alternatives are deemed tenable or impractical.

For example, a cancer patient who can't afford expensive chemotherapy will effectively rule this out as an option. Thus, chemotherapy 'framed' within an

---

[1] Emotion is treated as just one of many outcomes that the decision maker defines in terms of value and probability.

economic context may appear viable to one decision maker but not to another. Similarly, an individual who wishes to become more physically active, and lives next to a gym, may find that exercising more often is a highly plausible option. A teenager who plans to see the latest teenage movie may decide that going to the local cinema isn't an option because there is no one to go with, and going alone is unthinkable.

An option may seem more worthy of consideration if it is presented before or simultaneously with other options, or framed in a positive rather than negative fashion. For example, quitting smoking 'cold turkey' sounds more feasible if a smoker is informed, '50 per cent of quitters succeed' rather than '50 per cent of quitters fail'.

Framing can take other forms. For example, decision makers may first try to establish what is most important to them: maintaining good health, holding down a job, getting on with friends and family, and so on (Byrnes, 2002). This helps to simplify the problem. People try to work out which outcomes are gains and which are losses, usually in relation to some reference point, and disregard outcomes that are shared across alternatives, instead focusing on unique consequences that distinguish one option from another.

For example, an individual who feels healthy, and has a good social life, may perceive gain if this general situation is an improvement compared with the way things were the same time last week (the reference point). Furthermore, complex probabilities are simplified, so for example people cancel out probabilities for similar outcomes in evaluating available options, and make decisions on that basis.

Consider a smoker who learns that smoking entails a 20 per cent chance of dying from cancer, and a 20 per cent chance of developing heart disease, whereas not smoking carries a 20 per cent chance of succumbing to cancer but a 10 per cent chance of getting heart disease. The risk of cancer is effectively ignored, because it is similar across both options, and instead the decision maker focuses on heart disease since this distinguishes the two alternatives.

People also add probabilities together for choices that offer similar outcomes. For example, if living near a high-voltage cable entails a 10 per cent risk of cancer, and a 20 per cent reduction in property values, the decision maker assumes a 30 per cent probability of loss for living in this region when considering other possible places to live.

Overall framing helps the decision maker identify the feasible options, taking into account contextual factors. These may include social, cultural, environmental, political, economic and intellectual considerations, all of which define what choices the decision maker has. Framing also helps people simplify otherwise complex information, making the decision making process easier and more manageable.

Evaluation

What happens during evaluation is more or less similar to SEU theory: the decision maker considers the probabilities and values of outcomes associated

with each alternative, to identify the best option. However, there is one important difference compared with SEU theory: in addition to assigning a value to each outcome, people also consider the certainty or uncertainty of each outcome.

What happens at the evaluation phase can be summarised thus:

$$U = w(p_1), v(Z_1) + w(p_2), v(Z_2) + \cdots$$

Here, Z stands for each outcome, p denotes probability, while w and v indicate the weight and value functions respectively.

People tend to assign more weight to certain (i.e. guaranteed) over uncertain (i.e. merely probable) outcomes. For example, a teenager contemplating smoking may attach more importance to feeling 'cool' than to the risk of disease, simply because the former is guaranteed whereas the latter is uncertain.

However, the preference for certainty is moderated by good or bad situations. In general people are more cautious (risk averse) in good situations but take more risks (risk seeking) in bad situations.

In other words, when contemplating potential gains we prefer to keep what we have (or are guaranteed to receive) rather than gamble for a greater prize that isn't guaranteed. For example, teenagers who have never smoked often elect to experiment with cigarettes largely because the benefits – peer approval, feeling 'cool' and satisfied curiosity – are largely guaranteed. By contrast the merits of not smoking, notably reduced susceptibility to long-term health risks, impressive as they are, seem vague and uncertain. Why gamble with uncertain gains when there are guaranteed remunerations?

Curiously, people display the exact opposite attitude with regard to losses. We prefer an uncertain loss to a certain one, even if the certain loss is smaller. In effect people are prepared to take more risks when contemplating potential losses – they are risk seeking.

For example, teenagers often elect to have unprotected sex because the risks of STDs and unplanned pregnancy, serious as they are, are highly uncertain and may not materialise. Many youngsters may reason, 'I'll take my chances.' By contrast, the risks of using contraception – for example embarrassment, interruption, sense of distrust and reduced spontaneity – albeit less catastrophic, seem almost guaranteed to occur. This certainty is enough to put people off.

Furthermore, people have difficulty dealing with extreme probabilities. We do not like the idea of chance. Thus, highly probable events are seen as certain, while highly improbable outcomes are treated as impossible. So, for example, people are happy to travel by air, with no thoughts about the risks, simply because the possibility of a crash is extremely low. But of course, the plane could crash!

When people think about gains and losses, they do so relative to their current situation, or reference point. Any improvement relative to the starting point is regarded as a gain, while any deterioration is deemed a loss. Thus, what is a gain for one person may be a loss or 'no change' for another (e.g. a respiratory infection may not mean much to a terminally ill patient nearing death).

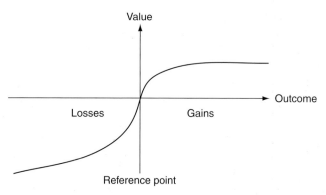

1.2 *Prospect theory. Assigning value to gains and losses. Changes near the reference point mean more; losses are more painful. Version 1.2, November 2002 Copyright (C) 2000, 2001, 2002 Free Software Foundation, Inc. 51 Franklin St, Fifth Floor, Boston, MA 02110-1301 USA.*

People react strongly to change that mirrors their current situation, but are progressively less sensitive to change that departs significantly from the status quo (see Fig. 1.2). For example, a teenage smoker who consumes sixty cigarettes per day (the starting point) will find it more stressful reducing this intake by sixty (i.e. close to the reference point), than by say five cigarettes per day (far from the reference point).

Finally, a loss is much more painful than an equivalent gain. In monetary terms, losing £100 can be far more annoying than gaining the same amount. The steeper shape of the curve within the loss domain depicts this aversion to loss. This indicates that increased losses sting more than comparable gains.

Applications and limitations

Prospect theory can be useful in making sense of various seemingly odd decisions, such as adolescents adopting risky behaviours despite full awareness of the inherent dangers. An option that entails uncertain risks (e.g. illness/disease) will be preferred to a lower-risk alternative whose outcomes are guaranteed (e.g. social disapproval).

What about research evidence on prospect theory? Do studies substantiate its postulates? In general, yes. However, very little of this research is health related (e.g. van Osch *et al.*, 2006), let alone relevant to health behaviour (McDermott, 1998). Most of the research has focused on decision making in commerce, marketing, consumer choice, politics, environmental issues and general psychology (e.g. Wong and Jessica, 2005; Fox and Hadar, 2006; Lasio-Morello, 2006; Saqib, 2006; Steinacker, 2006; Butler, 2007).

The paucity of prospect theory research on health behaviour is rather puzzling. After all, the model clearly offers certain advantages over SEU-based formulations, such as its emphasis on decision weights, and predictions about risk

aversion and risk seeking in gain–loss judgements (McDermott, 1998). Decisions about health behaviour entail a choice between alternatives, with varying degrees of certainty about outcomes. Thus, prospect theory can help predict health decisions, in a wide variety of scenarios.

Prospect theory is a largely mathematical model, and hence appeals more to economists and mathematicians than to psychologists. I am often sceptical about the applicability of mathematical models to solving riddles of human behaviour. Equations imply precision, order, predictability and reliability, ideals that are often at odds with the messiness and chaotic nature of human decision making.

People's decisions in the real world can be fuzzy, volatile, and with no apparent beginning and end (e.g. some people seem to 'drift' into decisions without being aware of it), or clear justification. Mathematical equations don't allow for this nonsensicality.

Like most rationalistic models of decision making, prospect theory assumes a certain degree of intellectual maturity in the decision maker, an ability for example to understand abstractions like 'gain', 'loss' and 'probability'. Yet, we know that certain sub-sections of the general population, notably children, adolescents, the uneducated and the mentally challenged, may lack this cognitive proficiency.

Finally, like SEU theory, prospect theory doesn't adequately address the pronounced and direct effect emotion often has on people's decision making (Janis and Mann, 1977), raising serious doubts about its relevance to adolescence. This imbalance is somewhat redressed by the model I'll discuss next.

The conflict-theory model

Up until perhaps the mid 1950s most theoretical accounts of human decision making arguably assumed rationality; people weighed up costs and benefits objectively before making a choice. However, around this time a group of social psychologists, including now renowned decision theorist Irving Janis, based at Yale University in the USA, began to undertake research into the role of emotional factors in decision making (Hovland *et al.*, 1953; Janis and Feshbach, 1953; Janis, 1967).

A series of studies published through to the 1970s demonstrated that strong emotions such as anxiety, stress and fear play a key role in the choices people make, transcending any influence rationalistic factors may have (e.g. Janis and Feshbach, 1953). Although decision theorists slowly began to incorporate the role of emotion into their thinking (Leventhal, 1970), it wasn't until the late 1970s that a full-blown comprehensive theory of decision making emerged which accounted for the role of stress in choice.

Known as the conflict-theory model, this formulation was developed by Irving Janis and Leon Mann, drawing largely from the accumulated research on stress up to that point (Janis and Mann, 1976, 1977, 1982; Janis, 1983, 1986).

Although conflict-theory has so far failed to generate the kind of extensive research inspired by models of health behaviour for example, it remains one of the most comprehensive accounts of human decision making in social psychology, and hence provides the basic foundation for this book. It is one of the few models of human decision making that thoroughly reconcile the role of emotion and rationality in choice.

According to this model, decision making is a process triggered by any development, for example a threat or challenge, in a person's environment that necessitates a change in current behaviour. In response, the individual may adopt one of several decision making styles, which may or may not be considered rational. These are: vigilance, panic, defensive avoidance, and complacency – adherence or change.

Vigilance

This simply denotes competent decision making. The decision maker carefully and objectively searches for relevant information, and then weighs up known costs and benefits, after which he or she makes an informed decision.

Vigilance entails progression through five critical stages: Stage 1: awareness of a threat or challenge that necessitates a decision; Stage 2: search for suitable alternatives; Stage 3: weighing up the costs and benefits of each alternative; Stage 4: making a commitment; Stage 5: adherence to one's commitment.

In Stage 1, the individual becomes aware of a new problem that necessitates a decision. For example, consider a teenage girl who looks in her mirror one morning and notices that she has gained a bit of weight. She resolves that something has to be done about this development. The decision making process is triggered.

Stage 2 involves surveying the available alternatives. Some options would be obvious to the decision maker, while others may be more obscure, or completely unknown. The individual may seek information and advice from friends, family members and professionals, such as a nurse, doctor or academic. For example, our teenage girl may speak to her best friend, consult her school nurse, or even scan through a magazine on teenage health for clues. Ultimately, she may decide that the only viable options available are to (a) do nothing; (b) go on a diet; (c) start exercising more regularly; and (d) both diet and exercise.

During Stage 3 the decision maker thinks about the costs and benefits of each available option, to find out which is best. The aim is to find a solution that offers the greatest benefits and/or fewest costs. The girl may reason that the best thing for her is simply to go on a diet, since exercising regularly, or trying to exercise and diet simultaneously, would be just too physically strenuous and time consuming, and offer no significant health benefits over her preferred option. Doing nothing is also out of the question since this would mean she continues to gain weight, with no advantages.

Stage 4 entails making a commitment. The decision maker 'goes public' with her decision, and begins to implement it. Friends and family are informed, and

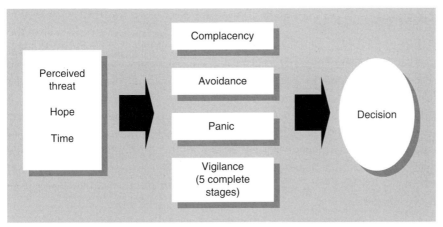

1.3 *The conflict-theory model (Source: Janis and Mann, 1977).*

various practical arrangements are made to execute the decision. For example our girl may tell her friend she has decided to go on a diet, and then accompany her mother to a local supermarket to buy the necessary foods.

Stage 5 involves adhering to the decision in the face of negative feedback. The decision maker encounters various difficulties and temptations that threaten to reverse her decision. For example, our teenager may find herself battling daily with strong cravings for tasty but fatty foods she has had to give up, as part of her new diet.

According to Janis and Mann (1977) these five stages depict competent decision making, and are only fully observed when vigilance is dominant. When other decision making preferences are preferred, the individual fails to observe all the stages, especially the second and third. In other words, defensive avoidance, panic and complacency are all defective decision making strategies, because the decision maker fails adequately to survey and evaluate her options.

Complacency

The decision maker responds with indifference. The individual calmly carries on as normal, seemingly oblivious to any threat. This tactic is based on unintended misjudgements about risks, resulting from insufficient and/or inaccurate information about the probability that the threat will actually materialise and/or about the seriousness of the danger should it manifest. Such misjudgements can readily be corrected by provision of complete and accurate risk information.

Alternatively, the decision maker may complacently adopt whatever protective action is most salient and/or strongly recommended. This strategy manifests when people promptly agree to adopt a preventive measure with little or no awareness of the risks or difficulties involved. This response is based on misjudgements about the risks of adopting a new course of action, and is defective in the sense that the individual is not psychologically prepared to deal with whatever losses are entailed in implementing the new action.

Defensive avoidance

This involves deliberate efforts to avoid a difficult decision because of the stress involved. Information that suggests the decision can be postponed (e.g. absence of a deadline) will encourage procrastination. The individual will stop thinking about the issue, and avoid discussing it with anyone who may disapprove. If the decision maker anticipates severe losses for postponement, he will consider shifting responsibility to someone else, arguing that others are in a better position to make an informed choice (e.g. 'My doctor/boyfriend/parents will decide') and hence should take the blame if things turn out badly. If responsibility cannot be shifted, for whatever reasons, then the person will resort to rationalisations to justify inaction.

Panic

This is also referred to as hypervigilance. The decision maker perceives an emergency, and frantically searches for any solution that promises immediate remedy. In such a state, the person becomes indecisive, as first one option and then another seems to be the best course of action. It is difficult to think straight, so that important risks or benefits associated with available options may be overlooked, or misinterpreted. There is a greater reliance on simplistic rules of thumb, to facilitate quick decisions.

Psychological antecedents

What psychological conditions determine which strategy will be adopted? Conflict-theory specifies four basic conditions: perception of risks in taking no action; perception of risks in taking action; optimism that a viable solution can be found; and finally, the perception that there is sufficient time in which to find a solution.

If the decision maker perceives no danger in continuing his present course of action, complacency will result: he will simply carry on as normal. Similarly, if the individual does not see any serious problems in changing to a new course of action, then again complacency sets in: he will change lethargically to any salient course of action.

If the decision maker perceives risks in changing and in not changing, then decisional conflict will result. The person is effectively caught between the deep blue sea and the devil; he is 'damned if he does and damned if he doesn't'. There is a price to pay whatever action is taken.

In this situation, lack of hope that a solution can be found will elicit defensive avoidance, while insufficient time in which to find a solution (i.e. deadline pressure) will result in panic. Vigilance predominates when there is decisional conflict, hope of finding a solution, and sufficient time in which to do so.

Applications and limitations

Empirical evidence on conflict-theory is patchy and inconsistent. When I began to explore conflict-theory in the early 1990s it quickly became evident that not much research had been published in this area. Although empirical research on the model has grown steadily there is still a dearth of studies in this area.

Nevertheless, existing evidence appears to fall into one of two strands. One has focused on the five stages of decision making (e.g. Friedlander *et al.*, 1984; Loneck and Kola, 1988; Moore, 1990; Chambers and Rew, 2003) while the other has investigated decision making styles[2] (e.g. van der Velde and van der Pligt, 1991; van der Velde *et al.*, 1992; Friedman and Mann, 1993; White *et al.*, 1994; Eiser *et al.*, 1995; Mann *et al.*, 1997; Umeh, 1998a; Tuinstra *et al.*, 2000). All in all, the evidence from these studies permits several tentative inferences.

First, people do observe some or all of the five decision making steps when making certain decisions, such as use of contraception (e.g. Friedlander *et al.*, 1984).

Second, factor analysis suggests people indeed employ distinctive decision making styles when making decisions, and these generally conform to the various decision modes specified by the model, notably vigilance, panic and defensive avoidance (e.g. Umeh, 1998; Tuinstra *et al.*, 2000).

Third, in general, vigilance is associated with 'better' decisions, such as opting to engage in health enhancing behaviour (e.g. exercising, using sun protection, using condoms), or to avoid health damaging activity (e.g. smoking, eating fatty foods). By contrast, defensive avoidance leads to risky decisions (van der Velde and van der Pligt, 1991; Eiser *et al.*, 1995; Umeh, 1998).

Evidence for the role of panic is inconclusive. It is not clear whether panicking leads to good or bad decisions (van der Velde and van der Pligt, 1991; Umeh, 1998). Other personal or contextual factors seem to be relevant in this regard.

Finally, studies focusing on children or teenagers are especially rare (but see Umeh, 1998; Tuinstra *et al.*, 2000). Nevertheless, what evidence there is generally conforms to the inferences made above.

Given the patchy body of evidence the model has had limited real-world application, at least within health psychology. This is quite curious given that Janis and Mann (1977) offer guidelines for possible interventions, such as a decisional balance procedure that compels decision makers to think systematically about costs and benefits before making a decision. This is achieved by asking the decision maker to prepare a detailed list of anticipated pros and cons around specific helpful categories such as 'gains and losses to significant others'. Studies have shown that people generally make better decisions when they undergo this procedure (e.g. Janis and Mann, 1977).

---

[2] There is a third strand of research dealing with the concept of decisional balance. This evidence is considered in the following section.

In my view the main problem with conflict-theory is its emphasis on decision making as a *process*. The idea that people make decisions in a sequential, deliberative and time-consuming fashion is highly questionable. Evidence has shown that adolescents sometimes make decisions on impulse, or in a haphazard fashion, without any particular organisation (e.g. Friedman, 1996). Severe time constraints can force snap decisions even in individuals who habitually think things through in an orderly fashion.

Despite these problems, conflict-theory offers a refreshing antidote to overly intellectual decision models, such as prospect theory and SEU, both of which lack realism and explanatory value in the emotional scenarios that often typify adolescent health behaviour.

Decisional balance

Decisional balance simply refers to the potential gains and losses considered by an individual during decision making (Janis and Mann, 1976, 1977; Andra, 2005). It is based on an assumption of human rationality. In other words, people are assumed to think about and weigh up potential outcomes during decision making. Research has shown that decision balance has some relevance. Adolescents do indeed distinguish between anticipated gains and losses, when making decisions (e.g. Berry *et al.*, 2005; Chen *et al.*, 2006; Drahovzal, 2007; Mauriello *et al.*, 2007), and are generally more likely to adopt a course of action if the perceived gains outweigh the losses, and less likely to take action if potential losses exceed the gains (e.g. Lauby *et al.*, 2006; Medvene *et al.*, 2007).

Originally, Janis and Mann (1977) identified four main gain–loss categories: utilitarian gains/losses to oneself; utilitarian gains/losses to significant others; self-approval/disapproval; and approval/disapproval from significant others.

The first category refers to the tangible things that a person might gain or lose, for example health, weight, income and material resources. Utilitarian gains/losses to significant others refers to the tangible consequences for one's friends and family, including days off from work to look after a sick child or sibling, loss of income, and diminished health (e.g. from passive smoking).

Self-approval/disapproval denotes having a good or bad self-image, for example on moral, political or religious grounds, or simply feeling good/bad about oneself. For example, an insecure girl may anticipate a boost in self-confidence from cigarette smoking.

The fourth category refers to the positive or negative attitudes of friends and family. For example, parental disapproval constitutes a 'loss', while their approval depicts a 'gain'.

Various questionnaires have been developed to measure decisional balance categories in relation to various health behaviours. Factor analysis of the data collected with these instruments has shown that adolescents do not distinguish between the four categories specified by Janis and Mann (1977). Thus, for

example, no significant distinction is made between a tangible loss, such as worsening health, and social loss, such as the expressed disapproval of one's parents. Instead, teenagers simply distinguish between what they stand to lose and what they stand to gain (e.g. Chen *et al.*, 2006; Lauby *et al.*, 2006).

Overall, decisional balance research highlights some of the cognitive appraisals that may influence an adolescent's decision making. As will be seen in the following section, predictable changes in decision balance have been implicated in progression through different stages of the decision making process.

In essence, adolescents think about pros and cons, and continue to do so as they become more and more committed to a course of action, modifying their thoughts accordingly to reinforce their current position. For example, a teenager considering using contraception during sexual intercourse will balance the benefits (e.g. reducing the risk of sexually transmitted disease and of unplanned pregnancy) against any costs (e.g. embarrassment, annoying delay prior to intercourse) and keep doing so, adjusting the importance attached to each outcome as he commits to and starts to initiate condom use.

Transtheoretical model of behaviour change

The transtheoretical model describes changes in a decision maker's anticipated gains and losses as he or she becomes increasingly committed to a course of action (Prochaska *et al.*, 1994). The gain–loss conceptualisation is based on decisional balance. Essentially, according to this model, the relative weightings of gains and losses differ significantly from when a person isn't considering adopting a behaviour to when she has adopted and implemented it (e.g. Otake and Shimai, 2001; Plummer *et al.*, 2001; Rossi *et al.*, 2001; Di Noia *et al.*, 2006; Spencer *et al.*, 2006; Svetlak and Kukleta, 2006).

Another way to interpret this model is that a person's gain–loss judgements change predictably as the decision making process commences, unfolds and finally terminates once a decision has been made and executed. Five 'stages of change' are specified: precontemplation, contemplation, preparation, action and maintenance.

A person in precontemplation has no plans to change his behaviour during the next six months. At contemplation the person is beginning to entertain the idea of changing his behaviour and adopting a new course of action during the next six months. An individual in preparation is beginning to make arrangements to change within one month, and has taken some tangible steps in that direction. At the action stage change has taken effect, but for less than six months. Finally, maintenance depicts change that has been ongoing for more than six months.

Let me illustrate these stages with an example, such as quitting smoking. At precontemplation, a smoker has no plans to quit in the next six months. However,

at contemplation he is beginning to think about quitting. In preparation he has started to make concrete plans to quit in the next four weeks. For example, he may start to destroy cigarettes in his possession, join a smoking-cessation programme at a local clinic, and announce his decision to friends and family. During the action stage the individual has quit smoking and not smoked for up to six months. In maintenance, he has avoided cigarettes for at least six months, or more.

The transtheoretical model postulates a relationship between decisional balance and stages of change. Essentially, the benefits of changing to a new behaviour increase steadily and the costs decrease, as the decision maker moves from precontemplation to contemplation. The costs of changing outweigh the benefits at precontemplation, but this situation reverses by the action and maintenance stages. The actual reversal in cost–benefit weights occurs during one of the intermediate stages, notably contemplation, preparation or even action.

For example, for a smoker at precontemplation, the costs of quitting will probably outweigh the benefits. However, as he progresses through to the action and maintenance stages, the benefits of change will start to outweigh the costs.

Additionally, the model incorporates several further cognitive processes that vary across stages of change, including self-efficacy (perceived ability to change) and temptations (cues that may hamper or facilitate change). Finally, people are motivated to progress from one stage to the next by various cognitive and behavioural resources, including perceived support from significant others (e.g. a partner), and monetary rewards.

One basic thesis that emerges from this model is that people modify their cognitive appraisals in order to justify their current position. Thus, a smoker who isn't planning to quit will be tempted to magnify the costs of quitting and discount the benefits. By contrast, someone who has managed to quit for six months will feel compelled to highlight the benefits and diminish the pain.

There has been a considerable amount of research on this model (e.g. see reviews by Hall, 2005, and Spencer *et al.*, 2006). Studies have shown that the framework has some validity in explaining adolescent health behaviour (e.g. Plummer *et al.*, 2001; Rossi *et al.*, 2001; Di Noia *et al.*, 2006; Svetlak and Kukleta, 2006). It certainly demonstrates that adolescents are much more delib-erative than some may think, and actively modify their gain–loss appraisals as they become increasingly committed to a course of action.

However, the theory has some important weaknesses. First, it places too much emphasis on cognitive factors, notably cost–benefit appraisals, in decision mak-ing, and hence may be difficult to apply in situations in which people are driven entirely by habit or emotion, for example.

Furthermore, it assumes that decision making and behaviour change occur sequentially in stages, and hence may be inapplicable to snap and impulsive

decision making. The model is revisited later in this book, as part of a discussion of decision making competence.

Decision making styles

Most people have a preferred way of making decisions. Like an air traffic controller who is 'trained' to make landing and take-off decisions in a particular way, in order to minimise the risk of an accident, most people have an established strategy or set of strategies for arriving at solutions to problems. Think about the last few major decisions you made. Notice any recurring thoughts, actions or emotions in the way you arrived at these decisions?

A decision making preference refers to the dominant strategy a person employs whenever he or she is required to make a decision. The preferred approach may affect the likelihood of a health enhancing or health damaging decision (e.g. van der Velde and van der Pligt, 1991; Umeh, 1998a). Thus, decision making preference is one of the most important aspects of decision making. It depicts how people actually make decisions in the real world, as contrasted with the way academics, researchers and theorists assume they make decisions.

I have already made the point that theories used by health psychologists to explain people's health behaviour, for example the health belief model (Rosenstock, 1974; Janz and Becker, 1984), often assume a rational approach to decision making: that is, people mentally weigh up various costs and benefits, before making their choice (Ogden, 2000; Milne *et al.*, 2000).

However, this assumption often isn't backed up by empirical studies. According to Janis (1984, pp. 331–332), 'the health belief model, like other models of rational choice, fails to specify under what conditions people will give priority to avoiding subjective discomfort at the cost of endangering their lives, and under what conditions they will make a more rational decision'. Psychologists have long recognised that people reach decisions in a variety of ways that often aren't rational (Hovland *et al.*, 1953; Janis and Feshbach, 1953; Rogers, 1983; Rippetoe and Rogers, 1987).

For example, acting on impulse, relying on simple rules of thumb or putting off decisions altogether are all common problem solving strategies people may employ that eschew rationalistic appraisals (Janis and Mann, 1976, 1977).

Curiously, there is no consensus on the exact number, type and meaning of people's decision making habits (Janis and Mann, 1977; Mann *et al.*, 1997, 1998; Friedman, 1996; Tuinstra *et al.*, 2000). Nevertheless, the decision making styles specified by Janis and Mann's (1977) conflict-theory have gained a certain degree of recognition and acceptance amongst decision theorists. This perhaps is largely due to development of the Decision Making Questionnaire (DMQ) (Mann, 1982; Mann *et al.*, 1997, 1998; Umeh, 1998a,

1998b; Tuinstra *et al.*, 2000), an instrument designed to measure decision making strategies based on the conflict model.

The Decision Making Questionnaire (DMQ)

Developed and updated by Leon Mann and his colleagues (Mann, 1982; Radford *et al.*, 1986; Beswick, 1988; Mann *et al.*, 1988, 1997; Burnett *et al.*, 1989; Tuinstra *et al.*, 2000), the DMQ measures the extent to which people utilise vigilance, panic, defensive avoidance and complacency during decision making.

The original version of the DMQ first appeared during the early eighties (Mann, 1982). Subsequently, however, there was a growing recognition that decision making in adolescence is unique. For example, adolescents seem less capable of rational decision making, compared with adults (Mann *et al.*, 1989), and thus may have a different repertoire of decision making preferences. Thus, the DMQ in its original form may not be suitable for this demographic group. Thus, during the late 1990s a special version of the DMQ, known as the Adolescent Decision Making Questionnaire (ADMQ), was developed.

One issue that often concerns psychologists is whether psychological constructs or dimensions that they identify are in fact 'real' and perceived as such by the general public. In other words, it is rather like a biochemist asking if the distinction between oxygen and carbon dioxide is in fact real, or an economist wondering if concepts like demand and supply actually exist. People will accept that different gases are probably involved when they inhale and exhale, or that there is indeed a difference between a buyer and a seller in a market scenario.

In a similar vein, it is reasonable to ask whether people actually display the various decision making preferences measured by the DMQ, or whether they perceive decision making as one aggregate activity, without varied approaches. Do people actually make a distinction between running away from a difficult decision and tackling it head on? Or is this all academic drivel, and unrealistic figments of Janis's and Mann's imaginations?

Research suggests that people do distinguish between the different decision making styles contained in the DMQ, rather than simply viewing decision making as one monolithic activity without any variations (Mann *et al.*, 1997, 1998; Umeh, 1998; Tuinstra *et al.*, 2000). For example, I factor analysed DMQ data from a large sample of adolescents and found three major dimensions: one depicted competent decision making, consistent with vigilance; another portrayed a tendency to avoid difficult decisions, or shift responsibility to others, reflecting defensive avoidance. The third factor illustrated hypervigilance, suggesting panic (Umeh, 1998a, 1998b). A similar study by Tuinstra *et al.* (2000) identified a similar set of decision strategies, albeit with an additional dimension depicting complacency.

Overall, the DMQ provides a much needed psychometric basis for conceptualising and measuring people's decision making. It has been shown to have cross-cultural validity (Mann *et al.*, 1998), and offers scientific confirmation of the existence and persistence of non-rational decision making habits.

Personal versus situational perspectives

There has been much debate about whether decision making preferences are best assessed as aspects of a person's personality, or tendencies determined by the prevailing situation (e.g. Janis, 1986; Leventhal *et al.*, 1993).

The DMQ conceptualises decision making as personality based. So, does this mean that the situation is unimportant in determining a person's decision strategy? Surely, the way someone makes decisions may vary considerably depending on circumstances. For example, a person may try to be more rational when making a life-or-death decision (e.g. whether or not to undergo vital surgery), but then act impulsively when faced with less consequential choices (e.g. what clothes to wear each morning).

Janis (1986, p. 473) notes that decision making preferences reflect personality traits, and hence influence most decisions a person makes, whether they involve health or otherwise. However, he also acknowledges that such personality attributes do not often account for very much of the variance in behaviour change (Umeh, 1998a, 1998b), suggesting that situation-based decision making may better explain people's choices. Indeed, there is some evidence that seems to support this idea (e.g. van der Velde and van der Pligt, 1991).

In formulating the conflict-theory model, Janis and Mann (1977) did place much emphasis on the distinction between situation- and personality-based decision making practices. However, the DMQ/ADMQ (e.g. Mann, 1982; Mann *et al.*, 1988) underscore the importance they attached to personality in decision making.

Whether one views decision making preferences as personality or situation derived, it is important to mention that reports of personality traits are more prone to bias. For example, asking people to report how they 'generally' make decisions may elicit recall of decision making activity they aspired to, or that was very remote in time but highly memorable, perhaps because the outcomes were especially satisfying. The result is that reports may be biased towards reporting on more impressive decision making experiences rather than how one actually tends to make decisions (Leventhal *et al.*, 1993).

What is health behaviour?

Since understanding health behaviour is the primary objective here, it makes sense to define this concept and its relevant dimensions. Health behaviour can be defined as any action or inaction that may affect one's health. Thus any activity that enhances or impairs a person's physical well-being qualifies. Thus common activities like cigarette smoking, alcohol consumption, eating fatty foods, exercising regularly, sexual practices (e.g. use of condoms, number of sexual partners) all qualify, not to mention problem or antisocial behaviours such as reckless driving, deliberate self-harm and suicide (e.g. Marks *et al.*, 2005; Morrison and Bennett, 2006).

In reality, it is possible to link almost any behaviour to adverse health outcomes. For example, using a mobile phone has been rumoured to cause long-term neurological damage (e.g. Hardell *et al.*, 2007), and sleeping on overly soft mattresses purportedly causes or worsens chronic back pain (e.g. McConnell, 2003). Thankfully, health psychologists have identified a finite number of behavioural categories that at the very least provide a certain degree of scope and clarity for anyone trying to decipher what is or isn't a health behaviour (e.g. Morrison and Bennett, 2006). These categories include the following:

- health compromising behaviours
- health enhancing behaviours
- health behaviours: sick role, illness and health behaviours.

Health compromising behaviours include any activity that is damaging to one's health. These include common behaviours like smoking cigarettes, drug use, alcohol consumption, excessive dietary fat intake, and more obscure activities like deliberate self-harm (e.g. cutting one's wrists).

Health enhancing behaviours denote activities that improve one's health, or at least reduce the risk of illness and disease. Examples are physical activity, fruit and vegetable intake, wearing a seatbelt, and using a condom during sexual intercourse.

Health behaviours refer to any behaviour associated with health, and may be health compromising or health enhancing.

Illness behaviour refers to people's reactions to illness symptoms, and typically includes self-medication, relaxation, or visiting a doctor, dentist or other health professional for advice or treatment.

Sick role behaviours denote responses to formal diagnosis of an illness, and include hospitalisation, adhering to a prescription regime, undergoing surgery, and follow-up visits to a doctor after treatment.

Most if not all of these behaviours may occur during adolescence, and it is fair to say that the majority originate during this period, or before (Nutbeam and Booth, 1994). Thus, teenagers continually have to make decisions about whether to engage in these activities.

Throughout this book I will repeatedly refer to all the behavioural terms mentioned here, especially health behaviour, and health compromising/enhancing behaviour. However, I invite readers not to allow jargon to interfere with their understanding of key arguments. However one chooses to define or label behaviour, emphasis should be on how adolescents' decision making informs our understanding of such activity. It is important not to lose sight of this point.

Defining adolescence

Clearly, adolescence is a troubled period during which children experience significant social, cognitive and physical changes as they make the transition to adulthood (Nutbeam and Booth, 1994; Petersen and Leffert, 1995). However,

I think it is essential to clarify precisely who is being discussed in this book, as not every individual or culture recognises adolescence as a distinct phase in the human lifespan, and even those that do don't always agree on exactly when it commences and terminates.

Furthermore, a lot of the scientific literature on which this book is based often fails to provide adequate information about its subjects, making it difficult if not impossible to establish what age group was used. Clarifying these issues now will help minimise confusion later in the book, when inescapable ambiguities about individuals, samples or populations become apparent.

In many Western countries, adolescence is generally marked by the onset of puberty (about 10 and 12 years for girls and boys respectively) and 'terminated' at around the point (about age 19) when the individual becomes economically independent, perhaps commencing a vocation. Thus, the age period from 10 to 19 years will be used as a rough definition of adolescence throughout this book.

However, I crave the reader's indulgence when discussing scientific literature. Many studies in social science employ university undergraduates and children, and a significant proportion fail to specify the average age or the age range of the sample, making it difficult to decide if the subjects were adolescents (aged 10 to 19 years). I have decided to include studies that use 'children', provided information about age is provided, and shows an average age of 12 years or a minimum age of 10 years.

Studies that use 'undergraduates' or 'college students' will be eligible provided the average age is 18 years, and the maximum age 19, or the subjects are clearly first-year students (i.e. freshmen). A review of archives from several US universities shows that the average age of first-year undergraduates is approximately 18 years, well within the age bracket I have specified.

Finally, studies that use 'young adults' are excluded, unless the average age is 18 years, and the maximum age 19.

Some readers may feel that these age criteria are somewhat arbitrary, but such definition is absolutely essential because it helps spell out the scope of this book, even if that scope does not necessarily fit other people's notion of adolescence. Furthermore, I must point out to readers that not every single study mentioned in this book satisfies these criteria. There are a few cases where the relevant information simply wasn't available. Nevertheless these studies were included because of the novelty or interest of their findings and inferences.

Decision making in adolescence

How do teenagers make decisions? Do they typically opt for a rationalistic approach or resort to defective strategies? Popular stereotypes would suggest the latter. Adolescents are regularly portrayed in the media (film, TV, etc.) as mindless and impulsive idiots who can't be trusted with their own welfare (Stepp, 2002).

But what does the science suggest? Well, empirical findings suggest a rather more complex picture than social prejudices would have you believe. On the one hand, studies have shown that teenagers are generally less competent decision makers than adults, with the former group for example showing less interest in cost–benefit considerations (e.g. Mann *et al.*, 1989; Halpern-Felsher and Cauffman, 2001). On the other hand, adolescents aren't averse to rationalistic thought (Plummer *et al.*, 2001; Rossi *et al.*, 2001; Di Noia *et al.*, 2006; Spencer *et al.*, 2006).

The preponderance of research shows that adolescents approach decisions in a variety of ways, and are capable of both competent and incompetent decision making. Research on the DMQ perhaps offers the strongest evidence for this view (e.g. Mann *et al.*, 1982, 1997, 1998; Friedman and Mann, 1993; Umeh, 1998a, 1998b; Tuinstra *et al.*, 2000).

Repeated factor analysis of data collected from adolescents using this instrument has consistently yielded several distinct decision making styles, principally vigilance, panic, complacency, and avoiding difficult decisions, for example by shifting responsibility.

Critics may argue that these decision strategies merely reflect the structure of the DMQ, and that respondents simply highlight themes presented to them by the researcher. However, research using different methodologies has verified at least some of these decision tactics.

For example, interesting evidence has emerged recently from research looking at how children and adolescents respond to projective psychological tests, notably the Thematic Apperception Test (TAT) (Morgan, 1995). The TAT typically involves presenting an ambiguous picture to a person, who is then required to tell as dramatic a story as possible about the picture, focusing for example on what is currently happening and what various characters are thinking and feeling. The assumption behind the TAT is that people will 'project' their own views, attitudes, emotions and preferences in the stories that they tell. Thus, responses to the TAT can provide valuable clues about a person's preferred way of dealing with problems or making decisions.

Psychologist Phebe Cramer conducted a series of studies spanning more than two decades in which the TAT was used to establish how children and adolescents prefer to deal with anxiety arousing situations (Cramer, 1987, 1991, 1999, 2007). Since decision making can often generate stress (Janis and Mann, 1977), Cramer's research is highly relevant to the present discussion, as it may yield clues about how teenagers prefer to make decisions.

In a recent study Cramer found that a preference for shifting responsibility and ignoring or distorting facts – in other words, defensive avoidance – is not just evident from late childhood through to early adolescence, but actually increases as teenagers get older (Cramer, 2007; but see Porcerelli *et al.*, 1998).

The tendency to avoid taking responsibility, notably by blaming others or passing difficult problems to others to solve, was especially pronounced. This is probably because there are people in the lives of most adolescents – parents,

teachers, guardians and other responsible adults available – who are willing and/or compelled to take responsibility.

Overall, yes, adolescents can be mindless and impulsive, as some stereotypes suggest, but that is only part of the story. Teenagers also behave quite rationally, for example by weighing pros and cons. They may also resort to problematic strategies such as avoidance and panic.

What are the implications of these decision making preferences for adolescent health behaviour? Is a particular style of decision making more likely to lead to health compromising or health enhancing behaviour? Can decision making preferences be used to make predictions about current and future behaviour? These issues are considered in greater depth later in this book.

Health behaviour in adolescence

Adolescents engage in a wide range of activities that may have serious implications for their health. There are the usual suspects such as cigarette smoking, alcohol consumption, risky sexual activity and diet-related behaviours.

The World Health Organization identifies several health behaviour groups associated with adolescence. These groupings are listed below. I adapted the list from an international report of a health behaviour survey in school-aged children undertaken by the WHO's regional office for Europe, in Copenhagen, Denmark (WHO, 2000):

- medication use (i.e. self-medication)
- exercise and recreational activities
- substance use (e.g. smoking, drinking and drug use)
- dieting, eating habits and dental hygiene
- sexual behaviour (e.g. sexual intercourse, condom use).

There are other important behaviours more often defined under the heading 'delinquent', 'antisocial' or 'behaviour disorder', rather than health behaviour. These include theft, arson, truancy, assault, vandalism, and other violent criminal behaviours. These activities often entail a considerable risk of physical injury to the person perpetrating the criminal act. For example, arson could result in severe burns, and assault could culminate in broken bones, after a physical fight. Although these are clearly criminal acts, such activities may nevertheless be categorised as health behaviours to the extent that they carry a real risk of physical injury if not illness and disease.

To complicate things a bit further, I am constantly aware of simple actions or pastimes that could impact on health but are rarely mentioned in health psychology textbooks under the category 'health behaviour'. These include activities like watching too much TV, viewing violent/dangerous movies or video games, riding bicycles recklessly or without appropriate protective gear, crossing the road without looking, playing rough/dangerous games with peers, such as climbing trees and fences or throwing stones, drinking soft drinks to excess, driving a car recklessly, for example by speeding or swerving, and playing loud music.

Box 1.3 Research spotlight: the Myers Briggs Type Indicator

How adolescents prefer to make decisions can be gauged using a variety of instruments. Although the Decision Making Questionnaire (Mann, 1982) formed the basis for my own research, the Myers Briggs Type Indicator (MBTI) has also been used to identify decision making preferences, albeit less explicitly so. The MBTI was developed by Isabel Briggs Myers and her mother Katherine Coole Briggs (Saunders, 1989; Myers, 1990; Myers *et al.*, 1998).

Isabel Myers contends that a person's preferred way of making decisions could be conceptualised around several bipolar dimensions: namely Thinking versus Feeling (e.g. objective thought versus subjective feelings), Sensing versus Intuition (preferring hard facts to abstract arguments), Judgement versus Perception (e.g. preferring to have matters settled or kept open) and Extraversion versus Introversion (being social versus being withdrawn). The first two dichotomies are typically associated with decision making and information processing.

Ugur Sak of the University of Arizona reviewed over a dozen studies that applied the MBTI to adolescent samples (Sak, 2004). His findings were intriguing. For starters, adolescents seemed to show preferences for all four personality types, suggesting that it may be incorrect to view teenage decision making in a primarily negative or one-dimensional way (e.g. Stepp, 2002). Your average adolescent has a wide repertoire of predilections – both good and bad – in how they make decisions.

For example, regarding the *Sensing/Intuition* domains, teenagers in general were rather more impressed by concrete observable facts and the 'here-and-now' (Sensing), than by remote and hypothetical possibilities of which they had little or no direct experience (Intuition). Thus an adolescent faced with a health behaviour decision, for example going on a diet or smoking, may attach more importance to immediate/short-term and tangible benefits, such as noticeable weight loss after a few days, than to long-term and seemingly abstract dangers, such as the risk of anorexia or greater susceptibility to disease.

For the *Thinking/Feeling* dimension, there was a slightly greater preference for subjectivity over objective thought. Teenagers were more likely to get emotionally involved in their decisions, attaching more importance to achieving consensus, and maintaining good relationships with others, presumably their peer group, boy/girl friend, and so on (Feeling). They were less disposed to logic and reasoning, for example by trying to remain detached and intellectual, and not allowing their personal feelings to get in the way.

Overall, the MBTI provides a highly useful instrument for measuring judgement in teenagers. However, unlike the DMQ, which focuses specifically on decision making, the MBTI has a wider emphasis, and is better regarded as a measure of personality. The DMQ's decidedly decision making theme makes it a more informative instrument in the context of this book.

Admittedly, the health consequences of some of these behaviours are unclear, even to health professionals themselves, let alone teenagers. Nonetheless, certain actions, such as crossing a road suddenly without stopping to look first, driving recklessly and climbing trees, are clearly dangerous activities, and most teenagers probably recognise the hazards. Thus, these habits can also be regarded as health behaviours.

Overall there is no limit to the type and number of lifestyle activities that can be considered health behaviours. Any behaviour, no matter how rare or obscure, that entails some degree of risk to one's well-being will qualify. For the purposes of this book, and to avoid getting distracted by ambiguities inherent in defining adolescent health behaviour, I will emphasise the WHO behaviour categories listed above throughout much of this text.

1.4 *Gender differences. Contrary to popular belief, teenagers have a variety of decision making styles, both rational and otherwise. However, while both genders can be rational, girls seem more subjective, emphasising good interpersonal relations over logic (Source: SXC).*

Current state of the literature

There is a paucity of research on decision making in adolescence, at least compared to the available literature on adults (Petersen and Leffert, 1995; Byrnes *et al.*, 1999; Byrnes, 2002). Thus, it should come as no surprise that studies focusing specifically on how decision making relates to health behaviour in teenagers are particularly rare. It may help to consider some hard facts, just to illustrate this point.

I recently conducted a literature search on the electronic database PsycINFO (from the year 1806 to 2007), configuring the system to look for studies containing the key words 'adolescents' and 'decision making'. This yielded over 1,200 results or 'hits'. However, given that a large chunk of these were simply studies on irrelevant or wider topics but which just happened to contain the relevant key words somewhere in the text, I decided to repeat the search, narrowing the selection criteria such that only studies that mentioned the aforesaid key words in their title were selected. This more stringent search yielded only ninety-seven results, and of these, only 20 per cent had a health or medical focus, with just thirteen specifically investigating health or risk behaviour.

Obviously, the search routine described here isn't the most reliable measure of the scope of available literature on a topic. Many highly relevant studies were probably omitted simply because the particular key words I chose weren't in the title. A search on another database (Academic Search Premier) designed to identify studies that mentioned the words 'adolescent' and 'decision making' in the abstract yielded over 400 hits! Even so, studies focusing specifically on health issues constituted less than half of the total, and many of these were medical in nature, with little or no reference to lifestyle factors.

Evidence for the importance of decision making

Despite the paucity of research available, evidence suggests that understanding how adolescents make decisions is crucial in understanding their health behaviour. Take for example a study by Victoria Miller and Dennis Drotar. They examined the ability of a group of diabetic teenagers to make good decisions in a variety of situations, and what bearing if any this had on their adherence to treatment (Miller and Drotar, 2007).

Participants provided information about their decision making habits and adherence to recommended treatments for diabetes, such as obtaining a glucose test. Evidence emerged indicating that poorer decision making practices were related to less compliance with treatment recommendations. Miller and Drotar's findings are by no means isolated. Zwane *et al.* (2004) interviewed small groups of 13 to 19 year olds from Swaziland, southern Africa, about the issues salient to them in relation to risky sexual behaviours (e.g. having multiple sexual partners, failing to use condoms). The teenagers were encouraged to speak freely and honestly.

Table 1.1 *What teenagers consider when deciding whether to use condoms during sexual intercourse. Emotional considerations such as trust seem to take precedence over objective risk–benefit appraisals (Source: Zwane* et al.*, 2004).*

Considerations	Meanings
Ideal age for first intercourse	Varies from person to person, but determines whether sex would occur
What it means to be sexually active	Economic, social and other benefits, slave to one's hormones, growing up
Trust in sexual partner	Suggesting condom use implies no trust
Pressure from peers	Whether other boys/girls are sexually active, or encourage sex

Several key themes emerged suggesting a lack of objectivity in decision making (see Table 1.1). For example, some participants felt under considerable pressure from others to be sexually active, and worried that suggesting condom use may show a lack of trust in one's partner. These seemingly subjective or emotional considerations increased the probability of risky sexual activity.

In the course of my own research I have found some evidence suggesting that emotion-laden decision making styles, for example panic and avoidance, may increase the likelihood of health damaging behaviour (Umeh, 1998a).

However, the lack of research in this area makes it difficult to form a conclusive picture on the relevance of decision making. There is a preponderance of studies on sexual behaviour (Scott, 1996; Schensul, 1998–9; Trierweiler, 1996; Langer and Girard, 1999; Zwane *et al.*, 2004) or pregnancy-related activity, for example abortion (Laird, 2001; Bailey *et al.*, 2003; Finken, 2005). This emphasis probably reflects the priorities of funding organisations (contraceptive use and pregnancy are 'hot' topics in the policies of many Western governments towards adolescent health).

Other studies have focused on decisions about medical treatment, for example in relation to diabetes (Levin, 1999; Miller and Drotar, 2007). Some research has looked at recreational and seasonal behaviours, notably sun tanning (Shoveller *et al.*, 2003).

Curiously, there is very little literature on health enhancing behaviours such as physical activity, or addictive behaviours, notably smoking, drinking and drug use (but see Ellermann, 2002; Ernst *et al.*, 2003). There is also limited interest in dietary activity.

Many of the studies I found examined decision making in clinical or ad hoc adolescent populations, for example pregnant girls, hospitalised teenagers with serious medical ailments such as schizophrenia or diabetes, or those considered 'gifted' or with behaviour disorder problems (e.g. McCabe *et al.*, 1996; Levin, 1999; Zuckerman, 1999; Garinger, 2001; Laird, 2001; Ernst *et al.*, 2003; Kester *et al.*, 2006). However, the use of clinical groups negates any inferences about adolescent decision making in general.

Overall, decision making preferences do seem to play an important role in adolescents' health behaviour. In general, vigilance, in other words objective and informed decision making, is associated with healthier lifestyles, whereas defective strategies such as avoidance seem to encourage risk taking (e.g. Langer and Girard, 1999; Zwane et al., 2004; Miller and Drotar, 2007; Umeh, 1998a, 1998b).

Relevance in professional psychology

How does a book on adolescent decision making and health behaviour fit in with the rest of professional and academic psychology? How is it relevant to existing university courses in psychology?

Health psychology

Health psychology generally addresses the contribution of psychological factors to health. A major part of this field involves trying to understand and predict health behaviour, in children, adolescents and adults, using rationalistic models, such as the health belief model, and protection motivation theory (Marks et al., 2005; Ogden, 2000).

Drawing largely from subjective expected utility theory, these formulations are regarded as models of decision making, and are able to predict significant albeit limited proportions of the variance in health behaviour (e.g. Janz and Becker, 1984; Milne et al., 2000), even amongst adolescents (e.g. Sturges and Rogers, 1996). For example, protection motivation theory has been useful in predicting dietary behaviour, condom use, physical activity, smoking and other health related habits in children and teenagers (e.g. Fruin et al., 1992; Abraham et al., 1994).

Despite this, existing literature remains inconclusive for one simple reason: these models assume a preference for rational decision making. This is clearly problematic since we know from research using the DMQ that teenagers may arrive at decisions in ways that clearly aren't rationalistic, such as acting on impulse or being evasive (e.g. Mann et al., 1997, 1998; Umeh, 1998a; Tuinstra et al., 2000).

There is a paucity of health psychology textbooks that comprehensively discuss both competent and defective decision making practices in adolescents. Thus, this book will serve as a useful handbook for anyone – student or academic – keen to obtain a more rounded understanding of the determinants of health behaviour in young people.

Social psychology

Decision making is a major topic in social psychology (Feldman, 2001). Many great decision theorists were/are social psychologists, including Irving Janis, Leon Mann (e.g. Janis and Mann, 1977), Howard Leventhal (Leventhal, 1970) and Carl

Hovland (e.g. Hovland *et al.*, 1953). Decision making is 'social' to the extent that groups make decisions and people are influenced by social considerations when they make decisions as individuals. Thus, most good social psychology courses discuss issues such as groupthink, group polarisation and the influence of social pressure on personal decisions (e.g. Brehm *et al.*, 1999; Aronson, 2002).

Therefore, this book should be a relevant supplementary text for any social psychology course that includes any discussion of decision making in specific population groups, specifically younger age groups. For example, discussions of the impact of social influence often elaborate on the problem of peer pressure and its capacity heavily to affect the behaviour of teenagers. The text should also provide an essential learning resource where social psychology discussions on decision making focus predominantly on the adult (or general) population, thereby raising questions about the generality of any assumptions, hypotheses, theories or conclusions to adolescents.

For example most textbooks in social psychology discuss the concepts of groupthink, group polarisation and decision making strategies, assuming an adult audience, for example by focusing on managerial, political or military scenarios (e.g. Feldman, 2001; Aronson *et al.*, 2002). The current text can help shed light on the relevance of these phenomena in social contexts that are relevant to adolescents.

Developmental psychology

A major topic in this field is the cognitive development of children and adolescents. Ever since Jean Piaget published his theory of cognitive development (e.g. Piaget, 1954, 1956) developmental psychologists have been interested in the brain's increased acquisition of intellectual skills from birth through to the late teens, and beyond (Nutbeam and Booth, 1994; Petersen and Leffert, 1995; Byrnes, 2002).

A particularly interesting feature of adolescence, and of Piaget's model in particular, is the idea that capacity for abstract, hypothetical, logical or rationalistic thought generally doesn't appear until the early teens. This ability continues to develop through late adolescence and early adulthood.

These views seem generally accepted in developmental psychology, and raise questions about the decision making competence of humans prior to adulthood (e.g. Mann *et al.*, 1989; Halpern-Felsher and Cauffman, 2001). There is now a general consensus that making a choice from amongst competing alternatives is rather a different experience in adolescence compared with adulthood (e.g. Albion and Fogarty, 2002; Crone *et al.*, 2003; Janis and Klaczynski, 2005).

Existing theories of choice based on adults – most of the decision making literature is adult oriented – may therefore not apply to teenagers. Thus, there is a need for appropriate academic literature focused specifically on adolescence. The present textbook meets this requirement, albeit with an emphasis on health. Since many of the day-to-day decisions teenagers make are health related (e.g. whether

to smoke, drink, go on a diet, drive fast, fight, play rough games, climb a high fence, etc.) the book covers a significant share of decision making activity in this age group.

Conclusion

The point of this chapter is to introduce the reader to some of the key concepts and arguments that make up the fundamental premise of this book, notably adolescent decision making, health behaviour and the link between them. There are several key points that need to be emphasised in this regard.

First, there is no universally accepted and applicable definition of decision making. This is important because textbooks and journal articles often refer to this universally recognised concept as though it has a clear meaning. The reality is that decision making is a multifaceted and perhaps even elusive concept, often difficult to measure or track. For example, it is not clear whether decision making is a process, a single event, a mathematical activity, or merely an instinctual act driven by simple rules of thumb. When adolescents avoid difficult decisions, can this be regarded as a form of decision making in itself, and so on? In the midst of this intellectual chaos, theorists have introduced the ADMQ, a highly useful and seemingly psychometrically sound instrument that provides some basis for scientific measurement of adolescent decision making. This scale forms the basis for many of the key research findings discussed throughout the rest of this book.

Second, health behaviour, like decision making, is multidimensional, but can be meaningfully dichotomised into health enhancing and health damaging activities. Although adolescents engage in many activities that may affect their health, there is particular emphasis on behavioural risk factors implicated in major health threats such as cardiovascular disease and AIDS, as well as responses to illness symptoms or medical diagnosis.

Finally, few behavioural scientists will dispute that how adolescents make decisions may have significant implications for their health behaviour. A youngster who thinks things through in great depth is less likely to adopt risky behaviour than a colleague who always acts on impulse based on what his friends are doing. It is this seemingly inescapable link between freedom of choice and health that underpins the whole book and, I hope, provides ample food for thought for most readers.

Key points

- There is no universally accepted definition of decision making although it generally entails choosing from among a selection of options. Decision making may resemble a sequential process or a single momentary event.
- Decision making can be understood from a variety of theoretical perspectives, including prospect theory, subjective expected utility theory, the conflict-theory model and the transtheoretical model of behaviour change.

- Health behaviour refers to any activity that potentially may affect one's health. Such behaviour may be health enhancing or health damaging.
- Adolescents approach decision making in a variety of ways, both rational and otherwise.
- How teenagers arrive at decisions may have significant implications for health behaviour.

Key terms

- Decision making
- Bias
- Rationality
- Models of decision making
- Conflict-theory
- Prospect theory
- Subjective expected utility
- Decisional balance
- Transtheoretical model of behaviour change
- Decision making styles
- Health behaviour
- Adolescence
- Professional psychology

Further reading

Hastie, R. and Dawes, R.M. (2001) *Rational Choice in an Uncertain World*. Thousand Oaks, CA: Sage.

Jacobs, J.E. and Klaczynski, P.A. (eds.) (2005) *The Development of Judgment and Decision Making in Children and Adolescents*. Mahwah, NJ: Lawrence Erlbaum.

Plous, S. (1993) *The Psychology of Judgment and Decision Making*. New York: McGraw-Hill.

Umeh, K. (1998b) A conflict-theory approach to understanding adolescents' health behaviour, PhD thesis, University of Leicester, United Kingdom.

2 Choice

Chapter summary

This chapter deals with the ancient but still relevant philosophical perspectives of free will and determinism, and their applicability to understanding adolescents' health behaviour. Free will contends that people retain the freedom of choice independent of genetic and environmental influences. Determinism argues that choice is predetermined by antecedent conditions, and hence not subject to free will. Implications of these perspectives for the prediction and alteration of adolescent health behaviour are considered, including the point that determinism constitutes an inadequate basis for predicting human activity. Determinism offers useful insights into human behaviour, and dominated social science research for decades. Nevertheless, the empirical value of this philosophy is limited. To gain a better understanding of adolescent health behaviour it is essential to account for freedom of choice. This in effect means understanding decision making and its various permutations.

Chapter outline

This chapter begins with a brief introduction to determinism and free will doctrine. Next, each philosophy is discussed in some detail, starting with determinism. I consider the historical prominence of this perspective and its

scientific merits. Next, free will is discussed, with emphasis on its philosophical underpinnings and scientific value. The rest of the chapter elaborates the concept of free will, with particular emphasis on its relevance in understanding adolescent health behaviour.

Philosophical background

One of the oldest arguments in philosophy and psychology is the notion of free will, the idea that human beings freely make choices that are largely independent of prior conditions, personal or situational (see review by Viney and King, 2003). In effect people retain the *freedom of choice*, regardless of the prevailing circumstances, including genetic and environmental constraints. This means human beings can foresee, evaluate and choose from a selection of options irrespective of social pressure, economic factors, political or legal restraints, personality traits and inherited characteristics, for example.

The concept of free will constitutes the primary foundation on which this book is based. Adolescents, like other humans, are free to choose what health behaviours to adopt or avoid. Consequently, psychological models and theories based entirely on the notion of *determinism* – that everything has a cause, and hence is predetermined, without the possibility of choice – cannot adequately explain and predict adolescent lifestyle factors.

This is an important argument, since the bulk of existing theoretical and empirical literature on adolescent health behaviour appears to be underpinned by determinism.

An example using social influence clearly illustrates the point. It is often argued that teenage smoking is caused by peer pressure, suggesting that this behaviour is dependent on certain antecedent conditions, and hence predictable.

While there is unarguably an element of truth in this contention, it is potentially flawed because it assumes adolescents are necessarily passive participants 'trapped' by causal forces (e.g. peer pressure) and unable to exercise free will. It can be argued that even the most insecure weak-willed teenager, faced with a barrage of threats from physically intimidating pro-smoking bullies, demanding he or she smokes a cigarette, can still choose not to smoke, albeit existing models of social influence may predict otherwise.

Determinism

Determinism is the philosophy that every human behaviour and experience has a cause. In essence, people's actions are predetermined by genetic and environmental factors. There is no freedom of choice: what appear to be freely

made decisions are in fact predestined preferences (van Inwagen, 1983; Suppes, 1993; Newall, 2005).

For example, an adolescent who smokes was preordained to do so by present or antecedent conditions (e.g. peer pressure, attitudes and beliefs). Hence, human behaviour is predictable, once its causes are known. If teenage smoking is caused by peer pressure, then we can anticipate future cigarette use on the basis of current social conditions. The future is fixed and inevitable.

Proponents of determinism, such as Watson, Freud and Pavlov, offer powerful counter-arguments discrediting the doctrine of free will. According to Viney and King (2003) these arguments relate to the historical longevity and increased dominance of deterministic reasoning and literature, the negative impact of free will on scientific inquiry and notions of personal responsibility and morality, and the capacity of determinism to satisfy our craving for prediction.

I will now consider each of these arguments with particular reference to adolescent health behaviour.

Historical dominance of determinism

Much of modern-day psychology is predicated on scientific doctrine. Psychology has been built on the basic premise that human behaviour has potentially identifiable causes, which, once discerned, will enable reasonably accurate prediction and control. As Viney and King (2003) point out, psychology textbooks are awash with theories of various sorts purporting to identify the causes, antecedents or determinants of cognition, emotion, behaviour, personality, and a host of other psychological characteristics.

This emphasis on determinism dates back to the origins of psychology, such as the establishment of the first psychological laboratory at the University of Leipzig. Here the legendary Wilhelm Wundt conducted and inspired hundreds of studies aimed at establishing causality in psychological phenomena (Diamond, 1980).

If modern-day psychology is heavily determinist, then one can assume this merely reflects the inherent superiority and 'correctness' of determinism over free will. After all, psychologists seem to have had tremendous success in establishing causality, confirming the dependence of psychological phenomena on antecedent forces. So, for example, we now know that teenage smoking can be caused by peer pressure, such that the stronger the pressure from peers to smoke the greater the likelihood of cigarette use (Marcell et al., 2005; Leatherdale et al., 2006).

A quick glance through any psychology journal of adolescence or adolescent health will indeed reveal a multitude of empirical studies identifying the antecedents of various delinquent, health or problem behaviours.

For example, browsing through a recent volume of the *Journal of Adolescent Health* (41, 6, December 2007), one is immediately struck by the apparent emphasis on antecedence, causality or correlations (which may point to causality).

Of eighteen articles in this issue, the vast majority seemed to focus on identifying personal and/or environmental factors (e.g. television viewing, self-control, self-esteem, demographics, congenital heart disease, taking hormonal therapy) that may explain, affect or predict some health behaviour (e.g. Kornblau *et al.*, 2007; Nelson, 2007; Wills *et al.*, 2007). Some articles were clearly aimed at establishing antecedence, in the form of longitudinal research (e.g. Schmalz *et al.*, 2007; Toulou-Shams, 2007), or causality by evaluating the impact of interventions designed to modify health behaviour (e.g. French *et al.*, 2007; Werch *et al.*, 2007).

The fact that such evidence exists and has been accumulating for decades suggests that causality and hence predictability are to be found in all adolescents' health behaviour, irrespective of free will. Other than a solitary review paper by Paula Duncan and some colleagues (Duncan *et al.*, 2007), not a single article appeared to address freedom of choice.

The paucity of health behaviour research examining adolescent free will is fairly typical of existing journal and textbook literature. It is difficult not to infer from such evidence that free will has somehow 'failed' to improve our understanding of adolescent health behaviour, and consequently is of little value in the pursuance of knowledge in this field.

In short, the history of theory and research on adolescent health behaviour seems to chronicle the scientific and explanatory value of determinism, and in particular its dominance over notions of free will.

Determinism and personal responsibility

Determinists point out that free will muddles personal responsibility. In essence, people are inescapably held responsible for their actions. Consequently they may suffer unfair and severe retribution or criticism in situations over which they have little or no control. Thus, free will magnifies what social psychologists refer to as the Fundamental Attribution Error (Brehm and Kassim, 1999), whereby the impact of an individual's personality on her behaviour is overestimated, while the contribution of situational or contextual factors is overlooked.

In this case free choice philosophers overestimate the amount of control people have over their behaviour and events around them. As an example, Viney and King (2003) make reference to the witch-hunts and burnings of the late Renaissance, in which the arraigned were deemed to have free will, and made a choice to worship evil. Modern-day anti-gay vigilantes often justify the persecution of homosexuals on the grounds that homosexuality is a lifestyle choice, rather than an inevitable result of genetic, biological and environmental conditions.

The emphasis on freedom of choice in most Western societies means that teenagers routinely blame themselves for negative events in their lives (Daigneault *et al.*, 2006). So, for example, an adolescent who uses drugs may

chastise himself for apparently choosing this behaviour of his own free will. Yet the truth may be very different. Often teenagers may have little choice, and be at the mercy of external conditions beyond their control, such as inexperience, attitudinal constraints, legal restrictions, and the requirement for others' approval (De Civita and Pagani, 1996; Ozer and Weinstein, 2004).

Holding teenagers responsible for their actions seems unfair under conditions of severe social pressure. For example, adolescents often cannot be held (entirely) accountable for health behaviours like condom use simply because free will is constrained by significant social factors. Using a condom requires the approval of one's sexual partner.

Similarly, most adolescents have limited responsibility for what they eat. They have little option but to consume whatever food they are served at home or at school. Making a unilateral decision at home is impractical because it is parents who own the kitchen, prepare the meals and do the grocery shopping. It is parents who have the money to shop, own the car to drive to the supermarket, and do the driving! An independent decision at school is also unrealistic. The school menu is fixed, and not many teenagers are prepared to do an 'Oliver Twist' just to get the diet changed.

Constraints associated with law, ethics and authority are especially pertinent to decisions concerning *medical treatment*. In most Western countries, including the United Kingdom and the USA, it is a legal requirement that the parents or legal guardians of teenage children below a certain age give informed consent for any medical decisions (Breeding and Baughman, 2003).

Some legal systems incorporate exceptions to this rule. Teenagers may be able to give consent for medical interventions pertaining to certain issues, for example treatment of a sexually transmitted or communicable disease, or care involving substance abuse, pregnancy, abortion, and injuries sustained from a sexual assault (Parekh, 2007).

Nevertheless, as a general rule, parental consent is required. This all means that under-age adolescents can't exercise free will in medical scenarios. Their behaviour is entirely a function of uncontrollable causal factors (e.g. the law, parents' preferences and doctors' opinion), hence mitigating personal responsibility.

Finally, there is the issue of cognitive ability. Adolescents, particularly those in their early teens, often lack the knowledge, experience and evaluative skills necessary to survey and weigh options (Mann *et al.*, 1989; Ormond *et al.*, 1991). In order to exercise free will, and hence be held responsible for their actions, people have to be able to process hypothetical arguments, such as making sense of risk probabilities (Byrnes, 2002). Yet this ability is still developing during adolescence (Petersen and Leffert, 1995).

Determinists will point out that the neurological or cognitive state of the brain is itself an antecedent condition that predetermines adolescent behaviour, hence negating personal responsibility. Thus, for example, a teenager who chooses to ingest dangerous drugs is blameless because he or she is 'predestined' to carry out this act by an a priori cognitive state.

Box 2.1 Media spotlight: power/status effects on free will

Teenagers are more likely to exercise their freedom of choice despite peer criticism if they enjoy power and status within the peer group.

Apart from power and gender issues associated with sexual relationships (i.e. boys often have the power, and hence make decisions about contraceptive use), youngsters considered 'cool', good-looking, popular, rich, in the football team or cheerleader squad, or known to be dating the coolest/most popular boy/girl on campus, may find their decisions passively accepted by other less privileged teens, notably the geeks and nerds.

In the Hollywood teen movie *Mean Girls*, starring Lindsay Lohan, Rachel Adams and Tina Fey, there are several interesting scenes involving a group of three girls considered by other teens on campus to be very popular. Amongst this trio, one girl, Regina George (Rachel Adams), routinely makes all the decisions, while her two loyal colleagues unquestioningly go along.

Regina's 'power' appears to derive from her status as a 'regulation hotty', a 'Queen Bee', on campus: in essence a spoiled rich girl, whom all the boys on campus consider 'hot', and whose friends and admirers think of as 'awesome'. In one particular scene, based in the school cafeteria, Regina expresses a desire to lose weight to three of her companions. One girl retorts, 'Oh God, what are you talking about?' A second girl quickly follows with another riposte, 'You are too skinny.' Regina stares silently at both girls for a second or two, and then dismisses both with the curt remark 'Oh, shut up.' There is no further challenge to Regina's decision to lose weight. What appears to be an issue thrown open for group discussion – and supposedly a group *decision* – is abruptly resolved by one individual, with no protest whatsoever from the rest of the group.

Not an ideal example perhaps – health isn't necessarily a key aspect of the dialogue. Nevertheless, it is a good illustration of how a particular individual's preference may enjoy a certain immunity from the usual social pressures that heavily influence decision making in adolescence.

Determinism and scientific prediction

One argument used to justify a determinist worldview is that, without determinism, it is effectively impossible to make reliable predictions about phenomena. Human beings need to be able to make reasonable forecasts, in order to control their environment and destiny (Viney, 1990; Viney and King, 2003). The ability to anticipate is crucial to our survival.

Thus, the notion that adolescent health behaviour has causality is extremely appealing to social scientists, irrespective of the truth of this philosophy. Determinism can be credited with inspiring decades of research aimed at

identifying the determinants of behaviour (e.g. see reviews by Tyas and Pederson, 1998; Umeh, 1998b; Spear and Kulbok, 2001; Rise, 2004).

Causality, once established, can then be used as the basis for predicting behaviour, and for developing interventions to improve adolescents' lifestyles (e.g. Cowan, 2002). Determinism offers health psychologists an escape from thinking the unthinkable – that adolescent health behaviour has *no* causes, and hence is entirely a function of free will, with its frightening randomness and unpredictability. It is more comforting to cling on to the idea of causality, with its promise of certainty, prediction and control.

Cumulative social science research has indeed identified various apparent 'causes' or 'predictors' of adolescent health behaviour, ranging from personal characteristics, such as personality, stress and perceptions of invulnerability, to situational forces like peer pressure and family cohesion (e.g. Tyas and Pederson, 1998; Spear and Kulbok, 2001; Rise, 2004).

However, this evidence is by no means conclusive. The concept of causality is deemed problematic by various philosophers, including David Hume (1711–76) and John Stuart Mill (1806–73) (Viney and King, 2003). For example, determinism aside, it is questionable whether causality can be unambiguously identified, in view of its plurality. Despite these concerns, the exponential growth of social science theory and research on adolescent health behaviour, and the use of accumulated literature evidence for developing useful interventions (e.g. Cowan, 2002; Rise, 2004) provide a powerful argument in favour of determinism.

It can be argued – and convincingly – that predictions of adolescent health behaviour are at best modest (see discussions of free will doctrine below). Nevertheless, in the real world, even moderate predictions can be hugely satisfying (Pimple, 2006). Take the example of teenage pregnancy. Correctly predicting that an adolescent will have unprotected sex is extremely valuable even if the prediction is correct less than half the time. After all, a single failure to use contraception can be costly.

Free will

Despite the above arguments in favour of determinism, decades of empirical research on health behaviour have shown that the predictive performance of determinist models is limited (Eagly and Chaiken, 1993; Umeh, 1998b; Floyd *et al.*, 2000; Milne *et al.*, 2000; Brewer *et al.*, 2007; Munro *et al.*, 2007). Thus, there is a need to consider the concept of free will, as a basis for improving our understanding of adolescent health behaviour.

Free will implies that a person retains freedom of choice, irrespective of situational and personal considerations (van Inwagen, 1983; Viney and King, 2003; Newall, 2005). Thus, the future is not set, or necessarily predictable. There has been a distinct lack of interest amongst psychologists in the importance of free will

doctrine to adolescent health. A recent search on PsycINFO using the key words 'free will' and 'adolescents' produced just four sources! Yet freedom of choice is a concept your average Western teenager seems to recognise (Sundberg *et al.*, 1970; Agnew, 1989).

In a pioneering study comparing free will amongst Indian and American adolescents, Sundberg *et al.* (1970) noted that the Western adolescent 'is frequently reminded that he should make his decisions himself and be willing to accept the responsibility for the consequences. It would not therefore be unreasonable to expect that American adolescents would score higher on items relating to free will and lower on items relating to external control than Indian boys and girls' (p. 376). In fact both groups equally endorsed free will, suggesting that freedom of choice may be more universal than previously thought.

Several months into writing this book I read an interesting email written by a teenage girl. The email, which had been sent to a website dedicated to helping adolescents cope with peer pressure and other problems, detailed how she had dealt with incessant hassle by peers trying to get her to smoke.

What drew my attention wasn't the bit about peer pressure, but rather her reference to decision making. She had apparently started smoking cigarettes after considerable pressure from friends to take up smoking. Yet, she blamed her smoking, not on peers, but rather on the fact that she had *chosen* to smoke in the midst of such pressure. In other words, it wasn't the demands of her peers that were chiefly at fault, but rather her decision making. This suggested to me that teenagers generally recognise and exercise their freedom of choice (Mann *et al.*, 1989; Petersen and Leffert, 1995).

Proponents of free will – known as libertarians, and including the likes of Carl Jung (1875–1961) and Gordon Allport (1897–1967) – present a number of compelling arguments to justify their position. One argument described by Viney and King (2003) is that believing in determinism is illogical since it suggests people do not have the freedom of choice to adopt a philosophical view. It means a preference for determinism, according to determinism, is effectively predetermined by certain antecedent conditions over which the individual has no control! A determinist cannot claim to have chosen to endorse determinism.

Another argument is that determinism negates personal responsibility. Hence, a teenager who drives recklessly, killing some pedestrians, has unprotected sex, smokes some pot and prefers to eat nothing but junk foods is entirely faultless and blameless, and merely a victim of uncontrollable causal genetic or environmental forces!

Yet another contention, perhaps the most objective and hence compelling one, is that deterministic models used to explain and predict adolescent health behaviour generally do not achieve very high levels of predictive accuracy. For example, studies reporting significant correlations between peer pressure and health behaviour rarely report strong correlations, say above 0.7, let alone perfect covariance. These arguments are considered in greater detail below.

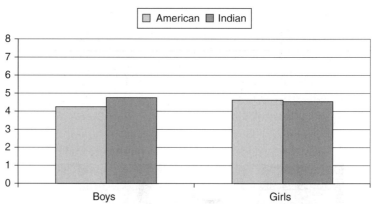

Endorsement of the statement 'What happens to me is my own doing: what I do is up to me.' A higher score indicates greater approval.

2.1 *How universal is the concept of free will? It is tempting to view free will as a doctrine embraced largely by adolescents born and raised in Western countries. However, the reality may be very different. A pioneering study conducted in the early 1970s showed equal endorsement of free will in American and Indian adolescents, notwithstanding the more restrictive cultural origins of the latter group. Evidence like this justifies inquiry into the role of free will in adolescent health behaviour (Source: Sundberg* et al.*, 1970).*

Free will and causality

Libertarians question the notion that every human behaviour or experience has a cause (Viney and King, 2003). After all, in exercising free will people can freely select particular actions or outcomes irrespective of any causal antecedent conditions. For example, let's once again consider the notion that peer pressure causes cigarette smoking amongst teenagers. An adolescent can freely choose not to smoke, irrespective of what his friends think, and he can repeatedly make the same decision in other situations, irrespective of the social conditions.

Now, if researchers find that peer pressure induces or predicts cigarette use in a particular study (e.g. Leatherdale *et al.*, 2006; Miller *et al.*, 2006), this is only because participants deliberately and *freely* elected to acquiesce to social influence, not because of any causal relationship between peer pressure and smoking. Subjects could just as easily have opted not to comply (Ungar, 2000). Thus the whole notion of causality seems highly questionable.

Causality has always been problematic for philosophers, dating back to the time of Aristotle (Viney and King, 2003). Different philosophers put forward different arguments and concerns, most of which are beyond the scope of this book. However, the English philosopher John Stuart Mill has offered a particularly compelling set of arguments worthy of mention here (Wilson, 1990).

One contention concerns the difficulties scientists experience trying to disentangle the never-ending 'chain' of causality, in order to identify an original cause.

2.2 *Freedom of choice. According to free will doctrine, every health behaviour, detrimental or otherwise, reflects a free choice that an individual has made, independent of personal and situational constraints (Source: SXC).*

This is known as the problem of 'first cause'. Consider for example the often-asserted notion that a perception of invulnerability causes risk taking among adolescents (Stauber, 1995; Milam *et al.*, 2000; Millstein and Halpern-Felsher, 2002).

Now, consider that invulnerability itself is caused by a lack of personal experience, which in turn is a consequence of a person's young biological age (e.g. see Greening and Dollinger, 1992). What then? Does causality not also reside in the antecedents of invulnerability, and if so, what was the original trigger?

The point here is that statements about cause–effect are often inconclusive simply because every cause has a cause, and identifying the original cause in this endless chain of causality may be impossible.

Another argument made by J. S. Mill is that there are usually multiple causes for an event. Simple cause–effect statements such as 'a perception of invulnerability causes risk taking' are in fact misleading because they ignore the plurality of causes for risky behaviour. Thus, is risk taking caused by perceived invulnerability, the raw sensory information (e.g. lack of physical pain) that we translate as a lack of danger, the neurological/brain electrical activity that occurs when we interpret sensory stimuli, or the memory that reminds us of the paucity of previous physical or emotional injury?

Take as another example the claim that social pressure causes smoking in teenagers (e.g. Leatherdale *et al.*, 2006). Is 'peer pressure' the real cause, or is it the threatening verbalisations, facial expressions, emotional displays or physical threats of the peer group, or indeed the stress caused by such pressure? Attributing causality will be problematic.

All in all, Mill viewed determinism as inadequate because, while on the one hand it suggests every event or behaviour has a cause, it fails to specify what the cause is, relying instead on scientific research to establish causality. Nevertheless, Mill vigorously defends determinism as essential in understanding human behaviour, arguing that failure to delineate causality in scientific inquiry need not invalidate determinist laws. It may simply be that the scientists aren't working hard enough to establish causality, or need to develop new causal hypotheses, suggesting other potential causes.

Despite Mill's optimism, it is accepted by many scientists today that not every event has an identifiable antecedent (see Kiel and Elliot, 1997), often for the precise reasons identified by Mill: a multiplicity of causes for any single event or behaviour, and the endless chains of causality with no discernible origins.

So, what does all this mean for understanding adolescent health behaviour? Well, it may never be possible to establish conclusively the causes of (and hence predict) health practices even if we embrace determinism as an underpinning philosophy. In this context the notion of free will does gain a certain appeal.

Why invest time and energy struggling in vain to establish the personal and situational causes of health behaviour if any causal relationship is probably mediated by freedom of choice? A complete understanding of teenage health habits requires, it appears, an understanding of their decision making.

Free will and prediction

One problem with determinism, libertarians point out, is its implication that human actions are predictable. Determinists argue that since human behaviour has causality, it should be possible to anticipate behaviour once the relevant precursors are identified. Thus, adolescent health behaviours should be perfectly foreseeable.

So, for example, if peer pressure causes cigarette smoking, then knowledge of the former should enable accurate prediction of the latter. Yet the reality is very

Box 2.2 Media spotlight: free will and economic constraints

Reading a lot of psychological literature on adolescent health behaviour, one could be forgiven for thinking that the main considerations entertained by teenagers when making a choice are social, primarily peer pressure.

One consideration rarely mentioned in this context is the financial consequence of choosing one option over another.

Since teenagers aren't particularly interested in economics and are often at the mercy of their parents when faced with financial decisions (e.g. pocket money), the monetary costs and benefits of competing alternatives may not at first appear to be a key consideration when teenagers are making health decisions.

However, a recent article in the *Liverpool Daily Post* (Wednesday, 3 October 2007) highlighted the importance of economic factors in choice. It reported that school children were increasingly shying away from healthy foods (e.g. low-fat meals) sold in their school canteen because these were becoming increasingly expensive to purchase. As a result, many pupils were going without food for the whole day, or simply opting for less healthy but cheaper meals from the chip shop.

Thus teenagers do consider economic factors in exercising their free will. However, determinists may argue they may have no choice in the matter: pocket money can only stretch so far, irrespective of other influences on choice such as peer pressure.

different. It would long have been evident, both to free will advocates and to determinists worth their salt, that behavioural science research (much of which is dominated by determinism) rarely reports strong let alone perfect predictions of behaviour (e.g. see reviews by Eagly and Chaiken, 1993; Milne *et al.*, 2000; Witte and Allen, 2000).

We can illustrate this problem by examining three studies investigating the link between adolescents' health behaviour and their perceptions (Misra and Aguillon, 2002; Marcelland and Halpern-Felsher, 2005; Wang *et al.*, 2006). There is an established school of thought in health psychology and aligned disciplines that people's beliefs about health affect their willingness to adopt preventive behaviours (Conner, 1993; Norman and Conner, 1996). Such is the ubiquity of this decidedly determinist mindset that health psychology is awash with various 'models' describing seemingly causal relations between health beliefs and protective action (e.g. Ogden, 2000). Yet decades of research have demonstrated the predictive limitations of this mindset, as the following studies will show.

I selected these studies partly because they employed multiple regression analysis, a procedure that quantifies the amount of 'variance' in a 'dependent' variable accurately 'predicted' by a set of 'independent' (potentially causal) variables (Tabachnick and Fidell, 1996). Predictive accuracy can be appreciated in percentages, with a higher percentage denoting better forecasting, and 100 per cent implying perfect prediction.

One study, conducted by Shiaw-Ling Wang and colleagues (Wang *et al*., 2006), examined the relationship between health beliefs and intent to perform various reproductive behaviours (using birth control during sexual intercourse, and seeking medical care/advice when anticipating a pregnancy). Subjects were a group of teenage girls suffering from diabetes, and recruited from various diabetic clinics in Pittsburgh.

Regression analysis showed that health beliefs accurately predicted just 24.4 per cent of the variance in their intentions, leaving over 75 per cent of the variance unexplained. To improve prediction the researchers incorporated additional explanatory variables, including personal attitudes towards reproductive behaviours and the belief that one could carry out such activity. However, these additional variables only improved predictability by a meagre 2 per cent: the bulk of variance remained unexplained.

Another investigation, by Marcelland and Halpern-Felsher (2005), examined the role of health beliefs in adolescents' intentions to see a doctor for four health problems – pneumonia symptoms, cigarette use, sexual intercourse and symptoms of depression. The sample consisted of high school students from northern California. Regression analysis revealed that health beliefs predicted less than 50 per cent of the variance, across the board. Prediction of intentions concerning pneumonia symptoms was particularly poor, at just 12 per cent! Thus, as in Wang *et al*.'s (2006) study, a substantial proportion of the variance was left unexplained.

Ranjita Misra and Sandra Aguillon report similarly dismal predictability in a study on the association between adolescents' health beliefs/knowledge (e.g. importance attached to health, and self-ratings of current health status) and their dietary habits and level of physical activity (Misra and Aguillon, 2001). Participants were high school students from north-east Missouri. In regression analysis health beliefs, together with other variables such as age and parental education, predicted only 24.8 per cent and 26.1 per cent of the variance in dietary behaviour and physical activity, respectively.

Findings from these studies are by no means atypical. A number of psychoanalytic reviews of research on health beliefs also report limited predictability (e.g. Janz and Becker, 1984; Floyd *et al*., 2000; Milne *et al*., 2000).

Poor predictability in scientific studies can be attributed to a variety of factors other than weak causal relationships (Tabachnick and Fidell, 1996). For example, questionnaires and similar instruments often used to measure people's health perceptions almost always suffer from some degree of unreliability and invalidity (e.g. Scandell and Wlazelek, 2002). Such measurement error diminishes predictive power (Bryman and Cramer, 1994).

Another possible reason for low predictive power is the failure of researchers to account for important predictor variables. Adding new variables to a regression model can improve predictive accuracy, at least in theory. This would be important particularly if, say, health beliefs are just one of several personal and situational determinants of behaviour.

The reality, though, is that 'saturating' a regression model with numerous variables rarely achieves strong, let alone perfect, prediction of 100 per cent (Tabachnick and Fidell, 1996). Thus, even with perfect measurement instruments, and a wealth of background and personal information, it would still be difficult, perhaps even impossible, perfectly to forecast adolescent health behaviour.

In effect, what we are looking at here is convincing evidence that determinist doctrine is insufficient for explaining adolescent health behaviour. There is clearly an element of human action that for some reason remains random, and hence difficult to anticipate, at least using basic cause–effect models. To libertarians, free will accounts for this arbitrariness in human behaviour.

There is simply no way of reliably determining what choice a person will make in any given decision making scenario. It is not inconceivable that adolescents, when in doubt about what to choose, may use a 'chance' strategy equivalent to reciting the children's counting rhyme 'eeny, meeny, miney, mo', to resolve their dilemma (Opie and Opie, 1959, 1992). This is equivalent to tossing a coin, or some other wholly chance-based activity. Any attempt at accurate prediction in this context will be severely negated, albeit not entirely (see Pimple, 2006).

Free will and personal responsibility

I have already discussed at length the determinist view on personal responsibility. To libertarians, determinism effectively obscures the notion of individual liability, effectively giving people free reign to commit all kinds of immoral acts on the grounds of inevitability and predetermination (Viney and King, 2003). Yet, in reality, both determinism and free will doctrine *distort* personal responsibility.

Whereas determinists view it from one extreme (people are never responsible for their actions), libertarians conceptualise it from the other (individuals are perpetually liable for their actions, because they are free to make their own choices). Thus free will, by definition, emphasises personal blame.

Take the example of unprotected sex. Free will doctrine suggests that adolescents who fail to use contraception have made a free choice, and therefore can and should be held responsible for their actions and any consequences. This indeed appears to be the dominant mindset in Western cultures and other individualist societies (Sundberg *et al.*, 1970). It is this very mindset that makes many adolescents blame themselves for negative outcomes (Daigneault *et al.*, 2006).

From a determinist's perspective, free choice cannot transcend a priori causality: what appears to be freely chosen behaviour is in fact already predetermined by antecedent conditions, so personal responsibility isn't applicable. Yet, this argument is disputable. Take, for example, adolescents' dietary habits. Food intake is often largely a function of what is served at home, or available in the school cafeteria (Shannon *et al.*, 2002). Despite these situational constraints, however, adolescents can have a say in what they eat.

For example, many youngsters can successfully negotiate with their parents what is cooked/served at home. Many (probably most) parents are happy to accommodate their children's preferences. Moreover, teenagers who regularly receive pocket money, to spend as they wish, are often the sole arbiter of what they eat. They can easily choose to buy a healthy meal, and/or even some fruits and vegetables, rather than the usual junk foods.

Like determinism, the problem with the free will perspective on personal responsibility is its *extreme* (and hence presumably atypical) position. Libertarians worry that a sense of diminished personal culpability can easily lead to an escalation in criminal, immoral and dangerous behaviour, and ultimately to a breakdown in social order and human survivability. According to philosopher Jean-Paul Sartre (1905–80), people may try to avoid personal responsibility by hiding behind determinism (e.g. 'it wasn't my fault', 'I was "forced" to do it') (e.g. Laing and Cooper, 1971).

Thus adolescents may be more disposed to indulge in risky activity, such as smoking, unprotected sex and dietary fat intake, believing they aren't responsible for their actions. And there is no shortage of personal and situational factors to which culpability may be attributed. Habit, parents, friends, TV and society can all be used to justify risk behaviour.

For example, adolescent smokers typically blame their cigarette smoking on social and physical demands, such as pressures to look 'cool' or 'popular', or to lose weight (Halpern-Felsher et al., 2004). There is rarely any reference to free will, such as accepting that cigarette smoking reflects a personal choice, and/or cannot be blamed on external forces. Diminished culpability begets a loss of self-restraint, with potentially catastrophic short- and long-term health consequences. Given this dismal portrayal it is no surprise that Western societies in general take the libertarian view on personal responsibility, especially when dealing with crime (Nagtegaal, 2004).

It is tempting to view adolescents as averse to accepting personal liability, especially in view of social stereotypes of teenagers as being irresponsible (Bostrom, 2001). Indeed adolescents may view their adolescence as itself an extenuating factor that mitigates personal responsibility (Steinberg and Scott, 2003). Nevertheless, a recent study using focus groups to explore personal responsibility in adolescents revealed a surprisingly encouraging picture (Mergler et al., 2007).

Participants indicated a keenness to take responsibility for their actions, even when there are clearly extenuating circumstances, such as peer pressure and parental input. There was a strong sense that one is responsible for one's behaviour and emotions, notwithstanding personal or situational factors. However, such views were by no means universal. Some adolescents felt they weren't in sufficient control of their own behaviour. Moreover, there was evidence that participants embraced personal responsibility primarily owing to a fear of punishment for bad behaviour, rather than out of any moral or philosophical convictions.

Box 2.3 Media spotlight: free will in Western culture

Freedom of choice is endemic in Western thinking. This was epitomised by a recent *Fox News* clip about the US President. On 11 December 2007 Fox News presented a news clip in which President George W. Bush was seen congratulating a teenage girl who had successfully quit drugs. In a speech showering accolades on the teenager, the President emphasised the fact that she had made a 'personal choice' to kick her drug habit. This comment illustrates the importance attached to free will in adolescence by those in the highest political echelons of Western society.

At first glance, choice may appear to be a readily available and free 'resource' that most teenagers have. Adult society often just can't understand why teenagers can't simply say 'no' to drugs, cigarettes, alcohol and other risky activities; after all, adolescents always have a choice! Or do they?

The problem with the notion of choice is that it requires the availability of (at least two) options to be workable: in the absence of options, there is no choice, and serious losses may be incurred as a result.

On 11 May 2004 a BBC News report illustrated how teenage unawareness about available options could lead to potentially catastrophic health decisions. It came to light that teenagers undergoing treatment for cancer were running the risk of future infertility, simply because they were unaware of their options. Only a minority were informed about measures such as freezing sperm or eggs, which could enable them to have children later in life. The charity Teenage Cancer Trust strongly recommended that teenagers be made fully aware of their options prior to treatment.

Yet, the acceptance of culpability, whatever its underpinnings, suggests that free will plays a particularly important role in adolescent behaviour. Mergler *et al.*'s (2007) study suggests adolescents are willing to embrace personal responsibility, irrespective of the circumstances. They exhibit a greater awareness of the consequences of one's actions, and an unwillingness to succumb helplessly to outside forces.

For example, a teenager facing incessant peer pressure to become sexually active will be continually aware that it is *her* decision, and may go through a period of soul searching and mental deliberation, before finally succumbing or abstaining. Overall, adolescents seem more libertarian than determinist in their attitudes towards personal liability.

Exercising free will

Free will is unworkable unless individuals know they have a choice (van Inwagen, 1983; Viney and King, 2003; Newall, 2005). Thus, at the very least, a person has to be aware of the available options (Byrnes, 2002).

For example, a teenage smoker cannot exercise free will if he believes smoking is his *only* option. Furthermore, once a person is aware of the alternatives, he must have a basis for making a choice, be that a carefully thought-out mathematical formula or a simple coin toss.

Adolescents on the whole can be very knowledgeable about the options available to them (Byrnes, 2002). They know what their alternatives are, and hence are in a strong position to make an informed choice.

Evidence for this comes from a study by Lita Furby, Catherine Thomas and Linda Ochs, from Eugene, Oregon (Furby *et al.*, 1995). They interviewed a small group of sexually active teenagers to gain a better understanding of how adolescents perceive their options when making decisions concerning STD[1] prevention during sexual intercourse. Encouragingly, the participants identified more than a hundred different methods of protection, which could be categorised into sixteen basic groupings. More interestingly, the researchers found that the average participant was aware of at least thirteen prevention methods, an impressive figure given that many adults struggle to come up with such a figure if quizzed about STD prevention.

I clearly remember receiving a comprehensive written list of pregnancy and STD protective options from my family doctor during a routine visit, shortly after my wife gave birth to our son. It was (and still is) standard procedure for doctors in Britain to discuss pregnancy prevention measures with new parents. If I recall correctly, the list contained fifteen or so methods. Now, if teenagers know about the majority of these measures then it suggests a remarkable awareness for any adolescent contemplating contraceptive use. Such familiarity isn't unusual. Research has shown that adolescent decision makers in general are very well informed, at least to the same degree as adults (Byrnes, 2002).

So how do they decide which option to choose? Contrary to stereotypical views, it appears that teenagers can be quite thoughtful and analytical when evaluating their alternatives. For example, in a study of food choices amongst 11 to 18 year olds, Isobel R. Contento and several colleagues found that participants not only developed personal decision making rules for determining what lunch to choose from a menu (e.g. establishing a suitable selection criteria, such as taste and health), but also engaged in negotiations (say, with the family) as a way of improving their options (Contento *et al.*, 2006).

Not surprisingly, adolescents (like adults) are heavily influenced by what options are actually available. Thus alternatives which aren't accessible or viable do not form part of the decision making process. For example, in another study of food choice Michelle L. Granner found that the availability of fruit and vegetables at home was the most reliable determinant of adolescent fruit and vegetable intake (Granner, 2004). This suggests a certain degree of realism, whereby choice is based on real-world options, rather than imagined or abstract possibilities.

---

[1] Sexually transmitted disease.

Box 2.4 Research spotlight: maximising choice

How much importance do teenagers attach to making good health choices? One way to find out is to consider how keen teenagers are to enlarge their options when required to make a choice: the more options available to them the greater the chances of a good decision (Janis and Mann, 1977).

Thus, if teenagers are keen to increase the available options in a given health related situation, then this could denote an emphasis on making a good decision.

Shannon *et al.* (2002) conducted a study that shed some light on this issue. They developed an eighteen-item questionnaire that measured various factors which teenagers believe influence their food choice in the school cafeteria. These factors included views about the availability of healthy foods on offer. Clearly, this issue relates specifically to the availability of options.

Respondents were required to indicate the extent to which they agreed with the following items:

- The school cafeteria should offer healthier low-fat foods.
- I would buy more low-fat foods from the school cafeteria if there was a larger selection of low-fat foods.

Data from nearly 300 high school students from the Minneapolis metropolitan area were analysed. Only 45.7 per cent and 46.1 per cent 'strongly agreed' or 'agreed' with the two items, respectively.

At face value, these findings suggest that most participants – at least a small majority – weren't bothered about maximising their options. Does this reflect an indifference to good decision making? It is difficult to say. Some teenagers may have genuinely believed the available food selections were sufficient to make a healthy choice. Others may have simply failed to grasp the value of having more options in a choice situation.

However, on a less positive note, a reliance solely on obvious options may indicate a reluctance to search for more alternatives. It is possible that some teenagers may not recognise that having more options improves their freedom of choice.

For example, only a minority of adolescents are likely to make a better choice if provided with more rather than fewer options. This phenomenon was clearly demonstrated by Shannon *et al.* (2002) using high school students. Fewer than 50 per cent of participants felt the school cafeteria should offer a wider selection of healthy foods, and that the greater choice would encourage them to purchase low-fat foods.

Perhaps one of the most intriguing discoveries is the setting of *boundaries*. It seems that when making certain types of decisions adolescents don't consider all the available options, but rather identify a select few they are prepared to entertain. A study by Michels *et al.* (2005) found that, when making sexual decisions, teenagers may consciously exclude particular forms of sexual activity

they aren't prepared to partake in, on grounds of personal principle. This attitude, narrow-minded though it may seem, suggests a rather more deliberate and attentive approach to decision making than some social stereotypes of teenagers may suggest (Stepp, 2002). Adolescents aren't as passive or indifferent as casual observation may sometimes suggest. Michels *et al.*'s (2005) study is considered in greater detail in Chapter 6.

The empirical value of free will

Can free will doctrine offer an improved or better explanation of adolescent health behaviour, over and beyond determinism? As already mentioned, decades of research have revealed the predictive limitations of determinist models (e.g. Eagly and Chaiken, 1993). The difficulties in establishing causality emphasised by John Stuart Mill and other philosophers (Viney and King, 2003) mean that determinism will struggle to offer even modest predictions of teenage health behaviour.

However, free will doctrine inherently negates predictability. Consider a boy faced with a choice between smoking and abstaining. To libertarians his decision cannot be reliably predicted since it is arbitrary and random, devoid of any discernible laws of causality. In fact the boy himself may not be able to predict his own decision, and even if he can, the forecast may prove unreliable over a number of trials.

Note that the randomness and unpredictability of choice applies notwithstanding individuals' prior decisions and behaviour, and other potential causal factors, such as peer group pressure, attitudes, knowledge and parental influence.

The historical dominance of determinism in psychological research and theory does accord some degree of empirical validity to causal philosophy (Viney and King, 2003). It is not difficult to find studies demonstrating seemingly causal relationships between health behaviour and various genetic, environmental and social factors, over which people have limited control (Eagly and Chaiken, 1993; Floyd *et al.*, 2000; Milne *et al.*, 2000; Brewer *et al.*, 2007). Yet the strength of such relationships is typically modest if not weak (e.g. Milne *et al.*, 2000; Munro *et al.*, 2007).

For example, in a comprehensive meta-analysis Munro *et al.* (2007) found that models which attribute causality to cognitive variables, such as health beliefs and attitudes, rarely explain more than one-third of the variance in health behaviour. It is tempting, in view of such gloomy evidence, to assume that incorporating free will parameters in health behaviour research will improve predictability and understanding.

However, this has not proved to be the case. I have found in the course of my own research that measures of how people exercise their freedom of choice – in essence, how they make decisions – provide at best marginal improvements in the prediction of adolescent health behaviour (Umeh, 1998a, 1998b).

For example, a preference for competent decision making improved prediction of sexual intentions, but only by a modest 2 per cent. Such evidence led me to concede that the common practice of excluding decision making variables from research on adolescent health behaviour (Umeh, 2002; also see Weinstein, 1993; van der Pligt, 1994) was somewhat justified (Umeh, 1998a). Yet, it may be premature and ill informed to dismiss free will doctrine, and embrace the notion that adolescents never really have a choice. There is a paucity of research investigating the relevance of free will (i.e. decision making) variables in health behaviour literature (Janis and Mann, 1977; Byrnes, 2002; Umeh, 2002). Factors such as the number of available options, freedom to choose and decision making style may explain significant proportions of the variance in health behaviour, after eliminating important genetic, environmental and social factors.

It is worth mentioning that the 2 per cent enhancement in predictability that I observed was statistically *significant* despite controlling for various personal and situational antecedents that, from the perspective of determinism, govern behaviour. This can be interpreted as evidence that free will may offer irrefutable, albeit modest, improvements in our understanding of human behaviour, over and beyond the input of determinism.

In any case, I examined free will from a general rather than a situation-specific perspective. So, for example, subjects were asked to respond to generic statements like 'I like to make decisions myself', which don't take into account how they will respond from one situation to the next. How a person chooses may vary across different scenarios (e.g. weighing several options in considering a diet change, but then only considering one alternative when offered a cigarette). Furthermore, people often have difficulty accurately summarising their general decision making habits and reporting this information accurately (Leventhal *et al.*, 1993). All these methodological constraints may limit predictive power.

Methodological issues aside, it may be unfair to expect more than modest improvements in prediction, given that free will doctrine emphasises randomness and spontaneity (Viney and King, 2003). Nonetheless, there is clearly a need for research that creates ideal conditions in a laboratory experiment in order to demonstrate the explanatory value of free choice in relation to adolescent health behaviour.

It is entirely possible, for example, that two adolescents (say identical twins), matched exactly on their genetic, environmental and social background, will make different choices when asked to choose between two options, over a number of trials. Would this conclusively demonstrate free will? Probably not. Determinists would argue that any difference in choice could be attributed to some disparity between the two individuals in antecedent conditions. After all, it is arguably impossible to create two exactly identical human beings, with matching genetic, neurological, psychological and social qualities, for example.

Nevertheless, the empirical value of free will, albeit yet to be demonstrated conclusively, is likely to remain a key consideration in trying to understand and explain adolescent health behaviour.

Further reading

Kiel, L.D. and Elliott, E.W. (1997) *Chaos Theory in the Social Sciences*. Ann Arbor: University of Michigan Press.

Van Inwagen, P. (1983) *An Essay on Free Will*. Oxford: Clarendon Press.

Viney, W. and King, D.B. (2003) *History of Psychology: Ideas and Context* (third edition). Boston: Allyn and Bacon.

3 Goals

Learning outcomes

By the end of this chapter readers should have an increased understanding of the following:

1 the relevance of goals in decision making
2 important background theory on goal directed behaviour
3 fear and danger reduction as fundamental objectives
4 the distinction between intrinsic and extrinsic goals, and their possible impact on the quality of decision making
5 the implications of goals for healthy and unhealthy choices
6 gender differences in goals, especially in relation to appearance issues
7 the significance of having a single goal during decision making.

Chapter summary

Goal setting is considered by theorists to be the first stage in the decision making process. Consequently I consider several key models of goal directed behaviour, notably goal theory, goal setting theory and the parallel response model. Although the first two frameworks originate outside health psychology, they are adaptable to a health behaviour setting. Distinctions are made between intrinsic and extrinsic goals, and dealing with danger versus resolving anxiety. Adolescents, it is argued, typically have multiple goals when making health behaviour choices. How one looks, health status and social approval seem to be particularly salient issues. Although good health is a key objective for teenagers, it is easily matched or superseded by social and appearance considerations. Furthermore, goals may impact significantly on the quality of decision making, with intrinsic objectives potentially more energising. Overall, this chapter highlights the importance of goals as incentives, or indeed disincentives, for the teenage decision maker.

Chapter outline

I begin this chapter by introducing the concept of goal setting in decision making, followed by a brief review of some relevant theories on goal directed behaviour. Next I consider salient goal categories, notably seeking to reduce

> anxiety and perceived threat, and chasing intrinsic versus extrinsic objectives. I then discuss the implications of goals for health behaviour, followed by a review of relevant gender differences in priorities. Finally, I look at the importance of feedback in goal attainment, the salience of fear and danger as key themes, and single-goal scenarios.

Goal setting

An adolescent faced with a health behaviour decision may ask the question 'what am I trying to achieve?' Most decision theorists accept that the very first step in decision making is setting a goal (Furby and Beyth-Marom, 1992; Byrnes *et al.*, 1999; Janis and Mann, 1977). People try to establish their priorities. Imagine a high school student considering whether to buy some 'junk food' from a fast-food outlet after class. His goal might be to satisfy hunger, kill boredom or simply enjoy a snack on the way home. Whether this objective is conscious or subconscious is debatable.

So, what goal(s) do adolescents set when contemplating health behaviour? There is no simple answer to this question, largely because there is little empirical evidence on the subject. It has been suggested that adolescents may not necessarily be aware of any particular objectives when making certain decisions, for example food choice (e.g. Subratty *et al.*, 2002).

However, social and health psychology literature suggests that people typically have two basic goals when confronted with a health risk. Presented with a threat, an individual has to decide whether to continue his present course of action, or adopt protective measures. His goal may be to deal with the danger (i.e. reducing personal risk), and/or resolve any associated anxiety (Leventhal, 1970; Leventhal *et al.*, 1983, 1993; also see reviews by Eagly and Chaiken, 1993; Witte and Allen, 2000). For example, an adolescent thinking about smoking may simply be preoccupied with making himself feel better. Thus, his goal is to reduce anxiety, and any option that allows him to achieve this is likely to be adopted.

It is difficult to find studies in which adolescents are simply asked about their priorities or objectives when making health behaviour decisions. Even if such evidence exists, the fact is that every person is a unique individual, with his or her particular mix of priorities. Thus, it is debatable whether one can identify goals that are universal to adolescents as a group.

Nevertheless, one productive way to approach this subject is by considering how much importance adolescents attach to being healthy (e.g. McKinney *et al.*, 1985). Another approach is to look at the things teenagers are most concerned or anxious about (e.g. Nowak and Crawford, 1998). People's anxieties often give a good indication of their priorities (Muris and Ollendick, 2002). Someone who becomes very anxious about health issues may attach considerable importance to reducing anxiety whenever they have to make a health related decision.

Perhaps, the best way to infer goals is simply by looking at the reasons adolescents choose to engage in a particular behaviour (e.g. Heinrichs, 1995; Rodham *et al.*, 2004; Macpherson, 2005; Wilson *et al.*, 2006; Alvord, 2007; Lee *et al.*, 2007).

I will consider each of these approaches separately, after first discussing relevant theoretical perspectives on goal setting.

Relevant theory

Psychologists have theorised about goal setting and goal directed behaviour for many decades (e.g. Lock, 1996, 2001). Given the vastness of this literature – spanning organisational, educational and social psychology, not to mention allied sciences – I have decided to narrow my discussion to several key theories that have some relevance or appear amenable to adolescent health behaviour and decision making.

Before progressing further, it is fair to say that none of these models is a theory of decision making (Janis and Mann, 1977). They consider goals and goal setting primarily as motivational or incentive variables, with little or no emphasis on decision making activity. Thus, it is important to guard against far-flung inferences about their relevance.

Goal theory

Goal theory is primarily a formulation about incentives that affect motivation to learn (Linnenbrink and Pintrich, 2000; Barron and Harackiewizc, 2001; Dowson and McInerney, 2001). Thus, it is typically applied in educational settings, but can be adapted to explain health behaviour (e.g. Vansteenkiste *et al.*, 2007). Essentially, a student's motivation to learn is driven by several goal dichotomies: mastery/performance, task/ego involvement and approach/avoidance goals.

The mastery/performance dichotomy denotes a student's desire for proficiency/ good grades, and may be associated with deeper commitment, and even anxiety. Both goals are intrinsic (Ryan and Deci, 2000) because achieving them generates a personal sense of satisfaction. Task/ego involvement refers to interest in a task because of its enjoyability and/or to boost one's ego. So, for example, a teenager may participate in physical education classes with the goal of having fun, or simply to look cool, for example by attracting praise. Approach/avoidance goals depict a desire to gain or avoid, respectively, favourable and unfavourable outcomes, for example obtaining good grades or avoiding failure.

All these goal dichotomies are applicable to health behaviour scenarios (see Fig. 3.1). For example, an adolescent may participate actively in physical activity (e.g. playing basketball), in order to perform well, and also to become more skilful (e.g. Allison *et al.*, 2005). Teenagers can be considered task/ego involved if they use drugs because it is fun, or simply to gain more 'street cred' amongst their peers

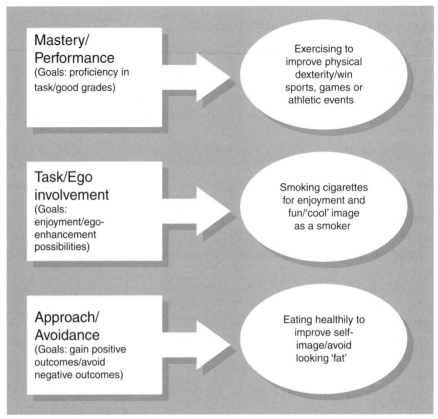

3.1 *Goal theory. Although this model (items on the left) is mainly applied to educational settings, the specified goal dichotomies are applicable to adolescents' health behaviour and decision making (see items on the right). For example, teenagers may entertain task/ego involvement goals when making decisions about cigarette use, alcohol consumption, drug use, and other enjoyable but 'cool' health behaviours. Similarly, their goals may be to avoid or gain specific health, social or other outcomes.*

(e.g. Lee *et al.*, 2007). A good approach/avoidance example is when a girl considers delaying sexual activity in order to avoid pregnancy/protect her health (e.g. Somers and Surman, 2004).

Overall, goal theory provides a useful basis for conceptualising adolescents' priorities when they are faced with health behaviour decisions. However, because of its educational background, health related empirical evidence is hard to come by. This negates any conclusive inferences about its relevance.

Goal setting theory

Developed by Edwin Locke, this framework comes from organisational psychology (Locke, 1996, 2001). It has philosophical underpinnings, inspired somewhat

by Aristotle's work on causality (see Viney and King, 2003). The basic thesis posits a positive correlation between goal difficulty and performance: the more difficult the goal, the greater one's performance. Furthermore, a clearly defined objective elicits better performance than a vague or ambiguous goal.

One appealing feature of this model is the proposed relationship between goals and performance. This has implications for adolescents' decision making. According to the model, goals focus one's attention on relevant goal-related activities, increasing effort and persistence. Take, for example, a teenage girl who is considering dieting in order to lose weight. Since weight loss (her goal) can be difficult to achieve, the girl will supposedly devote more time and energy to making her decision. She may survey more dieting options, to find the most effective solution, or think long and hard about the health risks associated with dieting, such as eating disorders, before finally taking the plunge. Thus, a difficult goal may improve decision making.

However, the goal–performance relationship is volatile and depends on a number of factors, including perceived attainability (not every goal is achievable, so putting in more effort is pointless), feedback (results indicating whether a goal is being achieved can highlight ways to achieve success) and self-confidence in one's ability to achieve a goal (doubts about one's abilities can undermine motivation). For example, weight loss may seem completely unattainable to a very obese adolescent, which in turn means little or no effort is expended trying to reduce fat intake.

The main problem with goal setting theory is that it is designed for an organisational rather than a health related setting. Empirical evidence testing this model in relation to adolescents, decision making or health behaviour is extremely rare. Nevertheless, like goal theory, it does provide a useful conceptual basis for understanding how goals might affect decision making performance.

The parallel response model

What goals do adolescents set when they are exposed to a health warning, or a similar threatening communication, such as illness symptoms? Social psychologists theorised as far back as the early 1950s about the objectives of a decision maker in this situation (Hovland *et al.*, 1953; Eagly and Chaiken, 1993).

Although much of this literature was based on observations of adults, subsequent research has demonstrated some applicability to adolescent decision making (e.g. Janis, 1958; van Wel and Knobbout, 1998). Adolescents are continually bombarded with health warnings designed to encourage healthy choices and minimise risk behaviour. Even if they don't find the warnings particularly threatening, they may be aware of other related threats that need to be addressed. This in turn may stimulate goal setting.

For example, a smoker who is warned by his parents about the risks of smoking may also worry about the threat of criticism or mockery from his peers if he quits. He may resolve that impressing his peers is the main priority, and hence carry on

smoking. A person who becomes aware of a threat has to decide how to respond. He has to decide what his priorities or objectives are.

The parallel response model, first elaborated in the early 1970s by psychologist Howard Leventhal (Leventhal, 1970; Leventhal et al., 1983), identifies two separate goals – danger control and fear control – that are evoked by threat.

Danger control is an intellectual 'problem solving' objective driven by a desire to avert danger. Achieving this goal involves thinking about both the nature of the threat (e.g. its seriousness) and potential coping behaviours (e.g. their effectiveness), and leads to adaptive action. For example, a teenager who becomes aware of the risk of AIDS may be motivated to avert this risk. She will consider the seriousness of AIDS ('It's life-threatening') and the effectiveness of condoms in reducing the risk ('These will enable me to protect myself'), and consequently plan to avoid unsafe sex.

Fear control by contrast denotes a desire to reduce anxiety, and typically involves a variety of defensive strategies that help to alleviate emotional discomfort. Examples include avoiding people or situations that remind one of the threat, denying that the danger has any personal relevance and simply trying to ignore the problem. For instance, a girl who suspects she's anorexic may start to worry. To reduce anxiety, she may try to avoid thinking about her weight, or discussing it with anyone. Her primary goal is to alleviate emotional discomfort, rather than address the medical problem.

The main problem with this model is its seemingly narrow focus. The idea that a decision maker has two basic goals – controlling danger and fear – comes across as a little simplistic. This criticism is strengthened when one compares the parallel response model with goal theory. Objectives such as mastery/performance and task/ego involvement do not seem to correspond with control of either danger or fear, yet these are objectives a teenager may realistically entertain. For example, an Ecstasy user, warned about the dangers of drug use, may resolve that having fun is all that matters. The parallel response model may not adequately accommodate this scenario. Despite these constraints, the model does provide some useful insights into goals adolescents may consider, and indeed prioritise, when making health behaviour decisions.

Reducing perceived threat

Conventional wisdom and theory suggest that one primary goal of any decision maker is to reduce any perceived threat to personal well-being (Hovland et al., 1953; Leventhal, 1970; Janis and Mann, 1977). Thus, when making decisions that may affect their health people may aim to reduce the threat of illness or injury.

However, threat may emanate from sources other than health. For example, Janis and Mann (1976, 1977) highlight the risk of social disapproval (i.e. criticism from significant others) and personal disappointment (e.g. a sense of immorality or low feelings of self-worth), as potential threats to the decision maker.

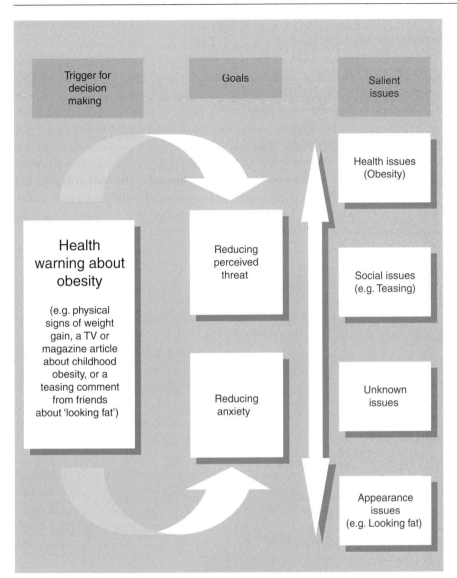

3.2 *Priorities for the decision maker. Psychological theory suggests that a decision maker has two basic goals: reducing any perceived threat to well-being and anxiety. For adolescents, perceived threat and anxiety are just as likely to emanate from social issues (e.g. image, criticism, teasing), appearance (e.g. shape, looking 'fat') and the unknown as they are from health risks. In fact, health may rank low in importance. For example, a sexually active teenager deciding whether or not to use a condom may be primarily concerned about not 'offending' his partner (i.e. implying lack of trust) rather than protecting his health.*

So to what extent is reducing perceived threat a goal for adolescents, and is health a key source of threat?

Research suggests that adolescents do attach some relevance to good health (e.g. Subratty *et al.*, 2002), albeit less so than adults (McKinney *et al.*, 1985). Although health is valued, considerable importance is attached to image issues, notably physical appearance (Evans *et al.*, 1995; Nowak and Crawford, 1998; Subratty *et al.*, 2002). Teenagers are often more concerned about their weight, shape and physical appearance than their health.

Consider a study by Nowak and Crawford (1998) in which high school students were asked to rate ten appearance and health related issues in order of importance to them. These included getting heart disease or high blood pressure later in life, becoming sick when they are older, physical fitness, weight, body shape and overall appearance, and the risk of developing diabetes.

Overall items relating to appearance were ranked the most important, with fitness and weight being the biggest priorities for boys and girls, respectively. Health issues enjoyed less priority. For example, only a small minority identified the risk of heart disease as being the most important. All in all, appearance was valued more than health, suggesting that physical attractiveness is more likely to be the primary goal in decision making.

It may be premature to infer from these findings that reducing perceived health threats is unlikely to be an important goal. A follow-up study by Subratty *et al.* (2002) asked adolescents to rank a similar group of items in order of importance. Results showed that a greater proportion of participants prioritised health concerns over appearance and looks. However, the difference was marginal. Appearance and looks still proved a very important issue (see Figure 3.3).

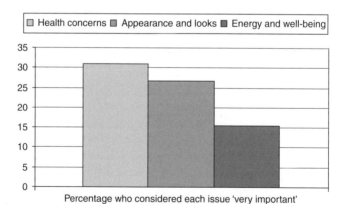

3.3 *Health as a goal. Although adolescents value their health they also prioritise physical appearance (e.g. looks, weight). A survey of adolescents' perceptions of health and nutrition revealed that although many respondents saw health as very important, appearance and looks weren't far behind (Source: Subratty* et al*., 2002).*

Another potential source of threat is peer pressure (Leatherdale *et al.*, 2006). Like appearance and looks, the risk of social ridicule or mockery is an ever-present threat that, to many teenagers, may override any health considerations. There is evidence that satisfying or impressing one's friends, or at least avoiding their disapproval, is an important goal during decision making.

Consider a study by Allison *et al.* (2005) that investigated the reasons given by adolescents for being physically active or inactive. Subjects participated in focus groups during which they were asked a variety of questions, including their reasons for not exercising. Pressure from friends and family emerged as key themes influencing their decision.

The researchers described the views of one participant: 'when asked to join a basketball game, his decision to play is based on whether most of his friends are also playing' (p. 163). Clearly, the goal of this individual was to blend in with his peer group, and hence elicit social acceptance. The fact that being physically active might be good for his health, reducing the risk of heart disease for example, was immaterial.

So what if anything can be gleaned from such evidence? Well, reducing perceived threats to well-being may indeed be an adolescent's goal. However, health risks may not be the top priority (Allison *et al.*, 2005). Threats like heart disease and cancer seem remote and hence far less important than more immediate risks, such as the danger of being considered 'fat' or 'unattractive' by other teenagers at school, or facing rejection by one's peer group (Smith and Smutts, 2003).

Finally, there is one crucial point to emphasise. Striving to reduce or eliminate a perceived threat – health or otherwise – is a largely intellectual goal (Janis and Mann, 1977). This is quite different from resolving the anxieties and other negative emotions that may be generated by the danger.

Essentially, an adolescent can make an intellectual judgement about the nature of a threat and what to do about it, quite separate from his efforts to address any emotional discomfort. For example, a girl who is gaining weight may lament, 'I don't want people to think I'm fat', and set about trying to achieve this goal, without experiencing any anxiety. Of course if she feels anxious, then reducing anxiety could also become an objective, pursued with equal vigour. Thus, as described by Leventhal (1970), the goals of reducing a perceived threat and of dealing with anxiety should not be confused.

Reducing anxiety

No one likes stress, and reducing anxiety or any other form of emotional discomfort is probably an important goal for most decision makers (Janis and Mann, 1976). Adolescence can be particularly stressful, for a variety of reasons, including developmental changes, interpersonal conflict (e.g. repeated arguments with parents) and self-esteem issues (Petersen and Leffert, 1995). Thus, the last thing a high school student wants to do is to add to his worries. And there are

many. Studies have shown that adolescents entertain a wide variety of anxieties (e.g. Ollendick, 1998; Ollendick *et al.*, 1989, 2001, 2002; Muris *et al.*, 2002; Muris and Ollendick, 2002).

Muris and Ollendick (2002) found that in addition to fears about health and medical threats (e.g. being killed, getting a cut, injury or serious disease, the sight of blood, going to the dentist), adolescents also harbour significant anxieties about the unknown (e.g. dark places, being alone, thunder and lightning, loud noises), animals (e.g. snakes, spiders), and difficult social situations (e.g. looking foolish, being teased or criticised, being punished by authority, looking different from others).

Teenage anxieties about social and image issues are considerable (indeed the two seem related; for example, many teenage girls want to lose weight in order to look good, and impress their peers, competitors or a prospective boyfriend). Muris and Ollendick (2002) unearthed a wide variety of such concerns, including fear of getting punished by a parent, teacher or school principal, gangs, having to go to school, being criticised by parents, looking foolish, being teased, having to meet someone new, and doing something for the first time. Many worries, such as being teased or looking foolish, relate to physical appearance. For example a fat girl may be teased about her weight, and the same applies for a frail unathletic looking boy.

We have already seen from research described in the preceding section that social approval can be the primary objective when making health behaviour decisions (Allison *et al.*, 2005). It is fair to assume that alleviating anxiety is a major underlying theme in such instances. For example, a boy whose friends routinely experiment with illicit drugs may feel compelled to join them, owing to worries about being ridiculed or laughed at for being a 'coward'.

Even when there is nothing in particular to be fearful about, adolescents may still find themselves feeling anxious. Fear of the 'unknown' (e.g. nightmares, dark places, being alone) was a key observation in Muris and Ollendick's (2002) work. It raises the possibility that teenagers become focused on reducing stress even when making trivial decisions for which there is little at stake (e.g. deciding whether to brush one's teeth or have chips for dinner). For instance, a student at boarding school may fail to practise proper dental hygiene out of fear of being alone in the washroom! His entire personal hygiene routine may be dictated by the need to contain this fear.

What about anxiety pertaining to health? Amongst the ten most common fears reported by Muris and Ollendick's (2002) subjects, AIDS was top of the list. Nevertheless, the majority of fears had little to do with health and lifestyle. The one fear that seemed most relevant to maintaining good personal health – fear of germs or getting a serious disease – was at the bottom of the list! Thus poor health isn't likely to be a major concern when making decisions.

Even so, adolescents clearly entertain palpable fears about certain health issues, most notably AIDS. Muris and Ollendick (2002) found that anxieties about 'danger and death', which included concerns about AIDS, physical injury, and contracting germs or a serious disease, account for the largest proportion of variance in their data. Thus, it is logical to expect that reducing these health

worries is an important goal during decision making. One study showed that teenage smokers participating in a smoking cessation programme cited anxiety about their health as the most important intrinsic incentive for quitting (Turner and Mermelstein, 2004).

The concern about AIDS is intriguing. On the one hand, research has shown that adolescents view avoiding STDs as a major priority when making sexual decisions, without specifically mentioning anxiety (e.g. Somers and Surmann, 2004). This suggests that emotional discomfort may not necessarily be a salient issue. Other research, however, suggests that alleviating anxiety is important in this context.

For example, Sonia Dias, Margarida Martos and Aldina Goncalves (2005) conducted a series of focus groups with a group of Portuguese adolescents during which the youths were asked about their attitudes and behaviours concerning HIV transmission and sexual activity. Several important themes emerged, one of which involved anxiety. In particular there were 'undefined fears' about HIV and the nature of its transmission, especially with regard to contact with infected people. Although it wasn't evident that alleviating this anxiety would be a key factor when making a decision, say whether to have sex with a new, potentially infected partner, it is likely to be relevant.

Unlike other health threats which seem far-fetched and remote, the risk of contracting HIV is immediate, and hence potentially much more worrying. Thus, for many teenagers, perhaps most, resolving this anxiety is likely to be a priority in any decision making about sexual behaviour. Any action that reduces one's fears, for example abstaining from sexual intercourse altogether, or insisting that one's partner has an HIV test, is likely to be adopted.

Intrinsic versus extrinsic goals

I said at the beginning of this chapter that a very good way of identifying the goal(s) of adolescent decision makers is to look at the reasons teenagers give for their decisions.

Research has revealed a particularly wide variety of reasons used to justify health behaviour, ranging from simple objectives like killing boredom and relaxation, to more involved or ambiguous goals such as ameliorating medical symptoms, looking cool or testing a partner's trustworthiness (e.g. Heinrichs, 1995; Rodham *et al.*, 2004; Somers and Surman, 2004; Turner and Mermelstein, 2004; Allison *et al.*, 2005; Macpherson, 2005; Wilson *et al.*, 2006; Alvord, 2007; Lee *et al.*, 2007).

One way to make sense of the multitude of incentives is to dichotomise them into intrinsic and extrinsic factors (Heinrichs, 1995; Cox and Klinger, 1988; Rodham *et al.*, 2004; Allison *et al.*, 2005; Macpherson, 2005; Wilson *et al.*, 2006; Alvord, 2007; Lee *et al.*, 2007). Intrinsic goals are those that are inherently enjoyable or interesting to the individual, while extrinsic goals are incentives that are separable or 'external' to the person (Ryan and Deci, 2000). To put it simply, intrinsic goals involve personal satisfaction in performing an activity, whereas

Table 3.1 *Reasons given by adolescents for selected health behaviours*

Behaviour	Intrinsic reasons	Extrinsic reasons
Postponing sex	Reputation and guilt Strong will and maturity Lack of trust Not ready	Partner reluctance or disapproval Desire not to get pregnant Parental disapproval
Using drugs (marijuana)	Enjoyment and fun Satisfying curiosity Killing boredom Relaxation coping (e.g. to relieve stress)	Conformity with peer group pressure Social benefits (e.g. bonding with friends, hanging out) Low health risks Activity enhancement (e.g. music sounds better)
Quitting smoking	Worried about health Performing better in sports Dislike for the way it makes one smell Stains fingers/teeth Dislike of reputation as a smoker Less enjoyment of smoking Dislike of how one looks when smoking	To save money Parental pressure to quit Pressure from boyfriend/girlfriend to quit Pressure from friends to quit To avoid punishment Difficulty in obtaining cigarettes
Physical inactivity	Low priority given to physical activity Involvement in other (technology-related) activities Being too young, short or overweight, or having a disability Laziness Desire to avoid stress Lack of confidence	Physical inactivity amongst peers and family members Negative parental attitudes (e.g. concern about injury, playing in the dark) Insufficient time caused by other commitments (e.g. school work, part-time jobs)

Sources: The information on sex, drugs, smoking and physical inactivity is based on the following studies, respectively, Somers and Surmann (2004), Lee *et al.* (2007), Turner and Mermelstein (2004), and Allison *et al.* (2005). Please note that the lists are not exhaustive, and some words or phrases have been altered to fit the table.

extrinsic goals denote the instrumental rewards of such activity. Examples of the former include reducing anxiety, improving self-esteem, having fun and being happy, whereas examples of the latter are receiving financial rewards, socialising, or impressing one's friends and/or family. Intrinsic motives satisfy innate psychological needs, for example the need for self-confidence, independence or happiness, and hence are often considered to have greater incentive value.

Table 3.1 lists intrinsic and extrinsic reasons given by adolescents for selected health behaviours. These motives provide some insight into potential decision

making goals. Consider the reasons given for postponing sexual activity: trying to avoid acquiring a bad reputation (presumably for sexual promiscuity or similar), and demonstrating strong will (i.e. being in control of one's affairs) and maturity, only engaging in sexual activities with trusted individuals, avoiding an unplanned pregnancy, and seeking the approval of significant others.

Similarly, reasons for being physically inactive suggest a wide variety of goals, including avoiding uninteresting (i.e. low-priority) activities, not exceeding one's physical limitations (e.g. height, disability), only doing what significant others seem to be doing or endorse, and only engaging in activities for which there is sufficient time.

By and large, intrinsic objectives seem to feature as much as extrinsic ones. But is there any tangible benefit in emphasising the distinction between intrinsic and extrinsic factors? The answer is yes. This is explained in the following sections.

Relative importance

Extrinsic goals can arguably be regarded as weaker incentives for the decision maker since they aren't inherently satisfying, which is the essence of intrinsic motivation (Ryan and Deci, 2000). Thus, it can be argued that intrinsic goals are pursued with greater vigour than extrinsic objectives. Ryan and Deci (1989) contend, based on existing literature, that the more extrinsic a goal is, the less interest, effort and importance the decision maker will demonstrate in pursuing that goal. They suggest an increased proclivity to shift responsibility and blame others, especially if things go badly.

Indeed, empirical research has demonstrated significant relationships between increased extrinsic motivation and diminished effort, such as less interest and commitment. This is probably because extrinsic goals are externally derived. They typically take the form of punishments or rewards suggested by others, in order to encourage a particular behaviour or decision.

So, for example, a boy who quits smoking in order to prevent mum and dad from cutting off his pocket money is unlikely to be enthusiastic about his decision, simply because it isn't inherently satisfying, but rather has been induced by others. His goal – preventing financial loss – is born out of the threats of others, rather than his own personal enjoyment, and hence is unlikely to be pursued with vigour. He may display great reluctance in destroying his cigarettes. By contrast, if he quits smoking because this is going to be inherently satisfying to him, an intrinsic goal, he'll be more enthused about avoiding cigarettes.

Not surprisingly, increased intrinsic motivation has been associated with greater effort and improved performance (Ryan and Connell, 1989; Miserandino, 1996). Overall, there seems to be a basic thesis: the less intrinsic a person's goal or the more extrinsic her incentive, the poorer the quality of her decision making.

However, much of the research on which Ryan and Deci's (1989) arguments are based is rather general. This raises questions about the applicability of their inferences to adolescent health behaviour. A brief literature search revealed a

number of studies suggesting that having an intrinsic goal does indeed lead to better performance in a health related task (e.g. Turner and Mermelstein, 2004; Vansteenkiste *et al.*, 2004; Fickenscher *et al.*, 2006; Gillison *et al.*, 2006; but see Breda and Heflinger, 2004). For example, psychologist Maarten Vansteenkiste and colleagues conducted two experiments to investigate the relative importance of intrinsic and extrinsic goals on exercise performance. A group of adolescents undergoing physical education classes at school were taught a new set of exercises: 'tae bo'.[1] Some participants were given an intrinsic incentive ('doing a little tae bo helps you to remain physically fit and prevents you from becoming sick at a later age'), while for others, an extrinsic goal was emphasised ('doing a little tae bo helps you to remain physically appealing to others and prevents you from gaining weight at a later age'). The intrinsic condition significantly improved task performance compared with the extrinsic goal. Interestingly however, this difference was mediated by a desire to achieve success or avoid failure, suggesting that deeper psychological dimensions relating to achievement may underpin intrinsic and extrinsic motivation.

In another study Turner and Mermelstein (2004) collected questionnaire data from adolescents enrolled in a smoking cessation programme. Participants indicated their reasons for quitting, including intrinsic goals (e.g. anxiety about health, needing to perform better in sport, reduced enjoyment of smoking, and not wanting stains on one's fingers or teeth), and extrinsic motives (e.g. to save money, pressure from friends to quit and the threat of punishment). The researchers also assessed subjects' motivation to quit, as well as their smoking status, at the end of the treatment programme.

Analysis of the data showed that, whereas at least two intrinsic goals predicted smoking cessation (reduce enjoyment and stains on fingers/teeth[2]), only one extrinsic factor was significant (pressure from friends to quit). Furthermore, only intrinsic goals were associated with desire to quit.

Overall, it seems reasonable to infer from existing literature that intrinsic goals increase the amount of effort put into decision making, resulting in better choices. Personal satisfaction is more energising than making others happy. If an adolescent is highly interested in and enthusiastic about pursuing a goal (e.g. contemplating going on a diet in order to feel better about herself), then she is likely to invest more time and energy in the decision making process, in order to maximise the chances of achieving her objective. She may conduct a more thorough search of the Internet for dieting options, consult friends, parents and experts for sound advice, and take more care in weighing this information, before deciding what to do. By contrast, lack of interest in a goal means less desire to find the best possible solution. Rather than spend time searching for and weighing information, the

---

[1] A sport similar to boxing, but with no opponent!

[2] The effect of this variable was inconclusive, as it was associated with failed cessation! However, the significant association still highlights the predictive importance of this intrinsic goal in the subject's decision making.

individual may simply make an impulsive choice, and blame others if things go wrong.

Nevertheless we have to be careful not to overstate the importance of intrinsic objectives to the decision making process. There are several important reasons for this. These are considered below.

Reality constraints on intrinsic goals

Intrinsic goals are self-centred needs that are often curtailed by situational restraints, and hence difficult to realise. For readers familiar with Sigmund Freud's work, this is analogous to the restraining effect the ego (social reality) has on the id (innate biological drives), whereby for example a need for aggression has to be met in a socially acceptable manner, such as becoming a boxer or using a punchbag (Viney and King, 2003, pp. 359–360).

Indeed, it has been suggested that, for this reason, the importance of intrinsic motives declines with age, as the individual experiences more and more pressure to conform, and respect the wishes and rights of others (Ryan and Deci, 2000). For instance, a juvenile who plans to use drugs for fun may find his path blocked by legal restrictions. Consequently, he may abandon the idea completely, or pursue it half-heartedly, with considerable ambivalence. Similarly, a boy whose goal is to have as much sexual excitement as possible on a Saturday night may find his options limited by situational constraints, such as difficulty finding a willing sexual partner, and potential criticism from family and friends. As a result he may settle for a less ambitious objective, such as merely having some fun, without any sexual activity (e.g. having a drink with friends), or settling for an unexciting sexual experience with a reluctant partner.

As intrinsic incentives decline in importance, extrinsic motives may assume greater significance. The views of others – friends, authority figures, society in general – start to matter more, with greater cognisance of the need for conformity, obeying the law, and other social standards by which adults are judged.

Overlap and predictive value

Intrinsic and extrinsic goals often overlap. Ryan and Deci (2000) emphasise this point several times in their paper. For example, they refer to several forms of extrinsic motivation, notably identification and integration, which overlap considerably with intrinsic incentives. Identification refers to a situation whereby a decision maker, pursuing an extrinsic goal, comes to appreciate the personal relevance of his objective, and hence identifies with it. The goal becomes as much intrinsic as it is extrinsic, because it is now highly valued by the individual and hence a potential source of personal satisfaction.

Take, for example, a boy who is considering quitting smoking because his parents disapprove. Thus, his primary motive for quitting is to please his parents, an extrinsic goal. However, what if he likes the idea of pleasing his parents,

perhaps because he values good interpersonal relations at home? He is identifying with what is effectively an extrinsic objective, thereby introducing an intrinsic dimension.

Similarly, consider a girl who is trying to lose weight in order to be accepted by the cheerleader squad at school. She is excited about the idea of becoming a cheerleader because it will improve her self-confidence and self-image. Thus, although being accepted by the cheerleader team is a decidedly extrinsic motive, it also has an intrinsic element, with innate psychological incentives.

Integration appears to be a more extreme form of identification, whereby an individual completely embraces an extrinsic goal as personally relevant.

Given the potential for extrinsic–intrinsic overlap, it can be difficult to establish which goal has greater motivational value. This was clearly demonstrated by Allison et al. (2005) in their study of physical activity. They noted that although participants gave both extrinsic and intrinsic reasons for being physically active, these incentives overlapped to a certain degree. According to them, the motives 'appear to satisfy internal needs as well as the need to impress others. Thus, the themes of physicality and challenge span both intrinsic and extrinsic reasons for participating' (p. 165).

Overlap aside, there is very strong evidence that extrinsic factors such as social approval or disapproval are more powerful incentives for certain health behaviours than intrinsic factors (Allison et al., 2005; Macpherson, 2005). For example, Allison et al. (2005) noted that participants placed greater value on extrinsic rather than intrinsic incentives for participating in physical activity.

It may be more important, for instance, to conform to peer group pressure by playing a basketball game, rather than declining simply to satisfy a personal dislike for sports. By the same token, minimising the risk of an unplanned pregnancy, or getting a pat on the back from mum or dad for good behaviour, can be far more powerful incentives when making sexual decisions than issues such as having a partner one can trust, or personal enjoyment.

Healthy versus unhealthy outcomes

Does a person's goal affect the likelihood of a healthy or unhealthy decision? For example, is a teenage smoker more likely to quit if he is motivated by concern about his health, or stains on his fingers and teeth, rather than a desire to please his parents? Clearly common sense suggests that if health protection is a primary goal then it follows that health behaviour is more likely to result. However, the reality is rather less clear-cut.

We know from research that health worries aren't necessarily the main incentive for wanting to quit smoking or actually doing so (e.g. Turner and Mermelstein, 2004). How so? One problem is that teenagers often have multiple goals when making health decisions, and it is often unclear which ones are considered top priority (e.g. Breda and Heflinger, 2004; Gillison et al., 2006; Lee et al., 2007).

Even a low-priority objective may still exert significant influence on the outcome, despite more powerful incentives, depending on situational factors. For example, an obese teenage girl keen to lose weight because of an overwhelming desire to boost her self-confidence may actually take concrete steps towards achieving her goal only after viewing an unflattering image of herself in a shop window. Thus, although improved self-confidence is the primary objective, physical attractiveness nevertheless exerts a significant impact on her decision making.

Even if an adolescent has only one goal, an extrinsic objective may undermine enthusiasm, so much so that decision making activity is perfunctory (e.g. not bothering to consider all the options), rather than thorough and competent. This in turn may reduce the likelihood of a healthy outcome. Indeed research has shown that a sloppy decision making style, characterised by procrastination, indecision, and little effort to find the best possible option, predicts greater levels of risky behaviour, such as physical inactivity, in adolescents (Umeh, 1998a, 1998b).

Consider an individual who is under pressure from family and friends to stop using illicit drugs, such as marijuana. Keen to obtain social approval – an extrinsic goal – he makes a snap decision to quit drugs for good. Because he is driven by a desire to impress others, rather than an intrinsic dissatisfaction with drug use, his efforts to stay 'clean' are half-hearted and lacking in determination. Within a short while he relapses, and finds himself using marijuana even more than before.

Overall, as we saw in the preceding section, the intrinsic versus extrinsic goal distinction can be crucial in determining the type of decision an adolescent will make. If intrinsic incentives inspire more competent decision making, and ultimately better health outcomes, then it is especially important to enable adolescents to establish the right objectives. Having an intrinsically satisfying or enjoyable objective may help diminish some of the lethargy and indecision sometimes associated with adolescent decision making (e.g. Friedman, 1996). Thus, risks and benefits may be weighed more thoroughly, so that serious health hazards are better appreciated, and impact significantly on choice.

The desire for good health is an important intrinsic goal that can elicit healthy decisions (e.g. Turner and Mermelstein, 2004). However, this objective isn't a priority for many teenagers. By contrast, as Allison *et al.* (2005) demonstrated, the need for social approval – an extrinsic factor – seems particularly pervasive, and can have wider health benefits, assuming the friends, family members and others who make up one's social milieu endorse good health.

Gender differences in goals

Are there gender differences in goal setting? The answer to this question seems twofold. On the one hand there are gender similarities in that both boys and girls seem to prioritise intrinsic over extrinsic goals, for certain health decisions. For example, research on food choice indicates that the most important goal for girls is to lose weight, whereas for boys it is to achieve physical fitness, and feel

energetic (e.g. Nowak and Crawford, 1998; Subratty *et al.*, 2002). These goals are all intrinsic.

On the other hand, there are gender differences in the kinds of intrinsic goals declared, and this is not just applicable to dietary decisions. For example, Turner and Mermelstein (2004) found significant sex differentials in the intrinsic goals that drive a decision to quit smoking. Girls were more likely to cite dislike for the way they smell after smoking, and stains on their fingers and teeth, as incentives, whereas boys were driven more by a desire to perform better in sports.

Notice that these goals seem to echo the incentives emphasised by boys and girls in the studies on food choice (e.g. stains relate to appearance, while participating in sports is associated with physical fitness) (e.g. Subratty *et al.*, 2002). Turner and Mermelstein (2004) found no gender variations in extrinsic motives, suggesting that males and females attach similar importance to such goals. Whether intrinsic goals were deemed more important wasn't clear from the data.

Gender dissimilarity in goals may have significant implications for our understanding of adolescent health behaviour. It may partially explain gender differences in health behaviour. Consider for example recent evidence pointing to a greater prevalence of cigarette smoking amongst girls compared with boys (e.g. Holm *et al.*, 2003; Rogacheva *et al.*, 2007; Vega *et al.*, 2007; but see Erbaydar *et al.*, 2005; Weiss and Garbanati, 2006). Faced with an opportunity to smoke, the priority for boys may be to avoid anything that may hamper their participation in sports (e.g. Turner and Mermelstein, 2004), whereas losing weight will be foremost in the minds of girls. We know from research that adolescent girls often associate cigarette smoking with weight loss (e.g. Hoerster, 2001). Of course, smoking is clearly detrimental to physical activity, especially regularly participating in sports. Thus, it follows that girls are more likely to opt for smoking, in order to control their weight, whereas boys are prone to decline smoking, consistent with their sporting aspirations. Hence goals are key in explaining and perhaps predicting whether particular health behaviours will be more prevalent amongst girls than boys, or vice versa.

Obviously this relationship isn't necessarily applicable in all circumstances. It is entirely plausible for males and females to arrive at the same decision, notwithstanding vast gender differences in objectives. For example, a couple may both feel inclined to use contraception during sex because the girl wishes to avoid an unplanned pregnancy, while the boy is keen to have sex at all costs, and will do anything to succeed. Although their goals differ, they both reach the same decision. This phenomenon has been clearly demonstrated in research on, for example, food choice (e.g. Nowak and Crawford, 1998; Subratty *et al.*, 2002) and deliberate self-harm (e.g. Rodham *et al.*, 2004).

For example, in a study of food choice perceptions and motives among a group of school children and adolescents (aged 12 to 20), Nowak and Crawford (1998) found that boys and girls had different goals for improving their diet. Whereas boys aimed for physical fitness, weight control was the primary objective for girls – the same decision, and yet different goals. In another study comparing reasons for

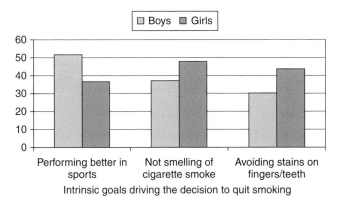

3.4 *Gender differences. Males and females may differ on intrinsic goals when making certain decisions, such as quitting smoking. Differences in extrinsic objectives were negligible in this context (Source: Turner and Mermelstein, 2004).*

deliberate self-harm, Rodham *et al.* (2004) found that girls who cut themselves were more likely than boys to cite a need to punish themselves, and relieve mental anguish – another example of a similar decision, but differences in emphasis.

All in all, the explanatory value of gender differences in goals may depend on the circumstances. It is possible that for most health behaviour decisions, males and females have both similar and disparate objectives, and the predictive importance of any differences in goals may vary over time and across behaviours.

Feedback and goal attainment

Do adolescents benefit from feedback indicating how well they are achieving their goals? According to Edwin Locke's goal setting theory, feedback helps, because it shows decision makers where they are in relation to their goal. The individual can then adjust performance accordingly to achieve their objective (Locke, 1996, 2001; Lathem and Locke, 2002). Any decisions that do not seem to be working as expected are modified, or replaced with new measures.

For example a girl who opts to use condoms to prevent an unplanned pregnancy may, after several 'late' periods, reason that condoms are not adequate. So she makes a new decision – abstain from sex altogether. Similarly, a smoker may find that ignoring a cigarette warning doesn't make him feel better. Furthermore, attempts to distract himself with other activities don't help either. So, in desperation, he simply shifts responsibility to others, blaming friends for encouraging him to smoke. He finds that this approach – relinquishing personal responsibility – provides him with considerable peace of mind.

Any new action taken is then subjected to the same evaluations. Is it working? Is one less susceptible to danger as a result? If the answer is no, then new measures are introduced, and the process continues indefinitely until an effective solution has been found.

Unfortunately, much of the scientific literature on feedback and goal attainment has focused on adults. Nevertheless, there is some very interesting research on this issue that examined adolescents. James Byrnes, David Miller and Marianne Reynolds conducted two experiments specifically to establish whether adolescents use feedback when making decisions (Byrnes *et al.*, 1999). These investigations are described in Box 3.1.

Previous studies had shown that adults progressively make better choices – that is, decisions that are most likely to achieve their desired goals, such as reducing the threat of an illness – when they receive feedback about the effectiveness of earlier choices. The key issue for Byrnes and his colleagues was whether adolescents behave like adults. Do they use feedback to improve their decision making, selecting options that achieve better 'results'?

The researchers suspected that children and adolescents might not benefit from feedback, and the findings seemed to confirm these suspicions, at least in part (see Fig. 3.5). Whereas adults altered their decisions in response to feedback, the same could not be said for adolescents. The latter group failed to modify their choices even after being informed about the shortcomings of their current decision.

Byrnes *et al.* (1999) suggested several reasons why children and adolescents may fail to learn from their mistakes. First, they may not get enough feedback. A good example of this is when a teenager chooses to use a condom during sexual intercourse, to avoid contracting HIV, but has no way of knowing if the condom actually 'worked' as it should (unless he later subjects himself to the ordeal of an HIV test). Condoms can develop small and inconspicuous perforations or tears, allowing passage of bodily fluids. Similarly, badly worn condoms may fail to offer maximum protection.

Alternatively, they may get enough feedback, but fail to understand fully what it means, let alone act on it. For example, a youngster informed that condoms are 80 per cent reliable may be unsure precisely how to interpret this information. Does it mean that condoms are effective or ineffective? It's possible that certain forms of feedback, such as how one feels at a given moment in time, or the verbal reactions of significant others, may be easier to interpret, and hence use to improve choice, than other hints, such as probability information (see Chapter 1) (Tversky and Kahneman, 1974).

Another possible explanation has to do with inattentiveness. Children and teenagers may not pay enough attention to feedback cues, perhaps owing to lack of interest and/or preoccupation with other more engaging activities. Consider an obese boy who embarks on a rigorous exercise routine, in order to lose some weight. After a few weeks he begins to suspect he has lost a few kilograms, but can't be bothered to climb on a weighing scale to be sure. Consequently, he fails to obtain accurate feedback, and hence doesn't realise he hasn't lost any weight at all. If he did, his current exercise regime could be doubled, or augmented with a modified diet, improving his chances of weight loss.

Overall, benefiting from feedback requires an ability to learn, that is, the capability to improve performance, on the basis of new information (Bandura,

Box 3.1 Research spotlight: does feedback facilitate goal attainment?

> Byrnes, J.P., Miller, D.C. and Reynolds, M. (1999) Learning to make good decisions: a self-regulation perspective. *Child Development*, 70, pp. 1121–1140.

Do adolescents benefit from feedback indicating how successful they are in attaining their goal? You would presume so. Take, for example, a girl who has decided to go on a diet with the goal of losing weight. Will she benefit from feedback about any subsequent increase or decrease in weight? You would assume so. Commonsense suggests that learning about a weight increase should cause her to re-evaluate her approach, and perhaps change strategy, to stand a better chance of achieving her goal. However, a study by Byrnes *et al.* (1999) suggests that adolescents may not necessarily learn from feedback.

They conducted two experiments. One focused on a medical/health issue, while the other dealt with a card-based decision task. I will only discuss the first experiment here since it is more in keeping with the health theme of this book. Moreover, both experiments generated roughly similar results so reviewing the two studies is unnecessary. Participants in the medical experiment comprised both adolescents and adults. All subjects were required to perform a medical decision making task over a certain number of trials. During the trials participants received feedback about how to arrive at the best decision. The task itself involved asking each participant to pretend he or she was a physician about to see sixteen patients suffering from a particular condition (high cholesterol or high blood pressure). Their job was to decide which of three medicines was the best one to enable the patient's recovery. They were provided with fictional information about the effectiveness, price and side effects of each drug.

After a subject decided on a drug for a patient the experimenter provided feedback on the outcome of this decision, in terms of the effectiveness of the drug in inducing patient recovery (e.g. the patient's blood pressure either increased or declined), and any resulting side effects (e.g. side effects were either present or absent). Following the trials, subjects were provided with verbal feedback designed to help them to more effectively evaluate the three dimensions of the drugs (i.e. their effectiveness, side effects and costs).

So, what did they find? Some results are shown in Figure 3.5. First, compared with adolescents, adults made significantly more correct decisions. Furthermore, although both adolescents and adults showed significant improvements in decision making after receiving verbal feedback, the improvement for adults was more impressive: 'adults were somewhat inclined to select the best drug prior to verbal feedback and the feedback served to enhance this tendency' (p. 1134). Most interesting, however, was that the number of correct choices for adolescents barely improved after verbal feedback was given. By contrast, decision making for adults significantly improved following verbal feedback.

Overall, these findings suggest that adolescents may alter their decision making in response to verbal feedback, but significantly less so than adults. The reason for this is unclear, but it is possible that factors such as inattentiveness and limited or poor comprehension may play an important role.

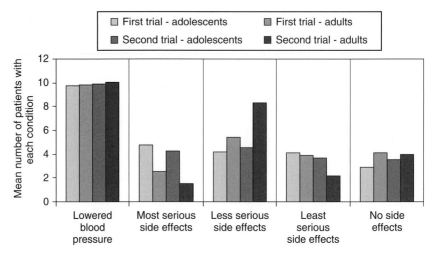

3.5 *Feedback and goal attainment. Adolescents and adults were asked to make a series of decisions about a patient's treatment. They were also provided with feedback showing how well they were doing in terms of patient improvement (e.g. side effects, blood pressure). Adults made better choices than adolescents, especially after verbal feedback. Differences between adolescents and adults were significant for 'most serious side effects' (both trials), 'less serious side effects' (2nd trial) and 'no side effects' (1st trial) (Source: Byrnes et al., 1999).*

1977). However, learning ability in children and adolescents can be somewhat constrained by underdeveloped reasoning abilities, lack of life experience and limited attention spans.

If adolescents fail to act on feedback, then they are less likely to improve their decisions to increase the chances of achieving their goals. This means that when a particular course of action (e.g. denial) fails to produce the desired results (e.g. improve one's appearance, elicit the approval of peers, make one feel better), adolescents may not necessarily modify or replace it. They would simply carry on as normal!

Fear and danger as underlying themes

We now know there is a wide variety of goals adolescents may have when making health behaviour decisions. We also know, based on the parallel response model (Leventhal, 1970), that reducing personal risk and/or anxiety are two fundamental objectives in health decision making. These points highlight an important question: do the various goals adolescents pursue all boil down to these two aims? Reducing anxiety and perceived danger may have as much to do with physical appearance, social considerations and the unknown as it does with health and medical matters (e.g. Muris and Ollendick, 2002).

Clearly, anxiety is a salient issue in adolescence (Muris and Ollendick, 2002; Ollendick *et al.*, 2001, 2002), and therefore is likely to be a major feature of their decision making. Most of the reasons adolescents give for adopting various behaviours seem fear related. For example, key incentives mentioned by teenagers for smoking cigarettes, such as wanting to feel good, being addicted and peer pressure (Palmqvist and Martikainen, 2005), may all be associated with stress. A teenager who finds he is more accepted by his peer group after smoking a cigarette may feel less anxious about being the target of ridicule and rejection (Muris and Ollendick, 2002).

In any case adolescents themselves cite reducing stress as a major reason for smoking (Tuakli *et al.*, 1990; Siqueira *et al.*, 2000). In fact, it may be the most important incentive. For example, in the study by Siqueira *et al.* (2000), a group of adolescent smokers were asked to select from a list of thirteen reasons what motivated them to progress from experimenting with cigarettes to smoking regularly. Coping with stress was the most common reason, cited by over 70 per cent of respondents. The stress in question probably derives from a multiplicity of sources, some of which I have already mentioned. It is interesting that smokers in this study also reported more negative life events (e.g. a severe accident, or serious illness of a family member) than non-smokers, raising the possibility that smoking is used to manage the stress from adverse experiences.

However, what about perceived threat? Is there any evidence that this represents an overarching theme for risks with multiple origins? About a third of smokers in Siqueira *et al.*'s (2000) study indicated that smoking helped them deal with problems. One has to assume that the word 'problem' was generic in this context, and hence may depict health, social, image, interpersonal and other troubles that typify the lives of adolescents.

Despite such evidence, defining adolescents' goals solely in terms of danger and fear control may be too narrow a conceptualisation. There are goals that do not fit tidily into either category. Some good examples are the need to satisfy curiosity, wanting pleasure, and a desire to feel 'grown up', all of which are difficult to define purely in terms of anxiety and risk.

Single-goal decision making

Research indicates that adolescents typically have multiple goals when making health decisions (e.g. Macpherson, 2005; Wilson *et al.*, 2006; Alvord, 2007; Cox and Lee *et al.*, 2007; Lee *et al.*, 2007). For example, they often cite multiple reasons for quitting smoking (Turner and Mermelstein, 2004), using drugs (Lee *et al.*, 2007) and engaging in physical activity (Allison *et al.*, 2005). Indeed models of goal directed behaviour, such as the goal theory (Locke, 1996, 2001), seem to imply goal multiplicity, for example ego/task involvement objectives and mastery/performance goals.

Box 3.2 Contextual issues: intrinsic goals and activity type

Intrinsic goals clearly play an important role in health behaviour decisions amongst adolescents. However, in discussing the nature of intrinsic motivation Ryan and Deci (2000) made an important point. Although intrinsic incentives exist within most, the salience of such motives in part depends on the context, specifically the type of task or activity one is considering. Some activities are inherently more satisfying than others.

This thesis has particular relevance here. Although adolescents do engage in a variety of health behaviours, not all of them can be motivated by intrinsic goals. Only the most enjoyable, exciting and hence satisfying activities are likely to be associated with intrinsic goals. This brings us to an important question. Which health behaviours are most associated with enjoyment and fun? There is no definitive answer, given the multiplicity of health activities and the incentives and reasons adolescents give for performing or rejecting them. Nevertheless, when asked to identify the reasons for performing various health habits, adolescents typically associate enjoyment and fun with substance use behaviours, notably smoking, drug use and alcohol consumption (e.g. Lee *et al.*, 2007), as well as physical activity (e.g. Allison *et al.*, 2005). Thus, these behaviours can be considered to have strong intrinsic value. Adolescents are likely to be intrinsically motivated for these activities, compared with other less entertaining behaviours such as contraceptive use, eating healthily or wearing seat belts. Enjoyment/fun is rarely given as a reason for enacting these latter behaviours (e.g. Rosenthal *et al.*, 1994).

However, note that any behaviour can be intrinsically satisfying, depending on the individual. To some teenagers, a seemingly bland activity like condom use can be the source of inherently intrinsic satisfaction, for example by imbuing a sense of mastery over one's sex life.

If an activity has strong intrinsic value, then an intrinsic incentive is likely to be set as the primary (or only) goal when one is deciding whether or not to engage in the activity. Judging from Ryan and Deci's (2000) work, the more intrinsic the goal, the more interest and effort one will demonstrate in pursuing the goal. This suggests greater intensity during decision making, and perhaps a more predictable outcome: teenagers may find it especially difficult to resist a health behaviour they enjoy, whatever the health hazards.

However, having a single goal may help simplify the decision making process, since the decision maker has just one target to pursue. Since there is only one priority, an individual may dispense with detailed appraisals of multiple incentives and disincentives, so that their decision making is largely perfunctory and ill considered.

For example, a teenager who is inclined to use drugs solely for the purpose of looking 'cool' may see little point in conducting a detailed analysis of the health risks of drug use, or indeed its pharmacological benefits. He is only interested in one outcome, and has an obvious means of achieving it. Important consequences that aren't priorities wouldn't seem worth considering.

This phenomenon is particularly evident when teenagers face peer pressure. Regardless of the issue for which they are making a decision – smoking, drugs, diet, use of medication, even undergoing surgery – the approval or disapproval of one's peers is often a major overriding consideration when evaluating options (e.g. Allison *et al.*, 2005). Any decision that is made will be designed primarily to placate friends and gain their approval.

Another good example is the preoccupation many teenage girls have with losing weight (Nowak and Crawford, 1998). Some opt to smoke cigarettes, regardless of the health risks, simply to keep their weight down. Headache tablets may be refused, despite a severe migraine, if it is suspected such medication can affect one's weight. This solitary goal may also supersede any other consideration when dietary decisions are being made.

Even decisions about seemingly unrelated factors – whether to use contraception, go to the dentist or drink alcohol – may be influenced by an overriding objective. For example, a girl may decline to visit her dentist simply because she wouldn't be allowed to smoke on the premises, and may gain some weight as a result.

This kind of 'single-issue' decision making may also affect the extent to which a teenager may benefit from feedback. Earlier in this chapter we reviewed a study suggesting that adolescents may not learn from feedback that could potentially help them to achieve a goal (Byrnes *et al.*, 1999). Perhaps the main goal of subjects in this study was unrelated to the criticism they received. Feedback was given about a hypothetical patient's recovery, an outcome that may have been of little interest to participants.

Adolescents may respond better to criticism if it pertains to their main incentive. Take, for example, a teenage girl who is trying to decide whether or not to go on a diet. Let's assume that she is hell-bent on looking 'cool'. Whatever decision she makes will be directed at achieving this goal. Say, she opts to go on a diet, and then is informed by a friend several weeks later that she still doesn't look cool, as she hasn't lost enough weight. This feedback may compel her to redouble her efforts, perhaps eating even less, or switching to a more aggressive diet.

Feedback is effective in this case because it is relevant to the goal set by the decision maker. But say her decision to diet is criticised by a parent as being unhealthy. Such feedback may be completely ignored, simply because being healthy isn't the girl's main priority.

Conclusion

I approached this chapter with a considerable degree of uncertainty. For many years I had clung stubbornly to the received wisdom in some areas of health psychology that a decision maker, faced with a threat, has two basic goals – reducing the danger and fighting anxiety. This is a view that dates back several decades to some of the earliest work on decision making in health scenarios. Yet I worried that there had to be more to this when trying to understand adolescent behaviour.

Indeed existing literature tells a rather confused and disorganised story. Adolescents, it seems, typically have a multiplicity of priorities when making any decision, including decisions that may affect their health. These objectives may involve fear and danger, but not necessarily so. They may be dichotomised as intrinsic and extrinsic objects, or even ego-, task- or achievement-oriented goals. Asked what motivates them to engage in a health behaviour adolescents often give many reasons, with no clear sense of which incentive enjoys top priority. Yet a number of things become clear after a while.

First, adolescents do indeed appear to have set goals or incentives when making health behaviour decisions. This seems obvious from the literature. Second, protecting one's health may be an important objective, but it probably competes with more immediate social incentives for priority, and can easily be relegated to secondary status. Third, goals may affect the quality of decision making. For example, it seems intrinsic objectives can energise an individual to put more effort into making an informed decision, whereas extrinsic incentives may evoke perfunctory decision making. Finally, and perhaps most importantly, goals affect the probability of a healthy or risky decision. It goes without saying that health enhancing behaviour is more probable if an individual's goal is to protect his or her health.

Key points

- There are several theoretic frameworks, from educational, organisational and health psychology, that can be used to understand goal setting in the context of adolescent health behaviour.
- Adolescents may have a variety of goals when making health behaviour decisions.
- Eliminating danger, and reducing fear, may be fundamental goals, but not necessarily so, as issues such as boosting one's ego and successfully performing a task are also important.
- Goals may be dichotomised as intrinsic, that is, personally satisfying incentives, or extrinsic, meaning motives external to the individual, such as social pressure.
- Maintaining good health may be an important goal but not necessarily so. Health objectives have to compete for priority with social concerns, and issues relating to physical appearance.

Key terms

- Goals
- Goal setting
- Goal setting theory
- Goal theory

- Parallel response model
- Perceived threat
- Anxiety
- Intrinsic and extrinsic goals
- Health outcomes
- Feedback

Further reading

Locke, E. A. (1996) Motivation through conscious goal setting. *Applied and Preventive Psychology*, 5, pp. 117–124.

(2001) Motivation by goal setting. *Handbook of Organisational Behaviour*, 2, pp. 43–54.

Ryan, R.M. and Deci, E.L. (2000) Intrinsic and extrinsic motivations: classic definitions and new directions. *Contemporary Educational Psychology*, 25, pp. 54–67.

Weir, M. (1984) *Goal-Directed Behaviour*. Newark, NJ: Gordon and Breach.

4 Fear

Learning outcomes

At the end of this chapter readers should have a better understanding of the following:

1 the importance of fear as a key factor in decision making
2 the pervasiveness of fear during adolescence
3 how adolescents react to fear associated with short- and long-term threats
4 the role of fear as a driving force
5 the importance of reassurance in dealing with fear
6 the extent to which fear can explain the gap between adolescents' knowledge of health threats and their lifestyle choices
7 the impact of irrational fears and exaggerated sensitivity to physiological arousal
8 defensive reactions to fear.

Chapter summary

This chapter considers the role of fear as a prominent influence in adolescent decision making. It is multifaceted, with health concerns competing side-by-side with social-, appearance- and image-related fears. Fear, it is argued, serves as a driving force, compelling teenagers to adopt any behaviour that helps alleviate stress, even if the action is damaging to their health. The effect of this emotion may vary depending on the short- or long-term nature of a stressor, and the presence or absence of reassurances. Fear may also trigger defensive reactions, for example denial and wishful thinking, whose sole purpose is to reduce anxiety. Protecting one's health may receive little or no priority in this context. Phobias, also known as irrational fears, can have a significant effect on choice. They may prevent teenagers from adopting health enhancing measures that magnify their phobia, for example visiting the dentist. Overall, fear seems an inescapable feature of the decision making landscape.

Chapter outline

The chapter begins by considering the significance of fear in decision making, followed by a review of the multiple sources of fear common in adolescence. Next I consider how teenagers react to fear, including anxiety associated with immediate and remote threats. Then I discuss the motivational property of fear, the role of reassurance, treatment of fear as a potential outcome, and the value of fear in explaining the knowledge–behaviour gap. The chapter rounds off with a discussion of defensive responses, phobias, anxiety sensitivity and the concept of 'freaking out'.

The significance of fear

As we saw in the previous chapter, dealing with fear can be an important objective for the adolescent decision maker. Thus, anxiety can have a significant effect on decision making. This is particularly the case in adolescence.

Remember the famous scene in Charles Dickens' novel *Oliver Twist*, in which a frail little boy plucks up the courage to request some more food? Dickens' tale, originally serialised, helped to raise public awareness of the various social evils that children face, notably cruelty, abuse and abandonment. However, a dominant theme that seems to pervade every aspect of this story – and indeed much of Dickens' book – is *fear*! This tale offers a chilling insight into the chronic and pervasive fear experienced by children who lived during the Victorian era. Fear seemed to infect almost every aspect of Oliver Twist's miserable existence. Fear determined where he slept, who he confided in, his willingness to comply with adult authority. Oliver agreed to participate in robberies, pick-pocketing and other petty crimes, probably because he was *too scared* to refuse. The consequences of refusal would have been dire.

During the Victorian era fear was widely used as an effective tool for coercing naughty children to behave better or comply with authority. The value of fear as a persuasive force that both enthralled and intimidated (perhaps in equal measure) children and teenagers – and governed their behaviour – was thoroughly exploited by adult authority figures, like Fagin.[1]

Today, the idea that fear is a major factor in an adolescent's daily living may seem laughable to some. Yet teenagers seem to rush in droves to see the latest horror movies, completely in awe of the sheer suspense and terror depicted on screen. Such is the level of enthusiasm that a separate 'teen-horror' movie genre has now emerged, with considerable yearly box office earnings. Some readers may recall the box office hits *The Blair Witch Project* and *Scary Movie*, both of which proved very popular with teenage audiences.

---

[1] This view forms part of the wider argument about the use of fear during the dark ages, for the purposes of intimidation or coercion. For example it has been argued that the church regularly used people's fear of the unknown to persuade them to repent of their sins and embrace Christianity.

The appreciation adolescents have for this genre of film may underscore a tacit acknowledgement of the importance of fear as a driving force in their lives, an emotion that all respect, and flee from, and which you ignore at your peril. It reminds me of the common theme that links most American Wild West movies. In these films even the toughest and most vicious cowboy is forced into submission once he is staring down the barrel of a gun.

Even the most complacent and carefree teenager – the kind who responds to every adult critique with the dismissive 'whatever', accompanied by a dismissive wave of the hand, as you often observe in some US teenage sitcoms and talk shows – will suddenly sit up and take notice once he or she experiences fear.

Sources of fear

As we saw in Chapter 2, teenagers often report feeling considerable anxiety about health problems, for example obesity, cancer, even death (Ollendick *et al.*, 1989, 2001; Muris and Ollendick, 2002). However, health per se is not the only issue that may generate fear. Teenagers also harbour other anxieties, each of which may have a unique impact on choice. Perhaps the best evidence for the multiple sources of fear adolescents face comes from the work of Peter Muris and Thomas Ollendick, of Maastricht University, and their colleagues (Muris and Ollendick, 2002; Ollendick *et al.*, 1989, 2001, 2002).

In one study, Muris and Ollendick (2002) administered a set of questionnaires to over 500 adolescents (aged 12 to 19 years). The questionnaires incorporated the FSSC-R (Fear Survey Schedule for Children – Revised), an instrument containing eighty-four statements that describe potentially frightening scenarios. Respondents indicated on a three-point scale ('none', 'some', 'a lot') the extent to which they feared each situation.

Exploratory factor analyses revealed initially five, and then later seven, fundamental sources of fear, with both models explaining the data satisfactorily. I have decided to present the seven dimensions here, as I find the greater variety more intriguing. The emerging factors are described below, together with examples of associated items:

Danger and death: Being killed or murdered, hit by a car or truck, raped or kidnapped, getting burned, germs or serious disease, rough or dangerous games, getting cut or injured, sharp objects, AIDS.

Aversive social situations: Getting punished by father/mother, gangs, getting sick at school, parental criticism, and being sent to the principal.

Anticipatory social situations: Meeting strangers, being teased, looking foolish, being criticised by others, being in a fight, and talking in front of the class.

The unknown: Dark rooms, being home alone, spooky places, nightmares, loud noises.

School and performance: Taking a test, failing a test, getting poor grades or getting a report card.

Medical situations: Getting a bee sting, having an injection, going to the dentist/doctor, the sight of blood, flying in a plane, going to hospital.

Box 4.1 Media spotlight: fear references in teenage magazines

Interestingly it didn't take me long to find multiple references to fear in just one teenage magazine. The 594th volume of *Mizz* (21 February to 5 March 2007), a magazine targeted at an adolescent and largely female audience, featured an article about a girl too scared to leave her home due to agoraphobia, an irrational fear of going out. This particular feature covered a full page, and described the girl's feeling of extreme anxiety so bad that it prevented her from going to school for two years!

Browsing through the rest of the magazine, I noticed quite a few subheadings alluding to fear, anxiety or stress, for example 'nicotine nightmare', 'boy stresses' and 'anxiety attacks'. The last item provided the heading for a letter from a reader complaining about 'fits of panic' and other symptoms of nervousness.

Overall, these direct references to fear seem to confirm the idea that anxiety is a salient issue in the lives of many teenagers, particularly girls. One thing I found interesting was the potential for fear to affect decisions regarding health behaviour. For example, the agoraphobic girl described how sometimes she refused to eat, because she was so worried. This is consistent with evidence associating irrational fears with unhealthy choices (e.g. Vika *et al*., 2006).

Animals: Snakes, worms, snails, big wild animals, sharks, spiders, strange or threatening dogs.

Perhaps one of the most interesting findings is that fear of danger and death accounted for the largest amount of variance in the data. This suggests that anxiety about health is an important issue for adolescents (albeit medical fears accounted for a comparatively small amount of variance). The emergence of two social dimensions shows how much adolescents worry about the views of others (Westenberg *et al*., 2004). Social concerns may be just as important as (if not more important than) health fears during decision making.

Initial reactions to fear

How do most teenagers initially react to fear? This is a difficult question to answer, but an extremely important one. Just as a first impression has a dispropor-tionate impact on how we relate to others (Miller *et al*., 2004), a person's first response to fear may have a more pronounced effect on their decision making than later reactions. For example, if one's initial reaction is to panic, this may severely hamper any subsequent attempts to think calmly and rationally (Janis and Mann, 1977).

As a starting point I decided to interview two teenage girls (Abbi Igwemma and Aishia Mills) one evening to get their personal opinions on things. Both girls were unequivocal in their response. Whenever they get scared, the first thing they do is talk to their friends. Depending on the circumstances, they may also talk to family members, for example their mother or a close aunt.

To verify their accounts I spent some time reviewing emails sent to a website that offers advice to teenagers. An initial search with the word 'fear' yielded a few dozen emails, several of which made specific reference to seeking advice from others. Of course, all the emails themselves were soliciting advice, in this case from an Internet source. Whether talking to others is the most common initial reaction to fear cannot be established from such a casual uncontrolled investigation. Nevertheless, it is clear that many teenagers will talk to someone else once they get scared.

Academic literature seems to support the argument that seeking advice is a strong initial reaction to anxiety. Byrnes (2002) argues that children and adolescents are indeed disposed to advice seeking, albeit somewhat less so than adults (Halpern-Felsher and Cauffman, 2001), and they tend to emphasise familiarity (e.g. asking a friend) over expertise (e.g. speaking to a parent or professional, such as a doctor) (Byrnes, 2002), especially if their decision making options are limited (Fuligni and Eccles, 1993).

Evidence on the link between fear and advice seeking is sparse. Nevertheless, a number of studies have explored how adolescents typically respond to stressful situations (e.g. Washburn *et al.*, 2004; Eyles and Bates, 2005; Balbinotti *et al.*, 2006; Compas *et al.*, 2006; Kuo *et al.*, 2006). These reveal a rather more convoluted picture than was previously suggested. Yes, adolescents do turn to others for advice: however, in general, they may respond to anxiety in various ways of which seeking advice is just one. Other evidence indicates that adolescents have no particular response to fear. Instead how they react is flexible and dependent on the prevailing situation (Campbell, 1996).

Whatever the response to fear, in any given scenario it is reasonable to assume the reaction will impact on decision making. For example, obtaining more advice from others may help a teenager identify more options and better appreciate their repercussions before taking further action (Byrnes, 2002). Alternatively, seeking advice from others can easily lead to a disastrous decision. This is particularly likely if the person approached for advice is ill informed, or well informed but offers incorrect advice for various reasons (e.g. forgetfulness, ulterior motives) (Halpern-Felsher and Cauffman, 2001).

It appears that the people teenagers most commonly approach for advice, at least initially, are their peers, consistent with research findings (Halpern-Felsher and Cauffman, 2001). Since a friend is unlikely to be significantly better informed about key health issues, any advice given may be flawed in some way, increasing the probability of an ill-informed decision.

Imagine a teenage girl named Sasha who suddenly becomes fearful that she is becoming obese. Frantic, she picks up the phone and rings her best friend, another teenager, who promptly suggests that she goes on a strict diet, one which amounts to eating little more than a small portion of vegetables per day. The friend confirms that she herself has been on a diet for several weeks and has lost a lot of weight. Unfortunately, what the friend doesn't say is that her strict diet and weight loss have made her anorexic. She isn't very well informed about eating disorders, and hence is not in a position to warn Sasha about this potential problem. Reassured by her friend's (wrong) advice, Sasha promptly decides to adopt a strict diet, and

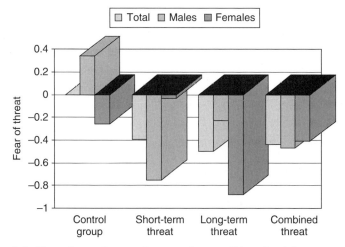

4.1 *Fear of immediate and remote threats. Although adolescents are often concerned about their health they may still make risky decisions. Conventional wisdom suggests that fear of remote health risks may have less impact on choice than more immediate social worries, such as anxiety about looking foolish, or being ridiculed by peers. However, a study on teenage smoking showed that gender plays an important moderating role. Among girls, long-term fears were in fact more influential than short-term worries, whereas the reverse was true for boys (Source: Smith and Stutts, 2003).*

loses weight rapidly over the next few weeks. After six months of starving herself she collapses one afternoon and has to be rushed to hospital. The way adolescents react to fear can have lethal consequences.

Fear of short- and long-term threats

The idea that fear affects a person's decision making has been recognised by psychologists for decades (e.g. Hovland *et al.*, 1953; Janis and Feshbach, 1953; Leventhal, 1970; Janis and Mann, 1977; Eagly and Chaiken, 1993). There appears to be considerable interest in social fears, and with some justification. We saw in the preceding chapter that anxiety about social situations is palpable during adolescence (Muris and Ollendick, 2002). Michiel Westenberg and several colleagues conducted a comprehensive study (Westenberg *et al.*, 2004) which revealed that social fears increase through adolescence, whereas anxieties about medical and health issues show a steady decrease.

Social fears may impact heavily on adolescents' decision making. One reason for this is that these worries are associated with immediate short-term threats. For example, public criticism and other forms of social mockery can be swift and instantaneous. By contrast concerns about health may have little or no impact on choice because most of the major health threats (other than the risk of HIV infection) seem long term and remote (van der Pligt, 1994).

4.2 *Social anxiety. Teenagers often fear social situations in which they may face public criticism. This anxiety is bound to affect their decision making (Source: SXC).*

Does this mean that short-term (social) fears always have a more powerful effect on health decision making than long-term (health) concerns? Not necessarily so, to judge from a study by Smith and Stutts (2003).

Two Professors of Marketing, Karen Smith and Mary Ann Stutts, designed an experiment to investigate whether fear emanating from long-term threats like serious diseases (e.g. cancer) is more or less persuasive than fear associated with more *immediate* social consequences, such as criticism from parents and other family members. Participants were high school students from several schools in the south-west region of the USA. They were assigned to one of three treatment conditions – two experimental groups exposed to a short-term or long-term fear message, or a control group that received no treatment.

All participants saw anti-smoking advertisements (which had been produced by a professional media organisation) portraying two students (boyfriend/girlfriend) having a dialogue in a typical high school setting. The short-term fear message incorporated references to bad breath, yellow teeth and stinking clothes, accompanied by the tag line 'Smoking Stinks', while the long-term fear message referred to the risks of lung cancer, heart disease and stroke, with the tag line 'Smoking Kills'.

They found that teenagers exposed to both the short- and long-term fear appeals smoked fewer cigarettes, smoked less frequently and were less likely to continue

smoking, compared with participants in the no-treatment control group. More interestingly, the long-term fear message seemed more effective than the short-term version, seemingly debunking the notion that teenagers generally feel invulnerable to remote health threats such as cancer and heart disease (see Fig. 4.1). However, this effect wasn't significant, meaning that both types of fear were in fact equally important in reducing adolescents' cigarette smoking. Curiously there were unexpected gender differences. Whereas short-term fears were significantly more influential than long-term fears in males, the reverse was true for females.

One problem with this study is that there wasn't any direct evidence that adolescents exposed to the fear messages in fact experienced a greater degree of fear compared with those in the no-treatment control group. Yet fear was assumed to underpin the observed effects of the messages. However, the social (i.e. short-term) and health (i.e. long-term) emphasis of the advertisements is consistent with the fears children and adolescents experience, as demonstrated by Muris, Ollendick, and other researchers (Ollendick *et al.*, 1989; Muris and Ollendick, 2002), so subjects in the treatment groups probably did feel frightened.

Thus, against conventional wisdom, this study showed that, overall, fears about one's health, remote as the threat might be, can influence adolescents' decision making, encouraging the abandonment of risky behaviour. However, males may be particularly sensitive to anxiety about short-term social pressures, whereas females may demonstrate greater foresight and intellectual aptitude, by basing their decisions on future health problems.

But what is the exact mechanism by which fear influences decision making? Why should teenagers prefer one option to another as a result of fear? In the 1950s Carl Hovland and two colleagues offered an intriguing account of why people, faced with frightening warnings about potential health problems, simply fail to adopt recommended preventive behaviours (Hovland *et al.*, 1953; Eagly and Chaiken, 1993). Their account, discussed below, shows how fear operates as the fundamental driving force in people's decision making.

Fear as a driving force

The movie blockbuster *The Blair Witch Project* offered excellent value for money, for both viewers and producers. Long sections of the movie involve whispered monologues uttered by a frightened teenage girl who seems to contemplate her fate, wondering what is going on, what has happened to everyone else, and how she might escape from the horrifying experience. What is interesting about this particular feature is that the girl continually 'rehearses' her predicament, trying to reassure herself.

Carl Hovland and his colleagues (1953) argued that this kind of mental rehearsal is key to understanding why some people are persuaded by fear to adopt healthier practices, while others seem unaffected (see review by Eagly

and Chaiken, 1993). Fear, they argued, is like a driving force that stimulates people into action, any action. Just like the law of conservation of energy in physics – which states that matter can neither be created nor be destroyed, but can only be channelled into a different form – fear cannot simply be 'destroyed', *it has to be 'managed' somehow*, otherwise the individual will become emotionally and physically incapacitated, unable to function normally.

Let's consider an example. A teenage boy who encounters a scary warning about unsafe sex, and the risk of contracting HIV, may become frightened. As a consequence he will try to do something about his anxiety. But what? The boy may deduce that it isn't really his responsibility to ensure that contraception is used during sex, leaving it up to his girlfriend. Or he could minimise the danger, focusing on the fact that he hardly knows anyone who is HIV positive, let alone sick with AIDS. Alternatively, the boy could simply practise safer sex.

According to Hovland *et al.* (1953), there are numerous ways a person may respond to fear. This premise formed the basis for a theoretical framework, known as the drive reduction model, which helps to explain the impact of fear on choice. The model contends that humans react to fear by considering and trying out various measures to reduce their anxiety. Any action that promises a reduction in fear is likely to be adopted (see Fig. 4.3). Thus, according to this theory, teenagers worried about their health should readily adopt health protective measures to the extent this reassures them. If choosing a healthy option fails to alleviate stress, then they will try out alternative measures irrespective of the health implications.

The priority is fear reduction, not health protection, according to the fear drive model. Thus, if ignoring a threat to one's health is reassuring then that is the course of action that will be chosen. Even if adopting a healthy measure alleviates anxiety, this option is still unlikely to be chosen if there are other alternatives that seem more effective in reducing fear.

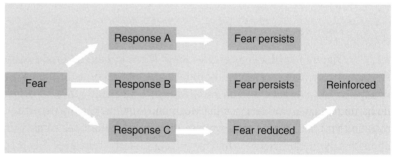

4.3 *A schematic representation of the drive reduction model. Adolescents may respond to fear in a variety of ways. Any response that promises to alleviate anxiety is likely to be reinforced, irrespective of the health risks (Source: Hovland* et al., *1953).*

The fear drive model helps explain why teenagers often persist in unhealthy activity, despite repeated warnings. Changing their behaviour isn't going to make them feel better – in fact they may feel worse if the change brings new concerns, most of which may have little or nothing to do with health. Take, for example, a smoker who is worried about the health risks. Quitting smoking may reassure him. However, the net reduction in fear may be negligible since he may no longer feel 'cool', which in itself is very worrying. He may find it much more reassuring simply to ignore the health risks for the time being, and carry on smoking. Although ignoring the danger is clearly not the healthier option, it is more effective in reducing anxiety! This explains why many teenagers carry on smoking even though they are fully aware of the risks (Siqueira *et al.*, 2000). Giving up cigarettes may not offer any emotional benefits.

The effect of reassurance

It is evident from the discussion so far that reassurance plays a key role in understanding the impact of fear on choice. The drive reduction model suggests that the most reassuring option is the one that is likely to be adopted by the decision maker.

But to what extent does this apply to adolescents? Are teenagers more likely to comply with a fearful health warning if it is accompanied by reassurances? Well, there isn't a clear-cut answer. Most of the research in this area has focused on adults (see reviews by Floyd *et al.*, 2000; Milne *et al.*, 2000; Witte and Allen, 2000). Nevertheless, in the mid 1990s, an experiment by James Sturges and Ronald Rogers (Sturges and Rogers, 1996) of the University of Alabama helped shed some light on the issue (see Box 4.2). Their findings showed that adolescents do in fact respond to reassurance, presumably because it alleviates emotional discomfort. Smokers were more likely to give up smoking if they heard reassurances that giving up would (a) effectively eliminate the danger to their health, and (b) be viable. Other experiments seem to corroborate these findings (e.g. Fruin *et al.*, 1992; Kaljee *et al.*, 2005; Simons-Morton *et al.*, 2006).

It is worth noting that studies in this area focus specifically on the perceived threat, rather than on feelings of anxiety. Thus, it is difficult to say with certainty that participants are motivated specifically by an anticipated reduction in fear rather than merely the cognitive perception of danger. However, since adolescents do harbour fears about their health (Muris and Ollendick, 2002), it is reasonable to assume that reassurances that promise the removal of a health risk will simultaneously calm the nerves.

The great psychoanalyst and philosopher Sigmund Freud argued that humans have an endemic preoccupation with avoiding anxiety, and will take whatever action is necessary to do so (Viney and King, 2003). Why should adolescents behave any differently?

Box 4.2 Research spotlight: the effect of reassurance

Sturges, J.W. and Rogers, R.W. (1996) Preventive health psychology from a developmental perspective: an extension of protection motivation theory. *Health Psychology*, 15, pp. 158–166.

This study tested the effect of reassurance on choice across three different age groups – children, adolescents and young adults. All subjects were non-smokers. They were exposed to health warnings highlighting the risks of smoking and their personal susceptibility. There were two versions of the warning: subjects heard either a strong or a weak variety. The former message emphasised that the subject was personally susceptible to serious health problems caused by smoking cigarettes, while the latter condition minimised the seriousness of the health problems and the subject's personal vulnerability.

To manipulate the level of reassurance contained in the warning, subjects heard either a message promising that not smoking cigarettes will help prevent health problems and was easy to do, or a message minimising the preventive value of not smoking while stressing the difficulty of avoiding tobacco. There were two dependent variables – desire to refrain from smoking cigarettes and using smokeless tobacco products.

The experimenters expected that since children are generally unable to reason like adults they may be less able to understand the information contained in the message, and therefore will respond differently. Closer to adults in their intellectual abilities, adolescents were expected to behave as Hovland, Janis and colleagues had theorised: that is, they will be more inclined to adopt a behaviour if doing so reassures them.

The researchers found that subjects given strong reassurances reported a stronger desire to avoid smoking. Those not given as much reassurance were less likely to avoid smoking in response to the high-threat communication. However, whereas adolescents and adults were happy to avoid smoking, if reassured, children exposed to the same conditions showed little or no reaction. However, children exposed to the strong warning were more likely to refrain from smoking if they received less reassurance. While the data for children were particularly intriguing, it is the behaviour of adolescents that is relevant here. The evidence shows that reassurance is critical when teenagers make health behaviour choices. Any option that makes them feel better – whether due to the inherently comforting features of the choice itself, or accompanying reassurances given by others – is likely to be embraced.

Fear as a potential outcome

In their book on decision making Janis and Mann (1977) note that the presence or absence of anxiety forms part of the costs and benefits that a decision maker may consider. Fear is distressing, thus any *increase* in fear amounts to a *cost*, whereas any *reduction* in fear is a *benefit*. The decision

maker will be drawn to any option that promises the greatest reduction and/or the least increase in fear.

We know from research that reducing anxiety is often a reason given by adolescents for adopting a particular health behaviour (e.g. Siqueira *et al.*, 2000; Allison *et al.*, 2005; Lee *et al.*, 2007). Thus, one's anticipated level of fear is a potential outcome that feeds into the decision making process, just like health threats, social approval/disapproval and other important considerations.

Take, for example, a girl deciding whether or not to go to see her dentist. Which alternative will she choose? Since staying at home is less stressful she is likely to prefer this option. However, in reality it may not be that simple. Forgetting the multitude of other costs and benefits that may also have to be considered (e.g. gum disease, disappointment in oneself), the girl may also have to weigh other worries she has. Other than her fear of dentists, she may also be anxious about being criticised by her parents, or even by her dentist, for not agreeing to attend her dental appointment. She may be anxious about developing some dental problem at some point in the future, having failed to have her teeth checked. The girl may also fear being laughed at by her friends if they find out she is too timid to visit the dentist. All or most of these fears will be taken into account when making her decision. The best option would be the one that offers the greatest overall reduction or least increase in anxiety.

However, making a decision may be far from easy. Choosing a healthy path may increase other fears, such as concerns about ridicule from peers. Alternatively, making an unhealthy choice could increase health worries, not to mention the anxiety about being punished by a parent, teacher or other authority figure.

Some teenagers may attempt to simplify things, for example by considering only one type of fear, or by simply postponing the decision altogether, or leaving it to others (e.g. parents, siblings, friends) to decide. As *goal setting theory* suggests (see Chapter 3) (Locke, 2001; Latham and Locke, 2002), establishing one's emotional priorities, that is, identifying the main fear, may help focus the mind, thereby facilitating a quick decision. For example the girl may decide that dealing with her fear of dentists is her primary goal, and promptly decline to visit.

Overall, adolescents may treat fear as a potential outcome, like any other, to which they may ascribe a favourable or unfavourable value (see Table 4.1). Decision alternatives will be weighed accordingly, to achieve the best emotional results.

Can fear explain the proverbial anomaly?

Can fear explain, at least in part, the proverbial anomaly whereby teenagers repeatedly make poor health choices, despite being fully aware of the risks (see Chapter 2)? Well, evidence suggests that fear is somehow implicated. We know that adolescents who choose to endanger their health report different levels of anxiety compared with individuals who elect to protect themselves (Umeh, 1998a; Lee *et al.*, 2007).

Table 4.1 *Teenagers associate different levels of fear with each decision option. Thus, anticipated fear is weighed like other potential outcomes in trying to decide what choice to make. Any option that offers a reduction in anxiety is likely to be adopted.*

Type of fear	Healthy option (e.g. quitting smoking)	Risky option (e.g. smoking)
Fear of medical and social situations	Fear reduction	Fear increase
Fear of danger and dying	Fear reduction	Fear increase
Fear of likely problems with peers	Fear increase (peers smoke)	Fear reduction (peers smoke)
Fear of being punished by adult figure	Fear reduction (parents approve)	Fear increase (parents disapprove)
Others (animal, school, the unknown)	Fear reduction (unknown risks of smoking)	Fear increase (unknown risks of smoking)

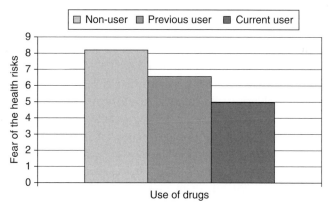

4.4 *Fear and the proverbial anomaly. Why do teenagers take risks despite being risk aware? Theory suggests that fear has motivational properties, such that any action associated with a reduction in fear is likely to be adopted. A study showed that teenage drug users are less fearful about the risks than non-users. One way to interpret this finding is that low fear encouraged risk taking (Source: Umeh, 1998b).*

For example, in my own research with teenagers (Umeh, 1998a, 1998b) I found that adolescents who avoided using drugs reported significantly more fear about the health risks of drug use, compared with individuals who were current users (see Fig. 4.4). One way to interpret this finding is that non-users were at least partly motivated by a need to avoid further emotional discomfort, since using drugs was likely to increase their anxiety. Users, by contrast, felt less fearful, suggesting that low fear had some incentive value, perhaps encouraging their risk taking. For example, drug use may help alleviate stress.

Thus, in accordance with Hovland *et al.*'s (1953) drive reduction model, it would seem non-users were deterred by the presence of fear, whereas users seemed encouraged by its absence. I observed similar fear–behaviour relations for other health habits, for example condom use, physical activity and dietary intake.

However, this interpretation is highly questionable. The problem is establishing the direction of causality. The vast majority of studies on fear and health behaviour have used a correlational design (see reviews by Milne *et al.*, 2000; Witte and Allen, 2000), resulting in a chicken-or-egg problem. Fear is just as likely to be a consequence of a decision as a cause of it. For example, drug users may deliberately minimise concerns about the health risks, in order to justify their risky behaviour (Janis and Mann, 1977).

Demonstrating causality would require a well-designed randomised controlled trial, in which adolescents' fear levels are manipulated, under controlled conditions. However, this type of study is impractical, simply because inducing very high (and hence potentially traumatising) levels of fear in subjects, just to see its effect on decision making, is unethical.

Some studies have demonstrated the effect of potential frightening communications on adolescent health behaviour, often with good manipulation checks suggesting that fear was indeed manipulated (e.g. Rippetoe and Rogers, 1987; Sturges and Rogers, 1996). These studies do confirm that fear may indeed have motivational properties. However, presumably for ethical reasons, such investigations tend to focus on health protective behaviour, rather than risky activity. Thus, the importance of fear as a factor in bad health decisions remains uncertain.

If the level of fear operates as an incentive or disincentive to behave in a particular way then it follows that what may appear a completely foolish decision to an observer may in fact be quite rational to the decision maker.

Fear from previous failure

Fear associated with an earlier experience may also help explain the proverbial anomaly. Anxiety associated with a previous decision that went badly can discourage a teenager from making the same decision in the future, irrespective of risk considerations.

Imagine a smoker who suffered intense withdrawal symptoms the last time he tried to quit smoking. Chances are anxiety associated with this previous failure may deter him from trying to quit smoking again, even if he is fully aware of the health risks.

This phenomenon highlights some of the complexity characterising the effect of psychological factors on decision making – current decisions are sometimes based, not on appraisals of the present situation, but rather on previous experience (e.g. van der Velde and van der Pligt, 1991; Kanvil and Umeh, 2000; Umeh, 2003; Grunfeld, 2004), which of course may include memories of previous anxiety.

For decades theorists have argued that previous experience plays a key role in learning. For example, in describing his highly influential social learning theory Albert Bandura noted that, through past experiences, people 'fear and avoid things that have been associated with aversive experiences, but like and seek those that have had pleasant experiences' (Bandura, 1977, pp. 58–59). Adolescent decision making is no exception.

This 'past coming back to haunt me' phenomenon was clearly demonstrated in a study on dental anxiety carried out by odontologists E. Skaret, M. Raadal, E. Berg and G. Kvale (Skaret et al., 1998). A group of 18 year olds were administered a questionnaire measuring their fear of dental treatment (e.g. drilling, use of needles), experiences of pain (and presumably fear) during their last dental visit, and dental decision making, including how long it has been since the last dental visit, attendance pattern (cancellation of or failure to attend appointments), and personal oral hygiene practices, notably tooth-brushing and flossing. Analysis showed that subjects who experienced pain during their last dental visit reported more dental anxiety. In turn, dental fears were associated with a significantly greater number of cancellations and missed appointments, as well as more delay in booking appointments.

Although the findings from this study aren't conclusive (the design was correlational, rather than experimental), they suggest a link between fears associated with earlier dental experiences on the one hand, and current decisions on the other (e.g. delay in making appointments).

A person's risk awareness may be of little consequence when past experience plays a dominant role in choice (Bandura, 1977). Thus, what appears to be a strange decision may in fact depict a logical process of learning in which concerns derived from previous experience overwhelmingly determine the choices one makes.

Defensive responses

I remember a graphic anti-smoking advertisement that was aired for some time on television channels in the UK. It was designed to highlight the damaging effects of passive smoking on very young children. Several scenes were shown in which a baby or very young child was sitting or playing in a room full of cigarette smoke, presumably produced by a non-visible smoker in the immediate vicinity.

What was particularly memorable about this health warning was the very close shots of the children's nostrils, in which thin plumes of passive cigarette smoking could clearly be seen entering the nasal canals each time the child inhaled. The effect was truly shocking – and frightening. Nevertheless I suspect that many teenage smokers who saw the advert would simply ignore it or minimise its significance. Why?

One reason is that it may be too disturbing for them to accept that smoking is dangerous, not just to themselves, but to babies as well. However, there is another

rather curious aspect to this anecdote. Suppose that the content was somehow *less* shocking? For example, what if there were no close-up scenes but just a written message about the dangers of passive smoking, without any of the alarming images? Perhaps the emotional effect might be less severe. Less repelled by the message, a smoker might be more willing to reconsider her behaviour.

In the late 1960s Irving Janis developed a theory, known as the family-of-curves model (Janis, 1967; Eagly and Chaiken, 1993), that elaborates this phenomenon.

The family-of-curves argument

The family-of-curves theory posits that fear generates two types of reactions – those that *facilitate* compliance and those that *interfere* with acquiescence. According to Janis (1967), the latter category incorporates a variety of defensive reactions, including minimising the seriousness of a threat or one's susceptibility to it, being hypercritical in evaluating message content, selectively attending to message content, and derogating the source of the message.

Janis reasoned that facilitating responses will predominate provided fear arousal does not exceed a certain level. If an individual becomes too scared, such that his fear exceeds this critical threshold, then interfering responses will take precedence.

Imagine an adolescent who isn't particularly worried about the risks of excessive alcohol consumption. As she is exposed to more and more warnings (e.g. on TV, in teenage magazines and from significant adults), her anxiety increases. For a while she exhibits mainly facilitative responses. She may drink less or avoid alcohol altogether. But as fear arousal exceeds the critical point, interfering responses become dominant. Avoidance, denial and other evasive strategies become the order of the day. She starts to ignore the warnings, or question their authenticity.

Janis's (1967) model effectively proposes a curvilinear (or curved) relationship between fear and compliance. In essence, an increase in fear is accompanied by a corresponding increment in acquiescence, but this relationship only applies up to a point. Beyond this threshold the association between both variables is reminiscent of the economic law of *diminishing returns*. As more fear is generated each increase yields less and less compliance. It is during this phase that adolescents may seem irrational, continuing to exhibit risky behaviour despite being aware of the dangers to their health. Plotted on a graph the resultant relationship between fear and acceptance of a health warning resembles an inverted U-shaped curve with the optimal point occurring at the level of anxiety at which compliance stops being facilitated.

Unfortunately there is insufficient empirical evidence to judge the applicability of this model to adolescent health behaviour. Few studies have been published that test the theory, and these focus mostly on adults, and generally report inconclusive results (see review by Eagly and Chaiken, 1993). There seem to be just as many studies reporting increased compliance associated with fear arousal as there are

investigations showing diminished compliance. Additionally, a large proportion of these studies are questionnaire surveys that simply test for correlations between self-reports of fear and compliance (or similar variables) (Witte and Allen, 2000).

Fear may indeed produce both healthy and unhealthy decisions, depending on various moderating factors. Level of fear may be one such factor, as Janis (1967) suggests. However, demonstrating this conclusively in adolescents would require a single experiment that clearly shows how increasing fear arousal first facilitates healthy choices, but begins to trigger unhealthy decisions once a critical threshold is reached.

But why have existing studies failed to demonstrate this effect? After all, the family-of-curves model has been around for many decades. One possible reason is that most experiments generate too *little* fear, so that only facilitative effects occur, or too much fear, in which case interfering responses predominate. Thus what is needed is a study that generates a sufficiently wide range of fear in subjects, in order to capture the curved relationship. Of course generating excessive fear can have ethical implications, and hence prove impractical.

The conflict-theory perspective

According to this formulation, defensive reactions result from anxiety, caused by pessimism about finding a solution to a threat (Janis and Mann, 1976, 1977; Janis, 1983). For example, a teenage smoker who recognises the risks of smoking, but doubts his ability to quit, may become defensive. According to Janis and Mann (1976, p. 658), the defensive decision maker 'evades the conflict by procrastinating, shifting responsibility to someone else, or constructing wishful rationalisations and remaining selectively inattentive to corrective information'.

Information or cues that suggest there are no serious penalties for postponing the decision will encourage the tendency to procrastinate. The individual will stop thinking about the issue, avoid discussing it with anyone who may disapprove of postponement, and stay away from social or other encounters where he may come under pressure to make a decision soon.

If the decision maker anticipates severe losses for postponement, he will consider turning responsibility for the decision over to someone else. The individual may rationalise that others are in a better position to make an informed choice (e.g. 'my boyfriend/parents will decide') and hence should take the blame if things turn out badly. If responsibility cannot be shifted because of pressure of a firm deadline (e.g. imposed by a parent) the individual may resort to rationalisations to justify his current position.

Although research on conflict-theory is scant, studies have shown that fear may indeed trigger defensive responses in both adolescents and adults (e.g. Umeh, 1998b; Witte and Allen, 2000). Whether the anxiety results from pessimism, as proposed by the model, is debatable, but it is worth noting that this argument

seems to be accepted by other influential theorists in health behaviour research, notably R. W. Rogers (1975, 1983). His view is considered next.

The view of R. W. Rogers

Rogers (1975, 1983; Rippetoe and Rogers, 1987) proposed a model of persuasion, protection motivation theory, which essentially posits that fear generated by a perceived threat may trigger defensive responses, including use of religious faith (use of one's spiritual cognitions and faith in God's will to cope), avoidance (attempts to evade or deny threat), wishful thinking (use of panaceas or unrealistic solutions), fatalism (complacent acceptance of threat as uncontrollable) and hopelessness (absence of belief in possible solutions to threat).

These evasive responses, Rogers suggests, are particularly likely if people do not see a viable way of dealing with a threat, specifically because of the perceived ineffectiveness of preventive measures, or doubts about their achievability. Unfortunately, although numerous studies have tested Rogers' model in the context of adolescents' health behaviour (e.g. Palardy *et al.*, 1998; Pechmann *et al.*, 2003; Grunfeld, 2004; Kaljee *et al.*, 2005; Mayes, 2006; Simons-Morton *et al.*, 2006; Boer and Mashamba, 2007), few have bothered to investigate defensive responses.

Nevertheless, a study by Fruin *et al.* (1992) demonstrated that threat might indeed generate defensive reactions in adolescents, especially in the absence of a feasible solution. High school students exposed to a health warning about the risks of physical inactivity, specifically cardiovascular disease, were more likely to act defensively, for example by resorting to fatalism and being pessimistic about finding a solution to the threat, if they doubted the benefits or feasibility of physical activity.

Other research suggests that merely experiencing fear, resulting from a threat, is enough to trigger defensive responses, regardless of the circumstances. For example, Rippetoe and Rogers (1987) examined how female college students respond to a health warning about breast cancer. Two adaptive coping styles (intention to perform regular BSEs, rational problem solving) and five maladaptive coping patterns (religious faith, avoidance, wishful thinking, fatalism, hopelessness) were assessed. Exposure to the warning energised both defensive and adaptive responses, irrespective of whether subjects were presented with a viable solution to the danger.

Overall, Rogers' view, like Janis and Mann's, emphasises a connection between defensiveness and difficulty resolving a decision making dilemma. If an adolescent is actively evasive, for example refusing to think about the risks of smoking, then he is probably facing a difficult problem or decision for which there is no clear solution. A smoker who wishes to quit, but doubts his ability to do so successfully, will find it tempting simply to ignore the problem, at least for the time being. Talk to a group of teenage smokers who wish to give up and you may easily find evidence of procrastination.

Box 4.3 Research spotlight: does fear impair good decision making?

Janis, I.L. and Feshbach, S. (1953) Effect of fear-arousing communications. *Journal of Abnormal and Social Psychology*, 48, pp. 78–92.

Janis and Feshbach presented a group of adolescents with one of three
frightening messages recommending better dental care. There was a strong
fear condition, a moderate fear condition and a minimal fear condition. In the
strong fear condition, subjects received a lecture emphasising the painful
consequences of poor dental hygiene, and illustrated by highly vivid photographs portraying tooth decay and mouth infections. By contrast those in the
moderate and minimal fear conditions were shown less severe photographs,
and administered a greatly 'toned down' version of the lecture. The strong fear
condition used personalised statements (e.g. 'this can happen to you').

Subjects in the strong group subsequently showed greater acceptance of the
communication compared with the other two groups. One week later, subjects
were assessed on their dental hygiene practices. The greatest amount of
conformity was observed in the minimal fear condition. The strong group (8%)
showed reliably less compliance than the minimal group (36%). Indeed, the
strong group did not differ significantly from a no-treatment control group,
whereas the minimal group showed a significant increase in conformity compared with the control group. Furthermore, the percentages in each group who
had followed recommendations to visit their dentist during the week following
the lecture were 10, 14, 18 and 4 per cent for the strong, moderate, minimal
and control groups, respectively.

Clearly, compliance seemed to depend on the level of fear aroused, with
those exposed to strong fear displaying the greatest evasiveness. This study
suggests that very intense fear can impair good decision making in teenagers,
by encouraging avoidance.

The impact of phobias

Fifteen-year-old David had a seemingly incurable fear of doctors. He knew
there was something rather idiotic about his anxiety. David would tremble uncon-
trollably when in close proximity to a doctor, and on several occasions had been
unwilling to go to hospital when he was obviously ill and in need of treatment. His
parents just thought he was acting silly, but the fear was real. David had a phobia.

Research suggests that teenagers sometimes have such irrational fears about
health related or medical issues (Ollendick, 1998). Such irrational worries play a
critical role in an adolescent's decision making. Since the fear is unreasonable, any
resulting decisions will probably be irrational too.

There is some empirical evidence indicating that irrational fears can indeed lead
to poor decision making. For example Vika *et al.* (2006) found that phobias
associated with having a medical or dental injection persuaded a small minority

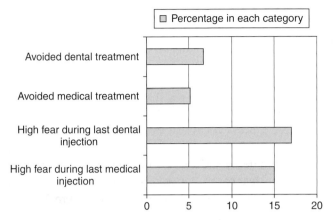

4.5 *Impact of phobias. Phobias about health or medical situations can deter healthy decisions. A study of dental and medical fears showed these anxieties hampered treatment, albeit in a minority of teenagers (Source: Vika et al., 2006).*

of teenagers, 5–7 per cent, to avoid medical or dental treatment, irrespective of the health risks (see Figure 4.5). Further analysis showed that fear was the sole reason for avoiding treatment, indicating that this factor receives the highest priority during decision making.

Phobias unrelated to health can also have a significant impact on choice. In one study, Jolanta R. Jablonska, Anna Dietrich-Muszalska and Agnieszka Gmitrowicz (2003) found that a large group of adolescents suffering from social fears (e.g. anxiety about meeting new people, talking in public, being criticised, looking foolish before others, or being in a fight or crowd) also showed tendencies towards alcohol consumption and abuse of psychoactive drugs. Since this study was correlational rather than experimental in its design, no firm conclusions can be drawn about causality. Nevertheless, since social phobias often originate in early adolescence, it isn't unreasonable to infer that interest in substances like alcohol is somehow linked to irrational fears.

Much of the research on teenage phobias has tended to focus on social fears (e.g. Walters, 2001; Jablonska *et al.*, 2003; Westenberg *et al.*, 2004). Thus, it isn't clear whether findings such as those reported by Jablonska *et al.* (2003) would generalise to health/medical fears. But perhaps that may be missing the point. Clearly, irrational fears seem to cause *poor* decision making, whereby teenagers prefer unhealthy activity like ingesting alcohol. It is possible alcohol and drugs serve as effective coping strategies for managing such anxiety (Carver *et al.*, 1989), especially when in a stressful social situation or when such a scenario is anticipated.

Social phobias can significantly hamper competent decision making. Kenneth S. Walters (2001) completed a postgraduate dissertation that demonstrated greater *submissiveness* amongst socially phobic teenagers, compared with adolescents with no irrational fear. This suggests greater susceptibility to social pressure. Fearful of and hence keen to avoid criticism, rejection or ridicule by others, teenagers with this particular fear may be overly keen to please others, especially

their peers. They may more readily succumb to peer pressure to smoke cigarettes, use drugs or engage in other risky behaviours.

Overall, phobic teenagers aren't particularly well placed to make health enhancing decisions. Overcoming or escaping their irrational fears is likely to take precedence over addressing any health concerns. Nevertheless, only a small minority of phobic adolescents may actually succumb to this pressure and make a bad decision.

Freaking out

Becky had been dating her boyfriend for several weeks now. Although the couple had only known each other a short time, they were already sexually intimate. Becky had always practised safe sex with previous boyfriends, insisting that they wore a condom if they wanted the relationship to continue. However, with this particular partner, she was unusually reckless. They used condoms occasionally but not all the time.

At first neither teenager was particularly bothered about their risk taking, until one day Becky noticed her period was a week late. She felt herself begin to panic. More days passed and still her period didn't arrive. After two weeks with no sign of menstruation Becky was in a frantic state. She rang her boyfriend early one morning, saying she was really 'freaking out' about the whole thing!

Teenagers often use the term 'freaking out' to describe extremely intense fear (Voice of America News, 2007). Typically, the anxiety is so severe they find it difficult to function normally. Although their reaction may fall short of sheer panic (see Chapter 8), many teenagers frantically try to contact friends, or family members, in a desperate search for empathy and reassurance. The fear is undeniably acute, at least from the point of view of the person experiencing it.

One thing that struck me during my research for this book was how events that seem quite benign and trivial generate considerable anxieties in adolescents. I became quite curious when a girl I was interviewing described her fear of spots (i.e. pimples). Apparently her anxiety was so intense she made a snap decision to change her diet (which, she was convinced, would alleviate the spots). This leaves one with the impression that teenagers may be unusually sensitive to *certain* types of fears. But if so, what are these fears?

Thomas Ollendick and various colleagues have identified the ten most intense fears experienced by children and adolescents in several studies (e.g. Ollendick *et al.*, 1989, 2001; Muris and Ollendick, 2002). This issue has already been addressed in this chapter. At least five of the top ten fears had something to do with death and disease, in other words health (Muris and Ollendick, 2002).

These threats are probably more likely to cause teenagers to freak out than other less frightening stimuli. However, another reason adolescents may freak out is an exaggerated sensitivity to anxiety. Adolescents who *easily* become highly stressed, and overreact to this aroused state, are understandably *more* likely to avoid things that may add to their anxiety, including health enhancing behaviours.

In one investigation, psychiatrists Kimberly Wilson and Chris Hayward found that adolescents with an overly nervous disposition were more likely to eschew situations or things they found threatening, including health related settings such as hospitals (Wilson and Hayward, 2006).

Now, it is tempting to infer from such evidence that being too anxious somehow *prevents* teenagers from confronting decisions head-on. In other words, anxiety triggers avoidance responses. However, we have to be cautious because much of the scientific evidence in this area is correlational, making it difficult to reach a consensus about cause and effect. Nevertheless it seems commonsensical that a teenager who easily becomes stressed may try to avoid aggravating his emotional state, by trying to resolve difficult health issues. Such youngsters may reason, 'Well if the jug is so full there's no point adding more water!'

However, the matter is rather more complicated than it may first appear. I've found that avoidant youngsters can experience *less* anxiety, at least when it comes to the dangers associated with one particular health topic – physical inactivity (Umeh, 1998b). Now, it is difficult to imagine that those adolescents who *aren't* particularly anxious are the ones who prefer to avoid problems. Why would they feel the need to be evasive if they weren't stressed?

Note that so far I have generally implied that it is anxiety that causes avoidance not the other way around. Things seem to make a bit more sense when avoidance is viewed as the cause, and anxiety as the outcome. For example, an anorexic teenager may feel less worried about her illness by denying or ignoring the problem: in essence, being avoidant should make her feel better, at least in the short term.

However, I have to warn readers that if they expect a simple explanation of the link between anxiety and avoidance in teenagers, they are unlikely to find one, certainly not in this book. As is often the case in behavioural science, any outcome is typically the result of a mishmash of personal and situational factors that are often impossible fully to disentangle and comprehend.

The best you can hope for is some sort of tentative position that wouldn't necessarily apply to every teenager in every situation. And the speculative position is this: avoidant teenagers are probably also struggling with anxiety. It is possible that each factor affects the other, so that for example a teenager who avoids making difficult health decisions may feel less anxious as a result, which in turn may encourage her to be more avoidant, and so on.

Persistent fear

Thirteen-year-old Tracy finds the whole thing extremely frustrating. No matter what she does she just can't get rid of her fear of becoming fat. She has tried not to think about it, distracting herself with other activities, but that hasn't worked. Tracy has resorted to outright denial, repeatedly declaring to herself 'I can never get fat', but that hasn't helped either. She even tried to convince herself

---

Box 4.4 Contextual issues: situational interpretation of fear

The way teenagers experience fear during decision making may depend on the situation in which they find themselves. This idea is based on the pioneering work of Schachter and Singer (1962), two psychologists who argued that how people interpret physical symptoms of fear (e.g. shivering) depends on their perception of situational factors. Two teenagers with exactly the same physiological signs of fear (e.g. same heart rate, breathing rate and amount of perspiration) may nevertheless experience this fear in completely different ways depending on the circumstances. A girl facing imminent disaster that requires a quick decision (e.g. possible pregnancy) may panic whereas a colleague facing a remote threat (e.g. heart disease from smoking) may feel only slightly perturbed.

But what are the key factors that characterise a decision making situation, and hence affect experience of fear? Is it the threat or risk to their well-being that people really worry about? Is the danger imminent or remote? Is it serious or benign? Can it be cured? Is the prognosis good? Is treatment painful and are there horrible side effects? A person's perception of these factors can easily create a sense that there is a serious crisis or nothing untoward.

But why does all this matter? Well, research has shown that adolescents do not understand fear as a single entity, but rather comprehend it in different ways. For example, adolescents seem to make a distinction between 'fear', 'anxiety' and physiological experiences of stress, concepts that to many may seem synonymous. This emerged in a study by Eleonora Gullone, Neville King and Thomas Ollendick (2000). Teenagers seem to understand fear essentially as 'being scared', whereas they may characterise anxiety using more moderate terms such as 'worrying' and 'hurt feelings'.

Then there are the physiological symptoms, such as difficulty breathing, sweaty palms and trouble sleeping. Fear is viewed as some sort of illness or practical problem, rather than an emotion. Such differences in how adolescents experience and define their fear can affect the quality of their decision making (Janis and Mann, 1977).

---

that being fat isn't such a bad thing, but that made no difference. Now a sense of helplessness and inevitability has started to set in.

What happens when an adolescent's fear persists despite repeated attempts to calm nerves? This is an important question to ask, because fear, as we now know, impairs decision making (Janis and Mann, 1977; Rogers, 1983; Witte and Allen, 2000). Thus, it follows that an adolescent who has very effective coping strategies for managing anxiety will make better and healthier decisions than a similar youth whose coping strategies are wholly ineffective.

Three psychologists – Jennifer Silk, Laurence Steinberg and Amanda Morris (2003) – conducted an empirical study that seems to support this argument. They asked a group of teenagers to record their emotions at regular intervals, each day, for a whole week. In practice this meant making a note at regular intervals

(i.e. each time they received a short electronic beep from their wrist watch) of their thoughts and emotions, and strategies used for dealing with these experiences, during the previous hour.

Certain strategies, such as denial, or doing whatever 'pops into' one's mind, proved to be quite ineffective in regulating *negative* emotions, albeit not anxiety specifically. Crucially, use of these unsuccessful tactics was associated with shoddy decisions, for example drinking alcohol, using drugs, smoking tobacco and various other activities that truanting children engage in.

All in all, unsuccessful management of fear remains an underresearched area, and so does its impact on health decision making in teenagers. Despite Silk *et al.*'s study (2003), we have to be careful to avoid jumping to conclusions. The impact of anxiety on decision making is very complex (Janis and Mann, 1977). Although failed management may impair choice, it is not difficult to imagine a scenario in which it has the exact opposite effect. For example, if fear is persistent it may actually persuade an individual to adopt health protective measures, whereas fear that is successfully suppressed may create a false sense of security, a lack of urgency that does little to deter risk taking!

Age and gender differences

Research has revealed significant gender differences both in the level of fear experienced and in its association with health behaviour decisions. In general, studies suggest that girls experience greater levels of fear than boys (e.g. Muris and Ollendick, 2002; Li and Prevatt, 2007; but see Westenberg *et al.*, 2004).

There are also significant age differences, but only for particular sources of fear, notably danger, death, social criticism, mockery or embarrassment (Westenberg *et al.*, 2004). In general these fears seem to decline with age, with 16–19 year olds reporting significantly lower levels compared with 12–15 year olds (Muris and Ollendick, 2002). However, Westenberg *et al.* (2004) report a more intriguing trend, whereby fear of punishment and fear of social evaluation decrease and increase with age, respectively. So, for example, adolescents aged 15–18 years were much more concerned about being mocked and criticised by their peers than 12–14 year olds.

Given these differences it is reasonable to assume that fear may be a much stronger influence in decision making amongst girls and/or younger adolescents. Indeed there is some evidence to support this view. My own survey data revealed not just significant gender differences in the level of fear – girls were more fearful of certain health risks, notably the dangers of drug use, unprotected sex and a poor diet – but also in the pattern of correlations between fear and health behaviour decisions (Umeh, 1998b). The reasons for gender differences in fear intensity seem obvious, albeit less so for drug use. Girls are bound to be particularly worried about getting pregnant, hence the group differences in sexual fears. Furthermore, girls are generally more concerned about their weight (e.g. Nowak and Crawford, 1998), and hence will be more anxious about diet-related risks.

The gender differences in drug-related fears are more difficult to explain. Girls may be more sensitive to and hence especially worried about social criticism, notably from peers (e.g. Schuman and Polkowski, 1975), introducing an added layer of fear to any existing health concerns.

What about the relationship between fear and decisions? Whereas, in girls, fear of the dangers of risky sexual behaviour (e.g. unprotected sex) was significantly correlated with contraceptive use decisions, with greater fear being associated with lower intentions to engage in risky sexual activity, in boys no such relationship emerged (Umeh, 1998b). This finding is particularly interesting given that fear was significantly correlated with decisions concerning other health behaviours, in *both* males and females, including dietary intake, physical activity and cigarette smoking. It is likely that the threat of pregnancy is so worrying that girls are compelled to address their fears by ensuring they always use contraception during sexual intercourse.

Overall, two main themes seem to emerge from some of the literature. The first is that there are significant age and gender differences in fear, particularly the latter. Secondly, despite these differences, fear seems to be a significant factor in health behaviour decisions of both genders, and across age groups, although the threat of unplanned pregnancy may magnify the impact of fear in females when making sexual decisions.

Conclusion

A basic thesis that emerges from this chapter is that fear plays a key role in decisions regarding health behaviour. The root of the problem perhaps lies in the multiplicity of fears adolescents entertain. They worry, even when there is nothing specific to worry about. Concerns about short-term social difficulties can be considerable and even anxieties about health threats such as AIDS, or medical issues like pregnancy, can play a substantial role in choice. Received wisdom has always suggested that teenagers are hardly perturbed by long-term risks, such as cardiovascular disease. However, evidence presented here suggests that girls may be genuinely concerned about remote health outcomes.

Ultimately, all these fears somehow have to be dealt with during decision making. Theory suggests that adolescents may simply select options that promise the greatest reductions in fear, perhaps notwithstanding the costs. However, this view is difficult to substantiate given the paucity of empirical research in this area. If it were true, it would suggest that fear is treated by the decision maker as merely another potential outcome that has to be considered when reviewing options.

What can be argued, with some degree of certainty, is that young people anxious about potential threats to their health may benefit from reassurances that emphasise the effectiveness of preventive measures, such as quitting smoking, and how easy it is to adopt such measures. Without such guarantees, adolescents may easily resort to defensive strategies, with the primary purpose of alleviating stress, irrespective of the health consequences.

Ultimately, perhaps the best way to understand the role of fear in health behaviour decisions is in terms of the theory of subjective expected utility, as described in the opening chapter of this book. Teenagers may be tempted to adopt *any* measure that offers the greatest and most probable reductions in anxiety! If such action is damaging to their health, well then, that problem may have to be dealt with another day.

Key points

- Adolescents have a multiplicity of fears, which may affect their decision making.
- Fear may operate as an incentive or disincentive that affects the probability adolescents will adopt or reject a course of action.
- Fear may trigger defensive reactions that encourage health compromising behaviour.
- Irrational fears may also have a significant effect on adolescent decision making.
- Reassurance can mitigate the negative effects of fear on adolescent health behaviour.

Key terms

- Fear
- Short- and long-term threats
- Driving force
- Reassurance
- Potential outcome
- Defensive responses
- Phobias
- Anxiety sensitivity
- Freaking out

Further reading

Eagly, A.H. and Chaiken, S. (1993) *The Psychology of Attitudes*. Orlando, FL: Harcourt Brace Jovanovich.

Muris, P. (2007) *Normal and Abnormal Fear and Anxiety in Children and Adolescents*. Oxford: Elsevier.

Ollendick, T.H., King, N.J. and Muris, P. (2002) Fears and phobias in children: phenomenology, epidemiology and aetiology. *Child and Adolescent Mental Health*, 7, pp. 98–106.

5   Consistency

Learning outcomes

At the end of this chapter readers should have a better understanding of the following:

1 the desire for consistency in choice
2 intention–behaviour consistency in adolescents
3 incentives for consistency, notably the hassle of making fresh decisions
4 the emotional consequences of inconsistency
5 the importance of anticipated regret, coercion, public commitment and social desirability bias
6 strategies for reducing inconsistency
7 the consequences of consistency for health behaviour.

Chapter summary

Decision makers often have a craving for consistency and adolescents are no exception. Consistency in adolescence seems partly dependent on personal and situational factors. Suspicion that one may regret a decision can cause vacillation, hence reducing consistency. Adhering to a socially acceptable position may be easier than maintaining a health damaging lifestyle that attracts criticism. Previous behaviour may encourage continuity more through habit than anything else. Consistency appeals because it eliminates the hassle of making fresh decisions and projects a favourable social image, such as making one look dependable. Also, public commitments are more likely to be maintained than private pledges. Adolescents may resort to various strategies to remain or at least appear consistent, including denial, and shifting personal responsibility, irrespective of the health consequences. The need for consistency may help explain why young people sometimes persist in behaviours that are clearly detrimental to their health.

Chapter outline

The chapter begins with a discussion of consistency and relevant background theory. Next, I consider some literature on the correspondence between intentions and health behaviour in adolescents. This is followed by a discussion of

incentives for consistency, and the moderating effects of contextual variables such as past behaviour, coercion, anticipated regret and public commitment. The chapter rounds off with a discussion of some strategies for reducing inconsistency.

A craving for consistency

One evening, soon after I began writing this chapter, I drove down to a small grocery shop near my home to buy some soft drinks. While waiting in a queue I noticed a newspaper lying in a stand just below the cash register. What really caught my eye was the conspicuous headline 'Teen killed in smash.' The story, written by journalist Khaleeli Homa, revealed a truly horrific incident. Two teenagers had apparently been driving recklessly, near Liverpool, in very bad weather, when the driver lost control and collided with a tree. The driver died, while his passenger was left with life-threatening injuries (Homa, 2007).

Back at home I couldn't help contemplating why the unfortunate youngsters had been driving recklessly. Presumably, the driver had consciously chosen to drive that way, with terrible repercussions. If so, why had he made such a poor decision? With insufficient information on the facts of the incident and the precipitating conditions, I was left to imagine a plausible scenario.

Perhaps this wasn't the first time the driver had driven recklessly. In this case he was merely driving as he usually did when the crash happened. If so, this high-lights one intriguing characteristic of human decision making – the importance of consistency.

Cognitive dissonance theory

Cognitive dissonance refers to an uncomfortable psychological state resulting from having inconsistent attitudes or behaviours. For example, according to this model an adolescent will experience tension if he or she engages in risky behaviour while simultaneously valuing good health. Since tension is uncomfortable people are motivated to reduce inconsistency by modifying their attitudes and behaviours, so that they are more congruous.

Proposed by Leon Festinger in the 1950s (see Festinger et al., 1956; Festinger, 1957; Festinger and Carlsmith, 1959; Harmon-Jones et al., 1996; Beauvois and Joule, 1999), cognitive dissonance theory has had a tremendous influence on the development of psychology and is relevant to any discussion on decision making. A decision represents an attitude (e.g. preference for smoking) and/or a behaviour (e.g. smoking). Thus, it follows that making two conflicting decisions

is bound to generate some degree of tension. Consequently people may feel compelled to be consistent in their decision making, and adolescents are no exception (Mann *et al.*, 1989).

Indeed, being consistent can be viewed as a distinct decision making strategy in its own right! Thus, if an individual chooses option A over option B today, then he or she is likely to choose option A over B in the future, to appear consistent. A critical point to make is that this striving for consistency may persist even if the individual realises option B is the better choice!

At the root of this tendency is the emotional discomfort caused when people have discordant thoughts or preferences. This unpleasant state constitutes a motivational force for attitude change (for a review, see Eiser and van der Pligt, 1988; Eagly and Chaiken, 1993; also see Festinger, 1957; Abelson, 1968; Janis and Mann, 1977). Festinger (1957) has likened it to extreme hunger for food. Just

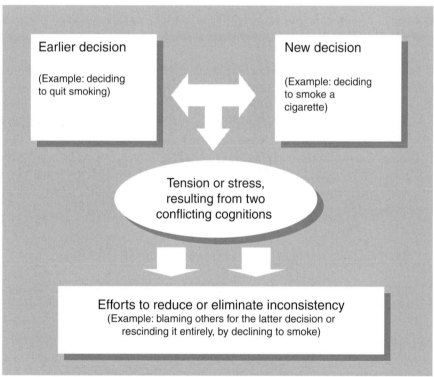

5.1 *Cognitive dissonance and decision making. According to cognitive dissonance theory, adolescents should experience tension when they make two inconsistent decisions. This tension stimulates efforts to reduce or avoid such inconsistency by ensuring that new decisions match old ones (see Festinger, 1957). This emphasis on consistency means that risky health behaviours, such as smoking, may be resistant to change, notwithstanding the significant threat to personal well-being.*

as hunger is stressful and leads to activity aimed at reducing it, so too does inconsistency. So, for example, a non-smoker who starts experimenting with cigarettes may try to attribute this U-turn to others (e.g. 'my friends forced me to smoke'). Passing the buck removes any sense of incongruity, because the decision to smoke is seen as someone else's choice, not his!

Unfortunately, there is precious little empirical evidence on the relevance of cognitive dissonance theory to adolescent decision making. The vast majority of the existing literature has focused on adults (Eagly and Chaiken, 1993). Nevertheless, the model does provide a useful theoretical basis for understanding why adolescents may adhere stubbornly to a bad health decision, despite its associated risks, or indeed why they might maintain a health stance, against all the odds.

Intention–behaviour correspondence

A common way to conceptualise decision making consistency in health psychology is by looking at the strength of intention–behaviour relations (Eagly and Chaiken, 1993; Norman and Conner, 1996). In other words, how much consistency is there between decisions and their implementation?

5.2 *Consistency in decision making. What at first glance appears to be a carefully considered choice (e.g. doing aerobic exercises) may in fact merely reflect unflinching adherence to an earlier decision (e.g. joining the gymnastics team), simply to ensure consistent decision making (Source: SXC).*

An adolescent who intends to quit smoking and actually does so, destroying all cigarettes in his possession, has demonstrated more consistency than a colleague who plans to exercise regularly in a local gym, but never actually makes it to the facility, let alone gets physically active.

The notion of intention–behaviour (sometimes referred to as attitude–behaviour) consistency was perhaps best popularised by Professors Ajzen and Fishbein, in the early 1980s (Ajzen and Fishbein, 1980), as part of their theory of reasoned action and planned behaviour (Ajzen and Fishbein, 1980; Ajzen, 1991). Although this model has had a considerable influence in health psychology, reliably predicting health behaviour in numerous studies (see review by Eagly and Chaiken, 1993), it is not strictly speaking a model of decision making. It does not really address the various facets of decision making, but rather merely lists various perceptions that may influence a decision. Thus, this model isn't discussed here. Interested readers can consult Ajzen and Fishbein's (1980) original work.

While the bulk of intention–behaviour research has focused on adults, a growing number of studies have used adolescent samples (e.g. Beck and Davis, 1980; Stults and Messe, 1985; Gillholm et al., 1999; Mazanov and Byrne, 2002; McMillan et al., 2005; Conner et al., 2006; van Empelen and Kok, 2006). However, some of these focused on college students (e.g. Gillholm et al., 1999), meaning that findings may not generalise to adolescents in their early and middle teens.

These studies seem to suggest that intention–behaviour consistency in adolescent decision making, far from being clear-cut, is significantly dependent on a variety of psychological factors, such as the degree of conscientiousness (i.e. the ability to discipline and organise oneself, to achieve set goals: Conner et al., 2006), fear that one may regret a decision, also known as anticipatory regret (e.g. Abraham and Sheeran, 2003), and how much preparation and planning goes into implementing a decision (e.g. van Empelen and Kok, 2006).

Despite these moderating influences, there is evidence that adolescents can show a remarkable degree of consistency in decision making, over a protracted period of time. A study by J. Mazanov and D.G. Byrne illustrated this capacity in relation to cigarette smoking (Mazanov and Byrne, 2002).

Questionnaire data were collected from a large sample of adolescents (almost 1,500 teenagers) at two different points in time, separated by a year. The first time they completed the survey, participants provided information about their current smoking behaviour as well as their intention to smoke during the next two years. During the second survey, a year later, respondents again indicated their current smoking status.

Analysis of the data for non-smokers showed a significant degree of consistency between intentions expressed at the initial survey and smoking behaviour by the follow-up evaluation. The results are presented in Figure 5.3. The vast majority of non-smokers who declared they had no intentions to smoke in the future behaved in accordance with their intentions a year later. The degree of consistency was extremely high – more than 90 per cent were consistent.

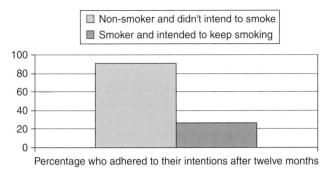

5.3 *Consistency in choice. Adolescents are capable of displaying a remarkable degree of consistency, although this may apply more to healthy than to risky behaviour. In one study on cigarette smoking, non-smokers who had no plans to smoke mostly adhered to this position over one period. By contrast, only a minority of smokers who intended to keep smoking adhered to this decision (Source: Mazanov and Byrne, 2002).*

Curiously, this figure was dramatically different for smokers. Less than a third of smokers who planned to keep smoking adhered to this decision, suggesting that social pressure to quit smoking, growing concerns about the health risks, and other disincentives for smoking, made it difficult to be consistent.

Note that the findings discussed so far pertain only to those whose original intentions matched their current behaviour. We haven't considered those who planned a U-turn – smokers who intended to avoid smoking, or non-smokers who planned to start smoking. Given the argument that decision makers are under pressure to be consistent, not to reverse their positions (Cialdini, 1993), you wouldn't expect much intention–behaviour correspondence in this group. Indeed, this is precisely what Mazanov and Byrne's data seemed to suggest. For example, only 6.1 per cent of original non-smokers who planned to start smoking were actually smoking after a year.

This evidence suggests that it is much easier to be consistent than inconsistent. Consistency also seems much easier if one's original decision is healthy and socially acceptable to start with, and hence not bound to attract criticism.

Cognitive incentives for consistency

According to psychologist Robert Cialdini (1993), being consistent in decision making is an extremely desirable way of dealing with the ambiguities and complexities of the modern world. Decision making can be complex, protracted, and characterised by uncertainty (Janis and Mann, 1977; Byrnes, 2002) and many adolescents find it intimidating, and demanding (Petersen and Leffert, 1995; Byrnes *et al.*, 1999). Paralysed with doubt, it may be tempting simply to do what one did previously in such a situation.

For example, a teenager who is offered a cigarette by peers may find it much easier simply to repeat her previous response to a similar offer, rather than get mentally bogged down trying to decipher the pros and cons of various options, just to make an informed choice. Similarly, a girl who is contemplating dieting but is unsure about the various pitfalls may be tempted to put off a decision if this is precisely what she did the last time she considered restricting her diet.

We know from existing research that adolescents who have prior knowledge or experience of a problem are less willing to analyse things afresh and learn more when faced with the same or similar problem again. For example, Professor of Marketing Stacy Wood and Professor of Business Administration John G. Lynch found that college students who already knew about allergy medications were less interested in learning new information on this subject (Wood and Lynch, 2006). This confirms the suspicion that adolescents readily defer to previous experience when faced with a decision dilemma they have encountered before.

Take the example of the girl considering dieting. If she has had to make this decision before – and many teenage girls have a history of making decisions about their weight – then there may be a 'feeling-of-knowing', the sense that one is already familiar with this problem and how to deal with it. Thus, instead of investing time and energy trying to work out a new solution, it would be very tempting simply to repeat the previous decision, or make a similar one.

The net effect is that health behaviour choices may show remarkable consistency over time, largely because each decision was derived from a previous one. Wood and Lynch (2006) hypothesised that adolescents with prior experience and knowledge on a subject will be particularly unwilling to learn anything new on the topic if their motivation to learn is low. Indeed, they found that teenagers who were motivated to learn by a monetary incentive showed much greater interest in new learning. This finding has some credence when considered within a decision making context. We know that making decisions can be difficult because there is often a lot of information to gather and digest, a considerable degree of uncertainty, and the risk of suffering losses (e.g. physical injury, illness, social disapproval) (Janis and Mann, 1977).

Some teenagers may be put off by this, and hence lack any incentive to dispense with the intellectual hassle involved in making new decisions. For example, a youth contemplating using protection during sexual intercourse may be put off by the wide variety of contraceptive methods available. Discouraged by the mass of information he has to sift through, the individual may resort to his old unsafe sexual practices. Thus, there would be high consistency in his decision making, albeit with potentially serious health consequences.

So what intellectual demands can discourage teenagers from approaching health decisions afresh, hence breaking a long history of consistent but risky decisions? The sheer quantity and complexity of information to learn and evaluate are obviously key factors. These issues are considered below.

Information overload

Research suggests adolescents have more difficulty making decisions if there is simply too much information to consider (Linn *et al.*, 1984; Sung and Kim, 1987). Consider a teenage girl who has just realised she's gained some weight, and is now seeking a solution to the problem. Now, imagine that she wishes to go on a diet. There is a bewildering array of dietary options available.

I did a quick search on Google using the word 'diet', and was rewarded with more than 100,000,000 hits. There is an abundance of not just diets, for example the Atkins eating scheme, Detox diets, Kalahari Cactus diet, GI diet and the Vita Top Slim Power, but a huge preponderance of sites offering advice to people who wish to diet, not to mention more medical-oriented articles, letters and research publications. And all this was available on the first three Google pages alone.

Any teenager, or adult for that matter, will probably be overwhelmed by all this information. Remember, I am not even including additional sources of dieting information, such as books, magazines, and keen parents, teachers and peers. Even if the girl is hell-bent on making an informed decision, based on a comprehensive and systematic evaluation of relevant facts, it might take a few weeks or months, if not years, to sieve through and make sense of the bulk of information.

Convoluted information

It isn't just the quantity of information that can be intimidating, but its complexity as well. For example, trying to work out which of a dozen dietary schemes is best is extremely difficult since the pros and cons of each aren't always obvious, or may be controversial. Even if things were clear, it may still be tricky comparing two different diet plans, simply because of the volume of information that has to be considered.

For example, trawling through Google I found a website dedicated to the Atkins diet. It identified specific advantages in taste, nutrition and ingredients. It further claimed that the nutritional advantage lies in its 'optimal mix' of key nutrients, such as proteins, fibre and vitamins. But when I tried to find out if competing diets offer the same benefits, I soon stumbled upon numerous letters written by dietary experts, expressing scepticism about the health benefits offered by various diets.

At this point things started to look very confusing indeed. Suddenly one couldn't be sure that claimed advantages were factual. To make things even more perplexing, it seemed to take a very long time to find out whether other diets also offered an 'optimal mix' of nutrients, as the Atkins diet claims to do.

I abandoned the search, suspecting that finding the right diet would entail a considerable amount of intellectual effort. Completely flummoxed, our teenage girl may be tempted to find a short cut, a quick and effortless method of resolving things, without having to wade through an ocean of dietary advice and facts. Difficult decisions can be a big turn off (Janis and Mann, 1976, 1977).

Emotional incentives for consistency

According to Festinger's theory of cognitive dissonance (Festinger *et al.*, 1956; Festinger, 1957; Festinger and Carlsmith, 1959) a decision that openly conflicts with an earlier position will make a teenager uncomfortable. In other words, inconsistent decisions produce stress, fear, tension or some other unpleasant emotion.

Let's try to imagine a realistic situation to gain a better appreciation of this argument. Fourteen-year-old Claire is convinced that drinking any form of alcohol is bad for her health. She always insists on having a soft drink whenever she goes out with friends or attends a party.

However, the other day, at a friend's birthday party, a boy she liked offered her some punch. To avoid disappointing him, and perhaps wanting to look grown up, Claire accepted the drink and found herself sipping punch for the rest of the evening. She felt extremely uncomfortable, later admitting, 'While I didn't drink that much, the whole thing just didn't seem right, and I felt like I was doing something wrong, something dangerous … it was very worrying indeed, and still is.'

Although Claire drank in moderation and didn't get drunk or disoriented, her sudden U-turn was a source of concern for several days. She felt disappointed with herself for succumbing to something that she has always objected to.

If Festinger's model is to be believed, people will do anything to be consistent. In essence if you want to know whether a teenager is likely to smoke tomorrow, find out if they smoked today, and/or yesterday. If they are current smokers, or have smoked previously, then they are likely to smoke again; it's as simple as that. Failure to smoke in the future would be discordant with the individual's current preference!

According to social psychologists, notably Irving Janis and Leon Mann (1977), inconsistency makes people uncomfortable for at least two reasons. First, they have to contend with a negative view of themselves as indecisive and unreliable. Many adolescents already suffer from chronic low self-esteem issues (Oregon Resiliency Project, 2003), and failure to adhere to a prior decision will further magnify this insecurity. Second, there is their public image. Few people want to be seen by others as unpredictable and erratic decision makers. Suffice it to say that teenagers (particularly girls) are very concerned about their public image, and especially fear negative evaluations by others (Ollendick *et al.*, 1989, 2001, 2002).

Parents may express disappointment at any deviation from a healthy lifestyle. Peers may frown at any change in behaviour, especially if that change is at odds with peer group activity. For example, a teenager who decides to stop smoking may attract ridicule and mockery from friends who think smoking is 'cool', and smoke on a regular basis.

According to Festinger (1957), people may reduce tension by ensuring new decisions match old ones, or distorting the facts about old decisions so that they match more recent ones. For example, a smoker who has decided to quit may convince himself and others that he never wanted to start smoking in the first

place. Alternatively, he can simply rescind the decision to quit, and carry on smoking.

The net effect of these cognitive changes is that the authenticity or significance of one decision is discounted, hence reducing any perceived duplicity or inconsistency with another otherwise conflicting choice.

The role of past experience

Clearly, one way to remove all the hassle from decision making is simply to do what one did when previously faced with the same problem. Indeed, studies have shown that one of the most powerful predictors of future health behaviour in adolescents is previous health behaviour (Umeh, 2003; Moan and Rise, 2006; O'Callaghan and Nausbaum, 2006).

There is an element of habit here, such that decisions which adolescents have become used to recur almost automatically, with little or no conscious thought. Old habits die hard, so for example a boy who has eaten chips all his life will find it much easier to carry on eating this diet rather than endure the hassle of switching to and maintaining a new nutritional regime.

Consistency serves as a useful 'quick-fix', allowing teenagers to circumvent difficult choices that otherwise may require considerable effort and will to resolve. Indeed, it seems logical to adhere to the last decision if that decision turned out well. In other words, if it isn't broken, then don't fix it – if the previous decision yielded good results, then it makes sense to take a similar stand in the current situation (Bandura, 1977).

Consider if you will the following scenario. A teenage boy has been experiencing ongoing medical symptoms. He has noticed that every few weeks he seems to experience a burning sensation when urinating. There isn't any blood, but the sensation is rather painful. The last time this happened, he reported it to his parents, who in turn promptly took him to see a doctor. The physician prescribed some antibiotics and painkillers that the boy subsequently found to be extremely effective. The burning sensation quickly disappeared.

However, after about four weeks the symptoms resurfaced. This time the pain was even more severe, and his urine seemed to be 'off colour'. The boy remembered that the last time this happened he had promptly alerted his parents, and the problem was quickly solved. Thus, he promptly informed his parents of this latest development.

A teenager may also consider it sensible to adhere to an earlier decision simply because of her inexperience in solving life's problems in general. It is a clever individual who acknowledges her naivety and relies on the little experience she has gained from a previous decision. Imagine an attractive girl who has had a slim figure for much of her life, but then suddenly begins to gain weight. One morning she declares, 'This is it. I have to do something before I get too fat.' Not knowing much about weight control and dieting, she decides to do some of the obvious

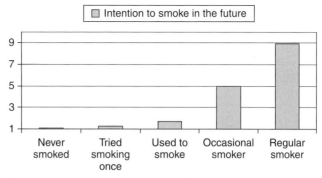

5.4 *Adherence to prior behaviour. Consistency may be the result of a long-established habit. Teenagers may find it much easier to continue rather than break an old addiction. Data from a study showed that the participants who currently smoked cigarettes had stronger intentions to smoke in the future compared with non-smokers. The difference between those who had 'never smoked' and participants who 'tried smoking once' was not statistically significant. This has no bearing on the argument, however. Current decisions were consistent with previous behaviour (Source: Umeh, 2003).*

things she reads about in teenage magazines, notably eating more fruits and vegetables, avoiding high-fat foods, and exercising regularly.

However, despite these measures she continues to gain weight. Soon, she is struggling to fit into some of her clothes, and starts to get really concerned. She has not been overweight before, and hence knows little about the subject. The girl decides that rather than 'messing about' with diets she has little or no experience of using, perhaps it would be better to simply stick to her regular diet, perhaps augmenting it with extra fruit and vegetables.

The key point here is that inexperience can be an incentive for consistency, especially in the absence of an obvious, effective and viable solution to a problem. It may even take the form of a simple rule of thumb whereby if in doubt one simply applies an old solution to an existing problem, rightly or wrongly.

The influence of coercion

We know from psychological research that if college students are forced to take a particular stance on an issue that is inconsistent with their actual position on the matter (e.g. by offering them an incentive, such as money, or threatening punishment) they don't experience any inconsistency (Festinger, 1957).

In other words, if a teenager makes a decision that is discordant with an earlier position, he or she will not actually sense any discrepancy if the latter stance was somehow coerced by external pressure (e.g. from a parent) offering incentives or threatening punishment. Since the person doesn't experience any contradiction he or she will not suffer any tension. Because there is no tension, little or no effort will be made to distort or reverse the latter decision so that it matches the earlier one.

Unfortunately, there is a paucity of evidence on this supposed link between coercion and consistency in adolescent decision making. Indeed, a recent review of several electronic databases revealed a pronounced lack of research on coercion in adolescents, let alone its relevance to consistency. This is unfortunate because there are important health implications for the influence of coercion.

For example, imagine an adolescent who is successfully forced against his will to reverse an earlier risky decision. Since the new decision was effectively coerced it doesn't reflect a genuine change in attitude – the individual is merely pretending to endorse a particular position, under duress, while privately harbouring strong reservations about the choice. In this context it is doubtful that the decision will be maintained or adhered to, especially in the long term. It is highly probable that the position will be reversed once the source of coercion has left the scene.

Consider a teenage boy who smokes cigarettes. One day his mum threatens to withdraw all of his pocket money unless he immediately quits smoking. Not smoking would clearly be at odds with the boy's earlier decision to smoke. Nevertheless, he may promptly comply with his mother's wishes, promising to quit smoking immediately. Because he is being coerced his decision to quit may be insincere. He is likely to resume smoking once his pocket money has been reinstated, only this time with a bit more secrecy to avoid being caught. His mother, for her part, may be under the mistaken impression that her son has quit smoking, when in fact this isn't the case.

Overall, coercion seems to trigger greater inconsistency in decision making. A decision which has been forced is unlikely to reflect the decision maker's true preference, and hence is prone to be abandoned once the source of coercion has disappeared.

However, I came across a rare study that disputes this thesis. Jonathan Tubman, Lilly Langer and Diana Calderon investigated whether being coerced to have sex affects how adolescents make decisions that may affect their sexual health (Tubman et al., 2001). Teenagers attending alcohol and drug treatment facilities in Florida were interviewed, and asked to complete various questionnaires about their sexual experiences, how they make decisions about sex, and other relevant issues.

The researchers were interested in the extent to which coercion affected will-ingness to make a rational decision. This calls for an individual to appraise the current situation (e.g. consider the options and their consequences) and make a fresh choice, rather than merely adhere to a previous or existing position. Analysis of the data showed that, compared to non-coerced subjects, coerced participants were less willing to engage in fresh decision making activity, such as thinking about available options and their consequences. Furthermore, the coerced group reported higher levels of risky sexual behaviour in the previous six months. Thus, coercion to have sex was associated with continued sexual activity.

Tubman et al.'s (2001) study shows that coercion may be associated with continuation of the coerced behaviour, in other words, greater consistency in choices made. Coercion discourages rational decision making, which requires a fresh analysis of a current situation, rather than adherence to a previous position.

Overall, given the paucity of literature in this area, much remains to be learned about the impact of coercion on consistency in adolescents, particularly in a health context.

Anticipated regret

Research has shown that intention–behaviour consistency is dependent on a number of psychological factors, notably anticipation that one may regret a decision, better known as anticipatory regret (Janis and Mann, 1977, pp. 219–242; also see Sheeran and Orbell, 1999). According to Janis and Mann (1977), anticipatory regret refers to 'the various worries that beset a decision maker before any losses actually materialise' (p. 222), and is typified by hesitation and doubt.

Almost every decision concerning one's health entails some degree of uncertainty, a nagging fear that one has made or is going to make the wrong decision, and experience regret. It denotes anxiety about the possible negative consequences of making the wrong choice.

For example a teenager who starts experimenting with cigarettes may subsequently rescind this decision out of fear that something bad is going to happen, like getting caught by his disapproving parents or a schoolteacher. Studies have shown that anticipatory regret plays a significant role in adolescent health decision making (e.g. Caffray and Schneider, 2000; McMillan *et al.*, 2005; Conner *et al.*, 2006). However, the key question here is this: does anticipatory regret cause adolescents to waver when making decisions, leading to inconsistent choices over time? Common sense suggests that it does. Often, health decisions, once made, are rarely forgotten. People continue to have doubts, wondering if they made the right choice, and adolescents are no exception. Fear that something dreadful may happen could quickly cause an individual to alter, reverse or abandon a decision.

Psychologists Mark Conner, Tracy Sandberg and Brian McMillan provide some empirical evidence to support this view (Conner *et al.*, 2006). A group of younger adolescents from selected schools in England completed questionnaires on anticipatory regret, cigarette smoking and other variables, at various points in time. Of particular interest was the extent to which participants who had developed strong intentions to smoke in the near future (the current school term) actually followed through and adhered to this decision months later.

Analysis revealed that anticipatory regret – measured with statements such as 'I would wish I had not smoked if I smoked this term' and 'I would feel depressed if I smoked this term' – was a key factor in the degree of consistency between smoking intentions and actual cigarette use. Specifically, significantly greater inconsistency was found amongst subjects with high levels of anticipatory regret about initiating smoking, compared with those reporting low levels. Thus, individuals who had originally decided to smoke were more compelled to rescind this decision due to foreboding and concern that they might regret their decision.

Anticipating regret is typically fuelled by uncertainty about the available options and their consequences (Janis and Mann, 1977). Sometimes people may suspect they've overlooked a better alternative, or worry that their preferred alternative may prove unworkable.

For example an adolescent may be unsure how best to suggest condom use to a girlfriend or boyfriend before sexual intercourse. Is there any way other than to suggest it outright? Or perhaps it is better just to produce a condom and attempt to use it without discussing it first? Or is it best to wait for the other person to suggest it first? There is no clear answer, leaving most teens bewildered. Of course every option available to a decision maker usually has various advantages and disadvantages, and adolescents may worry that they've overlooked a potentially serious outcome, and will come to regret their choice.

The net effect of these uncertainties is reduced confidence in one's decisions, and hence a low probability of short- or long-term adherence. Interestingly, some evidence suggests that anticipatory regret can actually enhance consistency. In a study on physical activity, Charles Abraham and Paschal Sheeran found that adolescents who intended to exercise were much more likely to exercise if they anticipated regret from failing to adhere to their original decision (Abraham and Sheeran, 2003).

Thus, consistency may be enhanced or diminished depending on what teenagers think they might regret. If they expect to regret a lack of adherence then decision incongruity will be minimal. By contrast, if regret is associated with health behaviour and its potential risks (Conner *et al.*, 2006), then inconsistency may prevail.

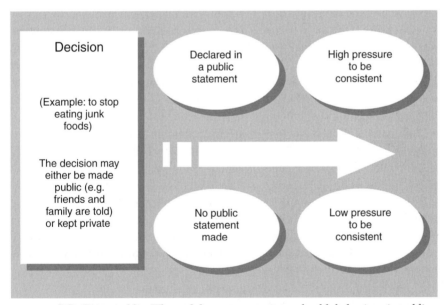

5.5 *Going public. When adolescents commit to a health behaviour in public they experience greater pressure to adhere to their choice, compared with when the same commitment is made in private. This may be partly due to a desire to come across as reliable and decisive.*

Going public

Why is consistency such a powerful force? Even if a teenager is completely bamboozled by the complexity of a situation, and is unsure what to do, why is it so tempting simply to adhere to a prior decision?

Adolescents aren't idiots and can recognise poor health choices when they make them. An individual who has previously elected to use an illicit drug will be fully aware that this wasn't a particularly good decision. So, why on earth would he or she insist on repeating this mistake when faced with another opportunity to use drugs?

Many behavioural scientists are adamant it has something to do with going public. According to psychologist Cialdini, once a person makes a public commitment, there is a natural tendency to adhere to this position, to avoid attracting criticism for unreliability or indecisiveness (Cialdini, 1993, p. 253). But is there really any scientific evidence showing that teenagers maintain consistency in their decision making following a public commitment?

In the early 1980s two psychologists Daniel M. Stults and Lawrence A. Messe carried out an interesting study, with college students, which demonstrated a link between public or private statements and intention–behaviour consistency (Stults and Messe, 1985). A group of girls were asked to play a Prisoner's Dilemma game (Plous, 1993). In this arrangement two 'prisoners' or 'players' can either 'cooperate' with or 'betray' each other, to obtain a reduction in their sentence or even go free. Each player has two options: either cooperate (i.e. stay silent and refuse to testify against the other) or defect in return for a lighter sentence.

Some subjects publicly declared their intentions to cooperate or defect, while others kept their preference private. A third group of control subjects weren't asked about their intentions. All subjects then played the prisoner game a number of times. Stults and Messe found that subjects who publicly declared their intentions were more likely to behave as intended during the game, compared with individuals who kept their plans private, and those in the control group.

Thus, making decisions in public can create pressure to adhere to one's commitment. Of course, Stults and Messe's (1985) study was based on a hypothetical scenario and didn't involve decisions about health behaviour. Thus, its relevance here is questionable.

However, David Wilson, Ronald Friend and colleagues conducted a classic study showing the importance of public commitments in health scenarios (Wilson et al., 2002). They tested the hypothesis that teenagers who freely and publicly choose to eat a particular quantity of fruits and vegetables per day, and increase their level of physical activity, are subsequently more likely to do these things than youngsters who make a similar decision, but in private.

The researchers asked a group of 11–15 year olds to take part in a project in which they had to advise others on the best way to increase their intake of fruits and vegetables, and also exercise regularly. Participants were encouraged to describe particular actions, thoughts and feelings they favoured, for example

sticking to a particular diet when socialising with friends, or when lacking in motivation, and remaining physically active when the weather is bad and one isn't in the mood.

Subjects indicated their preferences during a face-to-face interview with one of the researchers. Now, the crucial element in this study was that subjects had to go on record when stating their proclivities. Each participant was videotaped during the interview. Subjects had been led to believe that their views would be presented to others, presumably through the videotapes, so it was clear that their views would be made public.

As expected, the individuals who 'publicly' revealed their dietary preferences subsequently ate greater quantities of fruits and vegetables compared to other adolescents who had acted in 'private'. Furthermore, the former group also felt more capable of modifying their intake of fruits and vegetables, and levels of physical activity, and more confident they would not renege on their commitments.

These findings seemed to support the idea that if teenagers make a health behaviour decision in public, they would feel compelled to adhere to it, ensuring that subsequent choices match the original commitment.

5.6 *Public commitment. Once a decision becomes public knowledge, such as opting to drink alcohol in the company of friends, teenagers may feel compelled to adhere to this position in the future, to avoid 'losing face' (Source: SXC).*

Effect of social desirability bias

Social desirability bias denotes a desire to make a favourable impression on others (e.g. Miotto *et al.*, 2002; Helmes and Holden, 2003; Leite and Beretvas, 2005). Being popular is a highly valued commodity in adolescence. Few adolescents wish to be viewed unfavourably by others, particularly their peers.

Being an indecisive or unreliable decision maker can make one look erratic and unpredictable. According to Janis and Mann (1977), failure to maintain consistency in choice can be costly, in terms both of social criticism and of deterioration in one's self-image. Thus, a teenager who has made a public pledge knows others are watching and expect adherence. This can create tremendous pressure to 'follow through' with one's commitment, regardless of any health risks involved.

To change one's original stance on an issue, health or otherwise, is to acknowledge, in effect, that one is indecisive. This can be depressing, not just for the decision maker but also for significant others, notably peers. The humiliation is likely to be especially painful if the individual was advised by others not to make the decision in the first place.

Many teenagers would rather smoke themselves to death than give up smoking and face the dreaded words 'I told you so' from a gleeful parent, peer or other significant person. Some adolescents may simply be unable to acknowledge that a prior decision was wrong. They would rather adhere to a bad decision, and stomach the negative consequences, than allow someone else the satisfaction of being correct. I suspect many adolescents wouldn't just stick to a flawed position, but would try to convince themselves (and others) that it is the right choice.

But is there any direct scientific evidence for this? Are teenagers prone to maintaining a prior decision, simply to make a good impression, even when it becomes clear the decision is somehow flawed? Well, we know that social desirability is associated with health behaviour in adolescents (e.g. Miotto *et al.*, 2002; Moskowitz, 2004). Whether social desirability increases adherence and consistency is less clear.

Research suggests it may have a negligible, if any, effect. Psychologist Linda Tilgner and several colleagues conducted a study to determine whether social desirability has any effect on how teenagers respond to an eating disorder programme discouraging dieting (Tilgner *et al.*, 2004). Having consented to participate in such a programme it would be consistent if subjects decided, post-intervention, to avoid dieting. However, it is reasonable to assume that adolescents who are keen to make a good impression on others, say friends and family, will be particularly keen to appear consistent, by acting in accordance with programme objectives.

Results did show evidence of consistent decision making: subjects in the intervention group reported significantly lower intentions to diet post-intervention compared with a no-intervention control group, albeit this group difference had disappeared within a month.

Curiously, social desirability had no effect on consistency. In essence, subjects in the intervention group were not trying to impress anyone by refusing to diet, consistent with their participation in the anti-diet programme.

Byrnes *et al.* (1999) have found that children and younger teenagers do not change or reverse a decision even when they are informed their decision is wrong. If adolescents are happy to cling to a clearly bad decision, despite negative feedback, then they probably don't care much about what others think.

Psychologist Robert Cialdini refers to this phenomenon as the 'hobgoblin of little minds', whereby people in general refuse to rethink their position once they have made a decision (Cialdini, 1993). They stick stubbornly to their choice, even though it is clearly the wrong one, and they are beginning to suffer setbacks as a result.

People simply convince themselves they've made the right choice. Cialdini attributes this stubborn adherence to our need to be seen to be consistent. Sticking to a decision – no matter how flawed – gives the impression that the decision was carefully thought through, and the decision maker knows what he is doing. Thus, refusing to reconsider a decision can make adolescents feel good about themselves even if others disapprove.

Teenagers may be unwilling to rethink even the worst possible decisions, even where there is a lot at stake. For example, they may insist on having unprotected sex (Orr and Langefield, 2001) or declining to take vital medication after a kidney transplant (Feinstein *et al.*, 2005), even though they know they are risking life and limb. Refusal to take essential medication after undergoing major surgery, and hence risking serious medical complications (e.g. tissue rejection), is a particularly worrying example of how a craving for consistency can lead to disaster.

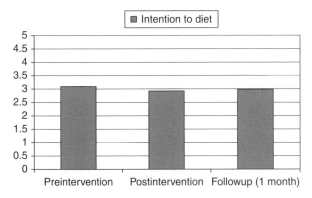

5.7 *Social desirability and consistency. Compared with a control group, girls involved in an anti-dieting programme subsequently reported slightly lower intentions to diet, consistent with their participation. However, social desirability had no effect on consistency, suggesting that making a good impression isn't necessarily a factor in consistent behaviour (Source: Tilgner* et al.*, 2004).*

Reducing inconsistency

What strategies do adolescents employ to reduce perceived inconsistency in choice? Research has shown that they may resort to denial, for example by refusing to acknowledge the significance of a decision or its associated risks (e.g. Gosling *et al.*, 2006; Peretti-Watel, 2006). Adolescents may also minimise inconsistency simply by diminishing personal responsibility, and blaming external factors for the incongruity (e.g. Cooper, 1971; Sakai and Kiyoshi, 1980; Gosling *et al.*, 2006; Chiou and Wan, 2007). The presence of someone (siblings, parents, schoolteacher) or something (e.g. addiction, coercion, opportunity) to blame is a highly convenient situation for teenagers experiencing inconsistency in their health habits.

Let's consider each of these factors in some detail.

Denial

Denial can take various forms. Pioneering psychologist Robert Abelson describes various ways of 'managing' the facts of a situation (Abelson, 1968). These comprise bluntly denying the existence of a real threat or danger, and developing convenient arguments that minimise the danger. Thus, apart from simply denying health risks, teenagers may also simply ignore the facts, or claim to have had insufficient time to consider them before making a decision. Hence, any inconsistency between choices is understood and excused.

Abelson portrays the act of denial as a person's 'direct attack' on threatening information that, if accepted, would produce inconsistency. He defines denial not only as incorporating mere rejection of facts (e.g. 'there is little or no evidence that smoking causes lung cancer') but also as reflecting the perceiver's deliberate efforts to counter-argue inconsistency provoking information (e.g. 'there is little or no evidence that smoking causes lung cancer; on the contrary, smoking actually improves your health by keeping your weight down').

In other words, teenagers may be quite deliberate and calculating when misrepresenting facts, rather than passive and unintentional.

Some evidence suggests that teenagers indeed resort to this kind of misrepresentation, apparently to 'excuse' incongruity between different positions (Gosling *et al.*, 2006).

Adolescents may resort to denial to avoid feeling awkward, idiotic, fickle and suggestible when they start smoking cigarettes. Usually the onset of smoking marks a significant change in their behaviour. The person may feel he is behaving out of character, and need self-assurance that this is not the case. Significant others, notably parents, would become concerned and demand an explanation for the sudden change in preference. Thus, the decision maker would be under significant pressure to resolve the inconsistency.

In this stressful situation denial may prove to be an especially useful way to explain things, and reassure oneself and all concerned that the discrepancy in behaviour might not in fact reflect any inconsistency after all.

Shifting responsibility

Minimising personal liability can also be effective in reducing perceived inconsistency. This situation is similar to one in which a person feels that she has been coerced into a particular course of action, and hence doesn't believe her decision is out of character since the decision was 'forced' on her. There is a sense that what is going on isn't of her own making, and if she could she would change things, but she can't (see Box 5.1).

One point to make about existing literature on this subject is that it is largely based on university undergraduates, and doesn't focus on health issues. Although

---

Box 5.1 Research spotlight: minimising personal control to explain inconsistency

Umeh, K (1998a) A conflict-theory approach to understanding adolescents' health behaviour. PhD thesis, University of Leicester.

Do teenagers minimise personal control or responsibility as a means of justifying inconsistency? I conducted a study that shed some light on this issue. A group of teenagers concerned about the danger cigarette smoking posed to their health attended a short one-to-one interview. The aim of the interview was to ensure that their anxiety pertained specifically to cigarette use, rather than health in general or nothing in particular.

I reasoned that any tension or anxiety associated with smoking cigarettes might reflect some perceived *inconsistency* between the choices an individual has made. In particular, an individual who currently smokes may feel this is at odds with his or her previous status as a non-smoker, and experience some discomfort as a result.

Participants completed a questionnaire and then were paid £1 sterling for attendance. The questionnaire measured feelings, thoughts and actions regarding smoking. Several items in the questionnaire depicted minimising personal control: 'I don't think I have enough time to find an effective way of avoiding the cigarettes'; 'I have not been able to think properly about the danger of smoking because of lack of time.'

Analysis of data showed *smokers* tended to agree *more* with these statements compared with non-smokers. It was as if smokers were trying to minimise any perceived contradiction between their current choice to smoke and previous self-restraint. There is no apparent inconsistency between smoking and not smoking if one doesn't recognize the risks associated with the former position. Similarly, perceived incongruity can be excused by claiming not to have enough time to think about and alter their current stance, to bring it more in line with their earlier position.

These results suggest that adolescents may minimise personal control as a means of justify behaviour inconsistent with one's concerns about potentials risks.

college students typically include adolescents in their late teens, the degree to which findings generalise to health behaviour is debatable. Nonetheless it isn't difficult to imagine a scenario in which personal responsibility is deflected in order to justify inconsistency.

For example, consider the following scene. A young girl named Sarah eats a lot of cakes, chocolates and potato crisps. She prefers not to eat such junk food because of the risk of obesity. Sarah claims she would like to improve her diet but is unable to because she is just so 'hooked' on junk food. She has apparently tried many times to lower her fat intake but failed miserably.

By convincing herself that she is powerless to control her diet, Sarah is able to eat unhealthily without experiencing any hypocrisy. In essence, her choice of food isn't really *her* choice, but rather a position she is stuck with.

Unfortunately there is a lack of research addressing the role of personal responsibility in health behaviour consistency. Although there is considerable evidence on the role of personal responsibility, or indeed locus of control (a similar construct, defining the extent to which people attribute their behaviour to themselves or external conditions), in adolescent health behaviour (e.g. Booth-Butterfield *et al.*, 2000; Ozolins and Stenstrom, 2003; Goggin *et al.*, 2007), it is difficult to find research relating these constructs to behavioural consistency.

It is entirely plausible that personal responsibility plays a significant role in justifying weak or inconsistent intention–behaviour relations, for example. When inconsistency is high, personal responsibility may be actively discounted, so as to deflect criticism and maintain feelings of self-worth as a reliable decision maker. By contrast, when inconsistency is minimal, personal responsibility may be magnified, to attract accolades for being a reliable decision maker.

Negative consequences of consistency

The consequences of blind adherence to a previous decision can be devastating, as illustrated in the following narrative.

It all began when Toby was 16 years old. He was getting a lot of headaches that seemed to last a long time and affect both the front and back of his skull. Toby's way of dealing with health problems has always been simply to ignore them, at least for a few weeks or even months. These headaches were no exception. He had ignored headaches in the past and the pain eventually went away – nothing terrible happened, like a terrible illness, or anything. Ignoring the headaches would save his parents – and himself – all the hassle of scanning medical books just trying to establish if he was coming down with something serious.

Toby successfully endured the headaches for two weeks, saying nothing to his parents about the pain he was in. However, the discomfort got progressively worse, not better. By the end of the second week the agony was excruciating and couldn't be ignored any longer. Toby reluctantly informed his mother, who immediately scheduled an emergency appointment with the family physician. After carefully

examining Toby, the doctor decided to refer him to a neurology specialist at the local hospital. He told Toby's parents that a scan was essential for an accurate diagnosis.

It emerged following several scans that Toby had a brain tumour. There was a large benign mass occupying a region near the back of the skull. The tumour was growing steadily, pushing outwards, and applying corresponding pressure on the brain. This was what was causing the headaches. The doctor pointed out that Toby's delay in notifying his parents about the headaches was potentially dangerous as every day a tumour goes untreated significantly increases the possibility of medical complications, and worsens the prognosis.

It is clear Toby felt compelled to adhere to an established habit of ignoring illness symptoms. However, this consistency had potentially dangerous repercussions.

Being consistent is fine, provided the earlier decision to which one wishes to adhere was health enhancing. Sticking stubbornly to a medically dangerous commitment can be disastrous.

We have seen earlier in this chapter that adolescents' previous health behaviour is a powerful determinant of their future decisions (e.g. Umeh, 2003; Moan and Rise, 2006; O'Callaghan and Nausbaum, 2006). Thus, if there is a long history of risky decisions then a teenager may effectively be trapped in a dangerous psychological 'web' from which it is difficult to extract himself.

Some final points

Is consistency a conscious phenomenon? According to Sigmund Freud's theory of psychoanalysis, seemingly unassuming behaviours may be rooted in the unconscious, serving hidden motives of which the individual is unaware (Viney and King, 2003). Consistency may depict an effort to avoid anxiety-provoking thoughts or memories that would otherwise require fresh decision making, and a change in position. For example a girl may smoke regularly because this helps distract her from memories of a painful childhood experience. Giving up smoking may allow these memories to surface, causing severe stress.

The behaviourist John B. Watson highlights the role of conditioning (Bandura, 1986), meaning that consistent decision making may be a tendency conditioned since birth or early childhood. Over time it becomes a habit and occurs almost automatically without an individual necessarily being conscious of what's happening.

Indeed most teenagers may be oblivious to any desire for consistency. It's not as if they go about their daily business thinking, 'Gosh, I must ensure that my decisions today are consistent.' I don't recall coming across such a sentiment in the dozens of emails, books and articles I studied while writing this book. The truth is that no one can say with certainty that any decision made by an adolescent at any given place and time was driven solely by a consistency craving.

This is an important point to make because we have to recognise that teenagers may behave consistently simply through force of habit (and old habits die hard), rather than any premeditated, conscious and deliberate intention. Ask a group of

adolescent smokers why they decided to smoke and consistency may not be mentioned once. Yet, from their utterances it may become apparent that many have, without realising it, ensured congruity by various means.

One cannot underestimate the importance of social influences in this regard. A sudden decision to give up smoking, stop using drugs or take up sports may be met with a barrage of jokes, teasing and other forms of verbal (or even physical) 'punishment' from peers. The possibility of rejection and isolation by the peer group is so frightening (remember Thomas Ollendick's work from Chapter 4) that many teenagers will feel compelled to adhere to any public commitments.

Conclusion

Can the consistency argument explain the proverbial gap between adolescents' lifestyle and health knowledge (Macfarlane and McPherson, 1993)? Common sense suggests it can. A teenager may choose to ignore a health warning simply because it is mentally and physically easier to maintain the status quo. One can then investigate the motives behind such adherence, for example habit, public commitment, uncertainty, information overload and complexity, and so on.

Making fresh decisions requires a renewed appraisal of the current situation, taking into account new knowledge, cues, and searching for more information to reduce any uncertainties. Why go through so much trouble if one is already familiar with the problem, and can simply respond as one has done previously? Similarly, if a person has made a public commitment, why risk instant mockery from peers, and a reputation as an unreliable person, by changing position just to protect one's health from some unlikely threats?

Consistency may explain why teenagers often make decisions on impulse. Such behaviour could merely be an instinctive response based on previous satisfying reactions to a familiar dilemma (Umeh, 2003; Moan and Rise, 2006; O'Callaghan and Nausbaum, 2006).

Of course human behaviour is noted for its complexity and I don't want to make the mistake of oversimplifying teenage decision making by the current discussion. As will be seen in the rest of this book, there are various other conventions, besides the need for consistency, that also govern choice.

Key points

- The need for consistency in choice is an important feature of human decision making, and adolescents are no exception.
- Adolescents show remarkable consistency in their health behaviour decisions.
- Consistency may be moderated by a variety of psychological factors, including anticipated regret, coercion and past experience.

- Making a public commitment may create a powerful urge for consistency, to avoid social criticism for unreliability or indecision.
- Adolescents can achieve consistency, or justify inconsistency, by resorting to defensive measures such as denial and buck-passing.

Key terms

- Consistency
- Inconsistency
- Cognitive dissonance
- Cognitive
- Emotional
- Denial
- Shifting responsibility
- Anticipated regret
- Social desirability

Further reading

Coats, E.J. and Feldman, R.S. (eds.) (2001) *Classic and Contemporary Readings in Social Psychology.* Englewood Cliffs, NJ: Prentice Hall.

Eagly, A.H. and Chaiken, S. (1993) *The Psychology of Attitudes.* Orlando, FL: Harcourt Brace Jovanovich.

Janis, I.L. and Mann, L. (1977) *Decision Making: A Psychological Analysis of Conflict, Choice, and Commitment.* New York: The Free Press.

Zanna, M.P. (1982) *Consistency in Social Behaviour.* Hillsdale, NJ: Lawrence Erlbaum.

6 Competence

Learning outcomes

By the end of this chapter readers should have a better understanding of the following:

1 what constitutes competent decision making
2 the extent to which adolescents satisfy criteria for competence during decision making
3 the impact of over-familiarity with a decision making scenario
4 the theory of compliant detraction, which describes the relationship between decision making competence and health behaviour
5 the effect of competence on health damaging and health enhancing behaviour
6 the effects of overconfidence, stress, and other personal and situational factors
7 the concepts of risk seeking and risk aversion tendencies in this context.

Chapter summary

This chapter discusses competence in choice. Contrary to popular belief, teenagers can display considerable proficiency in decision making, with potentially favourable implications for health behaviour. I introduce a new model, the theory of compliant detraction, which highlights the importance of decision making competence in understanding health behaviour decisions. Competent and incompetent decision makers are both capable of healthy and unhealthy choices. However, each group is motivated by qualitative differences in cognitive appraisals. Whereas competent teenagers engage in elaborate judgement, weighing alternatives and balancing risks and benefits, less proficient individuals take a more simplistic and narrow-minded approach, focusing solely on what they stand to gain. This model helps explain anomalies, such as a sensible teenager who inexplicably fails to use condoms, or a mindless youth who surprisingly says no to drugs.

Defining competence

A teenage boy offered a cigarette by peers pauses to contemplate his options before deciding to reject the offer. An obese adolescent girl consults friends and family for advice about how best to lose weight, ultimately deciding that a combination of dieting and physical activity would be best. A juvenile driver cautioned by the police for speeding pauses to evaluate the risks each time he starts to edge over the speed limit while driving.

All of these scenarios denote decision making competence in some form or another. But what does it really mean to be competent? In the late 1980s psychologists Leon Mann, Ros Harmoni and Colin Power identified some essential characteristics, based on their review of the literature on adolescent decision making (Mann et al., 1989). These include willingness to make a choice (i.e. take personal responsibility), accepting compromises, thinking about potential pros and cons, making a correct choice based on the information one has, showing a high degree of consistency, and making a commitment (i.e. following through with a decision).

These criteria generally echo the views of other decision theorists (Janis and Mann, 1976, 1977; Byrnes et al., 1999). According to Janis and Mann (1977) and Byrnes et al. (1999; Byrnes, 2002), competent decision making entails several fundamental steps:

- identifying a problem and setting a goal
- seeking advice or information about available options (e.g. consulting an expert)
- trying to work out which option is best, by weighing the pros and cons (e.g. using a condom is better than not using one)
- resolving the problem (i.e. making a decision and implementing it).

Popular stereotypes of teenagers portray them as incompetent decision makers, keen to take risks, act on impulse and behave recklessly (Gardner and Herman, 1990; Seginer and Somech, 2000; Jacobs et al., 2005; Reyna and Farley, 2006; Monastersky, 2007; Steinberg, 2007). Yet, as is frequently the case with human behaviour, popular myths often seem to lack truth the moment you start taking a closer look at things.

Research shows that adolescents can be quite rational in their decision making (Mann *et al.*, 1989; Byrnes, 2002), especially when there are serious health issues at stake (Michels *et al.*, 2005). However, such competence may be tempered somewhat by confusion and indecision (Friedman, 1996), and moderated by contextual factors (e.g. Brown and Mann, 1990). Nevertheless, a casual observer does not need to look far to find snippets of competent decision making.

A teenage undergraduate student once spontaneously mentioned during a routine academic meeting with me that she had quit smoking. When I questioned her about this decision, it became evident she had deliberated the pros and cons for a while, ultimately reasoning it was in her best interest to give up cigarettes.

Read through any random selection of letters/emails sent to teenage magazines and Internet websites, and you will find ample evidence of adolescents readily seeking advice about a wide range of health issues, for example weight gain, cigarettes, contraception, diet, eating disorders and drug abuse. Seeking relevant information represents an integral step in proficient decision making, as can be seen above.

It should become increasingly evident in this book that the quality of adolescent decision making is rather less bleak and much more convoluted than societal stereotypes would have you believe.

Recognising a problem

Recognising a problem and establishing priorities are essential first steps in finding an effective solution (Janis and Mann, 1977; Byrnes, 2002). For some people merely hearing a warning about a potential health problem (e.g. the risks of smoking) is enough to prompt decision making. For others the presence of a physical symptom (e.g. pain, an unusual lump or growth, or nausea) is sufficient to trigger alarm bells.

For instance a girl who wakes up one morning and discovers an unsightly pimple has to decide whether to ignore it and go about her daily business, or do something to remove, cure or disguise the blemish. Similarly, a benign social encounter, such as being offered a cigarette, drug or alcoholic drink by friends, can suddenly present a difficult dilemma.

We have already seen in Chapter 3 that adolescents may have a variety of goals when faced with a decision. These typically relate to health, social approval and image/appearance issues. But do teenagers readily recognise problems to begin with? Research findings have been patchy and inconclusive (e.g. Bauman, 1999; Zwaanswijk *et al.*, 2003; Coleman, 2006; Lindsey *et al.*, 2006; Edelen *et al.*, 2007; Molock *et al.*, 2007). These studies investigated a construct called 'problem recognition', meaning the willingness to recognise a (health) problem and take steps to remedy it (Cady *et al.*, 1996).

Some of this evidence suggests that teenagers may fail to grasp the true magnitude of a serious threat to their well-being. For example, Molock *et al.* (2007) conducted a series of focus groups with African American teenagers, to

determine how they might help a suicidal friend. Although the majority of participants had previous direct experience of this problem in their community, they harboured some uncertainty about the severity of the crisis and the need for any form of formal intervention to deal with it.

Teenagers who do acknowledge a problem may go on to engage in competent decision making. For example, Edelen *et al.* (2007) observed that adolescents undergoing treatment for substance abuse were more likely to opt to remain in treatment – clearly a good decision – if they recognised their problem in the early stages of treatment. Another study, based on in-depth interviews of depressed teenagers, found a willingness to recognise problems and seek advice from friends, family members or even professionals (Lindsey *et al.*, 2006).

Indeed, adolescents seem to be specifically aware of problem recognition as a distinct endeavour when dealing with issues such as substance abuse. Bauman (1999) factor-analysed data from a questionnaire administered to nearly 500 adolescent substance abusers, measuring various aspects of their desire to change. Several fundamental dimensions emerged, including problem recognition and willingness for change.

Ultimately, whether or not teenagers recognise problems may depend on a variety of personal and situational factors. A comprehensive review of the literature by Marieke Zwaanswijk and several colleagues (2003) showed that problem recognition in children and adolescents may depend on factors such as gender, age, single parenthood, parental attitudes and beliefs, family size, prior maltreatment or abuse, ethnicity, the presence/absence of psychopathology, and environmental factors, such as the availability of professional help. For example, problem recognition increased with greater psychological distress and was more common in boys during early adolescence and girls during late adolescence.

Once a problem has been acknowledged, most teenagers face a decision. Do they ignore the crisis and simply carry on as normal, or adopt a new remedial course of action? Assuming they are competent decision makers, the latter option is more likely to be selected. Having opted to take action, the next priority is to establish one's goals and start seeking relevant information that will help resolve the quandary.

Seeking relevant information

Once decision making is triggered, a competent individual will immediately begin to seek relevant information, with a view to finding a solution (Janis and Mann, 1977). Advice may be sought from friends, family and experts, books consulted, and the Internet surfed for useful clues about the available options and possible solutions.

Popular stereotypes would suggest your average teenager is lazy and reluctant when it comes to seeking information to facilitate an informed decision. Indeed some readers may struggle to visualise an adolescent spending considerable time and energy learning about a problem in order to find the best possible solution.

6.1 *Seeking information. Teenagers spend a considerable amount of time 'surfing' the Internet for possible solutions to health and other problems (Source: SXC).*

However, some adults who have regular contact with teenagers (e.g. parents, teachers) assume that they (the adults, that is) are the chief source of information for adolescents. Hence, they expect that youngsters who want to learn more about a health topic will approach them. Since few teenagers actually do this many adults presuppose that adolescents don't have the advice and guidance necessary to make informed decisions.

However, recent scientific evidence suggests that this view is far from the truth. Yes, few teenagers approach their parents for advice. In reality they simply go elsewhere to get the information they need, notably the Internet (Bleakley *et al.*, 2004). My own reviews of numerous websites that offer advice to teenagers have highlighted several things.

First, there are hundreds, perhaps thousands, of emails from teenagers requesting advice and guidance on a wide range of health issues, ranging from weight control, dieting and contraceptive use, to smoking, being physically active and alcohol consumption.

Second, these emails seem unprompted; that is, young people appear to take it upon themselves to write in, seemingly without any direct pressure from parents or other authority figures.

Third, many of those who write in appear to have surveyed and even tried out other options or potential solutions to their problem, before writing in for more advice and information.

Fourth, since the emails are completely anonymous, hence eliminating any fear of discovery and adverse consequences, such as parental reprimand, the actions and thoughts of those writing in are rather more believable than similar evidence obtained under contrived and unrealistic conditions, such as during face-to-face interviews or using questionnaires, as often happens in psychological studies. Thus, not surprisingly, many teenagers email about extremely personal issues, which presumably they would normally never reveal to and discuss with anyone.

Of course, it would be unscientific to reach any firm conclusions on the strength of correspondence sent to Internet websites. It seems plausible that those teenagers who write in represent a small minority of unusually open-minded and competent youngsters who prefer to make informed decisions. It is possible that the vast majority of adolescents, faced with a difficult decision, may be indifferent about seeking information, regardless of the source.

However, systematic research suggests otherwise. Public health experts Amy Bleakley, Cheryl Merzel, Nancy Vandevanter and Peter Messeri report that a majority of children and adolescents, at least 51 per cent, use the Internet frequently to obtain useful information about health problems. This claim is based on a comprehensive survey of various adolescent urban communities living in the New York area (Bleakley et al., 2004).

Pharmacist Nicola Gray and several colleagues seemed to reach a similar conclusion after conducting group discussions with teenagers, from both the USA and the UK (Gray et al., 2005a, 2005b). What I found particularly interesting about the observations of Amy Bleakley and her co-researchers was that adolescents seemed just as likely as adults in their 20s and 30s to use the Internet in this way, suggesting that the former group may not be quite as averse to good decision making as popular stereotypes suggest.

Surveying the available options

Seeking information from the Internet, or any other source, helps enlighten teenagers about the options available to them. For example, a smoker keen to give up smoking may learn a great deal about nicotine patches, local smoking cessation programmes, support groups, and other resources available to help him kick the habit. Similarly, a girl trying to lose weight may become aware of popular diets used by other girls, and enjoyable physical exercise routines that promise significant weight loss. A good decision maker will learn as much as she can, and then select the best option on the basis of what she knows.

Psychological literature suggests that adolescents are quite knowledgeable about the options available to them, if rather less so than adults (e.g. Furby et al., 1995; Byrnes, 2002). Indeed, teenagers seem to recognise that having more alternatives is an essential element of good decision making, increasing the likelihood of a satisfactory choice. For example, Ormond et al. (1991) found that 77 per cent of early adolescents, and 95 per cent of those in their middle teens,

correctly identified options generation as an essential step before making a decision. Thus, even very young teenagers appreciate the importance of this stage in the decision making process.

This emphasis extends to health behaviour decisions. For example, in Chapter 2, I mentioned a study by Shannon *et al.* (2002) on food choice, in which adolescents indicated a desire for a wider range of food items in the school cafeteria, in order to facilitate healthier food choices.

Although adolescents, like other decision makers, may prefer a wide range of options, this is by no means a guaranteed characteristic. In certain circumstances, teenagers actually prefer to limit rather than expand their options, ruling out certain alternatives on the grounds of principle.

Tricia Michels, Rhonda Kropp and others (2003) perhaps best illustrated this phenomenon in a qualitative study about decisions regarding sexual activity. They conducted one-on-one interviews with a small group of sexually active boys and girls, focusing on their sexual experiences, and using probes to gain some insight into their decision making. Analysis of the data yielded several themes, including one indicating a tendency to set boundaries. Essentially, some subjects (especially the girls) communicated to their partners various sexual practices that were off limits (e.g. manual or oral sex) or subject to preconditions (e.g. lack of interest, being 'ready' for sex, or being in a stable relationship). It is interesting that communicating these boundaries to others was itself a distinct theme, further highlighting the importance teenagers may attach to restricting their options.

Whether boundary setting extends to other health behaviours is debatable, since sexual activity is unique in terms of its moral significance, a strong emotional element and the involvement of a partner. However, I would be surprised if adolescents didn't impose restrictions in other scenarios that have moral or legal significance, for example drug use and alcohol consumption.

Weighing up risks and benefits

Ideally, choice should be based on the known pros and cons associated with each alternative. For example, faced with a choice between using or rejecting condoms, and given awareness of the various pros and cons of each alternative (e.g. condoms will help protect against sexually transmitted disease and unplanned pregnancy, but may spoil the sexual experience and be embarrassing to buy from a local pharmacy), a teenager may decide to use condoms because he or she perceives substantial benefits to well-being (e.g. reducing the risk of disease/pregnancy) and negligible risks (e.g. sexual inconvenience).

This raises a key question. Are adolescents actually interested in evaluating pro and con arguments?

Interest in argument

To what extent are adolescents interested in processing risk–benefit information or arguments? A person's level of interest in scrutinising arguments is known as his need for cognition (Petty and Cacioppo, 1986; Kao, 1994; Bakker *et al.*, 1995; Mesarosova, 1997; Ruiter *et al.*, 2004).

People with a high need for cognition enjoy thinking, reading, debating, studying and analysing, are generally good at intellectually demanding games, like chess, and perform well academically. They could obsess over a small trivial point raised by the physics teacher, and spend hours watching informative documentaries on TV. Overall, they seek out and engage in intellectual activities. Thus, when presented with a health warning they will naturally scrutinise and evaluate the arguments, trying to work out a rational solution.

Adolescents with a high need for cognition are persuaded more by argument than by superficial cues. For example, Bakker (1999) demonstrated that 'nerdy' teenagers are persuaded more by a written or verbal argument than by one based entirely on visual images, such as a picture or cartoon. He examined the impact of a written and cartoon message about HIV and safer sex on high school students who had either a high or a low craving for intellectual pursuits. Although both message formats improved attitudes towards safe sex, increasing the likelihood of condom use, the written message had a more pronounced effect in subjects with a high need for cognition, whereas the cartoon was more effective in subjects with a less intellectual orientation.

One obvious interpretation is that adolescents in the former group more carefully read and evaluated the written argument when making their decisions. Another possibility is that these teenagers were less impressed by the cartoon message, presumably because it did not present an intellectual challenge.

Findings such as Bakker's are important because many health warnings are issued primarily in written format, such as cancer leaflets at a doctor's clinic or an anti-smoking column in a teenage magazine or website. Clearly, such messages are likely to have a better impact on teenagers who like to read, think and argue. It is encouraging to note that individuals who hate reading, thinking or studying can still be persuaded to take steps to avert danger if they are presented with a suitable 'Charlie Brown' cartoon conveying the right message. The nerds cannot have it all their own way.

A health warning is likely to be met with indifference if an audience has no interest in the information to begin with. This was clearly illustrated by four experimental psychologists – Robert Ruiter, Bas Verplanken, David Cremer and Gerjo Kok – who asked a sample of first year psychology undergraduate women to complete a questionnaire measuring their need for cognition (Ruiter *et al.*, 2004). Subjects were then exposed to either a high or a low danger warning about breast cancer. They were also informed of the importance and ease of early detection. Finally subjects completed questionnaires measuring their responses.

The experimenters expected that high danger would elicit healthy reactions in subjects who enjoy cognitive activity, and defensive responses in individuals with low interest in intellectual pursuits. After all, participants in the former group were likely to think about the danger more thoroughly and carefully, and hence better appreciate the need for preventive measures.

Data analysis showed that subjects exposed to high danger were indeed more likely to perform breast examinations if they enjoyed cognitive activity. Curiously, high danger also seemed capable of producing defensive reactions (derogation of the message, suspicion of an ulterior motive in the message), irrespective of need for cognition.

The experimenters explained that people exposed to danger get anxious and hence respond defensively; the fact that they enjoy evaluating arguments makes no difference – anxiety is uncomfortable and has to be reduced, period!

This study seems to suggest that studious and inquisitive types who do well at school, and join the debating team, weigh up risks and benefits when making decisions that may affect their health.

It is worth noting that this study focused on older adolescents in their late teens. Healthy decisions may be easier to elicit in older teenagers simply because, as the French psychologist Jean Piaget theorised, intellectual development is sufficiently developed to allow better comprehension of the message contained in a health warning. Older teenagers may better understand threats like cancer, heart disease and obesity, in terms of both the danger they pose to health and their likelihood of occurrence.

For example, whereas a 12-year-old child may fail to grasp the nature of heart disease, a college freshman may recognise the damage caused by cholesterol and the real possibility of death from a heart attack. Thus younger teenagers may respond differently to a health warning, perhaps failing to comprehend the danger, owing to their limited intellectual abilities.

Research suggests that the need for cognition is a stable personality trait that persists across different decision making scenarios. Canadian academics Douglas Bors, François Vigneau and Francis Lalande carried out a survey of children and adolescents, in which subjects completed a questionnaire measuring their need for cognition (Bors *et al.*, 2006). Analysis showed that there was a common theme underlying subjects' responses, which the researchers interpreted as an enduring personality characteristic, rather than a situation-dependent construct.

Furthermore, adolescents with a high need for cognition probably reason better than those with less interest in intellectual matters (Kokis *et al.*, 2002). If so, the former group are perhaps more likely to weigh up their arguments effectively, enabling them to reach an optimal decision.

Research on decisional balance

Empirical evidence suggests that adolescents in general do consider risks and benefits in health decision making (e.g. Michels *et al.*, 2005; Abdullah and Ho,

2006). Research findings on Janis and Mann's (1977) decisional balance concept (see Chapter 1) show that adolescents are specifically mindful of various pros and cons when contemplating a health behaviour (e.g. Lowry, 2000; Hulton, 2001; Plummer *et al.*, 2001; Rossi *et al.*, 2001; Chen *et al.*, 2006a; Chen *et al.*, 2006b; Di Noia *et al.*, 2006; Yeh, 2006; Drahovzal, 2007).

Decisional balance denotes various perceived gains and losses people consider during competent decision making, including tangible gains and losses to oneself, such as worsening or improved health, and the approval or disapproval of significant others, notably friends and family.

Typically, a group of teenagers is administered a questionnaire – often known as a Decisional Balance Inventory – that evaluates their perceived outcomes in relation to some health activity, including fruit and vegetable uptake (Di Noia *et al.*, 2006), nutrition and physical activity (Drahovzal, 2007), weight management (Yeh, 2006), smoking (Plummer *et al.*, 2001; Chen *et al.*, 2006a) and dietary fat consumption (Rossi *et al.*, 2001). The data are then subjected to factor analysis, which typically yields two basic dimensions reflecting anticipated gains and losses.

All in all, these findings suggest that teenagers are cognisant of potential consequences when considering whether to adopt health behaviour. Of course, participants in these studies are usually presented with a questionnaire listing various pros and cons, to which they indicate their agreement/disagreement. Thus, it is difficult to say whether adolescents do spontaneously think about potential outcomes when making decisions under real-world circumstances.

Evidence from in-depth interviews

One problem with existing decisional balance research is its over-reliance on quantitative methods (Howitt and Cramer, 2005). Adolescents are 'forced' to respond to predetermined statements about pros and cons (e.g. 'do you agree with the following statement …?'). In a qualitative design, by contrast (Cormack, 2000), subjects are invited through open-ended questions to offer their views freely on the subject (e.g. 'what are your thoughts on …?'). The latter approach is bound to yield richer and more realistic data, since there are no artificial constraints on the information participants provide.

A number of studies have adopted qualitative methods, specifically using in-depth interviews and focus groups, to investigate cost–benefit evaluations in teenagers (e.g. Hanna, 1994; Michels *et al.*, 2005; Abdullah and Ho, 2006).

Kathleen Hanna, a registered nurse, was curious about whether teenage girls are conscious of the various costs and benefits associated with using oral contraceptives. She conducted in-depth interviews with a group of girls visiting family planning clinics to obtain oral contraceptives for the first time.

In addition to being interviewed, the girls were required to provide a written response to four questions regarding the consequences of oral contraceptives:

- In what ways do you think that taking the pill will be good for you?
- In what ways do you think that taking the pill will not be good for you?

- In what ways do you think that taking the pill will be good in relation to people important to you?
- In what ways do you think that taking the pill will not be good in relation to people important to you? (Hanna, 1994, p. 50)

These questions were based on the concept of decisional balance. Would the teenagers in Hanna's study perceive consequences in such an elaborate fashion? Her observations were intriguing. They seemed to contradict established stereotypes.

The girls described over seventy costs and benefits associated with birth control pills! Perceived benefits included the prevention of pregnancy, having a sense of personal responsibility, enjoying sexual intercourse, feeling satisfied that one is doing the right thing, and receiving approval from significant others such as friends and family. Of these, the prevention of pregnancy was one of the most frequently mentioned outcomes.

These findings suggest that subjects were very conscious of health consequences. Some of the costs identified were medical side effects, the prevention of a wanted pregnancy, concerns about having to take on such a 'big' responsibility (that is, in terms of going through the entire rigmarole of visiting a clinic, requesting and paying for oral contraceptives), the disapproval of significant others, presumably a partner who wants a child, and the financial costs of procuring birth control pills.

Whether the girls actually thought about these consequences when deciding whether or not to obtain oral contraceptive pills is debatable. It is entirely possible that they only really considered these issues when questioned – anyone can think up a list of potential consequences about an action they had never previously considered. On the other hand, if a person describes a particular consequence, prompted or not, it suggests that he or she is conscious of that particular outcome, and furthermore remembers it! It therefore seems improbable that such considerations wouldn't feature at all in their decision making.

Of course it can be argued that the sample in this study was unusual. After all, this was a group of individuals who, presumably, saw the logic and common sense in seeking oral contraceptives. In other words, they were unusually competent to begin with, and hence likely to have fairly well developed opinions about the consequences of using oral contraceptives.

However, one has to be careful not to be too presumptive here. Teenagers may seek oral contraceptives for numerous reasons other than merely being competent decision makers. For example, the girls may have been driven by anxiety about the possibility of becoming pregnant. Or they may have acted out of a desire for consistency (i.e. they had used oral contraceptives in the past, so wanted to adhere to this practice), or impulse (they made a snap decision to get some contraceptives), rather than carefully considered thought.

Nevertheless, Hanna's findings suggest that adolescents may contemplate pros and cons in much the same way as adults. This inference isn't just applicable to older adolescents, whose reasoning skills are more fully developed. Although

most of the participants were 15 to 17 years of age, the sample included a significant number of younger teenagers.

Experts suggest that children and younger teenagers are even less capable than older adolescents of evaluating hypothetical consequences, such as a non-figurative and remote disease. The work of Jean Piaget (1954; Piaget and Inhelder, 1956) suggests there is some truth to this. However, being less proficient at reasoning does not mean that no reasoning is possible!

Using risk–benefit information

Even if adolescents do think about costs and benefits, do they actually base their decisions on these thoughts? Social stereotypes suggest that they don't – decisions tend to be impulsive rather than competent (Stepp, 2002). Otherwise why do adolescents often make unhealthy decisions, despite their considerable knowledge of the risks? Why is it that many teenagers choose to smoke cigarettes even though they recognise the dangers? Why do adolescents fail to use condoms given the possibility of unplanned pregnancy? How come many youngsters continue to eat fatty foods even though they recognise the threat of obesity?

Research on decisional balance and behaviour change

Studies on decisional balance have shown significant changes in adolescents' risk–benefit evaluations as they progress through the decision making process (Smith, 1998; Hulton, 2001; Nigg, 2001; Otake and Shimai, 2001; Plummer *et al.*, 2001; Rossi *et al.*, 2001; Di Noia *et al.*, 2006; Svetlak and Kukleta, 2006).

By and large, the perceived benefits of adopting a new course of action (e.g. quitting smoking, reducing dietary fat intake) tend to outweigh the perceived risks by the end of the decision making process, when for example the behaviour has been selected and is being implemented, rather than at the beginning when for example change in behaviour is just being considered (but see Drahovzal, 2007[1]).

One way to interpret this finding is that behaviour change is *driven* by risk–benefit evaluations. Thus, an adolescent who is contemplating going on a diet may resolve to go ahead with this measure, having concluded that the benefits of dieting outweigh the costs. However, it is also plausible that teenagers conveniently adjust their risk–benefit perceptions, as they move towards their objective, in order to avoid any apparent inconsistency between their thoughts and actions. Hence, perceived outcomes are determined by the degree to which someone is

---

[1] Not all studies find a link between perceived pros and cons and behaviour change. Drahovzal (2007), for example, found no relationship between adolescents' cost–benefit appraisals and their self-reports of daily physical activity. However, an unreliable relationship was found when parents' proxy reports were considered.

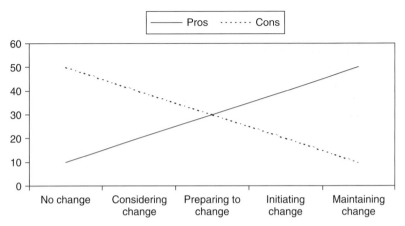

6.2 *Cognitive deliberations may drive decisions. The plot shows a rough representation between adolescents' cost–benefit evaluations and their degree of commitment to a decision, based on existing research. Stages of commitment are based on the transtheoretical stages-of-change model (Prochaska* et al., *1994). One interpretation is that pros and cons determine commitment. Another is that pros and cons are adjusted retrospectively to justify a commitment.*

committed to a decision, rather than the other way around. For example, an individual who has opted to quit smoking may conveniently emphasise the benefits, while simultaneously minimising its costs.

Nevertheless, findings from in-depth interviews and focus groups with teen-agers suggest that cost–benefits may in fact precede decisions (e.g. Hanna, 1994; Michels *et al.*, 2005; Abdullah and Ho, 2006). In fact some studies (e.g. Otake and Shimai, 2001; Di Noia *et al.*, 2006) have demonstrated that cost–benefit judge-ments still correlate significantly with behaviour more than six months after a decision has been implemented, suggesting that teenagers continue to appraise their decisions even after the horse has bolted, so to speak!

Uncertainty about how to exploit risk–benefit information

Many adolescents, particularly the younger ones, may be at a loss how to 'use' their knowledge of potential outcomes, especially if there are many issues to consider. Some evidence suggests that adolescent decision making can be sig-nificantly impaired by information overload (Linn *et al.*, 1984; Sung and Kim, 1987). With the brain deluged by a multiplicity of health, social and other considerations, trying to make sense of each incentive and disincentive may be extremely difficult. A child of 13, for example, may not know what to do with all this information.

What this means in practice is that competent decision makers will only consider those issues that seem important to them (see Chapter 2, on goal setting). Of course, the problem here is that outcomes that adolescents prioritise may not be the same ones that parents and wider society see as relevant.

We already know that adolescents may be motivated as much by social, appearance and ego considerations as they are by health issues (Heinrichs, 1995; Rodham et al., 2004; Somers and Surmann, 2004; Turner and Mermelstein, 2004; Allison et al., 2005; Macpherson, 2005; Wilson et al., 2006; Alvord, 2007; Lee et al., 2007; Vansteenkiste et al., 2007). So, even where a youngster painstakingly evaluates pros and cons before making a decision, observers may nevertheless view his choice as thoughtless because the 'important' consequences were not considered! For example, whereas the teenager may contemplate possible ridicule by his peers, his parents may be more concerned about potential health problems.

Over-familiarity

Some teenagers take pride in making good decisions. Studies have shown that when inventories such as the Decision Making Questionnaire (DMQ) (Mann et al., 1982) are administered to adolescents, the data typically reveal multiple decision making preferences, including a distinct preference for competence (e.g. Friedman and Mann, 1993; Mann et al., 1997; Umeh, 1998a, 1998b; Tuinstra et al., 2000).

Competent adolescents prefer to be logical, analytical and informed, rather than impulsive, evasive or panic-stricken, for example. Thus, you would expect such individuals to base their decisions on careful risk–benefit judgements. However, in reality, this may be easier said than done.

For example, the person may lack the ability or motivation to evaluate potential consequences (e.g. Petty and Cacioppo, 1986) (e.g. adolescents, especially the younger ones, may not have attained the cognitive abilities fully to appreciate hypothetical outcomes); there may be insufficient time to think (Janis and Mann, 1977) (e.g. avoiding being hit by a speeding truck while crossing a busy road); or it may seem sensible simply to rely on past experience (Bandura, 1977) (e.g. opting to go on a diet if this measure has worked previously).

As part of my postgraduate work I investigated the extent to which supposedly competent teenagers make decisions that are driven by rationalistic risk–benefit appraisals, compared with their less proficient colleagues (Umeh, 1998a, 1998b). The key findings are described in Box 6.1. Curiously, there was no evidence that high competence engenders more rational decisions than low competence. Why was this so?

There are many possible reasons. However, one plausible explanation relates to the issue of over-familiarity. Research has shown that people who have high prior knowledge on an issue often have little or no interest in learning more about it (e.g. Wood and Lynch, 2002). This has been attributed to what theorists call the 'feeling of knowing' phenomenon, whereby people believe they are already familiar with a problem, and hence simply refer to their existing knowledge or prior experience for a solution, rather than trying to reappraise the situation afresh (Hart, 1965).

Box 6.1 Research spotlight: are competent decision makers more reasonable?

Umeh, K. (1998a) Coping styles as moderators of cognition-decision relations amongst adolescents. *Psychology and Health*, 13, 987–1003.

What does it mean to be a competent decision maker? In particular, are decisions more likely to be based on reasoned thought or judgements?

To provide some sort of answer, I asked teenagers to indicate their intent to enact various health behaviours in the future and their perceptions of relevant risks and benefits (e.g. risk of cancer and heart disease; the benefits of preventive action). They also showed the extent to which they considered themselves good decision makers, by indicating their agreement with the following statements: 'Once I've made a decision then I don't change my mind'; 'When I make a decision I feel that I've made the best possible one'; 'I like to make decisions myself'; and 'When I decide to do something I get right on with it.'

These statements were derived from the Decision Making Questionnaire (Mann, 1982) mentioned in Chapter 1. The information provided was used to divide respondents into two groups: 'high competence' and 'low competence'. It was expected that intentions to engage in various health behaviours would correlate significantly with cost–benefit judgements, but only in 'high competence' teenagers. Common sense suggested competent decision makers will be more reasonable, ensuring decisions reflect perceived outcomes.

When the data were analysed the results seemed rather puzzling. The behavioural intentions of 'high competence' teenagers were no more (or less) likely to reflect risk–benefit judgements, compared with the intentions of the 'low competence' group. This suggests that competent decision makers weren't necessarily more reasonable in their decision making.

One curious finding pertained to decisions on sexual activity. Anticipating health benefits from condom use logically predicted increased willingness to use protection, but only in the 'low competence' group! 'High competence' subjects were keen to use protection irrespective of the perceived benefits, suggesting they considered the alternatives to safe sex unsatisfactory. Thus, although competent decision makers seem to weigh their options, less competent individuals aren't entirely thoughtless in their decision making!

The vast majority of adolescents are generally aware of the major threats to their health, such as cancer, heart disease, obesity and HIV/AIDS (e.g. Macfarlane and McPherson, 1993; Mazanov and Byrne, 2007). There has been so much publicity over the decades about these risks that most teenagers may suffer from the 'feeling-of-knowing' phenomenon. Faced with a health decision, they may simply rely on their preconceptions, rather than bother contemplating the pros and cons anew.

In an atmosphere of ubiquitous knowledge it may not matter whether an individual is competent or not, as everyone is generally well informed. But is

there any empirical evidence to support this view? Does high prior knowledge discourage new learning or information processing? Well, research in this area is extremely rare. However, Stacy Wood and John G. Lynch have conducted several illuminating experiments using college students (Wood and Lynch, 2002).

In one experiment, participants who knew little about allergy medications were asked to read an information booklet either on the subject of allergy treatment – thereby heightening their knowledge on the subject – or on an irrelevant topic. Later, they were informed about a new antihistamine allergy drug, accompanied by additional information presented either as new information or as similar to what they already knew about allergy medication. Finally, all subjects were tested on their knowledge of the new medication, to establish how much they had learned about the new product.

Analysis showed that subjects with high prior knowledge on allergy medication learned significantly less than those with low prior knowledge. However, this only occurred amongst individuals told that the additional information provided was similar to what they already knew. Amongst subjects given new information, those with high prior knowledge performed better.

This experiment clearly showed that adolescents and young adults are less willing to learn more about a subject if they are already familiar with it, and believe there is nothing new to be learned. Thus, teenagers may decline to consider risks and benefits during decision making because they are already familiar with these issues, and don't believe there is anything new to contemplate.

Wood and Lynch (2002) found in two other experiments, using university students, that high familiarity does indeed affect a person's motivation to process information. As in the previous experiment, subjects were assigned to either a high or low prior knowledge condition. They were then informed about a new product, after some participants were offered a $50 incentive if they performed well in a subsequent test to see how much they had learned about the new product.

Results showed that subjects with high prior knowledge learned significantly more than those with low prior knowledge, but only with the monetary incentive. This finding suggests that well-informed individuals may be willing to appraise things afresh if they have something tangible to gain.

Regardless, some evidence suggests that adolescents aren't quite as knowledgeable as they think they are (Wilson et al., 1990; Hastrup et al., 1992; Deb, 2005). Health hazards like heart disease, stroke and AIDS may be just too remote for them to understand their real significance (van der Pligt, 1994). Thus, a sense of familiarity may be misplaced.

Working out the best option

How do teenagers actually work out the best option given what they know about pros and cons of each alternative? Is there some simple mathematical

formula? Do they simply go for the option that offers the largest benefits and/or least costs? Or is it the importance attached to each consequence that matters? Or perhaps the whole process is all rather subjective, chaotic and heavily dependent on the prevailing situation.

Some research suggests that teenagers rely heavily on simplistic rules of thumb, in other words heuristics, (e.g. Klaczynski, 2000, 2001a, 2001b). This perfunctory approach falls short of criteria for competent decision making (Mann *et al.*, 1989), because the decision maker selects an option, not on the basis of its potential risks and benefits, but because it satisfies a seemingly subjective and arbitrary principle.

For example, Klaczynski (2001a) found that, asked to make a choice from a selection of options in a hypothetical decision task, adolescents relied heavily on a 'sunk cost' heuristic whereby a risky or worthless action is nonetheless pursued simply because one has already invested much in it (e.g. opting to smoke cigarettes simply because one has already bought several packets, and hence is unwilling to 'waste' their investment, despite the health risks). In effect, the decision maker is unduly influenced by a previous commitment, even though this decision was clearly flawed.

At least 50 per cent of adolescents in Klaczynski's (2001a) study used this heuristic when instructed to make a decision as they usually would. Furthermore, instructing them to be more competent in their thinking diminished but failed to eliminate reliance on this heuristic.

Adolescents may consider reliance on heuristics as entirely logical in view of the impracticalities of carefully weighing pros and cons every time one has to make a decision (e.g. Amsterlaw, 2006). Constraints like lack of time, information overload (e.g. a teenager seeking a low-fat diet faces a bewildering array of low-fat diets at the local supermarket or in a Google search) and emotional arousal make it extremely difficult to make a thorough survey of all the options and meaningfully evaluate their costs and benefits, such that the best option readily becomes evident (Janis and Mann, 1976, 1977).

Indeed, research has shown that teenagers may try to narrow their range of options, by excluding alternatives they consider personally disagreeable, often on morality or decency grounds (e.g. Jacobs and Klaczynski, 2002; Michels *et al.*, 2005). Readers may remember the study by Michels *et al.* (2005) in which adolescents set boundaries when making sexual decisions. Options that were considered too immoral or indecent were eliminated from further consideration.

The theory of compliant detraction

Mary is asthmatic. Since an asthma attack could happen at any time her doctor has advised that she carries an inhaler, especially when going out in public, with or without the company of others. If an attack occurred the inhaler would be

her only chance of survival. However, Mary feels that the inhaler isn't really that effective in helping her breathe more easily. Nevertheless, she continues to carry and use the device. She reasons, quite sensibly, that the alternative – not carrying an inhaler – is virtually suicidal, and hence not a realistic option.

This narrative epitomises an interesting phenomenon that has emerged from previous research with adults, and my own research on adolescents (Umeh, 1998a, 1998b). It is sometimes referred to in the general psychological/medical literature as reluctant compliance (e.g. McDermott, 2002; Benson and Britten, 2003).

Reluctant compliance

Previous research with adults has revealed a phenomenon whereby people reluctantly adopt a particular course of action despite having strong reservations about it (McDermott, 2002; Benson and Britten, 2003). One particularly interesting study by John Benson and Nicky Britten found that about 80 per cent of people taking tablets for high blood pressure had reservations about taking such medication, including concerns about side effects and an aversion to tablets for hypertension.

So, why did they continue to take their medicines? Well, it emerged that the majority of patients consciously 'balanced' their reservations against incentives for taking anti-hypertensives. 'When I started taking BP tablets, I weighed up any concerns about medicines I might have, with one or more of [my] reasons to take BP tablets' (p. 1315).

Cardiologist Aiden McDermott also found evidence of reluctant compliance during interviews with patients living with chronic but stable heart disease (McDermott, 2002). Several themes emerged, one of which highlighted a need felt by some patients to take regular medications to manage their symptoms, despite concerns about side effects, dislike for taking medication, and other reservations.

Like adults, adolescents may also display a willingness to adopt various preventive measures despite having reservations. They may balance their concerns against the perceived benefits of taking protective action. However, since this phenomenon involves logic and reasoning, specifically the meaningful weighing of pros and cons, perhaps only teenagers with a competent disposition are likely to perform it.

This is precisely what I found in the course of my research (Umeh, 1998a, 1998b). Adolescents high on decision making competence displayed a willingness to adopt preventive action, refusing to have unprotected sexual intercourse, irrespective of their views about the potential benefits (see Fig. 6.4). Thus, even those who were sceptical about the merits of using contraception – and many had such a reservation – were still disposed to this measure.

This finding partially forms the basis for a theory that describes how decision making competence affects health behaviour amongst adolescents.

The theory

Consider the following accounts: a seemingly mindless teenager makes a wise decision to quit smoking; a stupid boy seems just as willing as his sensible girlfriend to use condoms during sex; an obese girl embarks on a rigorous daily physical activity routine despite doubts about its merits

How can you explain these curious situations? The last item can be seen as an example of reluctant compliance, in which doubts about the merits of a behaviour are balanced against its riskier alternatives. However, the other two events may seem more puzzling. How is it that individuals with vastly different levels of decision making proficiency end up making the same decision? How can we explain the healthy choices of otherwise idiotic teenagers who barely pause to think before they act?

The concept of reluctant compliance forms part of a wider cognitive theory, which I propose, that provides useful insights into all three scenarios above. It is called the theory of compliant detraction (CDT). This model makes a number of predictions about the relationship between decision making competence and health behaviour in adolescents. It offers five basic propositions:

- A competent decision maker balances risks and benefits when contemplating a health behaviour.
- An incompetent decision maker may primarily consider potential gains when contemplating a health behaviour.
- A competent decision maker may still adopt a health behaviour despite scepticism about its benefits (see Fig. 6.4). It seems any doubts are set aside when the advantages, albeit questionable, are nevertheless judged to outweigh the disadvantages.
- An incompetent decision maker is unlikely to adopt a health behaviour given scepticism about its benefits (see Fig. 6.4). It seems any doubts are not balanced against the risks, leading to a narrow-minded and ill-considered decision.
- Both competent and incompetent decision makers are capable of health enhancing and health damaging behaviour (see Fig. 6.5), albeit for different reasons (see above). Competence does not necessarily produce healthy choices, nor does incompetence guarantee unhealthy decisions.

These principles assume a dispositional rather than a situational conceptualisation of decision making competence. In other words, competence is viewed as a stable personality trait, as measured by the DMQ (Mann *et al.*, 1997, 1998), which persists across time and situations.

Overall, competent teenagers engage in more elaborate cognitive deliberations when contemplating health behaviour, whereas less proficient individuals focus on a limited number of points, notably what they stand to gain. Nevertheless, despite these cognitive differences, one group is just as likely as the other to make a health protective or health damaging decision.

For example, both competent and incompetent adolescents may decide to quit smoking. However, while the former probably balance relevant risks and benefits in reaching their decision, the latter may be motivated solely by the perceived benefits of quitting. Thus, although their decision making is narrow minded and ill considered, the outcome may nevertheless be favourable. Competence level doesn't necessarily affect the probability of a healthy or unhealthy decision.

I found evidence for this view in relation to adolescents' food choice, alcohol consumption, cigarette smoking, drug use and use of contraception (Umeh, 1998a, 1998b). Competence was unrelated to decisions concerning each of these activities. Only in the case of physical activity was competence associated with an increased likelihood of healthy behaviour.

What is important here is the cognitive 'dance' that underlies adolescents' decisions. For example, if a competent decision maker adopts risky behaviour it is probably because he perceives no risk, or believes the incentives outweigh the disincentives. However, if the same decision is made by a less proficient individual, it is probably because he is focusing solely on the benefits. This might explain why occasionally seemingly mindless teenagers make healthy choices and apparently sensible ones take risks.

So, does this model have any practical significance? Well, there are important implications for health promotion. Cognitive-based health promotion interventions may be more effective if there is some assessment of the competence level of a target audience. Knowing whether adolescents try to weigh their options, or merely focus on the merits of one course of action, can be useful information for tailoring an intervention to a specific audience.

CDT assumes that adolescents do in fact think before they act. I had no direct evidence for this, although studies suggest that teenagers do engage in cognitive deliberations prior to and during commitment (Smith, 1998; Hulton, 2001; Nigg, 2001; Otake and Shimai, 2001; Plummer et al., 2001). The model also assumes that other personal and situational influences on decision making and health behaviour are held constant, or controlled for. Obviously, from an empirical standpoint, the model's predictions are likely to be qualified in many different ways by these wider influences. For example, past behaviour may nullify the effect of risk–benefit appraisals on health behaviour, irrespective of decision making competence (Umeh, 2003). However, these contextual constraints are a fact of life when considering almost any model of human behaviour, and have to be acknowledged.

The emphasis on risk–benefit appraisals is a familiar theme of long-established health behaviour models applied to adolescent health behaviour (e.g. Rogers, 1975, 1983; Eagly and Chaiken, 1993; Schwarzer and Fuchs, 1996; Milne et al., 2000). What is perhaps unique about CDT is its emphasis on decision making competence. The importance of this factor cannot be overstated. Whereas teenagers who scored high on competence seemed keen to adopt preventive behaviour, having apparently weighed their reservations against potential benefits, those with low competence scores exhibited strikingly different behaviour.

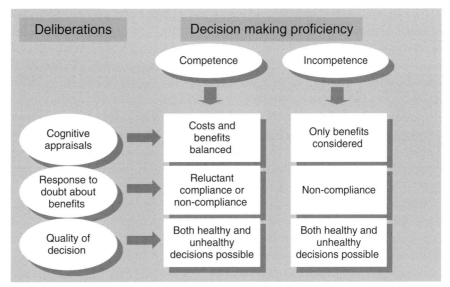

6.3 *The theory of compliant detraction. What happens when teenagers encounter health warnings and other messages recommending healthy behaviour? According to the theory of compliant detraction, competent decision makers engage in elaborate cognitive appraisals, balancing pros and cons. Those who doubt the potential gains of acquiescence may still comply, albeit reluctantly, if benefits are judged to outweigh risks. By contrast, incompetent decision makers take a more narrow minded view, focusing solely on perceived benefits of prevention, seemingly oblivious to risk. Thus, decision making is entirely driven by anticipated gains. Despite these group differences, both competent and incompetent individuals are capable of adopting and rejecting healthy recommendations, motivated by different cognitive appraisals (Source: Umeh, 2008).*

Those who doubted the value of contraceptive use simply weren't willing to use protection.

Since this group has little interest in sound reasoning and logic, they are unlikely to bother trying to balance their reservations against arguments in favour of safe sex. The net result is an ill-considered decision seemingly based on flawed reasoning.

In short, low competence can help explain why adolescents often seem to take undue risks with their health. Scepticism about the merits of healthy behaviour, combined with a limited grasp of the potential dangers associated with alternatives, leads to foolhardiness, and unwise decisions.

The role of competence

The role of competence in CDT is based squarely on the premise that adolescents differ in their level of decision making proficiency (e.g. Mann, 1982; Mann *et al.*,

1997; Umeh, 1998a, 1998b; Tuinstra *et al.*, 2000). A competent teenager will presumably be keen to learn as much as he can about the available options and their repercussions. Their characteristic mode of information processing is an open-minded interest in relevant information, with active search for both favourable and unfavourable evidence (Janis and Mann, 1976, 1977). If threats are ambiguous and vague, for example in terms of probability, they will go out of their way to obtain specific information, and other relevant data, no matter how threatening, in order to satisfy a need to be well informed.

Thus, faced with the option of using or not using contraception, they will carefully assess each alternative, weighing the various negatives (e.g. perceived ineffectiveness of condoms) and balancing these against the positives (e.g. some protection against sexually transmitted disease and unplanned pregnancy, both potentially devastating outcomes), echoing the cognitive appraisals reported by participants in Benson and Britten's (2003) study on hypertensive medication.

The individual will be keen to make a good decision. It would quickly become clear that the perceived demerits of safe sex, important as they might be, are decidedly outweighed by the benefits. Thus, he will be prepared to use contraception, albeit tinged with some reluctance.

It is fair to assume that adolescents who adopt health preventive measures have reservations about them. Avoiding cigarettes, for example, may be tinged with concern about the perceived health and social drawbacks, such as weight gain, increased stress, and loss of self-confidence (Halpern-Felsher *et al.*, 2004).

However, competent teenagers will balance these concerns against the perceived benefits of protective action. Even so, not every healthy decision reflects compliant detraction. For example, adolescents may be driven by panic or impulsivity into taking protective action (e.g. Mitchell, 1999).

Compliant detraction seems particularly likely in situations in which:

- there are no other alternatives (e.g. owing to intimidation or coercion), so the decision maker has no recourse but to adopt the only available course of action, or
- there are several options and the decision maker is competent, and aware of the various pros and cons associated with each.

A good example of the first situation is where an authority figure (e.g. a parent, teacher or policeman) forces a teenager to do something against her will, and leaves her no option. Imagine for instance a school principal who catches a pupil smoking and promptly yells at the child to stop ('destroy that cigarette, now!'). Faced with the threat of severe punishment, the teenager reluctantly complies. I suspect decisions made under such circumstances are unstable and hence easily reversed or abandoned (once the threat of retribution has receded).

The second situation is rather more interesting. It generally obtains when adolescents, of their own free will, adopt a behaviour that they have misgivings about, but nevertheless endorse, simply because the alternatives are unacceptable. Condom use is a prime example. The primary means by which a teenage boy may

protect himself (and his partner) from HIV/AIDS, during sexual intercourse, is to use contraception. While condoms aren't 100 per cent effective, the alternatives are even less acceptable. For example, attempting to withdraw prior to ejaculation can be difficult to remember or time properly. Even if this is achieved, it does not preclude the exchange of bodily fluids.

Another option is for both partners to undergo an HIV test before becoming sexually intimate. The problem with this approach is that even though a negative test result would be welcome, there is nothing to stop one or both individuals from committing infidelity and becoming infected. And finally, complete abstinence? Completely impractical – it is like asking birds not to fly, or fish not to swim.

The net result is that sensible teenagers who passionately dislike condoms may nevertheless use them. I may not particularly enjoy the taste of Coca Cola but it would still be preferable to drinking alcohol at a party! Unlike the 'no-choice' situation in which decisions are likely to be unstable and short-lived, this second scenario involves free will (see Chapter 2), meaning that decisions may be more genuine and hence stable.

A robust phenomenon

How robust are the observations discussed so far? This is an important question to ask. Behavioural scientists are often accused of conducting research in a kind of bubble, completely removed from a wider context. In the real world, there are many factors other than competence/incompetence that affect a teenager when he makes a decision relevant to his health.

For example, how he has behaved in the past is crucial – a youngster who has never smoked is more likely to reject a cigarette offer compared with a regular smoker (Umeh, 2003), even though both individuals may be equally competent

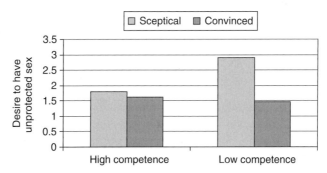

6.4 *Compliant detraction. Data from a survey showed that competent decision makers were no less willing to use protection despite scepticism about the benefits of contraception. It was as if they balanced their scepticism against the alternatives, deducing that using protection was still the less dangerous option. Incompetent teenagers by contrast seemed prepared to risk their health if they had reservations, seemingly oblivious to the alternatives (adapted from Umeh, 1998a, 1998b).*

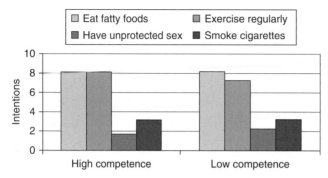

6.5 *Healthy and unhealthy decisions. Competent and incompetent decision makers are both capable of health enhancing or health damaging behaviour. Survey data revealed that although competent adolescents made healthier decisions regarding certain activities (physical activity, and use of protection), compared with their less competent colleagues, competence was unrelated to decisions concerning other behaviours (fat intake, cigarette use). Thus, competence may not necessarily deter bad choices. Similarly, incompetence doesn't necessarily negate good decisions (Source: Umeh, 1998b).*

decision makers. Similarly an adolescent who has always used condoms during sexual intercourse is likely to keep doing so, despite being deficient in decision making proficiency.

Then there are other considerations, for example fear. We know from Chapter 4 that adolescents have a lot of fears (Ollendick *et al.*, 1989; Muris and Ollendick, 2002), and these anxieties may have a tremendous effect on choice. Likewise, a teenager's wherewithal to carry out a particular course of action is crucial (Bandura, 1986). For example, a heavy smoker is unlikely to quit smoking if he lacks the support and strength of character to give up cigarettes. Then there are innate characteristics like gender – teenage boys and girls often make wildly different decisions when faced with the same situation.

In short, the list of potential influences on adolescent behaviour is endless. Although the evidence for the existence of compliant detractors seemed compelling, I was rather curious as to whether this was an ephemeral phenomenon that would be barely perceptible in a wider context, a milieu in which adolescent decision makers are pulled and pushed, back and forth, by multiple factors, of which prior behaviour, fear and confidence in one's abilities are just a few.

For the sake of argument, consider a scenario in which a teenage boy is about to have sexual intercourse with his girlfriend. He now has to decide whether to use a condom. The situation is tense, and time is short. He is well aware of the dangers of not using protection, but doubts that condoms are all that effective. Assuming the boy is a competent decision maker, CDT suggests he is likely to use protection notwithstanding his scepticism, because the alternatives are worse.

However, what if he is too anxious to think properly about the options and their merits and demerits? Maybe intimacy bothers him. Or perhaps he is a bit unsure of

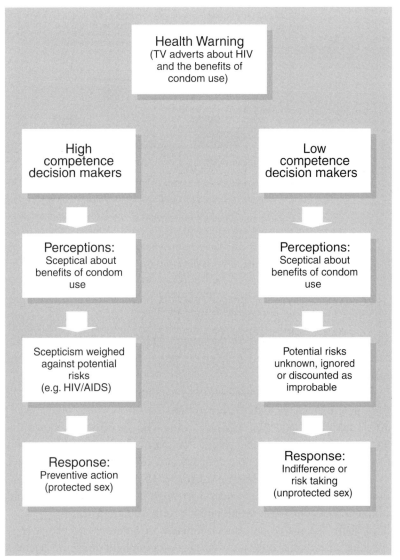

6.6 *An illustration of compliant detraction with respect to condom use. Competent teenagers may be sceptical about the preventive value of condom use (and with good reason – condoms aren't 100 per cent effective). Nevertheless, they will balance this doubt against the potential life threatening risks of not using condoms, and see sense in using protection, despite their reservations. Less competent adolescents may not be bothered about considering both sides of the argument – risks and benefits. Those who see little or no benefit in condom use may ignorantly act on this point oblivious to the risks they are taking (Source: Umeh, 1998a, 1998b).*

himself and doubtful that he has the social skills to negotiate condom use without suggesting distrust. Or maybe he isn't in the habit of using condoms, for whatever reason, and old habits die hard. What then? Would he still be compelled to use contraception, or be swayed by the other influences acting on him?

Intriguingly, robust evidence for compliant detraction remained even after making adjustments for previous sexual behaviour (i.e. past condom use), fear or anxiety associated with contraceptive use, perceived ability to initiate condom use successfully, and several additional factors, including gender (Umeh, 1998a, 1998b)! This suggests that the phenomenon, when it occurs, is probably quite robust, despite other psychological influences.

Adolescents often go along with an activity that they are sceptical about. You see this when, for instance, teenage girls decide to go on a diet to lose weight, despite having doubts about the effectiveness of dieting. Likewise, adolescents may quit smoking even though they don't personally know anyone who actually died from cigarette smoke. I suspect that, eventually, very strong doubts will prompt many youngsters to hesitate, and perhaps seek advice. On the basis of the feedback they receive, a decision may be maintained, modified or rescinded.

Confidence

Decision theorists posit a link between overconfidence and bungling decision making, specifically a failure to process information properly (Oskamp, 1965; Fischoff et al., 1977; Moorman, 1999; Alba and Hutchinson, 2000). Overconfidence can lead to a situation in which an individual is so sure of himself that he is prepared to make a decision without bothering to think about pros and cons. The person assumes he already knows what needs to be known to solve the problem, and hence sees no point in reappraising the situation afresh.

Other research suggests that confidence goes hand-in-hand with competence. Teenagers who score high in one also score high in the other (Mann et al., 1989; Friedman and Mann, 1993). It is possible that confidence may improve or worsen the quality of decision making depending on personal or situational factors. For example, a confident person may be willing to think more clearly about his options if he has access to the relevant information. In the absence of important facts, he may confidently rely on his instincts, with potentially disastrous results. Unfortunately existing research has been more concerned with the link between overconfidence and psychopathology (e.g. Faust et al., 1988; Garaigordobil and Dura, 2006), with little interest in decision making.

What we do know is that, in some instances, an adolescent's confidence in her ability to implement a course of action can elicit a decision to perform such action regardless of the potential consequences (Umeh, 2003; Zebracki and Drotar, 2004; Young et al., 2005). This isn't usually a problem, provided little is at stake. For example, in a situation requiring a decision about contraceptive use, an over-confident teenager may promptly opt to use condoms with little or no mental deliberation. The individual may have dealt with this problem before, and been happy with the results. Thus, although his decision making is virtually thoughtless and impulsive, he has clearly made the right choice.

Overconfidence can be valuable in situations that require quick decisions, if disaster is to be averted, with little or no time for risk–benefit appraisals. For

example, a confident teenage driver, reacting to a potentially deadly traffic emergency (e.g. an imminent head-on collision), may assume he already knows what to do in this situation. Consequently, he is able to react decisively in a situation where delay and indecision may be fatal.

Some decision theorists (e.g. Stewart *et al.*, 1999; Maddux *et al.*, 2005) have tested the idea that, in certain situations, a self-assured person will only make a decision if his perceptions of pros and cons justify it. Or alternatively, that cost–benefit deliberations may only lead to a decision if a person is confident he or she can carry out the chosen activity. However, evidence for this phenomenon is patchy and inconclusive.

Effects of stress

There appears to be a general consensus amongst decision theorists that stress somehow impairs competent decision making (Janis and Mann, 1977; Baumann *et al.*, 2001; Useem *et al.*, 2005; Driskell *et al.*, 2006). Indeed, research shows that teenagers who make poor health choices, such as smoking cigarettes, experience greater levels of stress (e.g. Siqueira *et al.*, 2000), raising the possibility that stress somehow impairs their decision making. Studies have shown that stress reduces the quality of decision making in adolescents (e.g. Ruisel *et al.*, 1994; Fishbein *et al.*, 2006).

In a review of the developmental changes that typify adolescence Petersen and Leffert (1995) noted that decision making in stressful situations is likely to be less sophisticated than when the situation isn't threatening. However, there is evidence associating stress with greater competence. For example Galotti (2001) found that, when making important real-life decisions, college students who reported more stress also tended to review more decision alternatives, before making a commitment.

The role of stress in health decision making is particularly hazy. One problem with making decisions about one's health is that the potential risks are so varied in terms of their perceived likelihood of occurrence, and hence so is the amount of stress they generate.

For example, teenagers face myriad potential threats. Problems like heart disease are rather far-fetched, no matter how much one smokes cigarettes or eats fatty foods. By contrast, risks like the HIV virus can be contracted immediately, following unprotected sex. This distinction between short- and long-term threats is important, because the way teenagers arrive at decisions may vary considerably depending on the immediacy of a threat (Gardner and Herman, 1990). Imminent dangers such as HIV create a sense of urgency and foreboding, generating more fear, and hence affecting decisions. The immediacy of risk became of particular interest to me when I realised that evidence for compliant detraction only emerged in relation to sexual behaviour. There was no evidence pertaining to other lifestyle factors.

While the medical consequences of smoking cigarettes, drinking alcohol or eating fatty foods wouldn't materialise for several years, if not decades, the repercussions of unsafe sexual intercourse are immediate, and hence more stressful. Physical evidence (e.g. missed periods, positive HIV test result) may become apparent in a matter of days, weeks or months. Thus, adolescents faced with a decision about contraception are probably under much greater emotional strain.

The possibility of an unplanned pregnancy is particularly worrying (Somers and Surman, 2004). Indeed, it is probable that the majority of adolescents who use contraception do so for protection against this urgent threat. Looking through various teenage websites, it quickly becomes apparent that adolescents seem far more preoccupied with the risk of unplanned pregnancy than STDs. Emails abound from teenage girls concerned about missed or late periods, contact with semen, the reliability of pregnancy test results, and what all this might mean. Some boys also write in, concerned about the same issues.

Faced with the possibility of an immediate crisis, teenagers may respond with more urgency. Thus any differences in decision making competence may become more pronounced. This would explain why the sceptical but compliant behaviour of competent teenagers, and seemingly narrow-minded appraisals of their less proficient colleagues, were only observed in relation to contraceptive use, and no other health behaviour.

By contrast, decisions concerning behaviours like smoking, diet and physical exercise will be less urgent, so that even a competent decision maker may be somewhat lethargic about surveying his options. Alternatively, he may consider fewer options than usual. An observer monitoring the activities of two teenage smokers – one competent the other incompetent – to see how they deal with the threat to their health may find it difficult to differentiate between them, in terms of the quality of their decision making. Both may probably quit smoking, eventually, but there may be little evidence of the balanced cognitive appraisals associated with skilled decision making.

Health promoters may find it particularly productive to focus on decisions concerning safer sex and unplanned pregnancy. They need not despair, for example, if adolescents question the necessity for condoms. Rather than try to convince them, it may be more constructive to present all the alternatives, and show why they are less suitable than what is being recommended. An audience that is open-minded and interested in learning more will probably end up using protection, notwithstanding their reservations about them. Even narrow-minded individuals may be persuaded if the benefits are suitably highlighted.

The dominance of contextual factors

Descriptive theories of competent decision making (e.g. Janis and Mann, 1977, 1976; Byrnes, 2002; Friedman, 1996) often seem to rely on a number of

assumptions about the prevailing context. These include the suppositions that the person making the decision:

- is able to carry out the decision once it has been made
- isn't bothered whether or not they like the decision, and
- is unaffected by her previous behaviour or experience.

Discussions about why teenagers make risky decisions often completely ignore the following:

- whether they are capable of making and implementing a healthy decision (they might need the approval and/or cooperation of their parents, for example when seeking to change their diet at home)
- whether she actually likes the healthy choice
- how they have behaved previously (i.e. a youngster who has smoked for years may find it more difficult to change than another teen who has only experimented with cigarettes once).

These issues have such a significant effect on decision making that they may completely overshadow the impact of decision making competence. This view is directly inspired by the work of Lucy Crabtree, who was one of my undergraduate students while I was working as a lecturer at Nottingham Trent University.

For her final year BA dissertation Lucy approached me with a proposal for a study originally aimed at understanding food choice in children and adolescents (Umeh and Crabtree, 2006). Using data collected from a large group of secondary school pupils, she was able to demonstrate that evaluations of costs and benefits, a key feature of proficient decision making, play an important role in fruit and vegetable intake. Essentially, those youngsters who opted to eat fruit and vegetables, and adhered to this decision, anticipated more benefits and fewer costs compared with colleagues who chose not to consume this diet. Initially this finding generated considerable excitement. Children and adolescents displayed competence in food choice.

Over the next few months Lucy and I agreed to publish the findings in an academic journal, and work on the paper soon began. Yet, as time went by, I began to suspect that there might be more to the findings than we had initially realized. Out of her own clever insight, and attention to detail, Lucy had also collected information from participants about the perceived ease or difficulty of eating more fruit and vegetables. Most children and teenagers require the cooperation of their parents when it comes to modifying their diet, and such cooperation isn't guaranteed.

Data were also collected on previous fruit and vegetable consumption. To obtain an accurate measure, participants were asked to keep a detailed record of their food intake over a seven-day period, in terms of both the type and the portions of items eaten. They were provided with suitable recording sheets, a detailed list of fruit and vegetables, and simple instructions on how to record what they ate each day.

Finally, Lucy also determined whether participants liked the idea of eating more fruit and vegetables. So, the key question was as follows. If children and adolescents choose to eat more fruit and vegetables, could this preference be the result of competent decision making, or is this decision driven by other influences, such as previous dietary behaviour or ability to change or maintain their diet?

It is plausible that even the most proficient decision maker may be overcome by the sheer momentum of his existing lifestyle, and other rather insurmountable factors, such as an impaired ability to get certain things done – like a fundamental change in diet – without support from others. Careful analysis of the data confirmed these suspicions. After making adjustments for prior consumption over the past seven days, perceived ability to control one's diet, and dietary likes or dislikes, it emerged that risk–benefit appraisals no longer played a significant role in determining food choice. Thus, whatever effect competent decision making had on choice was negated by more potent psychological influences.

Implementing a decision

Committing to and executing a decision are essential steps in competent decision making (e.g. Janis and Mann, 1976, 1977; Friedman, 1996; Byrnes, 2002). For many teenagers, struggling daily with peer pressure and other strong temptations, and hampered by limited resources, implementing a health related decision can be an uphill task.

Scientific evidence on decision implementation is abundant (Prochaska et al., 1992; Prochaska and Velicer, 1997), albeit evidence pertaining to adolescents specifically is patchy and inconclusive. Nevertheless, it isn't hard to find studies showing that teenagers often fail to implement crucial health decisions, often with terrible medical repercussions. Essentially, once adolescents have made a decision, only a minority actually follow through.

Paediatricians Sofia Feinstein, Rami Keich, Rachel Becker-Cohsen and others conducted one such study, providing a rather chilling insight into the deadly repercussions when teenagers fail to adhere to a medical decision. They investigated the decision to undergo a life-saving kidney transplant (Feinstein et al., 2005). Once a patient has undergone a kidney transplant she is administered immunosuppressive medications aimed at ensuring that the body doesn't reject transplanted tissue. Thus, adherence to this course of medication is vital if the transplant is to succeed, and the patient survive.

Feinstein and her colleagues noted that failure to keep taking the prescribed medication is particularly common amongst adolescent patients. For example, they found that non-compliance was many times higher in teenage patients compared with children under the age of 12. Furthermore, poor adherence was a problem with adolescent patients facing other life-threatening illnesses, notably asthma. Consequently many patients recover more slowly than normal, or fail to recover at all, culminating in premature death.

Why should this be so? Any decision, no matter how logical and carefully considered, is pointless if the decision maker fails to carry out the pronouncement properly. Opting to undergo a kidney transplant – a clearly competent choice given kidney failure – is pointless if one isn't going to follow through by taking the medicines necessary to ensure the transplant is a success.

Similarly, making a decision to change one's diet, stop smoking cigarettes or register with a gym is senseless if the decision maker is unable to stay the course, for example by disposing of all cigarettes and remaining abstinent, or actually attending the gym and continuing to do so. So what are the reasons for failed implementation?

There appear to be many. Perhaps one of the most prominent is a lack of adequate wherewithal. I am talking specifically about support from friends and family. Feinstein and colleagues found something rather interesting in their study. Adolescent patients who failed to take their immunosuppressive medication, as prescribed by the doctors, having agreed to and undergone a kidney transplant, tended to report insufficient care from family members. More specifically, the parents were less involved in supporting their child, for example by missing clinical appointments, not regularly accompanying them to clinic sessions, and failing to administer medicines at the times that they should.

Additionally, non-adhering teenagers faced more interpersonal problems or conflicts within the family, for example constantly quarrelling with parents, the chronic illness of other family members, for example an elderly parent, and other difficult family circumstances. This led the researchers to conclude that the support of family members is crucial in enabling the teenagers properly to execute their decision to undergo a kidney transplant.

Social psychologists Irving Janis and Leon Mann argue that, after making a decision, people often face various difficulties as they try to implement their choice (Janis and Mann, 1977). They become more aware of the negative consequences of their decision, repercussions that may have been less obvious, or completely unknown, at the time the decision was being made. For example, many adolescent smokers form the habit of opting to quit smoking only quickly to rescind their decision as soon as they realise how difficult it is.

Almost every decision that an adolescent has to make concerning his health will have potential negative consequences, no matter how competent the decision might be. I'm sure many youngsters realise in their early teens that you don't get something for nothing in life, and that there is always a price to pay for every decision made and action taken. In which case, most health decisions are unlikely to be properly implemented without help from significant others, notably parents.

In fact teenagers categorised as 'minors' would find it virtually impossible to execute certain decisions unless their parents were directly involved. This is particularly applicable to decisions about medical treatment, and outpatient medication. Parents can provide various resources, for example financial aid (e.g. paying for prescription drugs) and psychological support (e.g. providing reassurance). Unlike for adults, basic resources such as transportation (e.g. to visit a

hospital) may simply be unavailable to many teenagers without the cooperation of their parents.

Then there are ethical issues: in many countries minors under a certain age – usually 18 – cannot themselves legally consent to treatment or other medical interventions without the presence of a responsible adult who is usually their legal custodian (e.g. Brank, 2002). For example, a 13 year old cannot undergo surgery unless her parents consent to it. Thus, medical, legal and ethical restrictions may severely impede implementation. Therefore competence, or lack of it, may not necessarily be a central issue every time a teenager persists (seemingly willingly) in a behaviour that is damaging to her health.

Behavioural consequences of competence

Imagine a boy who, when offered a cigarette, pauses to contemplate the options and their associated risks and benefits. Is he likely to accept or reject the offer? Received wisdom suggests that he will reject the cigarette, in order to minimise the risks to his health (Rogers, 1975, 1983; Janis and Mann, 1977; Gardner and Herman, 1990; Eagly and Chaiken, 1993).

It can be argued that if an individual thinks carefully when making a choice, taking the trouble to obtain and evaluate all the relevant information, then he is more likely to make a healthy decision compared with a thoughtless person. However, there is some evidence indicating no association between decision making proficiency and risk behaviour (e.g. McKay, 1998; Zuckerman, 1999).

For example, McKay (1998) found no difference in competence between gang members and non-gang members.[2] Similarly, Zuckerman (1999) observed no variance in proficiency between teenagers who've attempted suicide and those who haven't. On the other hand, pausing to think carefully about sexual decisions has been shown to encourage abstinence and delay the loss of virginity (Trierweiler, 1996).

Minimising danger is just one of an innumerable number of potential goals that a teenage decision maker may prioritise. As we saw in Chapter 3, issues such as peer pressure, the opinions of one's parents and personal satisfaction are just a few of the possible outcomes that teenagers may consider, and with some urgency, during decision making (e.g. Turner and Mermelstein, 2004; Allison et al., 2005; Macpherson, 2005; Wilson et al., 2006; Alvord, 2007; Lee et al., 2007).

Competence is likely to lead to a healthy decision if self-preservation/good health is at the top of the list of priorities. And we know that this often isn't your average adolescent's primary concern (Ollendick et al., 1989; Muris and Ollendick, 2002). Peer pressure and wanting to be cool usually matter a great

---

[2] In fact analysis showed that competence was used more frequently by gang members.

deal more. In fact you could argue that health may not be on the list of considerations at all!

On the whole, insisting that adolescents be more proficient in their decision making would at best only elicit well-thought-out decisions. It wouldn't necessarily produce healthier choices. Much has been written about a British teenage pop star who suffered symptoms of anorexia for years and, despite continually reflecting on her problem and the damage it was doing to her health, continued starving herself, that is, until she collapsed in public and had to be rushed to hospital (Piper, 2006).

It can be argued that if a teenager adopts health damaging behaviour then her decision making can't have been all that competent. However, the decision may only seem bad to observers for whom health is a priority. If health, indeed life itself, were immaterial to the decision maker (e.g. a teenage boy with suicidal tendencies), then he would feel he has acted entirely logically, to the extent that his priorities have been met.

It is worth remembering that decision making is usually triggered by something (Janis and Mann, 1977). People don't spontaneously start making decisions, for no reason whatsoever. If a health problem triggers decision making, then in all probability health would be a major consideration for the decision maker.

For example, a girl who starts to gain weight rapidly may be prompted into making a decision to deal with her weight problem. She is likely to survey options related to weight loss, for example registering with a gym, or modifying her diet to reduce the proportion of fatty foods. It would be bizarre if she considered options completely unrelated to weight, for example studying for her maths exam! To give another example, consider the case of someone trapped in a burning house. The person has to make a decision – he can either try to escape and save his life, or stay where he is and be burned alive! Escaping the flames is likely to be the top priority in weighing the options.

If decision making triggered by a health problem fails to address the issue, then it is reasonable to assume there was some fault in the decision making process. Perhaps not all the options were considered. Or maybe they were, but the various costs and benefits weren't weighed up in a meaningful and systematic manner, perhaps because there were too many factors to consider (as is often the case) and the individual was simply overwhelmed.

There is also the issue of commitment. Even the most competent adolescent – or adult for that matter – who, having thoroughly evaluated a wealth of information, and made sense of it, has managed to make a healthy decision, may find that it is an endless struggle implementing her decision (e.g. Higgins and Conner, 2003; Feinstein et al., 2005; Daily and Mumford, 2006; but see Steadman and Quine, 2004). Commitment is particularly a problem in the early to middle teens (Mann et al., 1989). Exhausted and with nowhere to go, she may simply abandon the quest, leaving the health problem unsolved. Readers may be familiar with the reasonable teenage boy who agrees to stay away from drugs,

cigarettes and alcohol, but fails, or the overweight but logical teenage girl who has opted to cut down on her fat intake, but lacks the will power to follow through.

Whether competence leads to better choices may also depend, in part, on the health behaviour in question. Data from my own research revealed that competent decision makers made better health behaviour decisions, but only in relation to physical activity and use of contraception. Competence didn't seem to matter when deciding whether to smoke, use drugs, drink alcohol or eat fatty foods (Umeh, 1998a, 1998b). Adolescents may be selective about which health behaviours they are prepared to contemplate rationally, prior to adoption, and which they are happy to take up on a whim. This selectivity may be forced by circumstances beyond their command. Issues like past behaviour and control may matter a great deal in this regard.

Let's ponder the subject of past behaviour. Activities like smoking and drinking alcohol can become addictive, especially after several years, so that even the most level-headed adolescent, who, after careful reasoning, decides that such activities are bad for his health, may suddenly find that old habits die hard. Although a decision to avoid such behaviours may be the result of competent thought, carrying it out may be extremely difficult, if not impossible.

Then there is the issue of control. Adolescents sometimes have limited command over their decisions. Food choice is a good example. Teenagers can use their pocket money to buy snacks of their own choosing (e.g. during break time at school). However, it is their parents who generally decide what they eat for breakfast, lunch and dinner at home. For example, in Britain primary and secondary schools are encouraged by the government to offer their pupils specific portions of fruit and vegetables on a daily basis, whether the pupils like it or not.[3] In the absence of control it may be of no consequence whether one is a competent or incompetent decision maker.

Risk seeking or risk averse?

Competence generally implies risk aversion – a desire to minimise loss and/or maximise gain (Janis and Mann, 1977). However, readers may remember my discussion of prospect theory (Tversky and Kahneman, 1974) in Chapter 1, a model which suggests that an otherwise competent decision maker, keenly aware of potential gains and losses, may in fact prefer to take risks under certain circumstances.

For example, given a choice between a large but uncertain risk and a small but guaranteed risk, decision makers purportedly prefer the former option, despite the greater threat. That is, they are risk seeking. This is because, according to prospect

---

[3] Consumption is optional, but the key point is that the menu is predetermined, and hence beyond the control of pupils.

theory, people prefer uncertain outcomes when they have something to lose, but crave certainty when they stand to gain.

So, to what extent are teenagers risk averse or risk seeking? Popular myth suggests adolescents are risk seekers (Gardner and Herman, 1990). Indeed, research applying prospect theory to adolescents seems to support this view (e.g. Dahl, 2006).

In keeping with this model, teenagers should prefer safer options when the going is good (i.e. they stand to gain), but take more risks when things aren't going well. However, a study conducted by Yu Chin Chien suggests that adolescents aren't bothered by how they perceive the prevailing situation when making decisions. Participants in this study made the same choices irrespective of how the decision task was 'framed'; albeit for a minority, having something to gain led to caution, whereas anticipating losses produced risk taking (Chien et al., 1996; also see Dahl, 2006).

Overall, it appears adolescents are prone to make risky decisions, whether they expect gain (e.g. social approval) or loss (e.g. poor health). However the extent to which Chien et al.'s (1996) findings apply to health behaviour is debatable. It would be interesting to see whether risk aversion and risk seeking are somehow qualified by decision making competence in a health behaviour context. What appears to be risk taking activity may, on closer scrutiny, be quite reasonable behaviour to an unskilled decision maker. Consider a boy who has sex without contraception. He may appear to observers to be taking undue risks. To him, however, this behaviour may seem entirely reasonable if he has doubts about the effectiveness of contraception and is oblivious to the alternatives.

The notion of compliant detraction suggests risk aversion (Umeh, 1998a). If a competent decision maker is prepared to take steps to protect her health, notwithstanding scepticism about the merits of such measures, then this suggests a considerable degree of caution in her decision making.

Finally, there are contextual factors like fear, past behaviour and wherewithal to consider, all of which may affect risk taking (Umeh, 1998a, 1998b, 2003; Umeh and Griffiths, 2001). For example adolescents may take risks simply because they lack the wherewithal to change. Imagine a deprived youth who is hopelessly addicted to drugs. Although a skilful decision maker harbouring a desire to change, he may find it virtually impossible to kick his drug habit without sustained social support, from friends and family, and access to key health services.

Conclusion

Some sceptical readers may still find it laughable that adolescents can exercise good judgement when making health behaviour decisions. The idea of a juvenile investing considerable effort weighing his options, and making an informed choice, may be difficult to visualise. Yet, study after study has shown that competent decision making is a recurring feature of adolescence, rather than

just an occasional blip. There is evidence they readily seek information, particularly through the Internet, consider alternatives, and balance risks and benefits as they become increasingly committed to a particular course of action.

However, competence seems to be characterised by a number of curious quirks. One of the most interesting issues to emerge is the setting of boundaries when making sexual decisions. Teenagers who are clearly proficient in decision making may limit the options they are prepared to consider based on principle.

Another revelation is that competence may not necessarily elicit health enhancing decisions. By the same token, incompetence doesn't automatically predict health damaging behaviour. Overall the quality of decision making may have no bearing on health behaviour, for reasons that remain unclear. Nevertheless, competence may generate more open-minded appraisals, in which positive outcomes are weighed against negative consequences. The result is that an individual may be willing to adopt a health behaviour that lacks incentive, because it is the least objectionable of the available options.

Considered in the context of health promotion, this argument suggests that adolescents need to be convinced not about the merits of preventive behaviour, but rather about the inferiority of alternatives. Ultimately though, even the most competent decision maker, like any other person faced with a choice, has to contend with the moderating effects of factors such as stress, previous behaviour and overconfidence. These factors can exert a powerful impact on the quality of decision making that is difficult to resist.

Key points

- Adolescents can and do exhibit competence in decision making.
- The theory of compliant detraction is proposed. This model describes the relationship between decision making competence and health behaviour, an area hitherto neglected by current theories applied to adolescent health behaviour. The model offers testable predictions.
- Competence encourages more balanced judgements when making health behaviour decisions.
- Competence can but does not necessarily deter adolescents from engaging in health compromising behaviour. Indeed competence may not be associated with health behaviour at all.
- Personal and situational factors such as stress and past experience may moderate the effect of competent decision making on adolescent health behaviour.

Key terms

- Competence
- Risks and benefits

- Options, alternatives
- Problem recognition
- Commitment
- Stress
- Compliant detraction
- Risk aversion and risk awareness

Further reading

Arkes, H.R. and Ayton, P. (1999) The sunk cost and concorde effects: are humans less rational than lower animals? *Psychological Bulletin*, 125, pp. 591–600.

Ayton, P. and Hardman, D. (1997) Are two rationalities better than one? *Current Psychology of Cognition*, 16, pp. 39–51.

Byrnes, J.P. (2002) The development of decision-making. *Journal of Adolescent Health*, 31, pp. 208–215.

Smith, K., Shanteau, J. and Johnson, P. (eds.) (2004) *Psychological Investigations of Competence in Decision Making*. Cambridge: Cambridge University Press.

7 Avoidance

Learning outcomes

After reading this chapter readers should have a better understanding of the following:

1 the significance of avoidance in adolescent decision making
2 various dimensions of avoidance
3 the prevalence of avoidance amongst adolescents
4 explanations for the sources of avoidance in decision making
5 the childhood origins of avoidance
6 the effect of avoidance on health behaviour
7 health behaviours susceptible to avoidance
8 age and gender differences in avoidance.

Chapter summary

One way adolescents may approach difficult decisions is simply to avoid them altogether. In essence, they elect to continue their current course of action, ignoring any associated threat or problem that may necessitate a change in behaviour. Avoidance seems to stem from early childhood learning experiences, but may also be triggered by situational factors, such as the absence of viable solutions. Adolescents seem to utilise a variety of avoidance strategies, including suppressing disturbing thoughts; actively avoiding people, situations or events that remind them of a stressor; and shifting responsibility for decision making to others. Curiously, although avoidance facilitates health damaging behaviour, it does not necessarily prevent a teenager from contemplating potential health risks and benefits, and making a decision based on these cognitive deliberations. This evasive approach to decision making remains a common feature of adolescence and a major concern for health promoters.

Chapter outline

The chapter begins by looking at the significance of avoidance as a decision making strategy. This is followed by some discussion of different forms of avoidance, such as thought suppression and distraction, and the prevalence of

avoidance amongst teenagers. Next I consider some of the purported psychological antecedents of avoidance, and the possible childhood origins. This is followed by an analysis of the consequences of avoidance for health behaviour, and some discussion of shifting responsibility as an especially tempting form of evasiveness.

Avoidance in decision making

A team of researchers once interviewed a group of adolescent smokers about their experiences of smoking (Amos *et al.*, 2006). The interviews revealed something interesting. Although the majority of interviewees wanted to quit, they planned to do so sometime in the future, rather than promptly. Almost 50 per cent saw themselves quitting at some point in the distant future. This finding highlights an important feature of adolescent decision making – a tendency to avoid difficult decisions.

Quitting smoking, like many other preventive health behaviours, can be tough. So, many adolescent smokers deal with this problem by simply avoiding the issue altogether, or at least for the time being.

Difficult decisions can be a pain. Does one continue his current course of action, which is satisfying but bound to aggravate the problem, or change to a new course of action that may remedy the situation, but prove too costly to implement?

Take for example a girl who has a weight problem. She is faced with a choice: try to address the problem, or do nothing and simply carry on as normal. Whatever she decides, it is likely to be a very difficult choice. This is because both options have significant incentives and disincentives. Faced with a difficult dilemma it is very tempting simply to ignore the problem, hoping it will go away. There is evidence that this is how adolescents sometimes approach decisions, health related or otherwise (Mann *et al.*, 1997, 1998; Umeh, 1998b; Tuinstra *et al.*, 2000).

Avoidance in adolescent decision making is a multifaceted phenomenon. Before considering its various dimensions I will first discuss how teenagers view this approach to decision making. Given that avoidance is a recurring feature of adolescence one could be forgiven for thinking young people endorse this strategy. However nothing could be further from the truth.

Attitudes towards avoidance

Curiously, children and adolescents both seem to take a dim view of avoidance. Psychologist Jennifer Amsterlaw demonstrated this phenomenon while studying for her doctorate at the University of Michigan (Amsterlaw, 2006). She presented a sample of children and college students with different

everyday scenarios in which people were required to make a decision. In some scenarios the decision maker avoided thinking carefully about the decision, failed to survey available options, and refused to consider potential risks. In other scenarios, the decision maker did more or less the exact opposite, thinking carefully about alternatives and their consequences, and gathering rather than avoiding evidence.

It emerged that older children and college students tended to discredit those scenarios in which the person seemed to avoid rather than confront the decision. In other words, participants felt avoidance was a bad thing.

Granted, the scenarios used were not health related. Furthermore, participants were responding to a hypothetical situation, under contrived conditions (i.e. without any of the stresses and tensions associated with real-life decision making). Moreover, they weren't the decision maker in any of the scenarios, but instead were asked to evaluate someone else's actions.

Nevertheless, it is difficult to dismiss evidence like this. It suggests that teenagers recognise there is something specious about evading rather than facing tough choices. They know this is not the best way to make a decision, but nevertheless persist in this approach.

Factor analysis of the Decision Making Questionnaire (DMQ) (Mann *et al.*, 1982), an instrument that measures how people generally prefer to make decisions, has repeatedly generated a distinct strategy depicting avoidance (e.g. Friedman and Mann, 1993; Mann *et al.*, 1997, 1998; Umeh, 1998a, 1998b; Tuinstra *et al.*, 2000). Teenagers in these studies often identify strongly with avoidance statements, such as 'I avoid making decisions', 'I put off making decisions', 'I'd rather let someone else make a decision for me so that it won't be my problem', and 'I don't like to take responsibility for making decisions.'

Thus, although adolescents may strive for decision making competence, as outlined in the previous chapter, they also entertain an evasive approach that may ultimately prove seriously damaging to their health. They do what they can to avoid making a difficult choice, preferring instead to postpone the decision, shift responsibility to someone else, or rely on some other strategy that helps them evade the problem.

The purpose of avoidance

According to many theorists, the sole purpose of avoidance is simply to reduce fear or anxiety (Leventhal, 1970; Janis and Mann, 1976, 1977; Janis, 1986; Rogers, 1983). Difficult decisions can be stressful, so stressful in fact that a decision maker may become preoccupied with reducing emotional discomfort, rather than addressing the problem. An adolescent smoker, for example, may quickly realise that, by simply ignoring the health risks of cigarette use, he can save himself unnecessary anxiety. Similarly, by avoiding viewing herself in a mirror, or refusing to discuss her weight with anyone, an obese girl can avoid having to worry about her

health. Acknowledging a difficult problem, and trying to thrash out a solution, can be an intimidating prospect for many young people.

Facets of avoidance

How does avoidance manifest in adolescents? Psychological literature on coping generally depicts avoidance as a largely intellectual exercise (see review by Krohne, 1993; Leventhal *et al.*, 1993). This emphasis is conveyed in the use of the term 'cognitive' avoidance (Gosselin *et al.*, 2007). In essence, adolescents often think their way out of having to make a difficult decision, for example by simply refusing to consider a problem, or engaging in wishful thinking, to minimise its significance (Rippetoe and Rogers, 1987; Gosselin *et al.*, 2002, 2007; Kowalski *et al.*, 2006; Soetens and Braet, 2007; Sexton and Dugas, 2008). Of course avoidance can also involve physical efforts to avoid tough choices, such as ignoring information that reminds one about a threat (e.g. medical books or leaflets).

There appears to be a general acceptance that avoidance is multidimensional (e.g. Janis and Mann, 1977; Krohne, 1993). This view seems to be supported by evidence showing that adolescents use a wide variety of avoidance related strategies when faced with health related decisions. Table 7.1 lists some of these strategies, taken from selected studies.

The evidence from Kowalski *et al.*'s (2006) work is particularly illuminating. It is based on an in-depth analysis of open-ended descriptions by teenagers about how they cope with anxiety concerning issues relating to their physical appearance, such as diet, leisure activity, weight loss, physical activity, and even undergoing surgical procedures. I have not come across many studies that have provided such detailed insights into adolescents' use of avoidance in health scenarios, based on their freely expressed views![1]

The list is by no means exhaustive, or representative (it is biased towards physique, obesity and food choice), but it certainly gives one an idea of the wide repertoire of evasive measures young people may employ. Given the apparent emphasis on the concept of cognitive avoidance in the literature (e.g. Gosselin *et al.*, 2002; Eyles and Bates, 2005; Zanini *et al.*, 2005; Kowalski *et al.*, 2006; Soetens and Braet, 2007), I will now discuss some of its key components in some detail. There appear to be five main domains, as follows:

- thought suppression
- replacing disturbing thoughts with happy ones
- distracting oneself
- avoiding threatening stimuli
- transforming mental images into verbal thoughts.

---

[1] This is not to say that no other studies of this nature exist. For example, Friedman's (1996) work, which I discuss in some detail later in this chapter, also relied on a comprehensive unrestrictive qualitative approach, and yielded intriguing insights into adolescent decision making.

Table 7.1 *Some forms of avoidance utilised by teenagers in response to health related problems, based on selected studies. All these strategies may allow an individual to postpone making a difficult decision to discontinue risky behaviour, and instead adopt healthier habits.*

Avoidance strategy	Description and examples
Avoiding threatening stimuli (Kowalski *et al.*, 2006; Gosselin *et al.*, 2007)	Actively avoiding any cues that may trigger worrying thoughts. For example, a smoker may avoid looking at the health warning on a packet of cigarettes.
Physically keeping away from stressful stimuli – behavioural avoidance (Kowalski *et al.*, 2006)	Physically avoiding any situation that triggers disturbing memories. For example, an overweight girl may avoid social situations in which she may be called 'fat' by insensitive peers.
Thought substitution (Kowalski *et al.*, 2006; Gosselin *et al.*, 2007)	Replacing worrying thoughts with happier ones. A teenage kidney patient, worried about undergoing surgery, may try to think instead about all the fun he may have with other kids in the hospital ward.
Suppressing disturbing thoughts (Kowalski *et al.*, 2006; Gosselin *et al.*, 2007)	Refusing to think about any disturbing ideas or threats. For example, a girl who is anxious she may get pregnant from having unprotected sex with her boyfriend may simply refuse to entertain this thought.
Distraction (Gosselin *et al.*, 2002, 2007)	Trying to distract oneself to avoid thinking worrying thoughts. For example a teenage drug user who occasionally thinks about the risks to his health may sing to himself, play a video game or watch TV, to distract himself.
Transforming disturbing images into verbal thoughts (Gosselin *et al.*, 2002, 2007)	Worrying images are transformed into reassuring verbal utterances that help alleviate anxiety. For example, a boy who imagines himself growing obese, because of a lack of physical activity, may quickly retort, 'Ah, that will never happen to me.'
Wishful thinking (Rippetoe and Rogers, 1987; Kowalski *et al.*, 2006)	Trying to rationalise current risky behaviour by discounting the danger to oneself, and/or maximising the benefits of such behaviour. For example, an adolescent who refuses to visit his dentist may wishfully think, 'There's nothing wrong with my teeth or gums.'
Emotional discharge/expression (Eyles and Bates, 2005; Zanini *et al.*, 2005)	Venting one's feelings, to alleviate tension. A girl who is worried she's becoming anorexic may cry, scream, or pour her heart out to a friend, in order to relieve tension and feel better.

Table 7.1 (*cont.*)

Avoidance strategy	Description and examples
Shifting responsibility to others (Tuinstra *et al.*, 2000)	This is perhaps one of the most important but rarely mentioned avoidance strategies. It involves transferring responsibility for a problem to someone or something else. For example, a boy who buys unhealthy/junk foods at school may blame the school authorities for selling such foods in the school cafeteria.

Note: This list is not exhaustive, and the studies cited are not exclusive. Virtually all the strategies mentioned, with the exception of physically keeping away from stressors, are forms of cognitive avoidance. The last item – shifting responsibility – is rarely mentioned in the literature as a form of avoidance in adolescence. Tuinstra *et al.* (2000) found reliable evidence that this is indeed a distinct strategy teenagers use to avoid difficult decisions.

These dimensions can be measured using the Cognitive Avoidance Questionnaire (Gosselin, 2007). Research has shown that adolescents do in fact utilise each of these avoidance strategies to deal with anxiety, with greater anxiousness associated with more avoidance (e.g. Sexton and Dugas, 2008; Kowalski *et al.*, 2006; Gosselin *et al.*, 2007; Soetens and Braet, 2007). Each strategy has unique implications for decision making (Janis and Mann, 1977). Table 7.1 shows how each strategy may feature in decision making.

Thought suppression

A teenager may refuse to entertain any thoughts that remind him of a difficult problem. So, for example, a smoker who is troubled by the risks to his health may cope with his anxiety by simply suppressing any thoughts about his health. Gosselin *et al.* (2007) found that thought suppression wasn't a significant predictor of teenage anxiety, accounting for a negligible proportion of the variance. Its predictive value was weak compared with other avoidance strategies, suggesting that it may not be the easiest and most effective strategy for dealing with anxiety. This view seems to be supported by research findings.

For example, Soetens and Braet (2007) found that thought suppression was ineffective in subduing memories of high-calorie foods in obese adolescents. Participants, supposedly hypersensitive to food cues by virtue of their being overweight, were presented with a list of high-calorie foods (e.g. chocolate, French fries, pancake, pastry, pizza), together with a list of control words.

Prior to this some participants had been asked to suppress any thoughts about food or eating, while the rest received no such instruction. The teenagers were then given a few minutes to recall all the words they could remember and write them

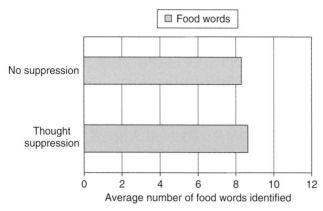

7.1 *Effect of thought suppression. How effective is thought suppression in coping with disturbing thoughts, hence negating the need for a difficult decision? In one study, overweight adolescents (supposedly hypersensitive to food cues) first suppressed food thoughts, then viewed a list of food words (e.g. French fries, cake), and then attempted to recall all the words they could remember. Suppression had no effect on recall, compared with a no-suppression group (Source: Soetens and Braet, 2007).*

down on a sheet of paper. Analysis revealed no difference between the suppression and no-suppression groups in the number of food words recalled (see Fig. 7.1). In essence, not thinking about food didn't prevent subjects from thinking about food!

In general, experiments on thought suppression suggest this is a rather ineffective strategy that may actually have a paradoxical effect, whereby the thoughts one is trying to suppress actually become more and more prominent during suppression (Wegner, 1989, 1994).

One suggested reason for this boomerang effect is that when disturbing thoughts occur, people try to distract themselves by turning to things or activities around them. These distractions then become retrieval cues that are reminders for the disturbing thought. Gradually, over time, the individual finds himself surrounded by numerous reminders. The presence of these multiple cues makes the thought much more difficult to suppress.

Take, for example, a teenager who is worried about her weight. She tries to avoid thinking about it, first by avoiding mirrors, then by reading a novel, and finally by calling her friends by telephone for a chat. Gradually, she finds that mirrors, novels and telephone calls all seem to remind her that she is overweight, making it almost impossible to ignore the problem. Given these arguments it is no surprise that thought suppression has failed to predict anxiety levels in adolescents (Gosselin *et al.*, 2007). This avoidance strategy may have a less disruptive effect on decision making, forcing teenagers to confront problems that 'just won't go away'. In view of its paradoxical effect, thought suppression may be quickly abandoned, and replaced by more effective evasive measures.

Substituting happy thoughts for disturbing ones

Thought substitution entails somehow 'removing' anxious thoughts from the mind and replacing them with happier ideas or imagery (Gosselin et al., 2002, 2007). A boy who is fearful because of thoughts he may get his girlfriend pregnant may try to stop worrying by reflecting instead on how much fun they have when they are together. Replacing worrying thoughts with happier ones can be effective because it obscures a disturbing fact, relieving anxiety, at least for the time being. Thought substitution requires an individual mentally to rehearse situations that are pleasing to him or her, and has been shown to be quite effective in suppressing disturbing memories (Hertel and Calcaterra, 2005).

Gosselin et al. (2007) have shown that adolescents may use thought substitution as an avoidance strategy, with increasing levels of anxiety associated with greater use. However, this technique failed to predict anxiety levels when considered within the context of other avoidance strategies, suggesting that it may be comparatively less effective, and/or popular. It's difficult to generate and maintain pleasing thoughts and ideas, especially if one is already in a very distressed state. For example, a girl who is panic-stricken about the possibility of being pregnant may have considerable difficulty visualising happy scenarios. Alternatively, disturbing thoughts may be too dominant and recurring to replace. The thought of being pregnant may be such a frightening notion it may completely dominate the girl's thoughts, and prove impossible to 'remove', no matter how hard she tries.

Unsuccessful at managing her fears, the girl will find herself having to confront the problem, and make some important decisions, such as planning to insist on condom use during any future sexual encounters, speaking to various abortion clinics, or resolving when and how to notify her parents, whose support will be invaluable in raising a baby. Overall, thought substitution requires considerable mental effort, concentration and sustenance, so that it ultimately defeats the purpose, which is to reduce tension, not increase it.

Distraction

Distraction involves engaging in activities that help one forget a disturbing thought. For example, a teenage drug user, rattled by a friend's comment about the dangers of drug use, may preoccupy himself by reading a book, listening to music, watching TV or 'hanging out' with friends. Empirical evidence suggests that distraction may have mixed results when used by adolescents to deal with medical or health related anxiety, or tension from other sources (e.g. Carlson et al., 2000; de Bourdeaudhuij et al., 2002; Jeffs, 2007; Wetzel and Schroger, 2007; Windich et al., 2007).

For example, Jeffs (2007) carried out a study that assessed the effectiveness of distraction for dealing with anxiety associated with allergy testing. Adolescents visiting an allergist were recruited as subjects. She found that greater use of distraction was associated with reduced anxiety. However, another study, by

Windich *et al.* (2007), produced more ambiguous findings. A group of teenagers with cancer were assigned to either an intervention or a control condition, to assess the effect of distractors on their experience of pain, fear and distress during a painful medical procedure.[2] The intervention group were allowed to select distractors, such as a book, hand-held video game or virtual reality glasses, in addition to receiving standard patient care. The control group received only care, with no distractors.

Following the medical procedure, subjects were asked to rate their level of fear and pain. Additionally, parents and a nurse also rated participants fear/distress levels, based on their observations. Although results showed that the intervention group experienced less fear/distress, this finding was based on the nurse's and parents' ratings. There were no group differences in self-reported pain and fear, suggesting that distractions didn't help.

Other research has shown that distraction can help manage stress, and hence improve performance during physical activity (de Bourdeaudhuij *et al.*, 2002). However, Gosselin *et al.* (2007) found that distraction wasn't a significant predictor of anxiety levels when considered within the context of other cognitive avoidance strategies. This suggests that distraction isn't as effective as other evasive measures.

Ultimately its effect may depend on the nature of the distractor itself, and how it is used. For example, a smoker who is worried about the dangers to his health may find that playing video games helps distract him from the disturbing thoughts, allowing him to postpone making a decision to quit smoking. By contrast, reading a book may do little to allay his concerns since this is a far less engaging activity.

Avoidance of threatening stimuli

In this scenario the individual actively avoids any stimuli that trigger disturbing memories. For example, a girl with a potential eating disorder may refuse to discuss the problem with anyone, and/or avoid books, TV programmes and people that are bound to remind her of the problem. Similarly, a newly qualified young driver, worried about his reckless driving, may pay little attention to news reports about gruesome traffic accidents, or his own 'near-miss' experiences on the road.

Psychological theory suggests that avoidance of triggers is arguably the most obvious evasive tactic an individual may adopt, generally manifesting as a distinct lack of interest in the problem, with endless postponement of any sort of remedial action (Janis and Mann, 1977, p. 87). Gosselin *et al.* (2007) report evidence that seems to support this view. Of the five forms of cognitive avoidance, this was one of only two that significantly predicted levels of anxiety in the adolescent participants. More importantly, avoidance of triggers accounted for the largest proportion of variance in anxiety, suggesting that this is perhaps the most salient and effective avoidance strategy. It is more likely than other tactics to be adopted by very anxious teenagers.

---

[2] Venous Port Access and Venipuncture. This involves inserting a needle into a vein.

The consequences for decision making are stark. The individual avoids having to make a decision, or if he does make a choice he delays commitment indefinitely. There is very limited if any mental deliberation about options and their costs and benefits, since any attempts to do this will simply remind the person of the problem, putting him under pressure to take remedial action.

Transforming mental images into verbal thoughts

Consider a girl who is anxious about becoming fat. From time to time she imagines herself in all sorts of unattractive and disturbing portly shapes. To prevent herself from worrying too much, each mental image is quickly followed by a reassuring verbal comment, such as 'wow, I will never be as fat as that', 'that's not me', or 'it can't happen', and 'it's all in my head, there's really nothing to worry about'. Research has shown that such verbalisations are associated with reduced nervousness in teenagers, indicating that this is quite an effective strategy for avoiding difficult decisions (Gosselin *et al.*, 2002, 2007). By verbally dismissing any disturbing thoughts about a threat or crisis, teenagers can alleviate considerable emotional discomfort. They can go about their daily activities as usual, without feeling compelled to make any tough choices that may be necessary to address a problem (Table 7.1).

Identifying worst case scenarios

One other way to avoid a difficult decision is by emphasising worst case scenarios, both to oneself and/or to significant others. In other words, a decision isn't really necessary since things aren't that bad after all.

Imagine the following scene. Fourteen-year-old Robert began drinking alcohol a few months ago, without his parents' knowledge. One day his parents found out, and summoned him for questioning. How had he obtained the drinks? Was he not aware of the damage that alcohol could do to his health? Robert retorted that while he understood his parents' concerns, his drinking wasn't such a 'big deal'; after all there were worse things he could be doing, such as using drugs or having unsafe sex. Robert carried on drinking alcohol.

This scenario was adapted from an episode of a US family comedy, *The Cosby Show*. It highlights yet another ploy that adolescents use to avoid acknowledging a problem and the tough decision it may necessitate. It is consistent with the findings of Patrick Peretti-Watel, a public health professional, who has studied adolescents' use of avoidance strategies, such as denial, to discount risk (Peretti-Watel, 2006).

Peretti-Watel argued that the more often teenagers engage in risky behaviour the greater their proclivity, when challenged, to highlight other scenarios that are worse than theirs. So, for example, adolescents who use cannabis are quick to point out the difference between cannabis and more dangerous drugs. The more cannabis is used, the more this differentiation is emphasised.

To test this idea he asked thousands of adolescents to complete a questionnaire measuring the extent to which they used cannabis and drew a distinction between addictive 'soft' drugs such as cannabis, and more dangerous 'hard' drugs. Using the information provided, he classified participants into those who 'never' used cannabis, 'occasional' users and 'regular' users. The three groups were then compared on their inclination to differentiate between drug types.

Consistent with expectations, those who used cannabis 'regularly' were more likely to discriminate between soft and hard drugs, compared with 'occasional' users, who in turn were more disposed to make such distinctions than the 'never' group. This finding seemed to point to evasiveness, a reluctance to acknowledge one's current behaviour is problematic, by comparing it with a more extreme case. Minimising or ignoring danger in this way allows teenagers to carry on as normal, obviating the need for them to reconsider their position, and perhaps make a new albeit tough decision to resolve the problem.

There is no reason why Peretti-Watel's findings should not generalise to other health behaviours besides drug use.[3] The more problematic a behaviour, the more teenagers try to draw a distinction between the level of danger to which they expose themselves and more dangerous scenarios. Consider the examples in Table 7.2.

These distinctions may work because there are always other situations one can identify which, correctly or incorrectly, are judged to be far more hazardous than a current one, thereby making the status quo seem less problematic than it actually is. Such arguments – which essentially equate to splitting hairs – of course completely ignore the fact that any exposure to danger can prove disastrous. Smoking cigarettes, eating high-fat foods and having unprotected sex can all have devastating health consequences, regardless of the number of cigarettes smoked, how many packets of crisps are consumed or how irregularly condoms

Table 7.2 *Health problems and worst case scenarios that may be used to justify inaction*

Problem or threat	Worst case scenario
Signs of an eating disorder	Emphasising the difference between oneself and more severe cases involving hospitalisation
Irregular condom use	Alluding to peers who never use any form of contraception, and hence are supposedly much worse off
Occasional smoking	Drawing a distinction between occasionally smoking the odd cigarette and 'heavy' or 'regular' smoking, in which whole packs of cigarettes are consumed daily

---

[3] Of course, this statement isn't particularly scientific. The only way to demonstrate the applicability of Peretti-Watel's ideas to other health topics is to test his ideas empirically. Short of that, any claims about generalisability are sheer speculation.

are used. Indeed exposure to *any* level of risk could be considered bad decision making, especially if there are less dangerous alternatives! Nevertheless, for a teenager, drawing such distinctions helps alleviate anxiety. That may be all that matters to the individual.

Prevalence of avoidance

In the mid 1990s Isaac Friedman, a psychologist from the Henrietta Institute in Jerusalem, decided to investigate the preferred decision making styles of adolescents. Friedman conceptualised decision making as essentially a two-stage process. The first stage involves deliberation (e.g. understanding the problem, surveying and weighing options), while the second stage entails resolution (making a choice and implementing it).

He conducted a comprehensive study during which over 600 teenagers completed a battery of questionnaires designed to measure how they typically tackle a variety of real-life problems, including personal and social issues. In particular, participants were required to indicate the extent to which various decision making practices were used, for example weighing options, looking for different solutions, and reversing a decision once it has been made.

From the data collected, Friedman identified a handful of fundamental dimensions. One of these domains was decidedly about avoidance, which Friedman regarded as being deficient in both deliberation and resolution. Curiously, questionnaire responses indicated that the majority of participants rarely used avoidance, but were more likely to vacillate, jump to conclusions or try to make an informed choice.

What can we infer from these findings? Is avoidance indeed a rare strategy amongst teenagers? Well, most studies involving the DMQ (Mann, 1982), an instrument that also measures decision making styles, seem to paint a different picture. Avoidance consistently emerges as a distinct decision strategy, accounting for substantial proportions of the variance in the data (e.g. Mann *et al.*, 1997; Umeh, 1998a, 1998b; Tuinstra *et al.*, 2000). However, I have found that the level of use is indeed significantly lower than that of other decision making strategies, such as careful deliberation and resolution (Umeh, 1998b) (see Fig. 7.2).

Overall, the preponderance of evidence suggests that avoidance in adolescence is anything but rare. Perhaps Friedman's (1996) data were somewhat skewed by a social desirability bias, whereby respondents wished to create a favourable impression of themselves.

Arguably, one particularly good source of evidence that may help resolve this issue is qualitative research. Data from workshops or interviews with focus groups are unencumbered by some of the artificiality of quantitative studies. Avoidance emerged as a recurring theme in Friedman's (1996) own workshops. However, the problem with the studies considered so far, including Friedman's (1996) work, is that they all assess decision making in a generic way. Teenagers are asked to

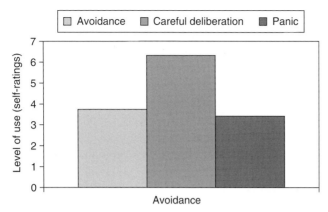

7.2 *Prevalence of avoidance. Secondary analysis of some of my data suggests that avoidance is less popular than competent decision making (Source: Umeh, 1998b).*

indicate how they make decisions in general, or with particular reference to unspecified personal or social problems.

Qualitative research on adolescent decision making in relation to a specific health issue paints a very interesting picture. A comprehensive qualitative study by Michels *et al.* (2005) on how adolescents make sexual decisions revealed no evidence of avoidance. Data from one-on-one interviews, conducted over several months, and then analysed using grounded theory methodology,[4] revealed several themes that pointed more to competent problem solving than evasiveness. Confronting risks and benefits emerged as a distinct theme, with active contemplation of the pregnancy and STD threat. At the very least, this study suggests that avoidance may indeed be very rare when adolescents are faced with consequential health behaviour decisions for which there is much at stake.

Psychological antecedents

What psychological preconditions predisposed teenagers to use avoidance? There is a school of thought that suggests people are more likely to avoid tough decisions if they think the situation is all but impossible to resolve (Janis and Mann, 1977; Rippetoe and Rogers, 1987; Mulilis and Duval, 2003).

A girl struggling to overcome an eating disorder may be at a loss how to address this problem. She is damned if she starts eating normally (she'll gain weight, and rapidly, with unbearable consequences for her self-image and the ways others view her appearance), and damned if she continues to starve herself (she will become very ill, and possibly die).

---

[4] Grounded theory is a form of thematic analysis (identifying themes) but with emphasis on developing a theory that explains the observed themes.

Health related decisions in particular are notorious for being difficult. Most activities which teenagers find pleasurable, such as smoking, drug use, unprotected sex and eating junk food, entail significant health risks, and so opting to perform these behaviours potentially creates a conflict of interest. Some adolescents may feel rather helpless, in the knowledge that they are bound to experience some pain or discomfort no matter what option they choose, and there is no way out of the situation. Feeling pessimistic, their only recourse may be to avoid a decision, or resort to some other defensive measures (e.g. passing responsibility for the decision to someone else, burying one's head in the sand, putting off the decision for the time being).

The psychological antecedents of avoidance are elaborated by at least two comparable theoretical perspectives in social psychology, the conflict-theory model (Janis and Mann, 1977) and the person-relative-to-event theory (Mulilis and Duval, 2003). Neither framework has been applied extensively to adolescent health behaviour, so their applicability in this domain is open to debate. Each perspective is considered next.

The conflict-theory position

According to advocates of this framework (Janis and Mann, 1976, 1977; Janis, 1986), problems arise when people face a difficult choice between equally attractive or unattractive options, but aren't hopeful that they can find a suitable solution to their predicament. Bewildered, they become very anxious and start looking for ways to reduce this anxiety. Thus, avoidance is triggered.

In Chapter 4 I considered evidence showing that providing adolescents with reassurances about the effectiveness and viability of health recommendations increases the likelihood that they will decide to comply, by modifying their lifestyles accordingly (e.g. Fruin et al., 1992; Sturges and Rogers, 1996; Kaljee et al., 2005; Simons-Morton et al., 2006). While the scientific evidence is far from conclusive, it does seem to support Janis and Mann's position that if people are hopeful a solution can be found they are more likely to tackle the problem rather than avoid it.

Consider the problem of teenage smoking. Many teenage smokers will attest that thinking about and trying to quit smoking can be very stressful (Amos et al., 2006). A smoker may find that she is just as keen to continue smoking cigarettes as she is to quit. Both alternatives are equally matched in the various advantages they offer (e.g. smoking looks cool, not smoking is healthy) and risks they entail (e.g. smoking is dangerous, not smoking could lead to weight gain). Furthermore, she may be sceptical that there is a realistic solution to this dilemma.

Compromises such as cutting down gradually on the number of cigarettes smoked, or switching to nicotine patches, may seem too impractical, unfamiliar or even expensive (e.g. it may be difficult to monitor the number of cigarettes smoked daily, and hence accurately gauge attempts to cut down). With no way out of this increasingly stressful quandary, the individual will be tempted to put off the

decision ('I will try quitting next month'), pass responsibility for making a decision to someone else ('it is up to my doctor/parents to help me quit'), or try to justify his current behaviour, so that it no longer seems so bad ('I don't know anyone who ever died from smoking, so what's the big deal?'). These measures, according to conflict-theory, all help to alleviate stress, at least temporarily. This in turn allows people to continue their risky behaviour unperturbed.

The person-relative-to-event perspective

Professors Mulilis and Duval developed an alternative school of thought that also offers some insight into the psychological origins of avoidance (Mulilis *et al.*, 2000; Mulilis and Duval, 2003). Their take on events is rather different because it is based on an analysis of how people respond to natural disasters, such as earthquakes and tornadoes, rather than more mundane threats, such as the risk of illness.

They contend that when people are faced with a problem they will respond inappropriately if sceptical about their abilities to cope with the crisis. The more convinced a person is that he lacks the wherewithal to manage a problem effectively the more likely he is to resort to avoidance, and similarly questionable strategies.

The feeling that one can't cope can emerge in two ways. One is that the magnitude of the problem is so great that it simply eclipses any resources an individual can bring to bear to solve it. The other reason is that the resources themselves are simply too deficient to be of any use in dealing with the crisis. Either way, the result is that the individual tries to avoid the issue altogether, focusing instead on reducing his anxiety by whatever means available.

For example, a teenage girl aware of the risk of pregnancy is nevertheless unlikely to use contraception if she doesn't think she is in a position to use protection. She may feel too embarrassed to buy condoms (e.g. Meekers and Klein, 2002), or unable to raise the issue of contraceptive use with her partner, for fear of implying mistrust (Zwane *et al.*, 2004). Or she may lack the necessary will power or negotiation skills (Smekal, 1975).

The net effect of these hindrances is that the girl feels incapable of doing what is necessary to reduce the risk of pregnancy. Consequently, she may become even more stressed, and hence motivated to reduce anxiety. The girl may put off using contraception until a later date, or simply refuse to think about the danger. These strategies will provide some emotional relief, making an immediate decision seem less urgent.

Mulilis and Duval (2003) further argue that people are likely to react inappropriately to a threat if they do not feel personally responsible for dealing with the problem. Now this is a crucial point, for both legal and economic reasons. From a legal perspective, younger adolescents (usually those below the age of 18) in most Western countries, including the United States and Great Britain, are considered 'minors' and so it is parents that are usually held responsible for their actions (Brank, 2002; Brank and Weisz, 2004; White *et al.*, 2007). Most teenagers are

Box 7.1 Contextual issues: do family circumstances negate avoidance?

Adolescents born into families of high socio-economic status may have access to resources that encourage competent decision making. They may have more material or financial options to choose from, and access to professional expertise that can help resolve difficult dilemmas. For example, a smoker considering quitting may be able to meet the financial costs of joining a local smoking cessation programme, and have a reliable means of transporting herself to sessions. These resources would make quitting smoking a viable option. Similarly, teenagers who have cordial relationships with their parents may be more willing to discuss difficult decisions with them, gaining valuable advice in the process. They may also participate more in family decisions, and hence improve their decision making skills. In short, a favourable family environment should discourage defective decision making practices, such as avoidance. Psychologists J. E. Brown and L. Mann conducted a study that seems to support this view (Brown and Mann, 1990). High school students from Adelaide, Australia, completed questionnaires measuring various family variables and their decision making preferences. Adolescents were less disposed to defective decision making strategies if they came from higher-income homes and loving families, and communicated well with their parents.

probably aware of this arrangement from a very early age, and hence are prone to exploit it when presented with difficult dilemmas they'd rather not face.

Adults unwittingly may also help perpetuate a sense of diminished responsibility in adolescents. Imagine a high school student caught smoking in class. The school authorities may well reprimand him for his bad behaviour. However, the same authorities may also attribute some responsibility to the parents, and wish to notify and/or speak to them about their child's antics (Johnson et al., 2000). Similarly, adolescents who fall sick and require medical treatment, such as surgery, may be informed by their doctor that they have to give written consent, in conjunction with their parents, before treatment can begin. With a reduced sense of personal responsibility many young people may be all too willing to ignore tough health behaviour decisions, leaving others to find a solution while they continue their risky activities.

Cigarette smoking – a case in point

Studies suggest many teenage smokers would like to quit smoking at some point in the future, but never quite manage to commit to and implement this course of action (Scheffels and Erik Lund, 2005; Amos et al., 2006). Others find it easier to place the responsibility for their habit on others, for example their peers ('I smoke because my friends do/make me'), or even wider society (Gittelsohn et al., 2001).

These findings suggest that the reason why adolescents may delay giving up smoking is the perceived hassle of making and implementing this decision. This perception of difficulty can be interpreted both as pessimism about finding a

viable solution, as suggested by Janis and Mann (1977), and a perception of resource inadequacy, as proposed by Mulilis and Duval (2003). Both versions overlap a great deal. However, some recent evidence suggests that teenagers don't view decisions involving risk as particularly difficult (Gambara and Gonzalez, 2005), indicating that any avoidance isn't necessarily triggered by pessimism about finding a resolution. Perhaps the use of avoidance may have deep-rooted origins dating back to learning during early childhood. This point is discussed in the following section.

Avoidance as a childish tactic

Behavioural scientists John Porcerelli, Suzanne Thomas, Stephen Hibbard and Rosemary Cogan carried out a study in the late 1990s (Porcerelli et al., 1998) which tested an interesting idea. They had become intrigued by psychological literature, inspired by the likes of the legendary Sigmund Freud and his disciples, which suggested that younger children become drawn to avoidant strategies, such as denial, because they are simple, easy and effortless. The rationality supposedly used by adults when resolving difficult decisions is simply too complex and intellectually demanding, and hence virtually incomprehensible, impractical and useless to a child. Thus, by the time children are entering their early teens avoidance has become an entrenched and established way of dealing with issues.

Porcerelli and his colleagues decided to test this thesis. They recruited children and adolescents representing several different age groups, ranging from 7 year olds to people in their late teens. All participants were required to respond to pictures depicting various scenes (e.g. a woman staring, feeding, rivalry between siblings). The task was for each subject to tell a story based on each picture. In doing so, it was expected that participants would impose their own thoughts, feelings and preferences, hence revealing any avoidance tendencies. A team of well-trained doctoral students presented the pictures following a standard protocol. The stories were recorded on tape and later studied by the researchers.

Of particular interest was any specific evidence of avoidance,[5] including failing to notice things which nearly all other subjects acknowledged, distorting information in the picture (e.g. perceiving a decidedly female character as male, or both genders), regarding negative events in a positive way, for example interpreting 'fear' as 'courage', refusing to acknowledge things or actions that may cause pain, displeasure or humiliation (e.g. death, injury), denying a fact or feeling (e.g. 'I don't know what that is'), claiming not to understand the meaning of information (e.g. 'What is it? I don't understand the picture'), and failing to recognise the reality of a situation (e.g. 'It didn't really happen', 'It was just a dream').

---

[5] Porcerelli and colleagues actually use the term 'denial' rather than 'evasion'. However, the two terms are synonymous, so I have decided to use the latter for clarity and consistency.

As expected, results showed that the youngest group displayed the strongest propensity for avoidance. This tendency was significantly lower amongst older subjects. Nevertheless, there was a noticeable rise in avoidance as age increased, albeit participants in their late teens showed the lowest levels of evasion. Overall, these findings confirm the idea that people are most likely to display avoidant tendencies in childhood and perhaps early adolescence, but become significantly less evasive by their late teens.

Porcerelli and colleagues suggested that any increase in avoidance with age perhaps reflects anxieties and uncertainties associated with the transition into adulthood and its associated responsibilities (e.g. going to college, finding work, moving out of their parents' home, etc.). An inescapable implication of these findings is that children and younger teens will be the ones most likely to run away from making difficult health behaviour decisions. For them, this would seem to be a simple and effective way of dealing with daily stresses.

Does avoidance impair competence?

According to theorists, avoidance is incompatible with proficient decision making (e.g. Janis and Mann, 1977). Indeed studies have routinely shown a negative relationship between avoidance and competence (e.g. Friedman and Mann, 1993).

By avoiding difficult decisions adolescents also escape having to go through the trouble of surveying options and weighing risks and benefits. Thus, a smoker doesn't have to think about the health hazards of smoking, and a junk food addict doesn't have to confront the risk of obesity. The same argument could apply to any other unhealthy behaviour – unprotected sexual intercourse, physical inactivity, excessive consumption of dietary fat, and so on. Since people who dodge making difficult decisions are preoccupied with avoiding stress, competent decision making will be way down their list of priorities.

Remember that by avoiding a tough decision a person is effectively making a decision to carry on as normal, to maintain the status quo. Clearly, such a decision is not based on sound reasoning, even though the individual may be in full possession of the facts necessary to make an informed choice.

According to Friedman (1996), avoidance entails low levels of mental deliberation (surveying and weighing options) and resolution (making a choice and implementing it). Other theorists have offered similar views (e.g. Janis and Mann, 1976, 1977; Janis, 1986). All in all, avoidance seemingly means ill-considered decision making.

But is there any evidence for this view? Are adolescents who are prone to avoidance less likely to weigh relevant information, such as perceived costs and benefits, when reaching health behaviour decisions? I examined this issue as part of my postgraduate work (Umeh, 1998a, 1998b). More details of this study are described in Box 7.2. In general, the results showed that avoidance had no bearing on the level of informed decision making. The extent to which decisions reflected risk–benefit deliberations was the same in high- and low-avoidance youths.

Box 7.2 Research spotlight: does avoidance hamper competence?

Umeh, K. (1998a) Coping styles as moderators of cognition–decision relations amongst adolescents. *Psychology and Health*, 13, pp. 987–1003.

Avoidance generally implies unwillingness to face worrying threats, and hence is incompatible with competent decision making, which entails confronting issues head-on, and making informed decisions, based on risk–benefit evaluations.

To test the influence of avoidance on competence, teenagers were asked to indicate the extent to which they identified with statements consistent with avoiding decisions. For example, 'I avoid making decisions', 'I put off making decisions', 'I'd rather let someone else make a decision for me so that it won't be my problem', and 'I prefer to leave decisions to others.' They also indicated their views about various health risks and benefits (e.g. the seriousness/probability of illness, such as heart disease, stroke and cancer, and the benefits of adopting preventive behaviours, such as exercising regularly, avoiding fatty foods and not smoking cigarettes). For a competent decision maker these cognitive assessments should form the basis for making a considered decision.

Since avoidance by definition denotes unwillingness to face disturbing thoughts, I expected that risk–benefit appraisals would poorly predict decisions in individuals prone to avoidance. After all, what is the point of considering potential consequences if you aren't going to make a decision?

Curiously, analysis of the data revealed no support for this view. Being avoidant did not seem to affect let alone impair competent decision making. 'High-avoidance' subjects seemed no more or less likely than their 'low-avoidance' counterparts to base decisions on cost–benefit evaluations. For example, irrespective of avoidance levels, participants tended to make healthier decisions (e.g. they reported lower intentions to smoke cigarettes, consume alcohol and eat fatty foods, and a stronger desire to use protection during sexual intercourse) if they believed that such choices would be beneficial to their health. Similarly, regardless of avoidance, decisions reflected perceptions of risk, for example the likelihood of contracting heart disease and cancer, and the seriousness of these illnesses.

All in all, these findings suggest that avoidance doesn't necessarily prevent teenagers from considering potentially disturbing outcomes and making decisions seemingly based on these evaluations.

So, how can this be so? How is it that teenagers who habitually shy away from tough choices are no less inclined to consider potential consequences in reaching decisions? There are several possible explanations.

One obvious explanation is that there is nothing particularly stressful about decisions concerning health behaviour, and hence little or no reason to shy away from making them. Another plausible explanation has to do with the way

avoidance was assessed. Participants indicated how they respond to decisions in general, without reference to a specific problem, threat or scenario. Janis (1986) notes that such generalised measures reflect personality traits that are so broad in scope they influence most decisions a person makes, whether they involve health or otherwise. However, he also acknowledges that such generic indicators may not account for situational variations in decision making.

Nevertheless, generalised measures of avoidance, and other decision strategies, form the basis for instruments such as the DMQ (Mann, 1982; Mann *et al.*, 1997, 1998; Tuinstra *et al.*, 2000), underscoring the importance theorists attached to a trait perspective on decision making. This issue continues to be a topic of debate (e.g. Janis, 1986; Leventhal *et al.*, 1993; Umeh, 2002).

Behavioural consequences of avoidance

Before writing this section I spent some time on the Internet reading the medical case history of a teenage girl who appeared to have undergone a psychological ordeal, culminating in her being admitted to hospital during the winter of 2000. She had deliberately been cutting herself, presumably in an attempt to relieve mental distress or punish herself. The girl had become aware, as early as the 5th grade, that all was not well. However, it wasn't until her freshman year in high school that she presented for treatment and was formally diagnosed with depression.

One thing that is striking about this story is the long delay from the moment the initial symptoms of depression appeared before a problem was acknowledged and treatment solicited. This suggests a certain degree of avoidance – she was unwilling (or unable) to acknowledge that she had a mental problem, and make the necessary decision to address it (e.g. seek treatment). Perhaps what's even more striking, and worrying, are the consequences of this delay in dealing with the crisis. By the time she finally made the decision to seek treatment, and was admitted to hospital, her condition had become sufficiently pathological to result in self-inflicted physical injury.

Teenagers who habitually postpone making tough choices are effectively flirting with danger, as whatever health problems they face remain unsolved, and possibly get progressively worse, perhaps to the point where life is at stake. From a purely decision making perspective, any unnecessary delay in making a choice amounts to incompetent decision making (Janis and Mann, 1976, 1977; Janis, 1983, 1986). The risk to personal well-being is considerable for two reasons.

First, the status quo is maintained, a position that is effectively ill considered and risky. Nothing is done to protect one's health. For example, adolescents who display high levels of avoidance are less physically active than less elusive youngsters, increasing their susceptibility to cardiovascular disease, obesity and other related health problems (Umeh, 1998a, 1998b). Other studies have found a similar association between avoidance strategies and unhealthy choices in teenagers (e.g. Abraham *et al.*, 1994).

Second, ignoring the threat of illness is one thing, but denying actual physical symptoms that require urgent medical attention is another. It is very worrying to think that adolescents facing critical medical emergencies may delay making vital decisions, such as notifying their parents or the school nurse, or booking a doctor's appointment. Any delay in seeking treatment could be catastrophic.

Yet, there is evidence suggesting that young people are prepared to postpone vital decisions in these particularly critical situations. Several physicians, led by Sofia Feinstein and Rami Keich, carried out a study to investigate a problem of non-compliance amongst teenage patients who urgently require kidney transplants (Feinstein et al., 2005). The doctors were concerned, arguing that organ transplants sometimes fail because adolescent patients often choose to stop taking immunosuppressive medications, depart from the recommended dose or frequency, or completely fail to take the medication for long periods of time. This in turn engenders severe deterioration in health, possibly even leading to premature death.

The physicians reviewed the medical records of seventy-nine patients and conducted interviews with each to try to ascertain the psychological reasons for non-compliance. They found evidence of excessive denial of their grave situation in at least 50 per cent of patients who failed to take their medication.

Clearly avoidance seems to facilitate risky behaviour, even if it doesn't significantly hamper cognitive deliberations. The key problem appears to be the delay caused by avoidance, resulting in continued risk taking. By the time an individual is ready to decide, it may be too late.

Susceptible health behaviours

It appears some health behaviours are more likely than others to encourage avoidance. I found empirical evidence for this, whereby only choices concerning physical activity were associated with avoidance (Umeh, 1998a, 1998b). Decisions regarding cigarette smoking, drug use, alcohol consumption, dietary fat intake and contraceptive use were not affected.

The risks associated with certain behaviours are ambiguous and hence more easily ignored and dismissed. And physical inactivity is a prime example. Whereas most teenagers recognise that unprotected sexual intercourse can lead to AIDS and unplanned pregnancy, that smoking can cause lung cancer, and that poor dietary habits can lead to weight gain, obesity and eating disorders like anorexia, the dangers of not exercising regularly may seem less obvious.

Furthermore, there is the issue of effort. Regular exercise involves initiating and maintaining rigorous physical routines, and hence requires sustained energy reserves, concentration, will power and an ability to deal with extreme fatigue. A study by Allison et al. (2005), based on a qualitative design, seemed to illustrate this problem succinctly. They found that the physical demand of regular exercise is a major reason why some adolescents remain physically inactive. It seems much

easier to reverse a behaviour that one has already initiated (e.g. quitting smoking), and which isn't unduly physically strenuous, than to commence an activity from scratch that entails considerable vigour.

Thus, decisions to exercise may be particularly difficult to accomplish (perhaps even more so than avoiding addictive behaviours like smoking), especially given that remaining physically inactive involves no effort at all, and can be extremely pleasurable, allowing one to relax and indulge in favoured pastimes (e.g. playing video games, chatting on the phone, watching TV). With such disincentives, it may be very tempting simply to postpone any plans to participate in sports or join the local gym.

Passing the buck

One of the biggest problems in trying to understand avoidance in adolescents is that they aren't the sole decision maker. Parents in particular are required to make many health related decisions on behalf of their teenage children, whether by choice, legal mandate or circumstance. The continual availability of someone else who can take responsibility for difficult decisions may encourage teenagers to 'pass the buck' (Janis and Mann, 1976, 1977), including youngsters who are ordinarily happy to shoulder responsibility.

This is precisely what the evidence suggests. In an analysis of the factor structure of the DMQ, Tuinstra *et al.* (2000) found a dimension consistent with shifting responsibility, with items such as 'I'd rather let someone else make a decision for me so that it won't be my problem', and 'When faced with a decision I go along with what others suggest.' My own analysis of the DMQ also generated an avoidance theme incorporating at least one item depicting buck-passing (Umeh, 1998a, 1998b). Clearly, many adolescents may find it particularly comforting to let someone else take responsibility and make their health behaviour decisions, rather than have to grapple with things themselves (Moore and Cartwright, 2005). If something goes wrong the fiasco can always be blamed on someone else.

Parental input

Other than decisions about advanced medical treatment (e.g. surgery), which parents are legally obliged to be involved in, there are certain mundane decisions that are usually made by parents, with or without their child's consent. Perhaps the best example is food choice. Most teenagers, particularly the younger ones, have little choice but to eat whatever food they are served at home, healthy or otherwise (Feunekes *et al.*, 1998; Kremers *et al.*, 2003; Kelly *et al.*, 2006).

Imagine a teenage girl who eschews difficult decisions. Also, imagine that this individual is overweight and has been advised to switch from eating high-fat junk foods to a diet high in fruit and vegetables. However, consider this. Since she lives at home with her parents, in reality it is the parents not the girl who decide what the

family eats for breakfast, lunch and dinner. The parents also decide what food items to purchase from the local supermarket. Of course the girl may be able to goad her parents into buying particular foods, but research suggests that such pestering generally has a limited effect on parental food choice (Kelly *et al.*, 2006). So, when this girl sits down for a meal, it is someone else who has decided what she is served, and subsequently eats.

An adolescent in this situation cannot be accused of buck-passing. The buck was never theirs to pass in the first place. However, this situation is rather more convoluted than it sounds.

For starters, the influence parents have on the dietary habits of their children partly depends on their parenting style. Parents with an authoritarian or indulgent parenting style seem to exert more influence on adolescents' food choice than parents who are neglecting (e.g. Kremers *et al.*, 2003). Nevertheless, even with very coercive parents, it can be argued that teenagers still retain some freedom of choice. For example, a schoolboy can use his pocket money to buy whatever snacks he wants during break time at school, even if mum and dad decide the content of regular meals at home. Avoidance could negate such acts of personal responsibility, with significant health implications.

Is buck-passing really avoidance?

Social psychologists view shifting responsibility as unmistakable evidence of avoidance (Janis and Mann, 1977). The reasoning is that by looking for ways to pass the buck, a much-needed decision that may reduce personal risk (e.g. quitting smoking, using condoms) is effectively avoided. Consequently, the person remains at risk, assuming the party to whom responsibility has been passed fails to take appropriate remedial action. For example, a teenager may fail to use condoms simply because she deferred responsibility for this task to her partner, but he failed to deliver.

Some empirical evidence supports the notion that buck-passing delays vital decisions. Sheri Lynn Turrell found that adolescents who were generally less keen to take responsibility in decision making were more likely to be hospitalised for an eating disorder (Turrell, 2005). One interpretation of this finding is that a reluctance to take charge meant that early symptoms of the eating disorder were probably ignored until things got so bad hospitalisation was inevitable.

A recent review of some relevant literature on asthma management revealed that adolescents are generally reluctant to assume responsibility for serious treatment decisions, such as undergoing surgery (Shaw, 2001). They seem to view assuming responsibility as a burden (Hanna and Guthrie, 2000). However, such reluctance may not always lead to negative outcomes. Children and teenagers often lack the knowledge and understanding that will enable them to make correct treatment decisions. Thus it makes a lot of sense for them to leave such matters to those 'in the know' – parents and doctors. In this context, relinquishing responsibility may in fact be a good thing. It can't really be regarded as evasiveness, since

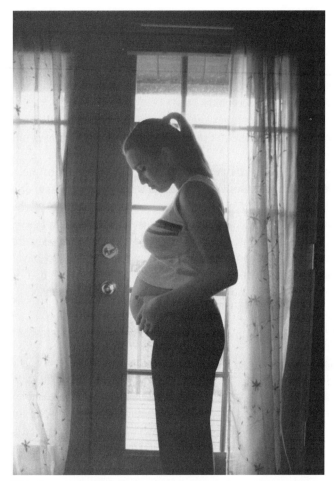

7.3 *Procrastination. Decisions concerning issues like an unplanned pregnancy are difficult to put off for very long. Physical evidence of the crisis quickly becomes too obvious to avoid (Source: SXC).*

the problem isn't being avoided per se, but rather is being passed on to someone else who is better qualified to tackle it.

Age and gender differences

Evidence on age and gender differences in avoidance is inconclusive. Take gender. Tuinstra *et al.* (2000) found that males obtained higher avoidance scores than females. However, Gosselin *et al.* (2007) observed the reverse – females were more disposed to cognitive avoidance than males. Yet again, Kowalski *et al.* (2006) found no significant gender difference, albeit boys showed a stronger preference for avoidance than girls. My own research has also revealed no significant gender differences in avoidance, as demonstrated in Figure 7.4 (Umeh, 1998b).

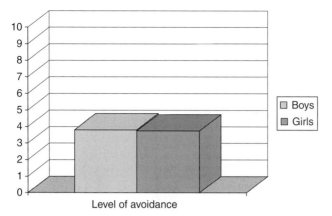

Figure 7.4 *Gender differences. Girls and boys seem equally prone to avoid difficult decisions, in a general sense (Source: Umeh, 1998b).*

So, what may account for these inconsistencies? Contextual issues probably play a key role. The likelihood that teenagers will use avoidance in decision making depends in part on the types of threat they face. Since boys and girls often encounter different kinds of stressors, health or otherwise, any gender differences in avoidance are likely to depend on the situation. For example, the risk of pregnancy is a more frightening issue for girls than for boys, and hence may elicit higher levels of avoidance in the former (Sowell *et al.*, 2002). By contrast, a more neutral subject, such as the threat of chronic illness, may generate no significant gender difference (Hampel *et al.*, 2005).

Even when both genders are confronted with the same problem, there may be gender differences depending on the particular form of avoidance in question. For example, Kowalski *et al.* (2006) found that, whereas girls were slightly more prone to employ cognitive avoidance to deal with anxieties concerning their physical appearance (20 per cent versus 18.7 per cent), there was a more pronounced gender difference in the use of behavioural avoidance – deliberate efforts physically to keep away from a stressor – to deal with the same problem (41.5 per cent versus 33.2 per cent).

Age differences in avoidance seem more reliable. I have already discussed the research by John Porcerelli and colleagues (Porcerelli *et al.*, 1998), suggesting that avoidance is much more prevalent during childhood and the early teens, compared with the late teens. Gosselin *et al.* (2007) also found what appeared to be a trend in the same direction – adolescents in junior grades at high school scored slightly higher on cognitive avoidance compared with those in senior grades.[6] I have also found a significant drop in levels of avoidance with increasing age (Umeh, 1998b).

Perhaps Porcerelli *et al.* (1998) offer the best explanation for any reduction in avoidance with growing maturity. Avoidance is learned and reinforced very early on in life because it is an easy and effortless strategy for dealing with difficult problems (e.g. delaying doing homework). It becomes a very costly measure as

---

[6] No test of significance is reported.

children become adolescents, and then adults, and take more responsibility for their health.

Ultimately however, like gender, any age differentials in evasiveness may depend in part on contextual factors, such as the type of avoidance. A recent study by Hampel (2007) showed that whereas middle adolescents scored significantly lower than late children on distraction, they scored significantly higher on passive avoidance, a form of evasiveness characterised by a sense of helplessness, resignation, and a propensity to capitulate so as to avoid difficult situations or decisions. A similar pattern in the use of avoidance strategies emerged for adolescents in their early teens, when compared with late children. It can be argued that the increased stress associated with the developmental problems of puberty can predispose middle adolescents to rely more on avoidance strategies, albeit selectively so.

Does avoidance really work?

Julie, a bubbly 15 year old, began to experience a very unusual numbing pain in the lower right-hand side of her abdomen. She did everything possible to distract herself – spending hours on the phone, trying to read, watching as much TV as possible, and even investing in an expensive video game. However, over subsequent days and weeks the pain got progressively worse. One morning Julie woke up in absolute agony. The discomfort was unbearable. Her attempts to disregard the excruciating pain were completely futile. She notified her parents, who promptly rushed her to hospital. A thorough medical examination revealed appendicitis.

So far in this chapter I have made an implicit assumption that avoidance works. That is, it effectively protects teenagers against the emotional discomfort (i.e. stress, anxiety, sadness, anger, etc.) caused by difficult decisions. However, there is no reason why this should necessarily be so – adolescents may find themselves still troubled despite their best attempts to deny or ignore a problem.

Not every decision can be avoided or dismissed. Some health risks have been so heavily publicised that they are firmly imprinted in the consciousness of most teenagers. A good example is AIDS, which ranks at the top of the list of adolescents' fears (Muris and Ollendick, 2002). Other threats can become so glaring, typified by blatantly obvious physical evidence (e.g. a developing pregnancy), that any attempts to ignore the problem and subsequent decision making are ineffective.

There may be another equally viable reason for the inefficacy of avoidance. Sometimes a health problem may simply be too prominent to be denied, ignored or dismissed. This is more often the case when adolescents experience actual physical symptoms of disease or illness, rather than just the threat of poor health. It is extremely difficult if not impossible to ignore the ache in a sprained ankle, an intense headache, diarrhoea, or bleeding caused by physical injury. In such a scenario, avoidance may eventually give way to competent decision making, as the individual is forced to confront the problem.

Box 7.3 Media spotlight: ignoring signs of illness

A well-known British teenager-turned-pop-singer provides a detailed account of her struggle with anorexia in a recent autobiography. Now in her twenties, she recounts how as a teenager she developed the eating disorder while on tour abroad.

She avoided food, and instead filled her stomach with decaffeinated coffee, coke, and even tissue paper! At first avoiding food in this way did not seem out of the ordinary; after all, she was working in an industry where dieting and weight loss were an established social norm. However, as the weeks and months rolled by she became more and more preoccupied with not eating. The girl convinced herself she was in complete control and could easily reverse her dietary habits whenever she wished. To her, it was very important to lose weight and she had never been entirely happy with her physical appearance.

She looked for ways to *justify* her actions. To convince herself that she was doing the right thing by not eating, and overcome severe hunger pangs, she studied photos of extremely skinny women. The girl overdosed on laxatives to empty her digestive system and simply refused to accept that she had a problem. Social situations were avoided that might force her to confront the issue. The girl also avoided viewing herself in the mirror, perhaps because her emaciated appearance might be too much to bear, forcing her to acknowledge she had a problem. She starved herself for many months. Eventually her periods stopped and she developed bladder and kidney infections. Finally she collapsed from exhaustion in a bar and had to be rushed to hospital.

Even after accepting she had a serious problem, this individual still felt compelled to minimise its seriousness, insisting that everything was well in hand. Avoiding signs of an eating disorder may occur in different ways: refusing to look at oneself in the mirror, insisting one is in control, minimising the severity of eating disorders, and so on. Like adults, adolescents often avoid facing facts that are too painful, disturbing or frightening. Accepting that one has an eating disorder can be extremely distressing. It would generate a whole repertoire of painful emotions, including anxiety, shame, guilt and disappointment. It would also require difficult decisions about whether, where, when and how to seek treatment.

I first became interested in the potency of avoidance after conducting an experiment about condom use with college students, mostly young adults in their 20s and early 30s (Umeh, 2004). This study showed that denying the threat of HIV failed to dissuade participants from using condoms if they were very frightened about the danger. It was almost as if denial provided little or no comfort to subjects for whom HIV was extremely salient and worrisome.

I never actually considered that this phenomenon might apply to adolescents. After all, this is a group of people for whom health threats often seem rather remote and intangible. Ignoring difficult health decisions should be easy.

However, evidence has shown that adolescents do harbour intense fears about health issues, particularly AIDS (Ollendick *et al.*, 1989; Muris and Ollendick, 2002), which makes one doubt that avoidance would be of any value, given the intensity of emotion.

A classic study conducted by psycho-pathologist Jennifer Silk and psychologists Laurence Steinberg and Amanda Morris shed some much needed light on this issue (Silk *et al.*, 2003). They arranged for adolescents from two US public schools to make a record of their current thoughts and feelings at regular intervals, each day, for a whole week! More specifically, participants had to record how mad, sad and nervous they felt. Subjects also indicated how they reacted to each of these emotions, using a checklist of strategies that included avoidance reactions such as denial, avoidance, wishful thinking, escape and inaction. The experimenters found that each time participants used avoidance their levels of anger and sadness remained high. In other words, avoidance didn't work, because subjects continued to feel emotionally perturbed.

Avoidance may also prove ineffective simply because a person is aware the problem still hasn't been solved. For example, a teenage smoker who postpones quitting smoking may continue to feel anxious because he still hasn't done anything to address the threat to his health. He may attempt repeatedly to give up cigarettes because attempts to deny the risks do little to alleviate his concerns. This argument may account, at least in part, for the absence of significant associations between avoidance and health behaviour reported in the literature (e.g. Umeh, 1998a, 1998b; Milne *et al.*, 2000).

Unlike the risks of physical inactivity, which are arguably hazy, hazards associated with unprotected sex (e.g. unplanned pregnancy, HIV), fat intake (e.g. gaining weight, obesity) and cigarette smoking (e.g. lung cancer) may be too blatant to avoid. Many adolescents eventually realise this, perhaps at great cost in some cases.

Conclusion

We saw in Chapter 4 that adolescents worry a lot. Thus, for them, avoidance is likely to be a highly appealing way to approach stressful decisions. The problem with avoidance is that it is incompatible with competent decision making: it delays important decisions, perhaps indefinitely, leaving the individual increasingly exposed to significant health risks; it prevents a person from thinking about options and their consequences, and formulating solutions.

The result is that health compromising behaviour goes unchallenged, even though one may be fully aware of the risks. A striking feature of avoidance in adolescents is its elaborate nature. Various avoidance strategies are employed, with varying degrees of sophistication and effectiveness. Shifting responsibility seems an especially tempting tactic, given the ample availability of adult figures to whom liability could be shifted. Parents may be legally required to take responsibility for certain health decisions, such as undergoing life-threatening medical

treatment, making buck-passing almost a default response for your average teen-ager facing a difficult choice.

Yet, avoidance does not necessarily produce the detrimental effect on health behaviour that its definition suggests. It doesn't unavoidably prevent teenagers from acting in accordance with their cost–benefit appraisals, nor does it necessarily predict health damaging behaviour. Nevertheless, avoidance goes some way in explaining the proverbial disconnect between adolescents' knowledge about health threats and their lifestyle choices.

There is some good news. Adolescents seem to rely less and less on avoidance as they get older, indicating that increasing maturity and resources provide an effective cure. However, older children and younger adolescents may find evasiveness an effortless strategy for dealing with everyday decision dilemmas.

Key points

- Avoidance is a recurring theme in adolescent decision making.
- Avoidance is multifaceted, incorporating a range of strategies, from thought suppression and the use of distraction, to shifting responsibility and thinking only happy thoughts.
- Avoidance does not necessarily cause adolescents to make ill-considered decisions. Health behaviours may still be driven by risk–benefit considerations.
- Avoidance can but does not necessarily facilitate health compromising behaviour. Indeed avoidance may show little or no association with lifestyle factors.
- Avoidance may be triggered by uncertainty about how to resolve a decision dilemma. It may also result form early learning experiences in childhood.

Key terms

- Avoidance
- Cognitive avoidance
- Thought suppression
- Distraction
- Threatening stimuli
- Transforming mental images
- Thought substitution
- Shifting responsibility

Further reading

Janis, I.L. and Mann, L. (1977) *Decision Making: A Psychological Analysis of Conflict, Choice, and Commitment.* New York: The Free Press.

Krohne, H.W. (1993) Attention and avoidance. Two central strategies in coping with aversiveness. In H.W. Krohne (ed.) *Attention and Avoidance* (pp. 3–15). Seattle: Hogrefe and Huber.

Umeh, K. (1998b) A conflict-theory approach to understanding adolescents' health behaviour, PhD thesis, University of Leicester.

8   Impulsivity

Learning outcomes

By the end of this chapter readers should have a better understanding of the following:

1 the meaning and nature of impulsive choice in teenagers
2 the different dimensions of impulsivity, such as sensation seeking and thoughtlessness
3 the impact of impulsive decision making on health behaviour
4 the notion of impulsivity as a sensible rather than a questionable strategy
5 the notion of impulsivity as a convenient strategy
6 the link between impulsivity and panic, especially with respect to deadline pressure and emotional arousal
7 the effect of panic on health behaviour.

Chapter summary

This chapter discusses impulsive decision making. Empirical evidence shows adolescents exhibit the characteristic symptoms of impulsivity, notably a sense of urgency, an inability to delay gratification, failure to think before acting, and craving excitement. Since decisions are by definition ill considered, impulsivity does seem to increase the probability of health damaging behaviour. The desire for instant gratification is particularly problematic, from a health promotion perspective. It suggests teenagers may prefer instant social- and image-related gains to long-term health benefits. Not surprisingly, panic-prone individuals may be particularly disposed to impulsive decision making. Panic has been found to be a distinct and recurring feature of adolescent decision making. Like impulsiveness, it tends to result in unhealthy choices, seemingly because decisions are made in a hurry, owing to a sense of impending doom. Overall, understanding impulsivity provides promising insights into adolescent health behaviour.

Chapter outline

This chapter begins with an introduction to the concept of impulsive decision making. This is followed by some discussion of the various dimensions of impulsivity, notably sensation seeking, thoughtlessness, a sense of urgency, and the need for instant gratification. Next, I examine impulsivity as a clever strategy that seems sensible in certain circumstances. The notion of panic and its association with impulsivity is soon considered. I consider the characteristics of panicky decision making, concluding with some discussion of age and gender differences in impulsivity.

Impulsive choice

An obese girl makes a snap decision to go on a diet. A boy unthinkingly accepts an alcoholic drink from a friend. A reckless teenage driver makes a sudden overtaking move without first looking out for oncoming traffic. These are all examples of impulsive decision making.

Impulsivity is generally defined in the psychological literature as a relative preference for smaller, easier and immediate outcomes over larger but delayed alternatives (Logue, 1995; Rachlin, 1995; Mitchell, 1999; Wulfert *et al.*, 2002). Impulsive people seek immediate thrills, gratification, excitement and novelty, and display impatience in the form of an inability to persevere at a task, especially one for which the rewards are long term rather than instant (d'Acremont and van der Linden, 2005).

It would be unthinkable to write a textbook about adolescent decision making without discussing, in some detail, the propensity for impulsive choice. It is generally acknowledged by academics, and society at large, that impulsivity is characteristic of adolescence, often leading to unhealthy choices (Shoda *et al.*, 1990; Krueger *et al.*, 1994; White *et al.*, 1994; Madden *et al.*, 1997; Wulfert *et al.*, 1999, 2002; d'Acremont and van der Linden, 2005).

There is indeed good reason to subscribe to this point of view. Media portrayals of adolescent decision making almost always depict impulsivity or some aspect of it, such as thoughtlessness (e.g. Stepp, 2002). It is rare to watch a movie or TV sitcom, for example, in which an adolescent is seen making a carefully considered decision involving patient and careful evaluation of options. Yet empirical evidence on impulsiveness in adolescence is patchy. Nevertheless, the available literature helps paint a discernible picture of the significance of this form of decision making in young people, and its impact on their health behaviour.

Dimensions of impulsiveness

Although many people think of impulsiveness as one-dimensional, it is in fact a multifaceted construct. Psychologists have identified several key domains,

8.1 *Impulsivity. This form of decision making generally denotes a craving for immediate gratification, whatever the risks, health or otherwise (Source: SXC).*

including a sense of urgency or emergency, lack of prior thought or meditation (i.e. thoughtlessness), an inability to delay gratification (i.e. a short-term mentality), and preference for sensation and excitement. These dimensions are largely derived from the UPPS[1] Impulsive Behaviour Scale developed by Whiteside and Lynam (2001), and incorporating items such as 'I have trouble controlling my impulses', 'I tend to give up easily', 'I'll try anything once', and 'I generally seek new and exciting experiences and sensations.' Respondents indicate the extent to which they endorse each item.

Although the scale was originally developed for adults, studies have shown that its four dimensions of impulsiveness are also applicable to adolescents. For example, a 2004 study by psychologists Mathieu d'Acremont and Martial van der Linden administered the scale to over 600 French teenagers and subjected the data to both confirmatory and exploratory factor analyses (d'Acremont and van der Linden, 2005). As expected, four themes emerged corresponding to the four original impulsivity dimensions. However, girls were more likely to have a sense of urgency, while boys were more prone to seek sensation.

So what effect does impulsiveness have on health behaviour? Are impulsive adolescents more likely to make poor health choices, or does their impetuous nature prove irrelevant when important health decisions are at stake? Before

[1] Urgency, Premeditation (lack of), Perseverance (lack of), and Sensation seeking.

discussing the influence of impulsivity on health behaviour let's delve more deeply into each of the four dimensions specified above.

A sense of urgency

An adolescent is more likely to act impulsively when he or she is in an emergency situation and panic-stricken. According to Janis and Mann (1977) the individual 'makes a quick survey of the situation and a snap judgement about the best thing to do, often being unduly influenced by what the people around him are trying to do' (p. 59).

Deadline pressure, or a sense of impending doom, can generate a considerable amount of fear (Janis and Mann, 1976). When extremely stressed and frantic, people hurriedly latch on to any course of action that promises immediate apparent resolution of the crisis, irrespective of the long-term consequences. Their haste and excitement mean that decisions are unlikely to be properly considered, increasing the possibility of illness, disease or physical injury.

Teenagers may experience a sense of urgency when making decisions about health, for example hastily lighting a cigarette to impress peers, hurriedly trying to decide whether to suggest condom use to a new boy/girlfriend prior to sexual intercourse, or facing a sudden traffic emergency while driving a car, with only seconds to act. Note that the sense of urgency in these examples has more to do with social concerns, and less to do with illness and disease. It is often suggested that the remoteness of many major health risks means that many adolescents simply don't feel susceptible to these theats (Moore and Rosenthal, 1991; van der Pligt, 1994; Whalen et al., 1994; Cohn et al., 1995).

Thus, while the impulsive teenager may be more sensitive to a health warning for example, this seems unlikely to create a sense that there is an emergency, thereby diminishing the need for quick decisions (Janis and Mann, 1976, 1977).

Another point is that few adolescents are totally unaware of the life-threatening potential of major health threats (e.g. Tilleczek and Hine, 2006; Mazanov and Byrne, 2007). This over-familiarity effectively eliminates any sense of urgency or 'shock value' that may otherwise trigger snap decision making. Thus, impulsivity may be a rare occurrence, to the extent that health threats aren't treated as emergencies. It is conceivable that adolescents will be more prone to impulsivity in situations where they face an unfamiliar threat, such as a new sexually trans-mitted disease, or diet-related illness. After all, we know from previous research that young people have a distinct fear of the 'unknown' (e.g. Muris and Ollendick, 2002), and hence may be in a hurry to escape when they encounter an unfamiliar health problem.

Take for example the issue of physical appearance. We know that teenage girls particularly are overly concerned about their weight. A slim girl who has never gained weight before may find herself in uncharted territory if she suddenly gains a few pounds. The shock could easily cause panic, and hasty adoption of any

Box 8.1 Media spotlight: impulsivity in emergency situations

The sense of urgency is understandably a recurring theme in horror movies made for teenage audiences. Readers may be familiar with Hollywood's successful *The Scream* movie trilogy, starring actresses Neve Campbell, Courtney Cox and Drew Barrymore.

In the series, a panic-stricken teenage girl, Sidney Prescott (Neve Campbell), and other teenagers are desperately trying to escape from a mysterious and vicious killer. Throughout each movie the frightened teenagers continually act impulsively, with little or no prior thought, as they frantically try to anticipate the killer's next move and the best means of escape each time the killer attacks. Although clearly unrealistic, the movies do illustrate the link between impulsivity and emergency situations.

measure that promises instantaneous weight loss. By contrast a girl who has lost and gained weight all her life, and therefore is extremely used to this problem, may experience little or no urgency upon discovering she has gained some weight. She is more likely to react with indifference, or follow a carefully thought-out weight-loss plan, based on years of experience.

Lack of prior thought

Impulsiveness implies acting without thinking. In other words, it depicts a failure to consider the available options, and their consequences, before reaching a decision (Whiteside and Lynam, 2001). The individual simply responds to superficial stimuli or cues that facilitate a quick decision. For example, teenagers often make snap decisions to smoke, use drugs or drink alcohol simply because this is what everyone around them seems to be doing (e.g. Wiltshire *et al.*, 2005; Leatherdale *et al.*, 2006), or because they have a craving for fun and excitement.

The idea that people may be persuaded by superficial cues, rather than reasoned argument, is not new. According to Petty and Cacioppo (1986), people will be persuaded by trivial stimuli, such as opportunity, emotion and attraction, especially if they have little interest in and/or are unable to engage in cognitive deliberations. Thus when adolescents are faced with a decision, they have at least two options. They can try to be thoughtful, and carefully evaluate their options, in order to make an informed choice that minimises loss and/or maximises gain. Or they can react impulsively to cosmetic cues, performing very little if any mental deliberation.

One reason teenagers may opt for the latter is the mental hassle of making informed decisions. Petty and Cacioppo (1986) contend that decision makers are more likely to be swayed by superficial cues if they lack interest in weighing relevant information, such as cost–benefit arguments, or find such information difficult to comprehend (see review by Eagly and Chaiken, 1993). For example,

an obese girl is more likely to make a spur-of-the-moment decision to diet, because it seems like a good idea, if she has little interest in carefully evaluating her options, and making a carefully considered decision.

Friedman (1996) presents rare evidence showing that thoughtlessness is indeed a distinct and recurring feature of adolescent decision making. He found that adolescents identified with questionnaire statements denoting thoughtless decision making, for example, 'I make a final judgement without prior extensive investigation or consideration', 'I make a decision without giving much thought to the problem', 'I reach a final decision without having checked, or even searched for very many possible solutions', and 'I make a decision and am ready to change it without seriously checking in depth other solutions to the problem.'

Friedman appropriately referred to this decision making style as 'undeliberated conclusion' (p. 889). Evidence like this shows that impulsivity in teenagers is characterised, at least in part, by a failure to think first before acting. It may also be typified by a desire for quick pleasure, a point elaborated in the following section.

Need for immediate gratification

I invite readers to try observing a group of teenagers socialising. Snap judgements may occur repeatedly as the interaction unfolds (e.g. someone opts to light a cigarette, drive recklessly, buy some alcohol or junk food, etc.). What is curious about these decisions is that they seem to involve immediate rewards. Teenagers are drawn to options that offer quick and instant gain, such as social approval, displaying impatience and indifference to alternatives that promise delayed results, like living longer (e.g. Gardner and Herman, 1990).

The need for immediate gratification can be defined as a preference for small but immediate incentives over larger but long-term gains. In other words, faced with a variety of options, youngsters will prefer the option that offers the most instantaneous, albeit small, benefits over alternatives that promise bigger but delayed advantages (Smith and Stutts, 2003[2]). For example, they will prefer to receive £10 now rather than £20 next week.

Clearly this preference for an immediate buzz creates a problem from a health promotion perspective. When making health related decisions, many adolescents are heavily swayed by a need for immediate gratification. Consider cigarette smoking. Asked why they smoke, many teenagers cite a range of potential benefits from smoking, most of which are short term if not instantaneous (e.g. Siqueira et al., 2006). This view is supported by empirical evidence. Bonnie Halpern-Felsher and several colleagues of the Division of Pediatrics, University of South California, compiled an inventory of the perceived benefits of smoking,

---

[2] This isn't quite as clear-cut as it sounds. Smith and Stutts (2003) found that although the short-term outcomes were more influential than long-term results in relation to cigarette smoking, this was only applicable to boys. The exact opposite effect was observed in girls.

which they found significantly differentiated between adolescent smokers and non-smokers (Halpern-Felsher *et al.*, 2004). These are listed below:

- You will look cool.
- You will be more popular.
- You will look more grown up.
- You will feel relaxed after smoking.
- You will be thinner.

With the exception of the last item, smokers perceived greater benefits compared with non-smokers. Notice that most outcomes will occur immediately, or at least very quickly, once a teenager starts smoking.

To his peers a smoker instantly looks 'cool' and more mature, and within a short time (a matter of minutes, hours or days) he may experience a rise in popularity on campus, for example by being more attractive to the opposite sex. Any increased feeling of relaxation will be instantaneous too. In short, by opting to smoke, your average teenager experiences immediate gratification on a multiplicity of levels.

Now consider the option of not smoking. For many adolescents the benefits are primarily health related (e.g. Turner and Mermelstein, 2004). One can effectively reduce the risk of contracting heart disease, lung cancer, emphysema, and other deadly medical conditions, but this advantage will only materialise much later in life – say middle age – when friends who smoked continuously for decades start to succumb to various medical conditions.

Clearly, the merits of not smoking are substantial; protecting oneself from death is a significant advantage, much more valuable (at least to anyone who values good health) than merely looking cool or grown up. However, health gains are extremely long term, and hence of no significance to an impulsive decision maker keen to reap immediate rewards. Thus, faced with a choice between smoking and not smoking, and given a desire for immediate gratification, it is no surprise that many adolescents opt for the former even though they may readily acknowledge the benefits of abstinence.

Since impulsivity involves a sense of urgency, the decision maker is in a hurry to resolve the situation. Thus, immediate or short-term outcomes get priority over long-term results. Any option that offers instant advantages (e.g. reduced stress, prompt admiration and respect from peers) will be much more attractive than one which promises long-term benefits (e.g. improved health, longer life expectancy).

Whether protecting one's health is perceived as an immediate or long-term benefit may vary from situation to situation, and across individuals. For example, a teenage driver fleeing from a police car, in the middle of the night, probably wants to achieve one thing – avoid getting caught (and hence facing severe reprimands from the police, his parents, and other aggravated adults). Preventing physical injury from a car accident may not be the major priority. Hence, little effort will be made to avoid reckless and dangerous driving antics that could cause an accident! By

contrast, a smoker alarmed by the death of a relative who contracted severe lung cancer, after a lifetime of cigarette smoking, may view cancer as a salient threat (Tversky and Kahneman, 1974), and consequently make a snap decision to quit.

Seeking sensation

Imagine an excitable youth who loves physically stimulating and dangerous activities, such as skiing, skateboarding, car racing, playing computer games, and enjoying a colourful sex life, with multiple sex partners. This individual also enjoys partying, and trying new and potentially exciting experiences, such as illicit drug use, and travelling. Psychologists would describe such an individual as high on sensation seeking.

The term sensation seeking generally refers to a craving for fun and excitement (Zuckerman et al., 1978). It is characterised by an aversion to boring, monotonous, repetitive or dull activities or people, an interest in social and sexual encounters, and other experiences that stimulate the mind and senses, and finally a desire for thrills and exciting ventures that involve speed or danger.

In a nutshell, psychologist Zuckerman and colleagues have identified four fundamental dimensions of this construct. These are as follows:

- thrill and adventure seeking
- experience seeking
- disinhibition
- susceptibility to boredom.

These domains are generally self-explanatory. The first two denote a craving for new and exciting activities, especially ones that involve speed and danger, and stimulate the mind and senses (e.g. skateboarding, driving fast and recklessly, and trying dangerous drugs). Disinhibition means the absence of psychological restraints (e.g. fear, embarrassment) that may hamper one's desire to meet new people, socialise and have sexual experiences. Susceptibility to boredom means precisely that – a tendency to get bored easily, especially when engaged in repetitive tasks or having unexciting social experiences.

When making decisions, people prone to seek sensations will readily select any option that promises excitement, with scant if any regard for potential health risks. Important steps in competent decision making, such as surveying and weighing available options (Byrnes, 2002), are likely to be performed superficially, if at all, with considerable bias in favour of thrilling rather than healthy outcomes.

Thus, there is a greater probability of health compromising behaviours, like smoking, drug use, unprotected sex and reckless driving, all of which are likely to offer the required thrills and physical stimulation, and sense of danger.

There is a considerable body of empirical literature demonstrating the deleterious effects of sensation seeking on adolescents' health behaviour (e.g. Crawford et al., 2003; Gutierrez et al., 2003; Bratko and Butkovic, 2004; Robbins and

8.2 *Sensation seeking. Impulsive decision makers exhibit a craving for excitement, fun and novelty (Source: SXC).*

Bryan, 2004; Roth and Herzberg, 2004; van Beurden *et al.*, 2005). Some of these studies are considered in the following section.

Behavioural consequences of impulsivity

Does impulsivity encourage health damaging behaviour? Well, since decisions aren't properly thought through there is a much greater chance of overlooking serious risks, resulting in unhealthy behaviour. Empirical evidence seems to support this view (e.g. Shoda *et al.*, 1990; Krueger *et al.*, 1994; White *et al.*, 1994; Madden *et al.*, 1997; Umeh, 1998a, 1998b; Wulfert *et al.*, 1999, 2002; d'Acremont and van der Linden, 2005).

Psychologist Edelgard Wulfert and several colleagues conducted an intriguing study in which high school students were offered a choice between a small but immediate benefit and a large but delayed reward (Wulfert *et al.*, 2002). Individuals who chose the former indicated a propensity for impulsive choice and, crucially, reported greater levels of risky health behaviour, such as illicit drug use, alcohol consumption and cigarette smoking.

An earlier investigation by psychologist Susanne H. Mitchell revealed similar findings (Mitchell, 1999). Young people in their late teens or early twenties completed a battery of questionnaires measuring impulsivity, including a measure of sensation seeking and novelty seeking, and a measure of extraversion. They also completed several tasks that gauged their affinity for impulsive decision making. These included a delay task in which participants had to choose between receiving a small financial reward, immediately, or after different levels of delay (e.g. 7, 180 or 365 days). Participants were also asked whether they smoked cigarettes, and were then classified as regular smokers (at least fifteen cigarettes per day) and non-smokers (never tried smoking).

Smokers reported significantly greater levels of impulsivity, scoring higher on unplanned decision making, extraversion, lack of inhibition, and seeking excitement, thrills, novelty and adventure.

Although the bulk of research on impulsivity and adolescent health behaviour has focused on the concept of sensation seeking (Baker and Yardley, 2002; Crawford et al., 2003; Gutierrez et al., 2003; Bratko and Butkovic, 2004; Robbins and Bryan, 2004; Roth and Herzberg, 2004; van Beurden et al., 2005), overall this evidence, together with other research on impulsivity (e.g. Mitchell, 1999; Wulfert et al., 2002), has shown conclusively that snap decision making does tend to support health damaging behaviour.

Impulsivity as a clever strategy

Research suggests that adolescents view snap decisions as sometimes necessary, for example during emergencies, when disaster is imminent. In an intriguing experiment, conducted by J. Amsterlaw (2006) as part of her doctoral dissertation at the University of Washington, a group of children and teenagers were presented with a number of scenarios in which people made a decision in one of three ways.

In one set of scenarios the decisions were made in a competent manner; another group of scenarios involved decision making using short-cut techniques, such as tossing a coin, or trial and error; finally, in the third set of scenarios decisions were made in an automatic, impulsive fashion, without thinking. The scenarios accurately depicted how people arrive at decisions in an emergency. There was a strong sense of urgency, with the individual desperate to escape danger, before it was too late.

Although the scenarios didn't involve health behaviour, the decision makers were still faced with a threat to their well-being (e.g. getting burned, broken bones, death), and stood to suffer severe penalties for making the wrong decision.

Amsterlaw asked participants to indicate how much thinking was involved in each scenario, how hard the character had to think, how long it took, whether there was some kind of problem to figure out, and how smart the character was. Analysis showed that all subjects felt the carefully considered decisions involved more thinking, mental effort and length of time. This seems to suggest that

teenagers may deem this approach to decision making impractical in an emergency.

However, what seemed most intriguing was that the competent and short-cut/ impulsive decision making scenarios were judged to be equally clever! One obvious inference from this is that children and adolescents will have little hesitation in making a snap decision if this is convenient to the situation. To them, this is no less brainy than trying to reason about things first, before acting.

This interpretation seems to be supported by another study, conducted by psychologist Paul Klaczynski of Pennsylvania State University (Klaczynski, 2001). He asked a sample of adolescents to find solutions to a range of decision making problems. Although the teenagers used reason and logic to solve the problems, they also employed simple, rapid and automatic decision making rules requiring little or no thought.

For example, subjects seemed to assume that if a particular outcome had not occurred as often as it should then it was likely to occur in the future, because things average themselves out (e.g. overestimating the probability of lung cancer simply because it has not yet occurred despite a lifetime of heavy smoking).

Another simple rule the adolescents used was to choose a course of action provided it promised favourable outcomes, completely ignoring the probability that those outcomes would actually materialise (e.g. deciding to quit smoking cold turkey because it would reduce the risk of cancer, ignoring the fact that the damage may already be done).

Overall, the findings from Amsterlaw's (2006) and Klaczynski's (2001) studies suggest that young people will have no compunction resorting to impulsive decision making, rather than bother trying to weigh things first. While some adults may take a dim view of this propensity, adolescents might think otherwise, viewing spur-of-the-moment action as clever, especially in the face of severe deadline pressure.

And they may have a point. An asthmatic boy on the verge of an acute respiratory attack would be idiotic to waste time evaluating his options instead of promptly reaching for his inhaler, and then calling for help. A girl who wakes up after a night of passion believing she may be pregnant has very limited time to take remedial action. A quick decision to take the 'morning after' pill would be a wise move.

Impulsivity as convenience

Adolescents, more so than adults, may have a good reason to be impulsive. Teenagers, particularly the younger ones, may lack the necessary cognitive abilities to fully understand the probability and seriousness of long-term health problems, of which they have little or no first-hand experience. Thus, faced with a decision, comprehensive mental deliberations may be unrealistic.

In one study Kate Tilleczek and Donald Hine (2006) conducted in-depth interviews with twenty adolescent smokers aged 18 to 19 years regarding the health

hazards of smoking. The data revealed that while older adolescents boasted a very elaborate understanding of the health and social risks associated with smoking, younger participants in their early teens lacked the same depth of awareness. For example, whereas almost all the older teenagers spoke about heart disease, only one younger adolescent mentioned this hazard. Overall, younger participants cited fewer health risks than their older counterparts.

Although research suggests that adolescents generally have good knowledge of the health threats associated with smoking and other unhealthy behaviours (e.g. Mazanov and Byrne, 2007), their understanding of this knowledge may be very limited. Yes, most teenagers receive health education at school, through the media and from their parents, but it is probable that the finer details of this information simply don't 'register', especially with youngsters in their early to mid teens. It therefore follows that, faced with health behaviour decisions, some may be inclined to make snap judgements, rather than struggle to juggle information they don't fully understand.

Panic

On 17 June 2005 a teenager accompanied by his friend was driving along a Los Angeles street in a family car. Both youths were rather tense. They were driving around in the middle of the night, probably without the knowledge and/or approval of their parents, and supposedly up to no good. Suddenly a police car appeared. The duo panicked. In a bid to escape, the driver made a sudden sharp turn that was so abrupt and violent that the car somersaulted and the engine caught fire. Trapped in the inferno both youths were suddenly in danger of burning to death. Luckily fire fighters promptly arrived on the scene and pulled the boys to safety. Neither teenager was seriously injured.

Impulsivity is sometimes associated with panic (Janis and Mann, 1976, 1977), a rare but distinct feature of adolescence (Ollendick, 1998). This narrative highlights something behavioural scientists have known for a while – panic is a fact of life during adolescence (Mattis and Ollendick, 1997; Reed and Wittchen, 1998; Hayward et al., 2000; Masi et al., 2000; Weems, 2000; Calamari et al., 2001; Ginsburg and Drake, 2002; Ginsburg et al., 2004; Leen-Feldner et al., 2006; Pfefferbaum et al., 2006). Behavioural science literature is awash with studies and review articles about panic disorder in children and teenagers (see review by Ollendick, 1998). It is clear from the literature that acute anxiety and a sense of impending disaster (e.g. death) are recurring symptoms (Lau et al., 1996; Weems, 2000; Calamari et al., 2001; Ginsburg and Drake, 2002; Ginsburg et al., 2004). Thus, anxiety symptoms in children and adolescents are now considered a risk factor for the development of panic symptoms (e.g. Ginsburg and Drake, 2002).

We know from this evidence that, just like adults, adolescents are prone to panic, displaying typical physiological symptoms, like shortness of breath, increased heart rate, heart palpitations, pain or pressure in the chest, trembling,

sweating, nausea, hot/cold flushes and choking sensations. They also exhibit the characteristic cognitive signs, including misinterpreting physical symptoms, and believing that one is 'losing control', 'going crazy' or 'freaking out'. For example, heart palpitations may be misconstrued as an imminent heart attack, or choking sensations interpreted as a cue that one is not really in command of one's body.

Indeed psychologist Thomas Ollendick reviews evidence suggesting that up to two-thirds of teenagers experience a panic attack at least once in their lifetime, and up to 5 per cent develop symptoms that are sufficiently extreme to be categorised as a psychiatric disorder (Ollendick, 1998). Furthermore, although panic or panic attacks may be triggered by specific situations, such as frightening physical symptoms (e.g. choking, shortness of breath), a disturbing health warning, or loss of a significant other (e.g. parent, sibling), they may also be a stable part of an individual's personality.

Overall, teenagers may panic when making decisions, irrespective of the prevailing circumstances (Umeh, 1998a, 1998b; Tuinstra et al., 2000). For example, a girl concerned about her physical appearance becomes alarmed after realising she has gained weight substantially. Frantic, she makes an impulsive decision to go on a diet, being too excited to weigh all her options carefully first (Janis and Mann, 1976). As will be seen later in this chapter, panicking can disrupt competent decision making, with potential implications for health behaviour.

Box 8.2 Media spotlight: panic in response to a traffic incident

During the latter part of 2006 in Britain the BBC ran a short television public health advertisement designed to reduce the number of teenage pedestrians injured or killed by speeding vehicles.

It featured several excited youngsters standing on a pavement next to a busy road engaged in lively teenage banter. In the enthusiasm a boy suddenly breaks away from the group and begins crossing the road, still chatting with his mates, barely pausing to check for oncoming traffic. All of a sudden he is struck by a speeding car, tossed into the air, and lands in a lifeless heap on the road. His friends are horrified – they scream and wail in terror. At this point the advertisement ends with a brief warning about the growing number of teenagers killed every day/week on British roads.

What really struck me about this advertisement was the behaviour of the unfortunate youngster who got hit. Although the incident was clearly staged, it came across as an extremely realistic portrayal of adolescent decision making. The victim appeared to make a snap decision to cross the road. Without further ado he proceeded to implement his decision, with devastating consequences.

Far from the orderly process of carefully searching for and evaluating alternatives, which decision theorists are fond of describing (Gardner and Herman, 1990; Byrnes et al., 1999), teenagers often make risky decisions on the hoof. And it gets worse. In an emergency, when disaster seems imminent (e.g. impending vehicle collision, missed menstruation, acute asthma attack), adolescents may simply panic, increasing the likelihood of snap decision making.

The idea that panic represents a form of decision making isn't new. Irving Janis and Leon Mann argued that panic-stricken decision making involves a frantic search for a solution, and the hasty adoption of any option that seems to offer rapid relief from anxiety (Janis and Mann, 1976, 1977; Janis, 1986). In such a frenzied state the individual is simply unable to survey the available options properly, and make an informed choice. Hence, decisions tend to be rushed and ill considered.

Panic is not a trait immediately associated with adolescence. It seems incompatible with notions of rebelliousness, invulnerability, risk taking, and other daring terms that are used to describe teenagers. Yet I have chosen to discuss it here. Why? Well, there are three reasons.

- As we have seen, there is evidence that children and adolescents do suffer panic disorders and panic attacks, much like adults (Ollendick, 1998).
- Evidence suggests that panic accurately characterises how adolescents sometimes make decisions (Umeh, 1998a, 1998b).
- There are significant implications for health behaviour decisions (Umeh, 1998a, 1998b).

It is not difficult to imagine scenarios in which decisions about health behaviour are made in a frantic or panic-stricken state. Typically, there is a sense of urgency, impending doom or deadline pressure.

Take for example a girl who realises she is gaining weight. Over the past few months she has been weighing herself regularly and has never gone above 110 lb. Most of her friends claim to weigh about the same, so she isn't unduly worried, until one Saturday morning. She gets up early, climbs on to the bathroom scales and is horrified. She has gained an additional 6 lb. The following week her weight increases even further. The girl starts to panic, feeling that something has to be done, quickly, before she becomes the target of ridicule at school. She makes a snap decision to restrict her food intake, only to suffer a relapse after finding the hunger cravings too difficult to bear.

This account seems to highlight two seemingly obvious facts about adolescent decision making. First, when adolescents make important decisions in a state of panic the normal rules of competent decision making, such as carefully surveying and weighing alternatives, may be difficult or impossible to apply. Extremely frightened and unable to think clearly, adolescents may find quicker and simpler ways to resolve the crisis (Janis and Mann, 1977; Mann *et al.*, 1997; Tuinstra *et al.*, 2000). Second, since decisions made in panic are by definition ill considered, a teenager may suffer adverse consequences as a result (Umeh, 1998a, 1998b).

Panic-like decision making seems to be a recurring feature of adolescence. When teenagers are asked to indicate how they make decisions, panic-like thoughts and behaviours often emerge as a distinct theme (Friedman and Mann, 1993; Umeh, 1998a, 1998b). Some findings from my doctoral studies (Umeh, 1998a, 1998b), and also from research by psychologists Isaac Friedman, Leon Mann and others, illustrate this tendency succinctly (Friedman and Mann, 1993; Mann *et al.*, 1997, 1998). Teenagers identify with DMQ statements such as

'I panic if I have to make decisions quickly', 'I feel as if I'm under tremendous time pressure when making decisions', and 'I can't think straight if I have to make a decision in a hurry' (Mann, 1982; Mann et al., 1997).

Deadline pressure

It can be argued that many decisions adolescents face involve deadline pressure, so that over time many develop a sense of impending doom, real or imagined, whenever they have to make a choice. From an empirical perspective not much is known about the effects of time pressure on adolescent decision making, especially within a health context. Some research suggests that teenagers make poorer judgements when operating under time pressure, resorting more to stereotypes and other simplistic rules of thumb (e.g. Lam et al., 2006), although the literature in this area is limited, dated, patchy and diverse (e.g. Jerusalem and Schwarzer, 1989; Matczak and Galinska, 1990; Svenson and Maule, 1993), precluding any firm conclusions on the subject.

Poor decision making under time pressure seems logical. Faced with a tight deadline, even the most sensible teenagers may find there just isn't enough time to survey all the relevant information, and make an informed choice (Janis and Mann, 1977).

Other than health emergencies (e.g. imminent asthma attack, traffic accident or undergoing surgery), most routine decisions adolescents have to make at home, at school or in the company of peers are arguably characterised by implied or stated deadlines (Shaw et al., 1996). These time constraints usually result from the threat of immediate social disapproval, or rapidly passing opportunities, which in turn places significant time constraints on decision making.

For example, decisions about what to buy in the school canteen have to be made fast before break time is over, or stocks run out. Similarly, a rare opportunity to smoke in the privacy of one's bedroom has to be exploited quickly before someone walks in.

It is also worth emphasising the decision making pressures within the peer group, as most adolescents spend a considerable amount of time amongst their friends. For example, a teenager may find himself amongst peers about to experiment with illicit drugs. Offered a 'joint', the youth has seconds to decide whether to accept, and suffer the potential health consequences, or decline, and face mockery and rejection from his peers.

The net effect of these scenarios is that many teenagers become accustomed to making decisions in a hurry. Eventually, they may come to associate time pressure with decision making.

Impaired thought

As we saw in Chapter 6, competent decision making requires an ability to process information. However, it may be difficult to think clearly in a state of panic.

8.3 *A sense of doom. The thought of imminent death or physical incapacitation resulting from a serious injury can trigger panic-like decision making (Source: SXC).*

Indeed, research has shown that adolescents indicate problems 'thinking straight' whenever they have to rush decisions (Umeh, 1998a, 1998b; Lam *et al.*, 2006). Remember the teenager driver who panicked upon seeing a police car? He reacted impulsively, in a state of high emotional arousal, and with a sense of impending doom (fear of getting caught by the police). In such an excitable state calm and logical thought may be difficult, even for a mature adult.

Consider the following scenarios. In each case a quick decision is required in the face of imminent danger (e.g. getting caught, severe reprimand, impending death or ill health, etc.), and thoughtlessness is evident or implied.

Terry is a plump 15-year-old girl who is rather anxious about her weight. Consequently, most of her friends and family are very careful not to talk about dieting or weight issues in her presence, to avoid upsetting her. Yesterday though, on her way back from school, she was verbally harassed by a group of teenage girls, who shouted words like 'fat' and 'gross' at her. Terry suddenly began to panic, feeling she would soon become horribly obese, unless something was done, quickly. Back at home she made a snap decision to purge herself to get rid of the calories.

Kevin is 16 years old. He and his girlfriend Amanda have been sexually active since they met six months ago. Neither Kevin nor his girlfriend was bold enough to suggest using contraception, so they simply had unprotected sex, oblivious to the health risks. One day, Kevin received a late night telephone call from Amanda. She had some horrible news. She had been to a local clinic, to have an HIV test, and the result was positive! Kevin panicked. He became so scared that he could

barely gather his thoughts together. The possibility that he may be HIV positive and perhaps soon die of AIDS was just too alarming to contemplate. He promptly broke up with his girlfriend and convinced himself he wasn't infected; after all, they had only had sex a few times.

Melissa is 14 years old and has been smoking since she was 12. She now smokes several packets of cigarettes daily and is heavily addicted to tobacco. However, recently her uncle Jim, who has smoked all his life and is now in his late 60s, was diagnosed with lung cancer, and admitted to hospital. Although Melissa already knew about the health risks of smoking, nothing prepared her for the shock of seeing her uncle slumped in a hospital bed, looking extremely frail, struggling to breathe and coughing up blood. Two days after undergoing surgery her uncle died. Melissa panicked, believing she was soon going to contract lung cancer too, and maybe even die from it. She promptly quit smoking, cold turkey. However, this hasty decision proved ill considered, as she suffered a relapse within two weeks, after developing severe withdrawal symptoms.

These scenarios highlight two points about panic-like decision making. First, decisions tend to be rushed, largely because of a sense of deadline pressure or impending doom (Janis and Mann, 1977). Second, since decisions are hasty, they tend to be ill considered. The individual fails to survey all the available options and weigh up the pros and cons, in order to establish the best course of action.

Studies suggest that panic may lead to greater uncertainty about which option to choose (e.g. Lam *et al.*, 2006), and more difficulty remembering important information. Unfortunately existing research is largely adult based, with emphasis on hospital patients. There is a paucity of evidence on the impact of panic on cognitive functioning in teenagers.

Ambivalence

Research suggests that adolescents in general can be quite resolute in making decisions (e.g. Gillison *et al.*, 2006; Boiche and Sarrazin, 2007). However, theoretical literature suggests that panic-prone individuals are prone to considerable vacillation (Janis and Mann, 1976, 1977). They become confused when faced with multiple options and limited time in which to decide which is best. Once a decision is made, it is immediately and repeatedly questioned, and hence easily rescinded, as new worries surface.

For example, faced with an emergency, many teenagers make numerous telephone calls to crisis hotlines and/or their friends, hoping for reassurance and useful advice (e.g. Teare *et al.*, 1995). These calls are made frantically, and often follow each other in rapid succession, as the individual exhausts the list of names and numbers in her diary or phone book. Of course, the danger is that, in such an excitable state, almost any advice offered by others will sound tempting, and is likely to be implemented without adequate thought. There is also a real risk of information overload as numerous suggestions arrive from multiple sources (Linn *et al.*, 1984; Sung and Kim, 1987).

It therefore follows that there is bound to be a lot of vacillation as one piece of advice is executed, and then promptly reversed or abandoned in favour of another newer suggestion (Katz, 1973; Becker *et al.*, 1974; Mann and Friedman, 1990; Friedman, 1996). Since the individual is in no state to evaluate all the information properly, a bad decision seems just as likely as a good one.

Katz (1973) emphasises the multiplicity of social, cognitive and biological pressures and conflicts that characterise adolescence, citing vacillation as an integral feature, a manifestation of hidden conflicts. Vacillation, according to him, has to be considered in trying to understand why teenagers engage in problem behaviours.

Conclusive empirical evidence for the existence of vacillation amongst teenagers comes from the aforementioned study by Friedman (1996). A large group of teen-agers completed a questionnaire measuring various decision making habits they employ when dealing with everyday problems. Factor analysis revealed three fundamental constructs, one of which clearly displayed vacillation (e.g. 'I weigh

8.4 *Frantic search. In a state of panic almost any advice will sound tempting and careful evaluation of the options is unlikely, possibly leading to a poor decision (Source: SXC).*

a number of solutions to the problem, get confused by the variety of options, and then choose nothing').

The pregnancy problem

Theories developed to explain adolescent decision making say little about panic (e.g. Rogel *et al.*, 1980; Gardner and Herman, 1990; Gordon *et al.*, 1996; Reyna and Farley, 2006). On a more optimistic note, there is a growing body of literature on emergency contraceptive use and the threat of unplanned pregnancies in teenagers (see review by Grunseit *et al.*, 1997; also see Walker *et al.*, 2004).

A serious emergency, and reason to panic, often arises when two adolescents have unprotected sexual intercourse and the girl is suddenly at risk of becoming pregnant. Teenagers typically panic in this situation, not sure what to do, and scared to death that they might be in serious trouble. Neither party may want to take responsibility, yet both will be fully aware that something has to be done, and quick! Even if both youngsters are particularly well informed and self-confident about their decision making competence, signs of panic may be evident. Snap decision making may prevail as a sense of impending doom takes hold.

And what about ambivalence? It seems teenagers may be indecisive about contraceptive use and pregnancy even where there is no apparent emergency. Psychologists James Jaccard, Tonya Dodge and Patricia Dittus found some evidence for this (Jaccard *et al.*, 2003). They interviewed nearly 5,000 adolescents, from diverse ethnic backgrounds, concerning their attitudes on pregnancy. Participants were asked whether they agreed with two statements – one depicting pregnancy as an extremely negative event ('getting pregnant at this time in my life is one of the worst things that could happen to me') and the other portraying pregnancy as a favourable experience ('It would not be all that bad if I got pregnant at this time in my life').

The researchers found that while most subjects agreed pregnancy was an inauspicious thing, a significant minority seemed ambivalent. Similarly, although a majority rejected the notion that pregnancy in adolescence is a good thing, a substantial minority were uncertain – some teenagers could not decide whether getting pregnant was something they wanted, suggesting indecisiveness.

The participants in the study were randomly selected from a large number of high schools across the United States, and there is no obvious reason to think that any ambivalence was caused by panic. However, since panic wasn't a variable in this investigation, no firm conclusions can be drawn. What seems evident is that the threat of pregnancy can be enough to induce panic, and hence ambivalence.

Consequences

We know that adolescents, like adults, can and do think carefully when making decisions (see Ormond *et al.*, 1991; Friedman, 1996; Mann *et al.*, 1997; Tuinstra *et al.*, 2000). For example, they often prefer options that promise some benefit,

such as approval from their peers, improved physique and better self-confidence, and minimise problems, such as health risks (e.g. Umeh, 2003; Turner and Mermelstein, 2004; Umeh and Crabtree, 2006).

Contemplating potential consequences is an essential part of competent decision making, as it is the only way the decision maker can work out which of several options is the most preferable (Janis and Mann, 1976, 1977). Yet, it is difficult to imagine panic-stricken youth thinking in a careful and balanced fashion. For example, a teenage girl who is made frantic by the possibility of being called 'fat' at her new school may impulsively decide to purge herself, without stopping to think about the consequences. Although fully conversant with the health dangers of purging, she may be too disconcerted to bother thinking about these risks.

In a state of panic a decision maker will be keen to find a solution quickly. Careful appraisal of options and their consequences would seem far too arduous and time consuming.

However, there is evidence suggesting that any effect panic has on the decision making process is minimal, in both adolescents (e.g. Umeh, 1998a) and adults (e.g. van der Velde and van der Pligt, 1991). Indeed, my own research suggests a rather intriguing picture (see Box 8.3). It appears that although panicking may not impair the quality of decision making in teenagers, it can nevertheless lead to unhealthy choices. For example I found that greater levels of panic were associated with reduced levels of physical activity. How so? It is possible that panicking does have some effect on cost–benefit deliberations that, although not significant, is enough to disrupt balanced judgement, so that dangers associated with a particular course of action aren't fully grasped.

For example, a panic-prone individual may recognise the risks of physical inactivity, but fail to give it much thought, to avoid worrying incessantly about the issue. With any worrying thoughts suppressed, the individual experiences a reduced sense of urgency, and remains inactive.

Even so, panic may have little or no effect on most health behaviours. Figure 8.5 shows some research findings relevant to this point (Umeh, 1998b). Although panic was associated with reduced levels of physical activity, it bore no relationship to decisions concerning other health behaviours, for example cigarette smoking and consumption of dietary fat.

The remoteness of major health risks means that even panic-prone adolescents may lack a sense of urgency when making lifestyle decisions (van der Pligt, 1994; Cohn et al., 1995). Although they may well be troubled by threatening cues such as a health warning, this seems unlikely to induce extreme fright of panic proportions. Indeed, research has shown that adolescents in general fail to acknowledge personal vulnerability to prominent health threats such as AIDS, heart disease and cancer (Moore and Rosenthal, 1991; Whalen et al., 1994). This in turn may produce widespread complacency that transcends panic tendencies.

One final point. Most teenagers are generally aware of the major threats to their health, especially if they engage in health damaging behaviour (e.g. Wiltshire

Box 8.3 Research spotlight: are panic-prone teenagers less sensible?

Umeh, K. (1998b) A Conflict-Theory Approach to Understanding Adolescents' Health Behaviour, PhD thesis, University of Leicester.

Are panic-prone teenagers less reasonable in their decision making compared with more relaxed colleagues? To test this idea I divided participants in my doctoral research into 'high-panic' and 'low-panic' groups, based on their responses to a questionnaire on decision making styles (the DMQ, see Chapter 1). Subjects also provided information about their perceptions of health risks and benefits (e.g. the likelihood and seriousness of various health risks, and the effectiveness of preventive action) and their desire to perform various health behaviours over the next few weeks.

Curiously, the extent to which decisions reflected risk–benefit judgements was the same in high- and low-panic subjects. This suggested that panicking does not necessarily impair the capacity for thoughtful decision making.

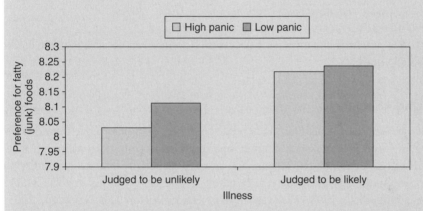

Despite this finding, a propensity to panic was associated with unhealthy decisions, in particular a reluctance to exercise regularly. This suggests that although panic may not significantly hamper considered judgement, it can still lead to bad choices. How so? It is possible that although panic may not impair decision making to a significant degree, it does have some effect. A jumpy teenager may spend some time weighing his options, only to act impulsively once he is ready to make a decision.

et al., 2005; Mazanov and Byrne, 2007). This familiarity means that the sense of urgency that may be associated with a new threat is non-existent or negligible. Thus, even panic-prone youth will be unperturbed when faced with a routine health behaviour decision. Even decisions concerning AIDS, a disease that adolescents find particularly worrisome (Ollendick *et al.*, 1989, 2001), may fail to inject any sense of alarm in characteristically jumpy teenagers. For example, I found that panic-prone adolescents were no more likely to use contraception compared with more relaxed colleagues. Years of publicity about AIDS means

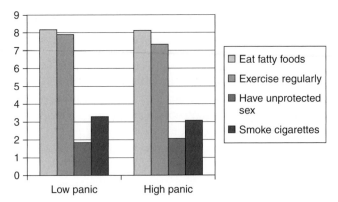

8.5 *Effect of panic on choice. Panicking may increase the likelihood of a bad decision, albeit not necessarily so. Survey data showed that although panic-prone adolescents were less likely to adopt health enhancing behaviour (physical activity), panic was not related to other health related activities (cigarette use, fat intake and use of contraception) (Source: Umeh, 1998b).*

even this potential calamity isn't necessarily going to rattle an otherwise easily alarmed youth.

Origins of panic

What psychological preconditions predispose adolescents to panic during decision making? Factors such as previous experience and social learning, self-confidence, temperament, attachment, anxiety sensitivity and susceptibility to phobias may be implicated (e.g. Bandura, 1977, 1986; Mattis and Ollendick, 1997; Ollendick, 1998; Hayward *et al.*, 2003; Wilson and Hayward, 2005; Leen-Feldner *et al.*, 2006). It is important to consider that any effect panicking has on choice might in fact be largely attributable to these factors. In other words, panic itself may not be the problem, but rather less obvious psychological precursors or correlates that significantly impair the quality of decision making.

Consider a plump girl who, alarmed by jibes about her weight, makes a snap decision to purge herself. While it is entirely plausible that her frantic state impairs her capacity or willingness to contemplate the potential alternatives (e.g. costs of joining a gym, going on a diet or doing nothing) before acting, it is also possible that prior experience concerning purging may magnify her sense of urgency and hence limit her ability to make an informed decision. For example, she may have learned from previous stressful experiences that getting worked up and acting impulsively can produce immediate and favourable results (Bandura, 1977). If so, she is unlikely to waste time conducting a thorough appraisal of relevant information, to find the best possible solution.

We know from existing literature that children and adolescents are heavily influenced by their previous experiences of trauma (Zubenko and Capozzoli, 2002; Williams, 2006). Unfortunately, there is little direct evidence to

substantiate the view that other psychological factors influence the effect of panic in this way.

Nevertheless, one variable that may play a particularly prominent role is adolescents' sensitivity to anxiety. This refers to a tendency to be alarmed by and overreact to symptoms of stress, such as a pounding heart or sweaty palms (e.g. Wilson and Hayward, 2005; Leen-Feldner *et al.*, 2006). Thus, anxiety sensitivity rather than panic per se may determine the nature of decision making, and its outcomes.

For example, a panic-prone teenager may struggle to think clearly about available options simply because he became extremely alarmed having noticed his heart was pounding and his palms were sweaty. Thus his propensity to panic isn't itself a key determining factor, but rather his oversensitivity to signs of distress. Alternatively, sensitivity to anxiety may determine when panic does or doesn't influence decision making. For example, panic may only impair thought in teenagers who are highly sensitive to anxiety, because this magnifies their panic symptoms.

This latter scenario seems particularly plausible if we take the view that panic isn't a chronic condition, but rather a rare occurrence subject to certain preconditions. Several times in this book I have mentioned the highly intriguing work of psychologist Thomas Ollendick, who critically reviewed some of the literature on panic attacks in children and adolescents (Ollendick, 1998). He noted that although panic episodes were becoming more common amongst teenagers, only a small minority of reported cases – around 15–20 per cent – are sufficiently serious to be diagnosed as a medical problem.

Furthermore, he argued that during their lifetime only very few adolescents ever experience a full-blown panic attack in which at least four of the thirteen or so psychological and medical symptoms are present (interestingly, cognitive deliberations such as believing that death is imminent tend to be reported rather less often than physical symptoms such as dizziness and fainting[3]). Finally, Ollendick noted that his own research conducted with other colleagues showed that although panic-stricken teenagers experience a considerable degree of anxiety, their symptoms are rarely serious enough to persuade them to seek treatment.

Overall, these observations suggest that panic in adolescence is quite rare. Even panic-prone youngsters may seldom be sufficiently alarmed that their decision making is seriously disrupted. Only under certain conditions, such as high sensitivity to anxiety, does panic become a serious threat to informed choice. This may explain why empirical research has revealed no connection between panicking and risk–benefit deliberations (Umeh, 1998a, 1998b).

But why do teenagers rarely experience extremely severe panic symptoms, as Ollendick (1998) suggests? One possible reason is that adolescents are hardly ever faced with emergency situations in which much is at stake and time is limited in which to find a resolution. This argument is particularly applicable to health scenarios. I have already argued in this chapter that most of the major health threats adolescents could face (e.g. cancer, heart disease) are just too remote to create a

---

[3] This may indicate that the ability to think clearly is somehow impaired.

sense of urgency (also see Chapter 4). These dangers seem far-fetched in both their apparent severity (e.g. most teenagers have never known or even heard of another adolescent who died from cardiovascular disease) and their probability of occurrence (e.g. full-blown AIDS can take over a decade to manifest, and cardiovascular disease and cancer only become serious problems from mid to late adulthood).

Furthermore, these dangers can easily be averted through the adoption of practicable preventive measures, and most teenagers know this. For example, school-based anti-HIV/AIDS education programmes typically highlight regular contraceptive use as an effective way to protect one's health from STDs. Similarly, programmes designed to reduce the incidence of heart disease and cancer specifically recommend regular exercise and not smoking cigarettes.

The presence of a salient solution is highly reassuring (Rogers, 1975, 1983; Rippetoe and Rogers, 1987). This may drastically reduce the amount of informational overload, and hence limit the level of emotional disturbance, even in panic-prone individuals. Perhaps the possibility of pregnancy is one of a few situations that may have the capacity to create a sense of emergency and induce full-blown panic. The threat is immediate, and hence probably a source of considerable anxiety for many teenagers.

Age and gender differences

Are there any reliable age and gender differences in impulsive decision making? A review of research on the UPPS revealed very patchy evidence on demographic differences amongst adolescents. Consequently, I decided to re-examine some of my own data, based on the DMQ (Umeh, 1998a, 1998b). Factor analysis of the DMQ generally fails to yield a separate impulsiveness scale (e.g. Mann *et al.*, 1997, 1998; Umeh, 1998a; Tuinstra *et al.*, 2000), even though the original instrument does contain items that seem to suggest impulsive decision making, for example 'Whenever I get upset by having to make a decision, I choose on the spur of the moment' and 'I tend to drift into decisions without thinking about them', and 'I put little effort into making decisions' (Mann, 1982).

I decided to test for associations between these items and demographic variables. Correlational analysis revealed a significant negative correlation between age and all three statements, showing that older teenagers were less impulsive than younger ones. This may point to a growing maturity in the former group, denoting a keenness to think things through first, before acting. We already know from other evidence that decision making competence improves with age during adolescence (e.g. Mann, 1989; Ormond *et al.*, 1991). As adolescents get older, and approach their late teens, they are much more likely to be held responsible for their actions, and suffer retribution for any negative outcomes. Thus, there will be a greater incentive to exercise better judgement when making decisions.

Further analysis revealed significant gender differences in the statements, 'Whenever I get upset by having to make a decision, I choose on the spur of the

moment' and 'I put little effort into making decisions.' Females identified more with the first item, and less with the second. In other words, girls were more likely to act on impulse, whereas boys were more nonchalant. However, group differences were small, and negligible.

There is some evidence that female impulsivity may be related primarily to shopping, rather than, say, health behaviour (Dittmar and Drury, 2000). Girls also score higher on the sense of urgency UPPS scale, although boys are more likely to seek sensation (e.g. d'Acremont and van der Linden, 2005).

Overall, gender differences in impulsivity seem marginal, and are probably partly explained by a social desirability bias in males (Helms and Holden, 2003). It's possible that boys are less willing to portray themselves as emotional, frightened, and effectively out of control, when making decisions. Impulsivity clashes with traditional male stereotypes of masculinity, toughness and 'being in charge' (Phillips, 2004). Thus, perhaps in reality, each gender is just as likely as the other to behave impulsively, at least in general. Whether this contention applies to health behaviour scenarios is difficult to say because of the paucity of empirical evidence in this area.

Box 8.4 Media spotlight: when peers provoke impulsive choice

One of the main features of impulsive decision making is a sense of urgency. An otherwise thoughtful and level-headed teenager can suddenly be compelled to make an impulsive choice – with potentially serious health consequences – because of a sense of urgency generated by peer pressure.

In an episode of the popular US teenage situation comedy *One-on-One*, titled 'Keeping it', a teenage girl and cheerleader named Breanna Barnes (Kyla Pratt) faces mockery and ridicule from other cheerleaders for being a virgin.

Well brought up by her father, Breanna is a reasonable girl who would prefer to avoid becoming sexually active until she is much older and the time is right. Up to this point she and her boyfriend Arnaz Ballard (Robert Ri'chard) had maintained a successful loving relationship without resorting to sexual intercourse. However, in the face of intense public mockery from her peers Breanna suddenly decides enough is enough, and makes a snap decision to lose her virginity. 'That's it, I can't take this anymore', she snaps, and then immediately proceeds to her boyfriend's home, making evident to him upon arrival that she 'came by to have sex'.

The astonished Arnaz agrees. There is no mention of contraceptive use. However, ultimately the sex never takes place – Breanna backs off at the last minute, disappointed to learn from Arnaz that he had already lost his virginity, to someone else. Perhaps the most worrying thing about this particularly realistic episode of *One-on-One* is the notion that even normally rational teenagers can, in the right circumstances, be 'panicked' by their fellow peers into acting impulsively.

Thus, having an essentially rational decision making style is no defence against a sense of exigency created by irresponsible peers.

Conclusion

In a comprehensive and thought-provoking article published in the *Washington Post* in 2002, journalist Laura Stepp discussed some of the popular stereotypes about teenagers that are prevalent in most Western societies, especially the United States (Stepp, 2002). While reading this article I became especially intrigued by the popular view many adults subscribe to that adolescents are impulsive, incapable of making sound decisions, and always getting into trouble. Indeed, adolescents do get into trouble, a lot of which is damaging to their health and seems to suggest poor decision making. Of particular concern is the ever-present threat of unplanned pregnancy, not to mention other serious problems like drug use, cigarette smoking and physical inactivity.

However, it can be argued that conceptualisations of adolescents as flawed decision makers may be a tad simplistic and gratuitous. Yes, adolescents do show all the signs of impulsivity, notably a craving for excitement, an inability to delay gratification, a sense of alarm, and lack of prior thought. However, impulsive choice may actually be quite sensible in situations of extreme deadline pressure. Furthermore, impulsivity associated with panic may not necessarily lead to risky behaviour. Data revealed that panic predicted only one of four health behaviours examined. There was no evidence that unsafe sex – the one activity that seems to fuel images of teenagers as rash and thoughtless decision makers – involves frantic and spur-of-the-moment decision making.

Nonetheless, it is important to point out that none of the evidence presented in this chapter totally explodes any myths. Rather, it merely compels one to question seemingly commonsensical notions about teenage decision makers, notably the idea that their hasty or impulsive decision making necessarily has adverse implications for health behaviour.

Key points

- Impulsiveness is a common feature of adolescent decision making.
- Like other decision making styles, impulsivity is multidimensional, characterised by a sense of urgency, an inability to delay gratification, thoughtlessness, and a craving for sensation and excitement.
- Adolescents may view impulsivity as a sensible decision making strategy in certain circumstances.
- Impulsive decision making is generally associated with health compromising behaviour, albeit not necessarily so. Since decisions are poorly thought through, there is a greater chance of important risks being overlooked.
- Impulsivity may be associated with panicky decision making, in which there is a sense of impending disaster, and an adolescent is in a hurry to find a solution.
- Panicking can lead to unhealthy decisions, but not necessarily so.

Key terms

- Impulsivity
- Sensation seeking
- Immediate gratification
- Sense of urgency
- Panic
- Deadline pressure
- Indecision
- Arousal

Further reading

Janis, I.L. and Mann, L. (1977) *Decision Making: A Psychological Analysis of Conflict, Choice, and Commitment.* New York: The Free Press.

Mattis, S.G. and Ollendick, T.H. (2002) *Panic Disorder and Anxiety in Adolescents.* Malden, MA: Blackwell.

Pogge, D.L., Borgaro, S.R., Horan, W.P., Stokes, J.M., Lord, J.J. and Harvey, P.D. (1996) Conduct disorder, impulsivity, and substance abuse in adolescents. *Biological Psychiatry*, 39, pp. 536–537.

Whiteside, S.P. and Lynam, D.R. (2001). The Five-Factor Model and impulsivity: using a structural model of personality to understand impulsivity. *Personality and Individual Differences*, 30, pp. 669–689.

9 Change

Learning outcomes

At the end of this chapter readers should have a better understanding of the following:

1 the significance of changeability in adolescents' decision making approach
2 different ways to conceptualise change in decision making
3 change in decision making amongst adolescents as a group
4 change in decision making at an individual level
5 change in the relative differences between two individuals' decision making approaches
6 change in the different aspects of an adolescent's decision making style
7 the degree of change that has been observed in adolescents over time
8 personal, situational and developmental factors that may affect the degree of change in decision making approach.

Chapter summary

This chapter discusses the issue of changeability in decision making style. Considerable instability can hamper accurate prediction of not just decision strategy, but also resulting health behaviour. Changeability in decision making can be conceptualised in different ways, including relative change between two youths, change in adolescents as a group, and also change between different aspects of an individual's decision making style. Surprisingly, empirical evidence suggests a remarkable degree of continuity in adolescents' decision making approach, not merely across days or weeks, but from year to year. In essence teenagers generally arrive at decisions in the same way, over time, although it seems they generally become more competent as they get older. Stability may be moderated to a certain extent by personal and situational factors, such as past experience and the stressful transition into high school. Overall, constancy can pose a problem for health initiatives designed to promote informed decision making concerning health behaviour.

Chapter outline

The chapter begins with a discussion of the notion of change and stability in adolescent decision making, followed by a discussion of the different ways of conceptualising the topic. There is particular emphasis on change at an individual level, with some discussion of the nature–nurture controversy. Finally I consider the role of developmental factors, prior experience and the identity crisis, all of which may moderate the degree of stability in adolescents' decision making.

Change and stability in decision making

One cold November morning, 16-year-old Michael decided to stop taking his medication. The consequences were immediate and catastrophic. Michael had recently suffered kidney failure and undergone a kidney transplant at a local hospital. After the operation he had been given some medicines, which he had to take several times a day without fail. The medication was needed to suppress Michael's immune system, and hence prevent his body from rejecting the transplanted tissue. However, after just three days Michael decided to stop taking his tablets, without telling anyone.

Within twenty-four hours he was rushed back into surgery suffering from hyperacute transplant rejection. He was lucky to survive, on this occasion. This wasn't the first time the boy had made a critical decision that almost cost him his life. Several months previously he had stupidly decided to drive a friend's car while under the influence of alcohol. He was involved in a terrible traffic accident and had to be rushed to hospital. The doctors said he was very lucky to be in one piece.

Is Michael's ill-considered decision making essentially part of who he is, or merely an occasional blunder forced by the peculiarities of a given situation? For the sake of argument, let us assume that Michael's decision making is a fundamental element of his personality. One issue that immediately comes to mind is whether his decision making changes, slightly or drastically, across time and situations, or remains essentially unchanged, irrespective of the circumstances.

Physicists often refer to the changeability of physical objects, for example the movement of the moon around the earth. They invest a lot of time studying change and the forces that produce or prevent it. Change is also an extremely important characteristic of human behaviour, and human decision making. Yet it is often overlooked or mentioned in passing, especially within current literature on adolescents' health behaviour.

Consider the popular negative stereotypes of teenagers (Stepp, 2002). You'd be forgiven for thinking adolescents are fundamentally mindless and impulsive. In other words, they rarely change their behaviour. Yet this may be far from the

truth. In reality young people can and do behave differently across time and in different situations, and teenage decision making is no exception. Adolescents may approach health behaviour decisions differently depending on the circumstances. Such changeability can make it difficult to characterise their decision making, as there is no continuity. It renders any stereotypes redundant, and makes it hard to identify and correct whatever flaws one may have as a decision maker.

It should be clear from the preceding chapters that the teenage decision maker is fairly well informed about most of the major threats to his health, such as obesity, sexually transmitted illness, unplanned pregnancy, cancer, asthma and heart disease, to mention just a few. Unlike very young children, who need round-the-clock supervision, teenagers enjoy more independence, and hence are in a position to make their own decisions. Yet, it is useful to know if their decision making style is stable or volatile over time. The emphasis here is rather different from the focus in Chapter 5, which was primarily about consistency in *decisions* (e.g. do smokers keep smoking?), rather than decision making *strategy* (e.g. does avoidance persist?). A steady decision making approach means predictable choices, whereas an erratic persona brings uncertainty.

Facets of change

Judging from existing psychological literature on personality, it can be argued that there are several ways in which change in adolescent decision making can be understood (Fruyt *et al.*, 2006; Pullman *et al.*, 2006).

One way is to consider whether teenagers as a group change their decision making style over time. For example, do a group of siblings at home, a classroom of pupils at school, or a group of peers at a nightclub generally make decisions in the same way all the time (e.g. acting on impulse, trying to be rational), or are there considerable shifts in group behaviour over time?

Another perspective is whether the decision making approach changes at an individual level over time. For example, one person may continually engage in competent decision making while another individual repeatedly replaces one avoidance strategy with another (e.g. switching between procrastination and shifting responsibility). Some teenagers will display a remarkable consistency in their decision making, over weeks, months, perhaps even years. They may use precisely the same arguments, consult exactly the same sources for advice, or perhaps panic in precisely the same frenzied fashion. By contrast, others may exhibit considerable variability, making them more difficult to characterise and hence predict. The idiom 'each to his own' appropriately encapsulates this view of change.

One can also consider whether there is any change in the decision making skills of one teenager in relation to another. So, for example, if John is a better decision maker than Mary today, will John still be a better decision maker than Mary next week, month or year?

Finally, there is the question of whether change occurs differentially amongst the various aspects of a teenager's decision making style. To understand this more fully it is important for readers to recognise that a person's decision making approach can be seen as multidimensional, incorporating a mix of characteristics unique to the individual.

Imagine a teenage girl prone to impulsive choice. As we saw in the previous chapter, impulsivity incorporates sensation seeking, an inability to persevere, and a strong sense of urgency or thoughtlessness. Let's say the girl's impulsiveness is characterised mainly by sensation seeking and lack of perseverance, with no sense of urgency and a lack of prior thought. This is her unique decision making profile. So the key question is this. Is she prone to maintain this profile over time, or are variations likely to occur in certain features (e.g. less interest in sensation seeking) while other characteristics remain unchanged?

Change in group behaviour

I use the term 'group' behaviour here to refer to stereotypical views of adolescents as decision makers, rather than characteristic features of group judgement described in social psychology, such as groupthink and group polarisation (Brehm *et al.*, 1999; Feldman, 2001). In Western societies adolescents as a group are generally considered to be not just poor decision makers (e.g. risk takers) (Petersen and Leffert, 1995; Byrnes, 2002), but also set in their ways, and, by implication, how they make decisions (Roberts *et al.*, 2001; De Fruyt *et al.*, 2006; Pullman *et al.*, 2006). Thus, to many adults, teenage decision making in general may be seen as typical, unchanging and largely predictable.

Adolescents are portrayed as characteristically thoughtless, heedless and impulsive, and hence prone to self-destructive or health damaging behaviours (Pechmann *et al.*, 2005; Carballo *et al.*, 2006). Those that habitually make good decisions, for example refusing to use drugs or drink alcohol, are regarded as 'good kids' (Crystal and Stevenson, 1995). Their decision making skills are considered to be part of their basic character. Similarly, adults dismiss as 'bad kids' youngsters who often flirt with danger. And, since this propensity is assumed to be part of who they are, no one expects any overnight change in their decision making proficiency.

Decision making is viewed as a matter of personality (Janis, 1986). It is in the nature of young people to be curious about smoking, to forget or refuse to use condoms, or to fail to take their medication. It is in their nature to experiment with alcohol, starve themselves to lose weight, or take drugs at a nightclub. In essence, the teenage decision maker is an individual unlikely to change, at least for the foreseeable future, or perhaps until young adulthood.

But is this cynical portrayal really true? Are adolescents as a group unwavering? Are their decision making habits that inevitable? Psychologist Helle Pullman and some colleagues conducted a study that may help answer this question (Pullman *et al.*, 2006). They monitored a large sample of youths over a two-year

9.1 *Group change. Despite the similarity in behaviour, each teenager is primarily an individual. Any continuity or change in decision making habits will differ for each girl (Source: SXC).*

period, to see if there would be any significant changes in their personalities, as a group. What emerged was rather curious. As a group there were only modest changes in personality. However, and this is where things got puzzling, these changes, although modest, were more pronounced amongst younger adolescents compared with those in their late teens.

It is important to emphasise that this study did not look specifically at decision making characteristics; rather, it merely investigated general personality features, such as how sociable the teenagers were and whether they were open to new experiences, ideas and encounters. Nevertheless, the findings do allow some tentative inferences, assuming that decision making forms part of a person's personality. One is that how teenagers in general make decisions essentially remains unchanged over time, given no outside intervention. Another is that children and younger teenagers are somewhat more erratic and hence less predictable than older adolescents.

Change in individual behaviour

Wendy has been very concerned about her health. She has gained a lot of weight over the past year or so, and now realises she has been comfort eating.

Wendy usually deals with such problems – indeed any health problem – by spending a considerable amount of time phoning friends or acquaintances who have had similar problems, to find out what their solutions were, and any pitfalls to be wary of.

Everyone Wendy spoke to about her putting on a few pounds doubted that she had a serious problem. Nevertheless, all recommended she should go on a strict diet and/or join a gym. After careful thought Wendy decided to take the advice. This is similar to how she dealt with an illness at school – she felt dizzy in class one afternoon and calmly decided to tackle the symptoms sensibly by going to see the school nurse. In short, Wendy is typically competent when making decisions.

What does this narrative demonstrate? It suggests that there can be considerable continuity in adolescents' decision making.

Individuals rarely change

Susan Harter and Nancy Whitesell, two psychologists who have done a lot of work on personality traits in adolescents (Harter and Whitesell, 2003), offer an intriguing thesis. Adolescents are first and foremost individuals, and it is extremely important not to lose sight of this fact. It is very easy to jump to conclusions about how teenagers as a group behave, and whether their personality changes over time, without allowing for the fact that every adolescent is different, unique and idiosyncratic.

Harter and Whitesell argue, on the basis of a series of studies, that some teenagers have personalities or personality traits that rarely change, regardless of the circumstances, while others have characters that alter considerably from one situation to the next (Harter and Whitesell, 2003).

I have already mentioned the study by Pullman et al. (2006) which found little or no change in various personality traits over a two-year period. What little change appeared was most pronounced amongst younger adolescents, that is, those in their early teens. Overall, the vast majority of participants – about four out of every five teenagers – did not report any change in any aspect of their personality.

Another study, by De Fruyt et al. (2006), assessed continuity and change in various personality dimensions, including emotional stability, extraversion, imagination, benevolence and conscientiousness. These personality dispositions, or variations of them, have been shown to be good reflectors of a person's decision making style, so that any change/continuity in any particular trait may indicate change/continuity in decision making practices (e.g. Cockroft, 1996; Denton, 1997; Bailey, 2003). For example Bailey (2003) found that high conscientiousness and a translation of imagination[1] predict greater competence in career decision making.

Nearly 500 children and younger adolescents (12 to 13 year olds) provided self-ratings on each personality trait at two different points in time, separated

---

[1] Openness to experience.

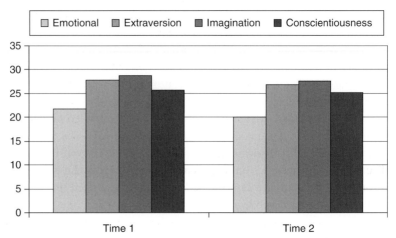

9.2 *Individual change and continuity. There appears to be considerable continuity in personality traits relevant to decision making. A study of younger teenagers showed little or no significant change over a 36-month period in major personality dimensions (Source: De Fruyt et al., 2006).*

by a thirty-six-month interval. Analysis revealed an amazing degree of stability. Although some significant changes were observed, especially amongst the adolescents, these variations were miniscule and hence almost irrelevant (see Fig. 9.2).

De Fruyt *et al.*'s (2006) findings I'm sure would concur with the experiences of many parents and other adults who have regular contact with adolescents. Short of undergoing shocking life-changing experiences, such as a near-death incident, most teenagers appear firmly set in their ways, with only the tiniest (if any) character changes occurring from time to time. However, it is important to reiterate the point that every teenager is different, and some, albeit a minority, do change considerably.

Although personality researchers like Harter, Whitesell, Pullman, De Fruyt and others don't specifically refer to decision making in their arguments, I see no reason why their ideas wouldn't apply to it (see Janis, 1986).

But how is it that teenagers, perhaps the majority, can be so unwavering in their approach to decision making?

Genetic and environmental constraints

A person's personality is essentially a consequence of inherited genes, the environment she grew up in, and the interface between these two factors (Heiman, 2004; Renaud and Guile, 2004). A teenager can inherit any number of behavioural traits from his parents, such as strong self-discipline, which would enable him to maintain a particular decision making strategy, regardless of the circumstances, or a propensity to be unduly influenced by situational factors, such as the opinions and actions of others. Susceptibility to situational influences would cause frequent

and sporadic changes in decision making strategy, depending on the social peculiarities or pressures of a particular circumstance.

Furthermore, the environment in which a youth grows up includes the care and education received from parents, not to mention other immediate family members, extended family, friends, other significant parties, notably schoolteachers, celebrities, doctors, the mass media, and so on. An adolescent taught from an early age to insist on competence when making decisions, and to adhere to this strategy regardless of the circumstances, is likely to grow up with a well-established and hence unchanging decision making style.

The effects of genetic and environmental factors on individuals can be complex and somewhat indecipherable. Genetic and environmental influences often interact. For example, imagine a teenage boy who customarily makes well-considered decisions, and has been this way ever since he can remember. Now consider that his father is exactly like him. It would be tempting to infer from this that the boy inherited his father's enduring knack for sensible decision making. While this may be true, it may only be part of the story. Social scientists have argued that the influence of genetic material on a person's personality depends partly, or entirely, on environmental factors (e.g. Bandura, 1977).

Thus, although the boy almost certainly inherited something from his father that predisposes him to informed choice, this potential has only been realised because of the care and education the young man received from his parents, not to mention school, and other sources of learning. Without social learning, any genetic potential for good or bad decision making would remain just that, a potential.

Predictability

One argument often made is that genetic inheritance is fixed. In other words, if an adolescent has inherited a propensity for fickleness and unpredictable decision making, no environmental factor would make any difference. The person isn't going to become suddenly more stable as a result of some intervention, trauma or other experience, no matter how intense and/or prolonged these environmental influences are. There are a number of possibilities to consider if we accept this argument.

The first is that a teenager who has inherited a knack for continuity is bound to be rather more predictable than usual. Thus, observers will neither expect nor ever experience a sudden change in the person's decision making style, whatever the circumstances. 'I know Tim', they would say. 'He is never going to do anything out of character!' They may be right.

The second thing to consider is that an adolescent who has inherited a jack-of-all-trades approach to decision making, always changing the way he responds to problems, is likely to be rather more fickle than usual, regardless of any environmental influences (e.g. criticism from parents, teachers and other significant persons). This in turn suggests even less predictability than usual. It would be

far less certain how this person may respond, for example, when offered a cigarette by peers. What will he do if he suddenly gains some weight and has to consider dieting, or suffers an asthma attack with no one around to help?

Of course, these points are speculative. Nevertheless, they are worth pondering. Bear in mind that even academics can't seem to agree on the relative contributions of heredity and the environment to human personality. Owing to the convoluted interplay of these factors, some teenagers may arrive at decisions in much the same way across a variety of situations, while others may use a different decision making approach depending on the situation. Ultimately though, every individual is a different kind of decision maker, and no firm assumptions can be made about the permanence or changeability of her decision making technique.

Change in relative differences

Adolescents may exhibit change in decision making style relative to others, over time. For example, an individual may find he is a more competent decision maker than his best friend under relaxed circumstances, but becomes less proficient in stressful situations. In a study on personality change in adolescents psychologists Pullman, Raudsepp and Allik made two key observations (Pullman et al., 2006).

First, relative differences among teenagers in the strength of various personality traits showed only average stability over a two-year period – correlations between personality features were around 0.5, give or take. This suggests that relative differences in the decision making styles of teenagers may persist over time, but only moderately so. This means there is also a distinct possibility of such differences vanishing.

The second observation is rather more intriguing. Relative differences in personalities seemed to get more stable with increasing age, and girls showed marginally more stability than boys. This means that as adolescents get older any differences between them become more and more permanent, especially if they are female. It is quite possible that by their early twenties relative variations in decision making skill are more or less fixed. In other words, some adolescents may consistently outperform their peers in decision making, through much of their adult life.

Change in profile

Psychological literature suggests that no significant change in a person's unique mix of decision making habits is likely to occur, over time. Filip De Fruyt, Karla Van Leeuwen and several other colleagues demonstrated this in an empirical study (De Fruyt et al., 2006). Parents were asked to describe their children's personality profile on two separate occasions separated by a three-year interval.

Personality descriptions at both times were highly similar, suggesting remarkable continuity. In other words these teenagers, in their parents' opinion, hardly changed their personality attributes over a considerable period of time.

It wouldn't be unreasonable to infer from this finding that the particular combination of personality traits that characterises an adolescent's decision making remains largely unchanged over time. Of course we have to be careful here, because parents' observation and recollection of their child's behaviour is subject to various biases, including a desire to portray their offspring as reliable. This may be particularly likely if that child has a generally likeable personality, so that the parents will naturally assume their child's 'good nature' is lasting rather than temporary. Teenagers themselves may be very clever at creating an impression of dependability, hiding any erratic tendencies.

Let's assume for the sake of argument that the findings from De Fruyt's study are compelling. How can we explain such remarkable consistency in adolescents' personality profile? It is difficult to ignore the role of genetics. There are so many emotions, thoughts and behaviours that characterise a person's decision making style that it is difficult to imagine all these facets remaining virtually unchanged for years unless they are rooted in that person's DNA.

Imagine a teenage girl who usually approaches difficult decisions with a mixture of avoidance and competence. Is she likely still to have this exact combination of personality traits if you bump into her in three years' time and observe her making a decision? Well, if the girl inherited these personality characteristics from one or both parents, then yes, she may remain the same basic person after three years, retaining even the most subtle nuances or idiosyncrasies, such as telephoning her best friend in the early hours of the morning for some advice about a problem, and then subsequently ignoring any recommendations.

Social learning dating back from early childhood may also play a key role in maintaining continuity (Bandura, 1977, 1986). A person may learn over the years that avoidance and competence can both yield significant rewards. For example, the former may be very effective at reducing stress, while the latter produces favourable decision outcomes. Consequently, the individual may exhibit these traits repeatedly until they become habitual.

Developmental factors

Any discussion of change in adolescent decision making must consider the role of developmental factors (Petersen and Leffert, 1995). It is generally acknowledged in the psychological literature that decision making competence improves as adolescents get older and begin to think more like adults (e.g. Mann *et al.*, 1989; Ormond *et al.*, 1991; Petersen and Leffert, 1995; Byrnes, 2002), although research findings are by no means conclusive (e.g. Brown and Mann, 1990).

There appears to be greater stability in an adolescent's character as she approaches adulthood (Byrnes, 2002). One obvious, if simplistic, reason is that

personality is still forming in late childhood and early adolescence, and hence is likely to be fluid and malleable at this point. Gradually, as teenagers get older, and 'discover' themselves, their character becomes more established, and hence less changeable.

Anecdotal evidence for this argument is not difficult to find. Watch a group of children playing together for a few minutes. The behaviour of some, perhaps most, would appear rather erratic. For example, a little boy may appear to enjoy playing rough and excitable games one minute, and then suddenly look composed and sedate the next. One girl may at first refuse to share a bar of chocolate with anyone else, and then suddenly offer some to another child. The same girl may suddenly ask for the chocolate back, bursting into tears if the other child fails to respond.

A child who seems responsible and decisive one minute could become impulsive the next. By contrast, a group of older teenagers playing or socialising in the same playground may display more stability and predictability. Some individuals will appear consistently competent while others may seem evasive. It could be argued that these youths would have roughly the same character tomorrow, next week, and perhaps next month, with only slight changes in personality. If adolescents' personalities are more established in their late teens, compared with late childhood and early adolescence, then it is also possible that their decision making styles will also become more permanent with increasing age.

Harter and Whitesell (2003) offer a more sophisticated insight as to why personality may vary more in early compared with late adolescence. When adolescents make the transition from elementary school to secondary school, usually in late childhood or early adolescence, they encounter new social pressures that substantially mould and remould their personalities, so much so that they may become less predictable (Harmon, 2007; Keller et al., 2007; Turner, 2007).

Moving to a new and unfamiliar environment is stressful, and would almost certainly require some adaptation. A decision making style which is incompatible with the new setting may be ditched, and replaced by a more amenable approach. For example, a boy may find that dealing effectively with intense peer group pressure to use drugs and alcohol requires quick thinking and snap decisions, rather than protracted deliberation aimed at finding an optimal solution. Whether this unsteadiness in decision making has implications for health behaviour is not certain. However, if over time a teenager forms the habit of switching between different decision making strategies, depending on the situation, then this volatility isn't suddenly going to disappear when the individual is confronted with difficult health behaviour choices.

Stable and unstable traits

When teenagers make bad decisions does this mean that they are intrinsically incompetent decision makers? According to psychologist M. Rosenberg

(1986) a person's personality may reflect both a core and hence unchanging aspect of their basic nature, and a changeable element that varies across time and situations. An unchanging personality is worrying because it suggests that poor decision making practices may be difficult if not impossible to change. A changeable personality, by contrast, is more encouraging because it implies that defective decision making habits aren't innate and can be corrected.

This notion of a core and adjustable personality is so well established in people's minds it is echoed in Western popular culture and entertainment. Anyone familiar with George Lucas's *Star Wars* series will know about the legendary Darth Vader. In the movies this figure is portrayed as an intrinsically bad character, someone prone to evil no matter the time, place or circumstances. He routinely makes snap decisions that involve having a person or persons (Luke Skywalker and his cronies) hunted and killed, or brought to him. Yet even a figure as fundamentally diabolical as Darth Vader displays a certain changeability from one situation to the next.

For example, in one scene, while dealing with a woman (Skywalker's sister and Darth Vader's daughter), Vader uncharacteristically fails to harm her with his supernatural powers. He will later display the same uncharacteristic sympathy to his son Luke (by refusing to kill him off during a sword duel). Yet, despite these positive lapses, most people who watch the *Star Wars* series – I suspect a large majority are teenagers – remain utterly convinced that Darth Vader is basically evil.

The folly of labelling

Is it sensible to label teenagers as bad decision makers when they make a few bad choices? Probably not, according to social science literature (Adelman, 1974; Al Talib and Griffin, 1994). According to labelling theory, a model that describes how an individual's self-image and behaviour are influenced by the way he is categorised by others (Link *et al.*, 1999; Phelan and Bruce, 1999), negative labels often lead to a self-fulfilling prophecy. To label a teenager an incompetent decision maker is unhelpful because it may trigger defective decision making in an individual who, although occasionally prone to poor judgement, is actually quite thoughtful and deliberative.

It is important for the reader to draw and maintain a sharp distinction between an adolescent's deep-rooted nature as a decision maker and his capacity to deviate occasionally from this basic character, albeit on a short-term basis. So, for example, an unrepentant teenage smoker who has a chronic habit of ignoring the health warnings on a packet of cigarettes may suddenly stop to read the warnings, reason that the benefits of smoking aren't worth the risks, and on the basis of this logic, decline to smoke. Similarly, a youth who is usually very open minded and thoughtful when making sexual decisions may occasionally display lapses of judgement, act on impulse, or completely ignore the threat of pregnancy or STDs. Unfortunately, occasional lapses in judgement negate predictability.

The role of prior experience

Any discussion about stability or change in adolescents' decision making would be incomplete without mention of the role played by prior experience (Bandura, 1977, 1986). Imagine two teenagers, Brian and Timothy. Brian has been plagued with health problems ever since he was little, including occasional acute asthma attacks. Over the years he has gradually developed a consistent way of deciding what action to take each time he has a medical emergency, such as scanning a short checklist given to him by his doctor to decide if his symptoms warrant calling an ambulance.

By contrast, Timothy's life couldn't be more different. He rarely falls sick and has only been to hospital on very few occasions since he was a child, mostly to receive some mandatory immunisation for children. Because of his inexperience in dealing with medical emergencies, Timothy's decision making is more erratic and unpredictable whenever he is faced with a medical crisis.

These two accounts highlight an important point. The stability of decision making may partly depend on the decision maker's experience in dealing with a problem. According to Bandura's (1977) social learning theory, people learn from their past experiences. Information acquired from prior learning 'serves as a guide for future action' (p. 16). So, for example, if deciding to smoke yielded favourable outcomes in the past, then this knowledge will increase the likelihood of a similar decision in the future.

Fazio, Zanna and colleagues (Fazio and Zanna, 1978a, 1978b; Fazio et al., 1982) contend that attitudes developed from past experience are more elaborate, easily remembered and hence stable than attitudes formed without prior experience. For example, an obese girl who has learned through experience that dieting never works will be readily aware of and hence act in accordance with her prior experiences, whenever she contemplates options for losing weight.

Literature concerning the impact of prior knowledge on new learning also highlights the importance of prior experience (Fischoff et al., 1977; Moorman, 1999; Alba and Hutchinson, 2000). People who already have high prior knowledge of a subject have been shown to be less willing to learn more on the topic (Wood and Lynch, 2002), because they assume they are already familiar with the issue, and don't need to learn more (Moorman, 1999). Thus, faced with a problem or decision, the individual makes judgements based on their prior knowledge, rather than a fresh analysis of the situation. For example, consider a teenager who is routinely offered cigarettes by friends. Presented with a new offer, he may assume he already knows what to do, and revert to his previous responses, rather than conduct a new appraisal of the circumstances, and work out a fresh decision. This would manifest as continuity in decision making.

Overall, prior experience of decision making may engender greater stability and hence continuity in one's approach to choice. An adolescent who is sexually active, and hence very experienced in making sexual decisions, is likely to have an established position on condom use. Faced with a choice between using and not using

contraception, he will be guided by time-honoured attitudes on the subject. The result is greater decision making stability over time. By contrast, a person who has never faced such a challenge before will have little prior experience to rely on and hence may be more unpredictable.

One reason why attitudes derived from past experience are more stable is that they are more resistant to counter-arguments. Janis and Mann (1977) argue that once a person makes a decision, he is repeatedly bombarded with counter-attacks, challenges and other threats, which could make him reconsider and perhaps reverse his position. This means more changeability in decision making. Previous experience makes people more resistant to such challenges, enabling continuity in choice patterns. An inspiring study by Chenghuan Wu and David Shaffer (1987) seems to provide some support for this argument.

A group of older adolescents (first-year undergraduates) were given an opportunity to develop a preference for one of two new and apparently different brands of low-calorie peanut butter. The items were simply wrapped in white paper, with no labels, but known as Product X and Product Y to the experimenters. Subjects were assigned to either a direct experience or an indirect experience condition. The former group were allowed to familiarise themselves with the butters by tasting them, while the latter group were merely provided with written information about the products, without being allowed to experience them directly.

Participants stated their preferences, and were then informed they had chosen Product X. They were then shown counter-arguments suggesting that Product Y was the superior butter. Analysis showed that direct experience subjects agreed less with, and hence were more resistant to, the counter-arguments (see Fig. 9.3). In other words, faced with a new opportunity to change their decision, adolescents with past experience showed less changeability.

However, to what extent do Wu and Shaffer's (1987) findings generalise to real-life health behaviour decisions? I remember reading about an investigation carried

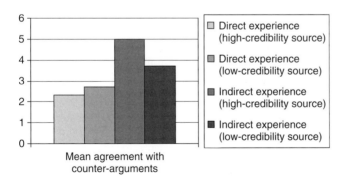

9.3 *Prior experience and resistance to change. Adolescents who are already familiar with a particular decision dilemma may be more resistant to challenges that undermine stability. A study showed that youngsters who had chosen one food product over another, based on past experience, were more resistant to counter-arguments challenging their decision (Source: Wu and Shaffer, 1987).*

out by two Dutch psychologists, F. van der Velde and J. van der Pligt, during the early 1990s (van der Velde and van der Pligt, 1991). The paper reported a study on how gay and heterosexual men coped with the threat of HIV and AIDS. It appeared that, whereas the former group had developed very elaborate and well-established ways of dealing with the problem, the latter group were more fragile in their decision making approach. The researchers argued that since gay men were much more experienced with HIV and AIDS – they've had to struggle with it ever since the problem appeared in the early 1980s – this group had the opportunity to develop an elaborate, tried-and-tested and hence more stable approach to dealing with the problem. Decisions are likely to be made using long-established protocols.

Overall, it seems anyone experienced in addressing health problems, or making health behaviour decisions, may have an established and hence predictable decision making style, whereas someone with significantly less experience will be more wavering and uncertain as they try to work out a fresh solution.

Effect of the identity crisis

Any discussion on changeability in adolescents' decision making will be incomplete without some reference to identity (Petersen and Leffert, 1995). Adolescence is characterised by a seemingly endless search for a personal and social individuality, a quest that continues for several years until adolescents enter their late teens, at which point many have developed a clearer understanding of who they are (Tani, 2001; Dunkel and Anthis, 2003; Burrow, 2005).

This search for an identity is particularly associated with junior high school. One identity many teenagers crave is 'coolness', both as a personal characteristic ('I'm cool') and as a social identity ('I'm one of the cool kids on campus', or 'I'm a cheerleader, and cheerleaders are cool'). Watch any Hollywood teenage movie and you will find innumerable references to the most popular boy/girl in school, the cool or coolest boy (usually some member of the football team) or girl (typically a pretty member of the cheerleading squad), the 'nerds' who are anything but cool, and so on.

Seeking an identity may depict both continuity and change to an adolescent's personality. Take for example ego identity, a concept proposed by renowned psychologist Erik H. Erickson to describe the identity adolescents acquire, after successfully negotiating the various developmental hurdles of adolescence, and which may incorporate personal and social identities (Tan et al., 1977). In one study, factor analysis of a questionnaire measure of ego identity, known as the Multidimensional Ego Identity Scale (MEIS), yielded several fundamental domains, including 'sameness' and 'continuity' dimensions (Tani, 2001). Other research has reported significant and irregular shifts in identity across different situations (e.g. Burrow, 2005).

Dunkel and Anthis (2003) suggest that having a negative self-image may trigger exploration for a better identity. Most teens would do anything to have a

positive self-image, including changing their character, albeit temporarily, just to be regarded favourably by others. Those who are already popular may strive to maintain their superior status. For example, they may be rather more sociable than normal with the opposite sex, or act more condescendingly to anyone thought to be their competition. It is at this stage in life that many youngsters develop a serious superiority or inferiority complex that stays with them for the rest of their lives. The net effect of this 'I want to be cool/popular' or 'I want to be like him/her' phenomenon is that personalities become quite fluid, changing on a regular basis.

This means that a teenager's approach to decision making is likely to change from time to time, to the extent that this helps identify and/or establish the right image. A normally level-headed youth with a knack for making well-considered decisions, but also a desire for popularity, may happily become impulsive if this is viewed favourably or demanded by significant others. Thus, decision making styles are likely to vary across time and situations, in accordance with identity requirements.

Conclusion

Whereas Chapter 5 discussed consistency in adolescents' decisions, this chapter looks at stability or change in their decision making style. The overall impression that emerges is that adolescents are rather unchanging and predictable in how they arrive at decisions. Thus, for example, someone prone to avoidance is likely to retain this disposition over time. This continuity seems to apply irrespective of how one conceptualises change, for example in terms of relative differences between two persons, decision making profile or group behaviour.

As teenagers grow older, and approach adulthood, it seems their decision making preferences only get more entrenched. Thus, attempting to improve the decision making competence of older teenagers, perhaps with a view to facilitating healthy choices, may be a futile exercise. Any such intervention is better off focusing on older children and younger adolescents, given that their decision making may be somewhat more malleable.

Overall, behavioural stability offers scientists the luxury of predictability. Being able to anticipate how a teenager may tackle a health behaviour decision in the future does empower health promoters to introduce appropriate safeguards to help compensate for a defective decision making strategy. So, for example, young people prone to impulsivity and avoidance can be made more aware of the shortcomings of these methods and given suitable corrective advice.

Key points

- Change in adolescent decision making can be conceptualised in several different ways, including variations in individual and group behaviour, and change across specific decision making attributes.

- Adolescents show remarkable stability in personality traits over time. This suggests significant continuity in decision making habits, given the significant association between personality and decision making.
- Adolescent decision making may have both a core unchanging element and a more volatile situational dimension.
- Continuity in adolescent decision making may depend somewhat on contextual factors, such as past experience, social transition and having an identity crisis.
- Change in decision making may also show a developmental trend, whereby decision making styles become more and more entrenched as adolescents get older and approach adulthood.
- Research in this area is sparse so any inferences have to be regarded with caution.

Key terms

- Change
- Continuity
- Decision making style
- Profile

Further reading

Cobb, N. (2004) *Adolescence: Continuity, Change and Diversity.* New York: McGraw Hill.
Heatherton, T.F. and Weinberger, J.L. (eds.) (1994) *Can Personality Change?* Washington, DC: American Psychological Association.
Siebert, A. (1996) *The Survivor Personality.* Berkeley, CA: Perigee Publishing.

References

Abdullah, A.S.M. and Ho, W.W.N. (2006) What Chinese adolescents think about quitting smoking: a qualitative study. *Substance Use and Misuse*, 41, pp. 1735–1743.

Abelson, R.P. (1968) Psychological implication. In R.P. Abelson, E. Aronson, W.J. McGuire, T.M. Newcomb, M.J. Rosenberg and P.H. Tannenbaum (eds.) *Theories of Cognitive Consistency: A Sourcebook* (pp. 112–139). Chicago: Rand McNally.

Abraham, C.S. and Sheeran, P. (2003) Acting on intentions: the role of anticipated regret. *British Journal of Social Psychology*, 42, pp. 495–511.

Abraham, C.S., Sheeran, P., Abrams, D. and Spears, R. (1994) Exploring teenagers' adaptive and maladaptive thinking in relation to threat of HIV infection. *Psychology and Health*, 9, pp. 253–272.

Adelman, S.I. (1974) Effects of labelling adolescents upon attitudes expressed by secondary teacher education students. *Dissertation Abstracts International: Section A: Humanities and Social Sciences*, 34, (12–A, Pt 1).

Agnew, R. (1989) Delinquency as a creative enterprise: a review of recent evidence. *Criminal Justice and Behaviour*, 16, pp. 98–113.

Ajzen, I. (1991) Theory of planned behaviour. *Organizational Behavior and Human Decision Processes*, 50, pp. 179–211.

Ajzen, I. and Fishbein, M. (1980) *Understanding Attitudes and Predicting Social Behaviour*. Englewood Cliffs, NJ: Prentice Hall.

Alba, J. and Hutchinson, J.W. (2000) Knowledge calibration: what consumers know and what they think they know. *Journal of Consumer Research*, 27, pp. 123–156.

Albion, M.J. and Fogarty, G.J. (2002) Factors influencing career decision making in adolescents and adults. *Journal of Career Assessment*, 10, pp. 91–126.

Albrecht, S.A., Higgins, L.W. and Lebow, H. (2000) Knowledge about the deleterious effects of smoking and its relationship to smoking cessation among pregnant adolescents. *Adolescence*, 35, pp. 709–716.

Allison, K.R., Dwyer, J.J.M., Goldenberg, E., Fein, A., Yoshida, K.K. and Boutilier, M. (2005) Male adolescents' reasons for participating in physical activity, barriers to participation, and suggestions for increasing participation. *Adolescence*, 40, pp. 155–170.

Al-Talib, N.I. and Griffin, C. (1994) Labelling effect on adolescents' self-concept. *International Journal of Offender Therapy and Comparative Criminology*, 38, pp. 47–57.

Alvord, E. (2007) Supportive and challenging social factors in a decision to be sexually abstinent. *Dissertation Abstracts International: Section B: The Sciences and Engineering*, 68 (2–B).

Amos, A., Wiltshire, S., Haw, S. and McNeill, A. (2006) Ambivalence and uncertainty: experiences of and attitudes towards addiction and smoking cessation in the mid-to-late teens. *Health Education Research*, 21, pp. 181–191.

Amsterlaw, J. (2006) Children's beliefs about everyday reasoning. *Child Development*, 77, pp. 443–464.

Andra, M.L. (2005) The relationship between coping styles, decisional balance, and smoking cessation outcomes. *Dissertation Abstracts International: Section B: The Sciences and Engineering*, 65 (8–B).

Arkes, H.R. and Ayton, P. (1999) The sunk cost and concorde effects: are humans less rational than lower animals? *Psychological Bulletin*, 125, pp. 591–600.

Aronson, E., Wilson, T.D. and Akert, R.M. (2002) *Social Psychology.* Upper Saddle River, NJ: Prentice Hall.

Ashbourne, D.T. (1995) Adolescent pre-pregnancy decision making: attitudes and behavioral intention relationships. *Dissertation Abstracts International: Section A: Humanities and Social Sciences*, 56 (1–A).

Ayton, P. and Hardman, D. (1997) Are two rationalities better than one? *Current Psychology of Cognition*, 16, pp. 39–51.

Bailey, C.J. (2003) Applying the five-factor model of personality to undergraduate career attitudes and beliefs: maturity, decision-making self-efficacy, and control. *Dissertation Abstracts International: Section B: The Sciences and Engineering*, 63 (9–B).

Bailey, P.E., Bruno, Z.V., Bezerra, M.F., Queiros, I. and Oliveira, C.M. (2003) Adolescents' decision-making and attitudes towards abortion in north-east Brazil. *Journal of Biosocial Science*, 35, pp. 71–82.

Baker, J.R. and Yardley, J.K. (2002) Moderating effect of gender on the relationship between sensation seeking–impulsivity and substance use in adolescents. *Journal of Child and Adolescent Substance Abuse*, 12, pp. 27–43.

Bakker, A.B. (1999) Persuasive communication about AIDS prevention: need for cognition determines the impact of message format. *AIDS Education and Prevention*, 11, pp. 150–162.

Bakker, A.B., Siero, F.W. and Buunk, B.P. (1995) Have safe sex or no sex: persuasive communication about AIDS among adolescents. *Gedrag and Gezondheid: Tijdschrift voor Psychologie en Gezondheid*, 23, pp. 166–178.

Balbinotti, M.A.A., Barbosa, M.L.L., Wiethaeuper, D. and Teodoro, M.L.M. (2006) Factorial structure of Coping Multifactor Inventory for Adolescents (CMIA-43). *PSICO*, 37, pp. 123–130.

Bamberg, S., Ajzen, I. and Schmidt, P. (2003) Choice of travel mode in the theory of planned behaviour: the roles of past behaviour, habits, and reasoned action. *Basic and Applied Social Psychology*, 25, pp. 175–187.

Bandura, A. (1977) *Social Learning Theory.* Englewood Cliffs, NJ: Prentice Hall.
    (1986) *Social Foundations of Thought and Action.* New York: Prentice Hall.

Barron, K.E. and Harackiewicz, J.M. (2001) Achievement goals and optimal motivation: testing multiple goal models. *Journal of Personality and Social Psychology*, 80, pp. 706–722.

Bauman, K.E., Fisher, L.A., Bryan, E.S. and Chenoweth, R.L. (1985) Relationship between subjective expected utility and behaviour: a longitudinal study of adolescent drinking behaviour. *Journal of Studies on Alcohol*, 46, pp. 32–38.

Bauman, S. (1999) The development and validation of a scale to assess motivation to change in substance abusing adolescents. *Dissertation Abstracts International: Section B: The Sciences and Engineering*, 60 (3–B).

Baumann, M.R., Sniezek, J.A. and Buerkle, C.A. (2001) Self-evaluation, stress, and performance: a model of decision making under acute stress. In G. Klein and E. Salas (eds.) *Linking Expertise and Naturalistic Decision-Making.* (pp. 139–158). Mahwah, NJ: Lawrence Erlbaum Associates.

Bazerman, M.H., Giuliano, T. and Appelman, A. (1984) Escalation of commitment in individual and group decision-making. *Organisational Behaviour and Human Performance*, 33, pp. 141–152.

BBC News (1998) Ecstasy victim's friend fined [online], BBC Online Network, Available from http://news.bbc.co.uk/1/hi/uk/145234.stm (accessed 23 February 2007)

Beauvois, J.L. and Joule, R.V. (1999) A radical point of view on dissonance theory. In J. Mills and E. Harmon-Jones (eds.) *Cognitive Dissonance: Progress on a Pivotal Theory in Social Psychology* (pp. 43–70). Washington, DC: American Psychological Association.

Beck, K.H. and Davis, C.M. (1980) Predicting smoking intentions and behaviours from attitudes, normative beliefs, and emotional arousal. *Social Behaviour and Personality: An International Journal*, 8, p. 185.

Becker, D., Dulong, O. and Igoin, L. (1974) The application of the Rorschach to adolescents on chronic hemodialysis. *L'Evolution Psychiatrique*, 39, pp. 605–619.

Benson, J. and Britten, N. (2003) Patients' views about taking anti-hypertensive drugs: questionnaire study. *British Medical Journal*, 326, pp. 1314–1315.

Ben-Zur, H., Breznitz, S., Wardi, N. and Berzon, Y. (2000) Denial of HIV/AIDS and preventive behaviour among Israeli adolescents. *Journal of Adolescence*, 23, pp. 157–174.

Berry, T., Naylor, P.J. and Wharf-Higgins, J. (2005) Stages of change in adolescents: an examination of self-efficacy, decisional balance, and reasons for relapse. *Journal of Adolescent Health*, 37, pp. 452–459.

Beswick, G., Rothblum, E. and Mann, L. (1988) Psychological antecedents of student procrastination. *Australian Psychologist*, 23, pp. 207–217.

Bleakley, A., Merzel, C., Van Devanter, N. and Messeri, P. (2004) Computer use and Internet access among urban youth. *American Journal of Public Health*, 94, pp. 744–746.

Boer, H. and Mashamba, M.T. (2007) Gender power imbalance and differential psychosocial correlates of intended condom use among male and female adolescents from Venda, South Africa. *British Journal of Health Psychology*, 12, pp. 51–63.

Boiche, J.C.S. and Sarrazin, P.G. (2007) Self-determination of contextual motivation, inter-context dynamics and adolescents' patterns of sport participation over time. *Psychology of Sport and Exercise*, 8, pp. 685–703.

Booth-Butterfield, M., Anderson, R.H. and Booth-Butterfield, S. (2000) Adolescents' use of tobacco, health locus of control, and self-monitoring. *Health Communication*, 12, pp. 137–148.

Bors, D.A., Vigneau, F. and Lalande, A. (2006). Measuring the need for cognition:item polarity, dimensionality, and the relation with ability. *Personality and Individual Differences*, 40, pp. 819–828.

Bostrom, M. (2001) *The 21st Century Teen: Public Perception and Teen Reality – A Summary of Public Opinion Data*. Washington, DC: The Frameworks Institute.

Brank, E.M. (2002) Paying for the crimes of their children: the legal and psychological perspectives on support of parental responsibility laws. *Dissertation Abstracts International: Section B: The Sciences and Engineering*, 62 (8–B).

Brank, E.M. and Weisz, V. (2004) Paying for the crimes of their children: public support of parental responsibility. *Journal of Criminal Justice*, 32, pp. 465–475.

Bratko, D. and Butkovic, A. (2004) Pet velikih faktora licnosti I predvidanje trazenja uzbudenja kod adolescenata I njihovih roditelja/The five-factor personality model and prediction of sensation seeking among adolescents and their parents. *Suvremena Psihologija*, 7, pp. 65–76.

Breda, C. and Heflinger, C.A. (2004) Predicting incentives to change among adolescents with substance abuse disorders. *American Journal of Drug and Alcohol Abuse*, 30, pp. 251–267.

Breeding, J. and Baughman, F.J. (2003) Informed consent and the psychiatric drugging of children. *Journal of Humanistic Psychology*, 43, pp. 50–64.

Brehm, S., Kassin, S. and Fein, S. (1999) *Social Psychology* (4th edition). Boston, MA: Houghton Mifflin.

Brewer, N.T., Chapman, G.B., Gibbons, F.X., Gerrard, M., McCaul, K.D. and Weinstein, N.D. (2007) Meta-analysis of the relationship between risk perception and health behaviour: the example of vaccination. *Health Psychology*, 26, pp. 136–145.

Brown, J.E. and Mann, L. (1990) The relationship between family structure, and process variables and adolescent decision-making. *Journal of Adolescence*, 13, pp. 25–37.

Brown, S.C. and Park, D.C. (2002) Roles of age and familiarity in learning health information. *Educational Gerontology*, 28, pp. 695–710.

Bryman, A. and Cramer, D. (1994) *Quantitative Data Analysis for Social Scientists*. London: Routledge.

Burnett, P.C., Mann, L. and Beswick, G. (1989) Validation of the Flinders' decision making questionnaire on course decision making for students. *Australian Psychologist*, 24, pp. 285–292.

Burrow, A.L. (2005) On the developmental continuity/discontinuity of early adolescent patterns of racial identity salience: relations with later identities and psychosocial adjustment. *Dissertation Abstracts International: Section B: The Sciences and Engineering*, 66 (3–B).

Butler, C.K. (2007) Prospect theory and coercive bargaining. *Journal of Conflict Resolution*, 51, pp. 227–250.

Byrnes, J.P. (2002) The development of decision-making. *Journal of Adolescent Health*, 31, pp. 208–215.

Byrnes, J.P., Miller, D.C. and Reynolds, M. (1999) Learning to make good decisions: a self-regulation perspective. *Child Development*, 70, pp. 1121–1140.

Cacioppo, J.T., Petty, R.E. and Morris, K. (1983) Effects of need for cognition on message evaluation, recall, and persuasion. *Journal of Personality and Social Psychology*, 45, pp. 805–818.

Cady, M.E., Winters, K.C., Jordan, D.A., Solberg, K.B. and Stinchfield, R. (1996) Motivation to change as a predictor of treatment outcome for adolescent substance abusers. *Journal of Child and Adolescent Substance Abuse*, 5, pp. 73–91.

Caffray, C.M. and Schneider, S.L. (2000) Why do they do it? Affective motivators in adolescents' decisions to participate in risk behaviours. *Cognition and Emotion*, 14, pp. 543–576.

Calamari, J.E., Hale, L.R., Heffelfinger, S.K., Janeck, A.S., Lau, J.J., Weerts, M.A., Taglione, P.A. and Schisler, R.L. (2001) Relations between anxiety sensitivity and panic symptoms in nonreferred children and adolescents. *Journal of Behaviour Therapy and Experimental Psychiatry*, 32, pp. 117–136.

Campbell, T.A. (1996) Coping and perceived control in older children and young adolescents during three stages of a stressful event. *Dissertation Abstracts International: Section B: The Sciences and Engineering*, 57 (2–B).

Carballo, J.J., Oquendo, M.A., Giner, L., Zalsman, G., Roche, A.M. and Sher, L. (2006) Impulsive–aggressive traits and suicidal behaviour in adolescents and young adults with alcoholism. *International Journal of Adolescent Medicine and Health*, 18, pp. 17–19.

Carballo-Dieguez, A., Remien, R.H., Dolezal, C. and Wagner, G. (1997) Unsafe sex in the primary relationships of Puerto Rican men who have sex with men. *AIDS and Behaviour*, 1, pp. 9–17.

Carlson, K.L., Broome, M. and Vessey, J.A. (2000) Using distraction to reduce reported pain, fear, and behavioural distress in children and adolescents: a multisite study. *Journal of the Society of Pediatric Nurses*, 5, pp. 75–85.

Carver, C.S., Scheier, M.F. and Weintraub, J.J. (1989) Assessing coping strategies: a theoretically based approach. *Journal of Personality and Social Psychology*, 56, pp. 267–283.

Cecil, H., Evans, R.I. and Stanley, M.A. (1996) Perceived believability among adolescents of health warning labels on cigarette packs. *Journal of Applied Social Psychology*, 26, pp. 502–519.

Chambers, K.B. and Rew, L. (2003) Safer sexual decision making in adolescent women: perspectives from the conflict-theory of decision-making. *Issues in Comprehensive Pediatric Nursing*, 26, pp. 129–143.

Chen, H.S., Sheu, J.J. and Chen, W.W. (2006a). Psychometric testing of the Chinese version of the Decisional Balance Scale (CDBS). *Health Education and Behaviour*, 33, pp. 812–820.

Chen, H.S., Sheu, J.J., Percy, M.S., Brown, E.J. and Yang, R.J. (2006b) The Chinese version of the Decisional Balance Scale: further validation. *Nursing Research*, 55, pp. 225–230.

Chien, Y.C., Lin, C. and Worthley, J. (1996) Effect of framing on adolescents' decision making. *Perceptual and Motor Skills*, 83, pp. 811–819.

Chiou, W.B. and Wan, C.S. (2007) Using cognitive dissonance to induce adolescents' escaping from the claw of online gaming: the roles of personality responsibility and justification of cost. *CyberPsychology and Behaviour*, 10, pp. 663–670.

Cho, H. and Salmon, C.T. (2006) Fear appeals for individuals in different stages of change: intended and unintended effects and implications on public health campaigns. *Health Communication*, 20, pp. 91–99.

Cialdini, R.B. (1993) *Influence: Science and Practice* (3rd edn). Boston: Allyn and Bacon.

Clayton, C.S. and Bray, S.R. (2007) Keep it real: do behavioural entreaties change first-year students' intentions to exercise? *Journal of Sports and Exercise Psychology*, 29, p. S153–S154.

Coats, E. J. and Feldman, R. S. (eds.) (2001) *Classic and Contemporary Readings in Social Psychology*. Englewood Cliffs, NJ: Prentice Hall.

Cobb, N. (2004) *Adolescence: Continuity, Change and Diversity*. New York: McGraw Hill.

Cockroft, R. D. (1996) Personality and authoritarian moral systems. *Dissertation Abstracts International: Section B: The Sciences and Engineering*, 56 (10–B).

Cohen, R., Rinat, C., Schwartz, S. B. and Frishberg, Y. (2005) Is non-compliance among adolescent renal transplant recipients inevitable? *Pediatrics*, 115, pp. 969–973.

Cohn, L. D., Macfarlane, S., Yanez, C. and Imai, W. K. (1995) Risk perception: differences between adolescents and adults. *Health Psychology*, 14, pp. 217–222.

Coleman, D. K. (2006) Parental problem recognition, help-seeking and service utilization for adolescent mental health: do age, gender and the presence of school problems affect parental decisions? *Dissertation Abstracts International: Section B: The Sciences and Engineering*, 67 (5–B).

Compas, B. E., Boyer, M. C., Stanger, C., Colletti, R. B., Thomsen, A. H., Dufton, L. M. and Cole, D. A. (2006) Latent variable analysis of coping, anxiety/depression, and somatic symptoms in adolescents with chronic pain. *Journal of Consulting and Clinical Psychology*, 74, pp. 1132–1142.

Connell, J. P. and Wellborn, J. G. (1990) Competence, autonomy and relatedness: a motivational analysis of self-system processes. In M. R. Gunnar and L. A. Sroufe (eds.) *The Minnesota Symposium on Child Psychology*, vol. 22 (pp. 43–77). Hillsdale, NJ: Erlbaum.

Conner, M. (1993) Pros and cons of social cognition models in health behaviour. *Health Psychology*, 14, pp. 24–31.

Conner, M. and Norman, P. (1996) The role of social cognition in health behaviours. In M. Conner and P. Norman (eds.) *Predicting Health Behaviour* (pp. 1–22). Buckingham: Open University Press.

Conner, M., Sandberg, T. and McMillan, B. (2006) Role of anticipated regret, intentions, and intention stability in adolescent smoking initiation. *British Journal of Health Psychology*, 11, pp. 85–101.

Contento, I. R., Williams, S. S., Michela, J. L. and Franklin, A. B. (2006) Understanding the food choice process of adolescents in the context of family and friends. *Journal of Adolescent Health*, 38, pp. 575–582.

Cook, A. J., Moore, K. and Steel, D. G. (2005) The taking of a position: a reinterpretation of the elaboration likelihood model. *Journal for the Theory of Social Behaviour*, 35, pp. 143–154.

Cooper, J. (1971) Personal responsibility and dissonance: the role of foreseen consequences. *Journal of Personality and Social Psychology*, 18, pp. 354–363.

Cormack, D. (2000) *The Research Process in Nursing* (fourth edition). Oxford: Blackwell Science.

Couturier, J. L. and Lock, J. (2006) Denial and minimisation in adolescents with anorexia nervosa. *International Journal of Eating Disorders*, 39, pp. 212–216.

Cowan, F. M. (2002) Adolescent reproductive health interventions. *Sexually Transmitted Infections*, 78, pp. 315–318.

Cox, W. M. and Klinger, E. (1988) A motivational model of alcohol use. *Journal of Abnormal Psychology*, 97, pp. 168–180.

Cramer, P. (1987) The development of defense mechanisms. *Journal of Personality*, 55, pp. 597–614.

(1991) *The Development of Defense Mechanisms: Theory, Research, and Assessment.* New York: Springer-Verlag.

(1999) Ego functions and ego development: defense mechanisms and intelligence as predictors of ego level. *Journal of Personality,* 67, pp. 735–760.

(2007) Longitudinal study of defense mechanisms: late childhood to late adolescence. *Journal of Personality,* 75, pp. 1–23.

Crawford, A.M., Pentz, M.A., Chou, C.P., Li, C. and Dwyer, J.H. (2003) Parallel developmental trajectories of sensation-seeking and regular substance use in adolescents. *Psychology of Addictive Behaviours,* 17, pp. 179–192.

Crone, E.A., Vendel, I. and van der Molen, M.W. (2003) Decision making in disinhibited adolescents and adults: insensitivity to future consequences or driven by immediate reward? *Personality and Individual Differences,* 35, pp. 1625–1641.

Crystal, D.S. and Stevenson, H.W. (1995) What is a bad kid? Answers of adolescents and their mothers in three cultures. *Journal of Research on Adolescence,* 5, pp. 71–91.

D'Acremont, M. and van der Linden, M. (2005) Adolescent impulsivity: findings from a community sample. *Journal of Youth and Adolescence,* 34, pp. 427–435.

Dahl, M.J. (2006) Adolescent decisions in situations of uncertainty: the impact of risky choice framing and decision making competency. *Dissertation Abstracts International: Section B: The Sciences and Engineering,* 66 (12–B).

Daigneault, I., Tourigny, M. and Hebert, M. (2006) Self-attributions of blame in sexually abused adolescents: a mediational model. *Journal of Traumatic Stress,* 19, pp. 153–157.

Daily, L. and Mumford, M.D. (2006) Evaluative aspects of creative thought: errors in appraising the implications of new ideas. *Creative Research Journal,* 18, pp. 367–384.

de Bourdeaudhuij, I., Crombez, G., Deforche, B., Vinaimont, F., Debode, P. and Bouckaert, J. (2002) Effect of distraction on treadmill running time in severely obese children and adolescents. *International Journal of Obesity,* 26, pp. 1023–1029.

Deb, S. (2005) Knowledge, attitude, and perception of adolescents about different aspects of reproductive health: a cross-sectional study. *Social Science International,* 21, pp. 70–92.

De Civita, M. and Pagani, L. (1996) Familial constraints on the initiation of cigarette smoking among adolescents: an elaboration of social bonding theory and differential association theory. *Canadian Journal of School Psychology,* 12, pp. 177–190.

De Fruyt, F., Bartels, M., Van Leeuwen, K.G., De Clercq, B., Decuyper, M. and Mervielde, I. (2006) Five types of personality continuity in childhood and adolescence. *Journal of Personality and Social Psychology,* 91, pp. 538–552.

Denton, D.W. (1997) A structural equations analysis of the relationship between personality and performance in a supervisory assessment center. *Dissertation Abstracts International: Section B: The Sciences and Engineering,* 57 (10–B).

De Vries, H., Mudde, A.N., Kremers, S.P.J., Leijs, I. and Uiters, E. (2000) The European Smoking Prevention Framework Approach (ESFA): an example of integral prevention. *Health Education Research,* 18, pp. 611–626.

Diamond, S. (1980) Wundt before Leipzig. In R.W. Rieber (ed.), *Wilhelm Wundt and the Making of a Scientific Psychology* (pp. 3–70). New York: Plenum Press.

Dias, S.F., Matos, M.G. and Goncalves, A.C. (2005) Preventing HIV-transmission in adolescents: an analysis of the Portuguese data from the Health Behaviour

School-aged Children study and focus groups. *European Journal of Public Health*, 15, pp. 300–304.

Di Noia, J., Schinke, S.P., Prochaska, J.O. and Contento, I.R. (2006) Application of the Transtheoretical Model to fruit and vegetable consumption among economically disadvantaged African American adolescents: preliminary findings. *American Journal of Health Promotion*, 20, pp. 342–348.

Dittmar, H. and Drury, J. (2000) Self-image – is it in the bag? A qualitative comparison between 'ordinary' and 'excessive' consumers. *Journal of Economic Psychology*, 21, pp. 109–142.

Dowson, M. and McInerney, D.M. (2001) Psychological parameters of students' social and work avoidance goals: a qualitative investigation. *Journal of Educational Psychology*, 93, pp. 35–42.

Drahovzal, D.N. (2007) Decisional balance of nutrition behaviour and physical activity among children and adolescents. *Dissertation Abstracts International: Section B: The Sciences and Engineering*, 67 (7–B).

Driskell, J.E., Salas, E. and Johnston, J.H. (2006) Decision making and performance under stress. In A.B. Adler, T.W. Britt and C.A. Castro (eds.) *Military Life: The Psychology of Serving in Peace and Combat,* vol. 1: *Military Performance* (pp. 128–154). Westport, CT: Praeger Security International.

Duncan, M.P., Garcia, A.C., Frankowski, B.L., Carey, P.A., Kallock, E.A., Dixon, R.D. and Shaw, J.S. (2007) Inspiring healthy adolescent choices: a rationale for and guide to strength promotion in primary care. *Journal of Adolescent Health*, 41, pp. 525–535.

Dunkel, C.S. and Anthis, K.S. (2003) The self across time and space in late adolescents: a test of temporal–spatial continuity in identity. In S.P. Shohov (ed.) *Advances in Psychology Research*, vol. 20 (pp. 131–143). Hauppauge, NY: Nova Science Publishers.

Eagly, A.H. and Chaiken, S. (1993) *The Psychology of Attitudes*. Orlando, FL: Harcourt Brace Jovanovich.

Edelen, M.O., Tucker, J.S., Wenzel, S.L., Paddock, S.M. and Dahl, J. (2007) Treatment process in the therapeutic community: associations with retention and outcomes among adolescent residential clients. *Journal of Substance Abuse Treatment*, 32, pp. 415–421.

Edwards, W. (1961) Behavioural decision theory. *Annual Review of Psychology*, 12, pp. 473–498.

Eiser, J.R., Eiser, C., Sani, F., Sell, L. and Casas, R.M. (1995) Skin cancer attitudes: a cross-national comparison. *British Journal of Social Psychology*, 34, pp. 23–30.

Ernst, M., Grant, S.J., London, E.D., Contoreggi, C.S., Kimes, A.S. and Spurgeon, L. (2003) Decision making in adolescents with behaviour disorders and adults with substance abuse. *American Journal of Psychiatry*, 160, pp. 33–42.

Eiser, J. and van der Pligt, J. (1988) *Attitudes and Decisions*. London: The Guernsey Press.

Elkind, D. (1967) Egocentrism in adolescence. *Child Development*, 38, pp. 1025–1034.

(1985) Egocentrism redux. *Developmental Review*, 5, pp. 218–226.

Ellerman, C.R. (2002) Starting and stopping: adolescents' decision-making about drug use. *Dissertation Abstracts International: Section B: The Sciences and Engineering*, 62 (11–B).

Elliott, M.M., DeSilva, N.K. and Middleman, A.B. (2007) Sexual activity and teenage females taking hormonal therapy for medical indications. *Journal of Adolescent Health*, 41, pp. 616–619.

Erbaydar, T., Lawrence, S., Dagli, E., Hayran, O. and Collishaw, N.E. (2005) Influence of social environment in smoking among adolescents in Turkey. *European Journal of Public Health*, 15, pp. 404–410.

Evans, N., Gilpin, E., Farkas, A.J., Shenassa, E. and Pierce, J.P. (1995) Adolescents' perceptions of their peers' health norms. *American Journal of Public Health*, 85, pp. 1064–1069.

Eyles, D.J. and Bates, G.W. (2005) Development of a shortened form of the Coping Responses Inventory-Youth with an Australian sample. *North American Journal of Psychology*, 7, pp. 161–170.

Fallon, B.J. and Bowles, T.V.P. (1998) Adolescents' influence and cooperation in family decision-making. *Journal of Adolescence*, 21, pp. 599–608.

Faust, D., Hart, K., Guilmette, T. and Arkes, H.R. (1988) Neuro-psychologists' capacity to detect adolescent malingerers. *Professional Psychology: Research and Practice*, 19, pp. 508–515.

Fazio, R.H., Chen, J., McDonel, E.C. and Sherman, S.J. (1982) Attitude accessibility, attitude-behaviour consistency, and the strength of object-evaluation association. *Journal of Experimental Social Psychology*, 18, pp. 339–357.

Fazio, R.H. and Zanna, M.P. (1978a) Attitudinal qualities relating to the strength of the attitude–behaviour relationship. *Journal of Experimental Social Psychology*, 14, pp. 398–408.

(1978b) On the predictive validity of attitudes: the roles of direct experience and confidence. *Journal of Personality*, 46, pp. 228–243.

Feinstein, S., Keich, R., Becker-Cohen, R., Rinat, C., Schwartz, S.B. and Frishberg, Y. (2005) Is non-compliance among adolescent renal transplant recipients inevitable? *Paediatrics*, 115, pp. 969–973.

Feldman, R.S. (2001) *Social Psychology*. Upper Saddle River, NJ: Prentice Hall.

Festinger, L. (1957) *A Theory of Cognitive Dissonance*. Evanston, IL: Row Peterson.

Festinger, L. and Carlsmith, J.M. (1959) Cognitive consequences of forced compliance. *Journal of Abnormal and Social Psychology*, 58, pp. 203–211.

Festinger, L., Riecken, H.W. and Schachter, S. (1956) *When Prophecy Fails*. Minneapolis: University of Minnesota Press.

Feunekes, G.I., de Graaf, C., Meyboom, S. and van Staveren, W.A. (1998) Food choice and fat intake of adolescents and adults: associations of intakes within social networks. *Preventive Medicine*, 27, pp. 645–656.

Fickenscher, A., Novins, D.K. and Beals, J. (2006) A pilot study of motivation and treatment completion among American Indian adolescents in substance abuse treatment. *Addictive Behaviours*, 31, pp. 1402–1414.

Field, M., Christiansen, P., Cole, J. and Goudie, A. (2007) Delay discounting and the alcohol Stroop in heavy drinking adolescents. *Addiction*, 102, pp. 579–586.

Finken, L.L. (2005) The role of consultants in adolescents' decision making: a focus on abortion decisions. In J.E. Jacobs and P.A. Klaczynski (eds.) *The Development of Judgement and Decision Making in Children and Adolescents* (pp. 255–278). Mahwah, NJ: Lawrence Erlbaum.

Fischoff, B., Slovic, P. and Lichtenstein, S. (1977) Knowing with certainty: the appropriateness of extreme confidence. *Journal of Experimental Psychology: Human Perception and Performance*, 3, pp. 552–564.

Fishbein, M. and Ajzen, I. (1980) *Understanding Attitudes and Predicting Social Behaviour.* Englewood Cliffs, NJ: Prentice Hall.

Fishbein, D.H., Herman-Stahl, M., Eldreth, D., Paschall, M.J., Hyde, C., Hubal, R., Hubbard, S., Williams, J. and Ialongo, N. (2006) Mediators of the stress–substance–use relationship in urban male adolescents. *Prevention Science*, 7, pp. 113–126.

Floyd, D.L., Prentice-Dunn, S. and Rogers, R.W. (2000) A meta-analysis of research on protection motivation theory. *Journal of Applied Social Psychology*, 30, pp. 407–429.

Forsythe, A.C.L. (2003) Key grade-related periods for anti-tobacco campaigns and interventions: trends in tobacco use, risk and protective factors for high and low sensation-seeking White pre-teens and adolescents. *Dissertation Abstracts International: Section B: The Sciences and Engineering*, 63 (8–A).

Fox, C.R. and Hadar, L. (2006) 'Decisions from experience' = sampling error + prospect theory: reconsidering Hertwig, Barron, Weber and Erev (2004). *Judgement and Decision Making*, 1, pp. 159–161.

French, R.S., Mercer, C.H., Kane, R., Kingori, P., Stephenson, J.M., Wilkinson, P., Grundy, C., Lachowycz, K., Jacklin, P., Stevens, M., Brooker, S. and Wellings, K. (2007) What impact has England's teenage pregnancy strategy had on young people's knowledge of and access to contraceptive services? *Journal of Adolescent Health*, 41, pp. 594–601.

Friedlander, M.L., Kaul, T.J. and Stimel, C.A. (1984) Abortion: predicting the complexity of the decision making process. *Women and Health*, 9, pp. 43–54.

Friedman, I.A. (1996) Deliberation and resolution in decision-making processes: a self-report scale for adolescents. *Educational and Psychological Measurement*, 56, pp. 881–890.

Friedman, I.A. and Mann, L. (1993) Coping patterns in adolescent decision-making: an Israeli–Australian comparison. *Journal of Adolescence*, 16, pp. 187–199.

Fruin, D.J., Pratt, C. and Owen, N. (1992). Protection motivation theory and adolescents' perceptions of exercise. *Journal of Applied Social Psychology*, 22, pp. 55–69.

Fruyt, F.D., Van Leeuwen, K.G., Ciercq, B.D., Decuyper, M., Mervielde, I. and Bartels, M. (2006) Five types of personality continuity in childhood and adolescence. *Journal of Personality and Social Psychology*, 91, pp. 538–552.

Fuligni, A.J. and Eccles, J.S. (1993) Perceived parent–child relationships and early adolescents' orientation toward peers. *Developmental Psychology*, 29, pp. 622–632.

Furby, L. and Beyth-Marom, R. (1992) Risk-taking in adolescence: a decision-making perspective. *Developmental Review*, 12, pp. 1–44.

Furby, L., Thomas, C.W. and Ochs, L.M. (1995) Preventing sexually transmitted diseases: how adolescents perceive the options. *Journal of Applied Developmental Psychology*, 16, pp. 143–162.

Galotti, K.M. (2001) Helps and hindrances for adolescents making important real-life decisions. *Applied Developmental Psychology*, 22, pp. 275–287.

Gambara, H. and Gonzalez, E. (2005) What choices do adolescents have? *Infancia y Aprendizaje*, 28, pp. 277–291.

Garaigordobil, M. and Dura, A. (2006) Neosexism in adolescents aged 14 to 17: relationships with self-concept/self-esteem, personality, psychopathology, behavioural problems and social skills. *Clinica y Salud*, 17, pp. 127–149.

Gardner, W. and Herman, J. (1990) Adolescents' AIDS risk taking: a rational choice perspective. *New Directions for Child Development*, 50, pp. 17–35.

Gardner, M. and Steinberg, L. (2005) Peer influence on risk taking, risk preference, and risky decision making in adolescence and adulthood: an experimental study. *Developmental Psychology*, 41, pp. 625–635.

Garinger, H.M. (2001) An examination of the decision making process in gifted female adolescents: the relationship with a sense of self, a sense of morality, and at-risk behaviour. *Dissertation Abstracts International: Section A: Humanities and Social Sciences*, 61 (10–A).

Gibbons, R.D., Brown, C.H., Hur, K., Marcus, S., Bhaumik, D.K., Erkens, J.A., Herings, R.M.C. and Mann, J.J. (2007) Early evidence on the effects of regulators' suicidality warnings on SSRI prescriptions and suicide in children and adolescents. *American Journal of Psychiatry*, 164, pp. 1356–1363.

Gilbert, M.A., Bauman, K.E. and Udry, J.R. (1986) A panel study of subjective expected utility for adolescent sexual behaviour. *Journal of Applied Social Psychology*, 16, pp. 745–756.

Gillholm, R., Ettema, D., Selart, M. and Garling, T. (1999) The role of planning for intention–behaviour consistency. *Scandinavian Journal of Psychology*, 40, pp. 241–250.

Gillison, F.B., Standage, M. and Skevington, S.M. (2006) Relationships among adolescents' weight perceptions, exercise goals, exercise motivation, quality of life and leisure-time exercise behaviour: a self-determination theory approach. *Health Education Research*, 21, pp. 836–847.

Ginsburg, G.S. and Drake, K.L. (2002) Anxiety sensitivity and panic attack symptomatology among low-income African American adolescents. *Journal of Anxiety Disorders*, 16, pp. 83–96.

Ginsburg, G.S., Lambert, S.F. and Drake, K.L. (2004) Attributions of control, anxiety, sensitivity, and panic symptoms among adolescents. *Cognitive Therapy and Research*, 28, pp. 745–763.

Gittelsohn, J., Roche, K.M., Alexander, C.S. and Tassler, P. (2001) The social context of smoking among African-American and white adolescents in Baltimore City. *Ethnic Health*, 6, pp. 211–225.

Goggin, K., Murray, T.S., Malcarne, V.L., Brown, S.A. and Wallston, K.A. (2007) Do religious and control cognitions predict risky behavior? Development and validation of the alcohol-related God Locus of Control Scale for adolescents (AGLOC-A). *Cognitive Therapy and Research*, 31, pp. 111–122.

Gordon, C.P. (1996) Adolescent decision making: a broadly based theory and its application to the prevention of early pregnancy. *Adolescence*, 31, pp. 561–584.

Gosling, P., Denizeau, M. and Oberle, D. (2006) Denial of responsibility: a new mode of dissonance reduction. *Journal of Personality and Social Psychology*, 90, pp. 722–733.

Gosselin, P., Langlois, F., Freeston, M.H., Ladouceur, R., Dugas, M.J. and Pelletier, O. (2002) The Cognitive Avoidance Questionnaire (CAQ): development and validation among adult and adolescent samples. *Journal de Therapie Comportementale et Cognitive*, 12, pp. 24–37.

Gosselin, P., Langlois, F., Freeston, M.H., Ladouceur, R., Laberge, M. and Lemay, D. (2007) Cognitive variables related to worry among adolescents: avoidance strategies and faulty beliefs about worry. *Behaviour Research and Therapy*, 45, pp. 225–233.

Granner, M.L. (2004) Individual, social, and environmental factors associated with fruit and vegetable intake among adolescents: a study of social cognitive and behavioural choice theories. *Dissertation Abstracts International: Section B: The Sciences and Engineering*, 64 (7–B).

Gray, N.J., Klein, J.D., Noyce, R.P., Sesselberg, T.S. and Cantrill, J.A. (2005a) The Internet: a window on adolescent health literacy. *Journal of Adolescent Health*, 37, pp. 243.e1–243.e7.

(2005b) Health information seeking behaviour in adolescence: the place of the Internet. *Social Science and Medicine*, 60, pp. 1467–1478.

Green, L. and Dollinger, S.J. (1992) Illusions (and shattered illusions) of invulnerability: adolescents in natural disaster. *Journal of Traumatic Stress*, 5, pp. 63–75.

Griffiths, F., Green, E. and Bendelow, G. (2006) Health professionals, their medical interventions, and uncertainty: a study focusing on women at midlife. *Social Science and Medicine*, 62, pp. 1078–1090.

Grunfeld, E.A. (2004) What influences university students' intentions to practice safe sun exposure behaviours? *Journal of Adolescent Health*, 35, pp. 482–492.

Grunseit, A., Kippax, S., Aggleton, P., Baldo, M. and Slutkin, G. (1997) Sexuality education and young people's sexual behaviour: a review of studies. *Journal of Adolescent Research*, 12, pp. 421–453.

Gullone, E., King, N.J. and Ollendick, T. (2000) The development and psychometric evaluation of the fear experiences questionnaire: an attempt to disentangle the fear and anxiety constructs. *Clinical Psychology and Psychotherapy*, 7, pp. 61–75.

Gutierrez, J.L.G., Puente, C.P., Rodriguez, R.M., Arjonilla, N.M., Puertas, C.P. and Herrador, M.R. (2003) Busqueda de sensaciones, consumo de alcohol y de extasis (MDMA) en adolescents/Sensation seeking, alcohol and ecstasy (MDMA) consumption in adolescents. *Analisis y Modificacion de Conducta*, 29, pp. 705–735.

Hall, K.L. (2005) A meta-analytic examination of decisional balance across stage transitions: a cross-sectional analysis and cross-sequential cross-validation. *Dissertation Abstracts International: Section B: The Sciences and Engineering*, 65 (9–B).

Halpern-Felsher, B.L., Biehl, M., Kropp, R.Y. and Rubinstein, M.L. (2004) Perceived risks and benefits of smoking: differences among adolescents with different smoking experiences and intentions. *Preventive Medicine*, 39, pp. 559–567.

Halpern-Felsher, B.L. and Cauffman, E. (2001) Costs and benefits of a decision: decision making competence in adolescents and adults. *Journal of Applied Developmental Psychology*, 22, pp. 257–273.

Hampel, P. (2007) Brief report: coping among Australian children and adolescents. *Journal of Adolescence*, 30, pp. 885–890.

Hampel, P., Rudolph, H., Stachow, R., Labeta-Lentzsch, A. and Peterman, F. (2005) Coping among children and adolescents with chronic illness. *Anxiety, Stress and Coping*, 18, pp. 145–155.

Hanna, K.M. (1994) Female adolescents' perceptions of benefits of and barriers to using oral contraceptives. *Issues in Comprehensive Paediatric Nursing*, 17, pp. 47–55.

Hanna, K.M. and Guthrie, D. (2000) Adolescents' perceived benefits and barriers related to diabetes self-management – Part 1. *Issues in Comprehensive Paediatric Nursing*, 23, pp. 165–174.

Hardell, L.O., Carlberg, M., Soderqvist, F., Mild, K.H. and Morgan, L.L. (2007) Long-term use of cellular phones and brain tumours – increased risk associated with use for >10 years. *Occupational and Environmental Medicine*, 64, pp. 626–632.

Harmon, M.A. (2007) Facilitating the transition from elementary school to middle/junior high school for culturally and linguistically diverse and/or exceptional early adolescents. *Dissertation Abstracts International: Section A: Humanities and Social Sciences*, 68 (4–A).

Harmon-Jones, E., Brehm, J.W., Greenberg, J., Simon, L. and Nelson, D.E. (1996) Evidence that the production of aversive consequences is not necessary to create cognitive dissonance. *Journal of Personality and Social Psychology*, 70, pp. 5–16.

Harrell, T.K., Davy, B.M., Stewart, J.L. and King, D.S. (2005) Effectiveness of a school-based intervention to increase health knowledge of cardiovascular disease risk factors among rural Mississippi middle school children. *Southern Medical Journal*, 98, pp. 1173–1180.

Hart, J.T. (1965) Second-try, recall, recognition, and the memory-monitoring process. *Journal of Educational Psychology*, 58, pp. 193–197.

Harter, S. and Whitesell, N.R. (2003) Beyond the debate: why some adolescents report stable self-worth over time and situation, whereas others report changes in self-worth. *Journal of Personality*, 71, pp. 1027–1058.

Hastie, R. and Dawes, R.M. (2001) *Rational Choice in an Uncertain World*. Thousand Oaks, CA: Sage.

Hastrup, J.L., Phillips, S.M., Vullo, K., Kang, G. and Slomka, L. (1992) Adolescents' knowledge of medical terminology and family health history. *Health Psychology*, 11, pp. 41–47.

Hattne, K., Folke, S. and Twetman, S. (2007) Attitudes to oral health among adolescents with high caries risk. *Acta Odontologica Scandinavica*, 65, pp. 206–213.

Hayward, C., Killen, J.D., Kraemer, H.C. and Taylor, C.B. (2000) Predictors of panic attacks in adolescents. *Journal of the American Academy of Child and Adolescent Psychiatry*, 39, pp. 207–214.

Hayward, C., Killen, J.D. and Taylor, C.B. (2003) The relationship between agoraphobia symptoms and panic disorder in a non-clinical sample of adolescents. *Psychological Medicine*, 33, pp. 733–738.

Heatherton, T.F. and Weinberger, J.L. (eds.) (1994) *Can Personality Change?* Washington, DC: American Psychological Association.

Heiman, N. (2004) The genetic and environmental structure of Cloninger's model of personality. *Dissertation Abstracts International: Section B: The Sciences and Engineering*, 65 (6–B).

Heinrichs, G.A. (1995) Adolescent sexual attitudes and behaviours: the effects of intrinsic–extrinsic religiosity. *Dissertation Abstracts International: Section B: The Sciences and Engineering*, 56 (5–B).

Helmes, E. and Holden, R.R. (2003) The construct of social desirability: one or two dimensions? *Personality and Individual Differences*, 34, pp. 1015–1023.

Hertel, P.T. and Calcaterra, G. (2005) Intentional forgetting benefits from thought substitution. *Psychonomic Bulletin and Review*, 12, pp. 484–489.

Higgins, A. and Conner, M. (2003) Understanding adolescent smoking: the role of the theory of planned behaviour and implementation intentions. *Psychology, Health and Medicine*, 8, pp. 173–186.

Hilda, G. and Elena, G. (2005) What choices do adolescents have? *Infancia y Aprendizaje*, 28, pp. 277–291.

Hine, D.W., McKenzie-Richer, A., Lewko, J., Tilleczek, K. and Perreault, L. (2002) A comparison of the mediational properties of four adolescent smoking expectancy measures. *Psychology of Addictive Behaviours*, 16, pp. 187–195.

Hoerster, C.M. (2001) The influence of gender on smoking behaviour as mediated by social factors and weight concerns in 8th graders: a path analysis. *Dissertation Abstracts International: Section B: The Sciences and Engineering*, 62 (6–B).

Holm, K., Kremers, S.P.J. and de Vries, H. (2003) Why do Danish adolescents take up smoking? *European Journal of Public Health*, 13, pp. 67–74.

Homa, K. (2007) Teen killed in smash. *Liverpool Echo*, 17 January, pp. 1–2.

Hovland, C.I., Janis, I.L. and Kelley, H.H. (1953) *Communication and Persuasion*, New Haven, CT: Yale University Press.

Howitt, D. and Cramer, D. (2005) *Introduction to Statistics in Psychology*. Harlow: Prentice Hall.

Hulton, L.J. (2001) The application of the transtheoretical model of change to adolescent sexual decision-making. *Issues in Comprehensive Paediatric Nursing*, 24, pp. 95–115.

Jablonska, J.R., Dietrich, A.M. and Gmitrowicz, A. (2003) Wystepowanie leku spolecznego wsrod reprezentatywnej grupy mlodziezy z Lodzi/The prevalence of social phobia in a representative group of adolescents from Lodz. *Psychiatria Polska*, 37, pp. 87–95.

Jaccard, J., Dodge, T. and Dittus, P. (2003) Do adolescents want to avoid pregnancy? Attitudes toward pregnancy as predictors of pregnancy. *Journal of Adolescent Health*, 33, pp. 79–83.

Jacobs, J.E., Chhin, C.S. and Shaver, K. (2005) Longitudinal links between perceptions of adolescence and the social beliefs of adolescents: are parents' stereotypes related to beliefs held about and by their children? *Adolescence*, 34, pp. 61–72.

Jacobs, J.E. and Johnston, K.E. (2005) 'Everyone else is doing it': relations between bias in base-rate estimates and involvement in deviant behaviours. In P.A. Klaczynski and J.E. Jacobs (eds.) *The Development of Judgement and Decision Making in Children and Adolescents* (pp. 157–179). Mahwah, NJ: Lawrence Erlbaum.

Jacobs, J.E. and Klaczynski, P.A. (2002) The development of judgement and decision making during childhood and adolescence. *Current Directions in Psychological Science*, 11, pp. 145–149.

(eds.) (2005) *The Development of Judgement and Decision Making in Children and Adolescents* (pp. 255–278). Mahwah, NJ: Lawrence Erlbaum.

Janis, I.L. (1958) Methods: case studies and survey research. In I.L. Janis (ed.) *Psychological Stress: Psychoanalytic and Behavioural Studies of Surgical Patients* (pp. 223–238). Hoboken, NJ: John Wiley and Sons.

(1967) Effects of fear arousal on attitude change: recent developments in theory and experimental research. In L. Berkowitz, (ed.) *Advances in Experimental Social Psychology* (pp. 166–224). San Diego, CA: Academic Press.

(1983) The role of social support in adherence to stressful decisions. *American Psychologist*, 38, pp. 143–160.

(1984) The patient as decision maker. In W.D. Gentry (ed.) *Handbook of Behavioural Medicine* (pp. 326–368). New York: Guilford Press.

(1986) Coping patterns among patients with life-threatening diseases. *Issues in Mental Health Nursing*, 7, pp. 461–476.

Janis, I.L. and Feshbach, S. (1953) Effect of fear-arousing communications. *Journal of Abnormal and Social Psychology*, 48, pp. 78–92.

Janis, I.L. and Mann, L. (1976) Coping with decisional conflict: an analysis of how stress affects decision making suggests interventions to improve the process. *American Scientist*, 64, pp. 657–666.

(1977) *Decision Making: A Psychological Analysis of Conflict, Choice, and Commitment*. New York: The Free Press.

(1982) A theoretical framework for decision counselling. In I.L. Janis (ed.) *Counseling on Personal Decisions: Theory and Research on Short-Term Helping Relationships* (pp. 47–72). New Haven, CT: Yale University Press.

Janz, N.K. and Becker, H.M. (1984) The health belief model: a decade later. *Health Education Quarterly*, 11, pp. 1–47.

Jeff, D.A. (2007) A pilot study of distraction for adolescents during allergy testing. *Journal for Specialists in Pediatric Nursing*, 12, pp. 170–185.

Jerusalem, M. and Schwarzer, R. (1989) Selbstkonzept und Angstlichkeit als Einflüsgrüsen für Strëserleben und Bewaltigungstendenzen (Self-concept and anxiety as predictors of stress experiences and coping tendencies). *Zeitschrift für Entwicklungspsychologie und Pädagogische Psychologie*, 21, pp. 307–324.

Johnson, H.C., Cournoyer, D.E., Fisher, G.A., McQuillan, B.E., Moriarty, S., Richert, A.L., Stanek, E.J., Stockford, C.L. and Yirigian, B.R. (2000) Children's emotional and behavioural disorders: attributions of parental responsibility by professionals. *American Journal of Orthopsychiatry*, 70, pp. 327–339.

Jorgensen, S.R. (1980) Contraceptive attitude–behaviour consistency in adolescence. *Population and Environment: Behavioural and Social Issues*, 3, pp. 174–194.

Kahneman, D. and Tversky, A. (1973) On the psychology of prediction. *Psychological Review*, 80, pp. 237–251.

(1979) Prospect theory: an analysis of decisions under risk. *Econometrica*, 47, pp. 313–327.

Kaljee, L.M., Genberg, B., Riel, R., Cole, M., Tho, L.H., Thoa, L.T.K., Stanton, B., Li, X. and Minh, T.T. (2005) Effectiveness of a theory-based risk reduction HIV prevention program for rural Vietnamese adolescents. *AIDS Education and Prevention*, 17, pp. 185–199.

Kanvil, N. and Umeh, K.F. (2000) Lung cancer and cigarette use: cognitive factors, protection motivation and past/current behaviour. *British Journal of Health Psychology*, 5, pp. 235–248.

Kao, C. (1994) The concept and measurement of need for cognition. *Chinese Journal of Psychology*, 36, pp. 1–20.

Katsenelinboigen, A. (1997) *The Concept of Indeterminism and Its Applications: Economics, Social Systems, Ethics, Artificial Intelligence, and Aesthetics*. Westport, CT: Praeger.

Katz, J. (1973) Adolescents: are they normal? *Australian and New Zealand Journal of Psychiatry*, 7, pp. 235–242.

Keller, T.E., Cusick, G.R. and Courtney, M.E. (2007) Approaching the transition to adulthood: distinctive profiles of adolescents aging out of the child welfare system. *Social Science Review*, 81, pp. 453–484.

Kelly, J., Turner, J.J. and McKenna, K. (2006) What parents think: children and healthy eating. *British Food Journal*, 108, pp. 413–423.

Kester, H.M., Sevy, S., Yechiam, E., Burdick, K.E., Cervellione, K.L. and Kumra, S. (2006) Decision making impairments in adolescents with early-onset schizophrenia. *Schizophrenia Research*, 85, pp. 113–123.

Kiel, L.D. and Elliott, E.W. (1997) *Chaos Theory in the Social Sciences*. Ann Arbor: University of Michigan Press.

Klaczynski, P.A. (2000) Motivated scientific reasoning biases, epistemological beliefs, and theory polarisation: a two-process approach to adolescent cognition. *Child Development*, 71, pp. 1347–1366.

(2001a) Framing effects on adolescent task representations, analytic and heuristic processing, and decision-making: implications for the normative/descriptive gap. *Applied Developmental Psychology*, 22, pp. 289–309.

(2001b) Analytic and heuristic processing influences on adolescents' reasoning and decision-making. *Child Development*, 72, pp. 844–861.

Kochenderfer-Ladd, Becky (2004) Peer victimization: the role of emotions in adaptive and maladaptive coping. *Social Development*, 13, pp. 329–349.

Kokis, J., Macpherson, R., Toplak, M., West, R.F. and Stanovich, K.E. (2002) Heuristic and analytic processing: age trends and associations with cognitive ability and cognitive styles. *Journal of Experimental Child Psychology*, 83, pp. 26–52.

Kornblau, I.S., Pearson, H.C. and Radecki, C. (2007) Demographic, behavioural and physical correlates of body esteem among low-income female adolescents. *Journal of Adolescent Health*, 41, pp. 566–570.

Kowalski, K.C., Mack, D.E., Crocker, P.R.E., Niefer, C.B. and Fleming, T.L. (2006) Coping with social physique anxiety in adolescence. *Journal of Adolescent Health*, 39, pp. e9–e16.

Kremers, S.P., Brug, J., de Vries, H. and Engels, R.C. (2003) Parenting style and adolescent fruit consumption. *Appetite*, 41, pp. 43–50.

Krohne, H.W. (1993) Attention and avoidance. Two central strategies in coping with aversiveness. In H.W. Krohne (ed.) *Attention and Avoidance* (pp. 3–15). Seattle: Hogrefe and Huber.

Krueger, R.F., Caspi, A., Moffit, T.W., White, J. and Stouthamer-Loeber, M. (1994) Delay of gratification, psychopathy, and personality: is low self-control specific to externalising problems? *Journal of Personality*, 64, pp. 107–129.

Kuo, B.C.H., Roysircar, G. and Newby, C.I.R. (2006) Development of the Cross-Cultural Coping Scale: collective, avoidance, and engagement coping. *Measurement and Evaluation in Counseling and Development*, 39, pp. 161–181.

Kuther, T.L. (2002) Rational decision perspectives on alcohol consumption by youth: revising the theory of planned behaviour. *Addictive Behaviors*, 27, pp. 35–47.

Laing, R.D. and Cooper, D. (1971) *Reason and Violence: A Decade of Sartre's Philosophy, 1950–1960*. New York: Pantheon.

Laird, H.M.G. (2001) Ego development and decision-making in pregnant adolescents. *Dissertation Abstracts International: Section A: Humanities and Social Sciences*, 61 (10–A).

Lam, S., Chiu, C., Lau, I.Y., Chan, W. and Yim, P. (2006) Managing intergroup attitudes among Hong Kong adolescents: effects of social category inclusiveness and time pressure. *Journal of Social Psychology*, 9, pp. 1–11.

Langer, L.M. and Girard, C. (1999) Risky sexual behaviours among substance-abusing adolescents: assessing the effect of decision making and avoidance motives. *International Journal of Adolescence and Youth*, 7, pp. 327–348.

Lasio-Morello, M.V. (2006) A climate for personal well-being: an integration of prospect theory and psychological climate. *Dissertation Abstracts International: Section A: Humanities and Social Sciences*, 67 (3–A).

Lathem, G. and Locke, E. (2002) Building a practically useful theory of goal setting and task motivation. *American Psychologist*, 57, pp. 705–717.

Lau, J.J., Calamari, J.E. and Waraczynski, M. (1996) Panic attack symptomatology and anxiety sensitivity in adolescents. *Journal of Anxiety Disorders*, 10, pp. 355–364.

Lauby, J.L., Bond, L., Eroglu, D. and Batson, H. (2006) Decisional balance, perceived risk, and IIIV testing practices. *AIDS and Behaviour*, 10, pp. 83–92.

Leatherdale, S., Cameron, R., Brown, K., Jolin, M. and Kroeker, C. (2006) The influence of friends, family and older peers on smoking among elementary school students: low-risk students in high-risk schools. *Preventive Medicine*, 42, pp. 218–222.

Lee, C.M., Neighbors, C. and Woods, B.A. (2007) Marijuana motives: young adults' reasons for using marijuana. *Addictive Behaviours*, 32, pp. 1384–1394.

Leen-Feldner, E.W., Zvolensky, M.J. and Feldner, M.T. (2006) A test of a cognitive diathesis stress model of panic vulnerability among adolescents. In A. J. Sanfelippo (ed.) *Panic Disorders: New Research* (pp. 41–64). Hauppauge, NY: Nova Biomedical Books.

Leite, W.L. and Beretvas, S.N. (2005) Validation of scores on the Marlowe-Crowne Social Desirability Scale and the Balanced Inventory of Desirable Responding. *Educational and Psychological Measurement*, 65, pp. 140–154.

Leventhal, E.A., Suls, J. and Leventhal, H. (1993) Hierarchical analysis of coping: evidence from lifespan studies. In H.W. Krohne (ed.) *Attention and Avoidance* (pp. 71–99). Seattle: Hogrefe and Huber.

Leventhal, H. (1970) Findings and theory in the study of fear communications. In L. Berkowitz (ed.) *Advances in Experimental Social Psychology* (pp. 119–86). New York: Academic Press.

Leventhal, H., Safer, M.A. and Panagis, D.M. (1983) The impact of communications on the self-regulation of health beliefs, decisions, and behaviour. *Health Education Quarterly*, 10, pp. 3–29.

Levin, B.W. (1999) Adolescents and medical decision making: observations of a medical anthropologist. In J. Blustein, C. Levine, and N. N. Dubler (eds.) *The Adolescent Alone: Decision Making in Health Care in the United States* (pp. 160–179). New York: Cambridge University Press.

Lewin, K. (1951) *Field Theory in Social Science: Selected Theoretical Papers*. New York: Harper and Row.

Li, H. and Prevatt, F. (2007) Fears and related anxieties across three age groups of Mexican American and White children with disabilities. *Journal of Genetic Psychology*, 168, pp. 381–400.

Liao, S. (2005) Good advice for bad backs. *Prevention*, 57, p. 39.

Lindbladh, E. and Lyttkens, C.H. (2002) Habit versus choice: the process of decision making in health-related behaviour. *Social Science and Medicine*, 55, pp. 451–465.

Lindsey, M.A., Korr, W., Broitman, M., Bone, L., Green, A. and Leaf, P. (2006) Help-seeking behaviors and depression among African-American adolescent boys. *Social Work*, 51, pp. 49–58.

Link, B.G. and Phelan, J.C. (1999) The labelling theory of mental disorder (II). The consequences of labelling. In A.V. Horwitz and T.L. Scheid (eds.) *A Handbook for the Study of Mental Health* (pp. 361–376). New York: Cambridge University Press.

Linn, M.C., Delucchi, K.L. and de Benedictis, T. (1984) Adolescent reasoning about advertisements: relevance of product claims. *Journal of Early Adolescence*, 4, pp. 371–385.

Linnenbrink, E. and Pintrich, P.R. (2000) Multiple pathways to learning and achievement: the role of goal orientation in fostering adaptive motivation, affect, and cognition. In S.S.J.M. Harackiewicz (ed.) *Intrinsic and Extrinsic Motivation: The Search for Optimal Motivation and Performance* (pp. 195–227). New York: Academic Press.

Liu, X., Tein, J.Y. and Zhao, Z. (2004) Coping strategies and behavioural/emotional problems among Chinese adolescents. *Psychiatry Research*, 126, pp. 275–285.

Locke, E.A. (1996) Motivation through conscious goal setting. *Applied and Preventive Psychology*, 5, pp. 117–124.

—— (2001) Motivation by goal setting. *Handbook of Organizational Behavior*, 2, pp. 43–54.

Logue, A.W. (1995) *Self-Control: Waiting until Tomorrow for What You Want Today*. Englewood Cliffs, NJ: Prentice Hall.

Loneck, B.M. and Kola, L.A. (1988) Using the conflict-theory model of decision making to predict outcome in the alcoholism intervention. *Alcoholism Treatment Quarterly*, 5, pp. 119–136.

Lowry, C.R.S. (2000) Testing the transtheoretical model of change in young adult male smokeless tobacco users. *Dissertation Abstracts International: Section B: The Sciences and Engineering*, 61 (6–B).

Macfarlane, A. and McPherson, A. (1993) Suffer the not-so-little children. *The Guardian*, 23 March, p. 19.

Mackey, K., Arnold, M.L. and Pratt, M.W. (2001) Adolescents' stories of decision-making in more and less authoritative families: representing the voices of parents in narrative. *Journal of Adolescent Research*, 16, pp. 243–268.

Macpherson, L. (2005) Examination of a process model of adolescent smoking self-change efforts in relation to gender. *Dissertation Abstracts International: Section B: The Sciences and Engineering*, 66 (3–B).

Madden, G.J., Petry, N.M., Badger, G.J. and Bickel, W.K. (1997) Impulsive and self-control choices in opioid-dependent patients and non-drug-using control patients: drug and monetary rewards. *Experimental and Clinical Psychopharmacology*, 5, pp. 256–262.

Maddux, J.E., Sherer, M. and Rogers, R.W. (2005) Self-efficacy expectancy and outcome expectancy: their relationship and their effects on behavioural intentions. *Cognitive Therapy Research*, 6, pp. 207–211.

Mann, L. (1982) Decision making questionnaire II. Unpublished questionnaire, The Flinders University of South Australia.

Mann, L., Burnett, P., Radford, M. and Ford, S. (1997) The Melbourne decision making questionnaire: an instrument for measuring patterns for coping with decisional conflict. *Journal of Behavioural Decision Making*, 10, pp. 1–19.

Mann, L., Harmoni, R. and Power, C. (1989) Adolescent decision-making: the development of competence. *Journal of Adolescence*, 12, pp. 265–278.

Mann, L., Harmoni, R., Power, C., Beswick, G. and Ormond, C. (1988) Effectiveness of the GOFER course in decision making for high school students. *Journal of Behavioural Decision Making*, 1, pp. 159–168.

Mann, L., Radford, M., Burnett, P., Ford, S., Bond, M., Leung, K., Nakamura, H., Vaughan, G. and Yang, K. (1998) Cross-cultural differences in self-reported decision-making style and confidence. *International Journal of Psychology*, 33, pp. 325–335.

Marcell, A.V. and Halpern-Felsher, B.L. (2005) Adolescents' health beliefs are critical in their intentions to seek physician care. *Preventive Medicine*, 41, pp. 118–125.

Marks, D.F., Murray, M., Evans, B., Willig, C., Woodall, C. and Sykes, C.M. (2005) *Health Psychology: Theory, Research and Practice* (second edition). London: Sage.

Masi, G., Favilla, L., Mucci, M. and Millepiedi, S. (2000) Panic disorder in clinically referred children and adolescents. *Child Psychiatry and Human Development*, 31, pp. 139–151.

Matczak, A. and Galinska, D. (1990) Wpływ premji czasowej na wykonanie przez dzieci zadań testu Ravena (Effect of time pressure on children's performance on the Raven Test). *Psychologia Wychowawcza*, 33, pp. 150–160.

Mattis, S.G. and Ollendick, T.H. (1997) Panic in children and adolescents: a developmental analysis. *Advances in Clinical Child Psychology*, 19, pp. 27–74.

(2002) *Panic Disorder and Anxiety in Adolescents*. Malden, MA: Blackwell.

Mauriello, L.M., Rossi, J.S., Fava, J.L., Redding, C.A., Robbins, M., Prochaska, J.O. and Meier, K.S. (2007) Assessment of the pros and cons of stress management among adolescents: development and validation of a decisional balance measure. *American Journal of Health Promotion*, 22, pp. 140–143.

Mayes, S. (2006) Protection motivation theory and knowledge of household safety hazards as predictors of parental home safety behaviour. *Dissertation Abstracts International: Section B: The Sciences and Engineering*, 67 (6–B).

Mazanov, J. and Byrne, D.G. (2002) A comparison of predictors of the adolescent intention to smoke with adolescent current smoking using discriminant function analysis. *British Journal of Health Psychology*, 7, pp. 185–201.

(2007) Changes in adolescent smoking behaviour and knowledge of health consequences of smoking. *Australian Journal of Psychology*, 59, pp. 176–180.

McCabe, M.A., Rushton, C.H., Glover, J. and Murray, M.G. (1996) Implications of the patient self-determination act: guidelines for involving adolescents in medical decision making. *Journal of Adolescent Health*, 19, pp. 319–324.

McConnell, J. (2003) Mattresses for a pain in the back. *The Lancet*, 362, p. 1594.

McDermott, A.F.N. (2002) Living with angina pectoris – a phenomenological study. *European Journal of Cardiovascular Nursing*, 1, pp. 265–272.

McDermott, R. (1998) Adolescent HIV prevention and intervention: a prospect theory analysis. *Psychology, Health and Medicine*, 3, pp. 371–385.

McKay, M.A. (1998) An investigation of the decision making process and self-esteem in adolescent gang membership. *Dissertation Abstracts International: Section B: The Sciences and Engineering*, 59 (2–B).

McKinney, J.P., Chin, R.J., Reinhart, M.A. and Trierweiler, G. (1985) Health values in early adolescence. *Journal of Clinical Child Psychology*, 14, pp. 315–319.

McMillan, B., Higgins, A.R. and Conner, M. (2005) Using an extended theory of planned behaviour to understand smoking amongst school children. *Addiction Research and Theory*, 13, pp. 293–306.

Medvene, L.J., Base, M., Patrick, R. and Wescott, J. (2007) Advance directives: assessing stage of change and decisional balance in a community-based educational program. *Journal of Applied Social Psychology*, 37, pp. 2298–2318.

Meekers, D. and Klein, M. (2002) Understanding gender differences in condom use self-efficacy among youth in urban Cameroon. *AIDS Education and Prevention*, 14, pp. 62–72.

Mergler, Amanda G. and Patton, Wendy A. (2007) Adolescents talking about personal responsibility. *Journal of Student Wellbeing*, 1, pp. 57–70.

Meriweather, A.L. (1997) The influence of self-led discussions on the learning of problem-solving skills with adolescent females. *Dissertation Abstracts International: Section B: The Sciences and Engineering*, 57 (12–B).

Mesarosova, M. (1997) Selected motivational dispositions and their correspondence with intellectual potential and school achievement. *Psychologia a Patopsychologia Dietata*, 32, pp. 22–34.

Michels, T.M., Kropp, R.Y., Eyre, S.L. and Halpern-Felsher, B.L. (2005) Initiating sexual experiences: how do young adolescents make decisions regarding sexual activity? *Journal of Research on Adolescence*, 15, pp. 583–607.

Milam, J.E., Sussman, S., Ritt-Olson, A. and Dent, C.W. (2000). Perceived invulnerability and cigarette smoking among adolescents. *Addictive Behaviors*, 25, pp. 71–80.

Miller, C.H., Burgoon, M., Grandpre, J.R. and Alvaro, E.M. (2006) Identifying principal risk factors for the initiation of adolescent smoking behaviors: the significance of psychological reactance. *Health Communication*, 19, pp. 241–252.

Miller, J.K., Westerman, D.L. and Lloyd, M.E. (2004) Are first impressions lasting impressions? An exploration of the generality of the primacy effect in memory for repetitions. *Memory and Cognition*, 32, pp. 1305–1315.

Miller, V.A. (2005) Parent–adolescent communication and adherence to diabetes treatment in adolescents with diabetes: the mediating role of decision-making competence. *Dissertation Abstracts International: Section B: The Sciences and Engineering*, 66 (5–B).

Miller, V.A. and Drotar, D. (2007) Decision making competence and adherence to treatment in adolescents with diabetes. *Journal of Pediatric Psychology*, 32, pp. 178–188.

Millstein, S.G. and Halpern-Felsher, B.L. (2001) Perceptions of risk and vulnerability. *Journal of Adolescent Health*, 31, pp. 10–27.

(2002) Judgements about risk and perceived invulnerability in adolescents and young adults. *Journal of Research on Adolescence*, 12, pp. 399–422.

Milne, S., Sheeran, P. and Orbell, S. (2000) Prediction and intervention in health-related behaviour: a meta-analytic review of protection motivation theory. *Journal of Applied Social Psychology*, 30, pp. 106–143.

Miotto, P., De Coppi, M., Frezza, M., Rossi, M. and Preti, A. (2002) Social desirability and eating disorders. A community study of an Italian school-aged sample. *Acta Psychiatrica Scandinavia*, 105, pp. 372–377.

Miserandino, M. (1996) Children who do well in school: individual differences in perceived competence and autonomy in above-average children. *Journal of Educational Psychology*, 88, pp. 203–214.

Misra, R. and Aguillon, S. (2001) Predictors of health behaviours in rural adolescents. *Health Education*, 101, pp. 22–31.

Mitchell, S.H. (1999) Measures of impulsivity in cigarette smokers and non-smokers. *Psychopharmacology*, 146, pp. 455–464.

Moan, I.S. and Rise, J. (2006) Predicting smoking reduction among adolescents using an extended version of the theory of planned behaviour. *Psychology and Health*, 21, pp. 717–738.

Molock, S.D., Barksdale, C., Matlin, S., Puri, R., Cammack, N. and Spann, M. (2007) Qualitative study of suicidality and help-seeking behaviors in African American adolescents. *American Journal of Community Psychology*, 40, pp. 52–63.

Monastersky, R. (2007) Who's minding the teenage brain? *Chronicle of Higher Education*, 53, A14–A18.

Moore, J.W., Jensen, B. and Hauck, W.E. (1990) Decision making processes of youth. *Adolescence*, 25, pp. 583–592.

Moore, S. and Cartwright, C. (2005) Adolescents' and young adults' expectations of parental responsibilities in stepfamilies. *Journal of Divorce and Remarriage*, 43, pp. 109–127.

Moore, S.M. and Rosenthal, D.A. (1991) Australian adolescents' perceptions of health-related risks. *Journal of Adolescent Research*, 7, pp. 177–191.

Moorman, C. (1999) The functionality of knowledge illusions. *Paper presented at the Association for Consumer Research Conference*, Columbus, Ohio.

Morgan, W.G. (1995) Origin and history of the Thematic Apperception Test images. *Journal of Personality Assessment*, 65, pp. 237–254.

Morrison, V. and Bennett, P. (2006) *An Introduction to Health Psychology*. Harlow: Prentice Hall.

Moskowitz, J.M. (2004) Assessment of cigarette smoking and smoking susceptibility among youth. *Public Opinion Quarterly*, 68, pp. 565–587.

Muir, S.L., Wertheim, E.H. and Paxton, S.J. (1999) Adolescent girls' first diets: triggers and the role of multiple dimensions of self-concept. *Eating Disorders: The Journal of Treatment and Prevention*, 7, pp. 259–270.

Mulilis, J.P. and Duval, T.S. (2003) Activating effects of resources relative to threat and responsibility in person-relative-to-event theory of coping with threat: an educational application. *Journal of Applied Social Psychology*, 33, pp. 1437–1456.

Mulilis, J., Duval, T.S. and Bovalino, K. (2000) Tornado preparedness of students, non-student renters, and nonstudent owners: issues of PrE theory. *Journal of Applied Social Psychology*, 30, pp. 1310–1329.

Munro, S., Lewin, S., Swart, T. and Volmink, J. (2007) A review of health behaviour theories: how useful are these for developing interventions to promote long-term medication adherence for TB and HIV/AIDS? *BMC Public Health*, 7, p. 104.

Muris, P. (2007) *Normal and Abnormal Fear and Anxiety in Children and Adolescents*. Oxford: Elsevier.

Muris, P., Merckelbach, H., Ollendick, T.H., King, N.J., Meesters, C. and van Kessel, C. (2002) What is the Revised Fear Survey Schedule for Children measuring? *Behaviour Research and Therapy*, 40, pp. 1317–1326.

Muris, P. and Ollendick, T.H. (2002) The assessment of contemporary fears in adolescents using a modified version of the Fear Survey Schedule for Children – revised. *Journal of Anxiety Disorders*, 16, 567–584.

Myers, I. (1990) *Introduction to Type: A Description of the Theory and Applications of the Myers-Briggs Type Indicator*. Washington, DC: Center for Applications of Psychological Type Inc.

Myers, Isabel Briggs, McCaulley, Mary H., Quenk, Naomi L. and Hammer, Allen L. (1998) *MBTI Manual (A Guide to the Development and Use of the Myers-Briggs Type Indicator)* (third edition). Palo Alto, CA: Consulting Psychologists Press.

Nagtegaal, M. (2004) Het dilemma van de vrije wil in de forensische psychologie / The dilemma of free will in forensic psychology. *Psycholoog*, 39, pp. 3–9.

NASPE (National Association for Sport and Physical Education) (2003) Adults'/teens' attitudes towards physical activity and physical education [online], The Sport Journal, available from www.thesportjournal.org/2003Journal/Vol6-No2/nasp.asp (accessed 23 March 2007).

Nau, R.F. (2006) Uncertainty aversion with second-order utilities and probabilities. *Management Science*, 52, pp. 136–145.

Nelson, M.C. (2007) The prominent influence of race on weight-related health among children and adolescents. *Journal of Adolescent Health*, 41, pp. 523–524.

Newall, P. (2005) Free will and determinism [online]. The Galilean Library, Manuscripts, available from www.galilean-library.org/int13.html (accessed 20 December 2007).

Nigg, C.R. (2000) Predicting, explaining and understanding adolescent exercise behaviour using longitudinal and cross-sectional approaches. *Dissertation Abstracts International: Section B: The Sciences and Engineering*, 60 (9–B).

(2001) Explaining adolescent exercise behaviour change: a longitudinal application of the transtheoretical model. *Annals of Behavioural Medicine*, 23, pp. 11–20.

Norman, P. and Conner, M. (1996) The role of social cognition models in predicting health behaviours: future directions. In M. Conner and P. Norman (eds.) *Predicting Health Behaviour* (pp. 197–225). Buckingham: Open University Press.

Nowak, M. and Crawford, D. (1998) Getting the message across: adolescents' health concerns and views about the importance of food. *Australian Journal of Nutrition and Dietetics*, 55, p. 3.

Nutbeam, D. and Booth, M.L. (1994) Health behaviour in adolescence: risks and reasons. In G.N. Penny, P. Bennnett and M. Herbert (eds.) *Health Psychology: A Lifespan Perspective* (pp. 53–66). Chur: Harwood.

O'Callaghan, F.V. and Nausbaum, S. (2006) Predicting bicycle helmet wearing intentions and behaviour among adolescents. *Journal of Safety Research*, 37, pp. 425–431.

Ogden, J. (2000) *Health Psychology*. Buckingham: Open University Press.

Ollendick, T.H. (1998) Panic disorder in children and adolescents: new developments, new directions. *Journal of Clinical Child Psychology*, 27, pp. 234–245.

Ollendick, T.H., King, N.J. and Frary, R.B. (1989) Fears in children and adolescents: reliability and generalizability across gender, age and nationality. *Behaviour Research and Therapy*, 27, pp. 19–26.

Ollendick, T.H., Langley, A.K., Jones, R.T. and Kephart, C. (2001) Fear in children and adolescents: relations with negative life events, attributional style, and avoidant coping. *Journal of Child Psychology and Psychiatry*, 42, pp. 1029–1034.

Ollendick, T.H., King, N.J. and Muris, P. (2002) Fears and phobias in children: phenomenology, epidemiology and aetiology. *Child and Adolescent Mental Health*, 7, pp. 98–106.

Olukoya, A.A., Kaya, A., Ferguson, B.J. and AbouZahr, C. (2001) Unsafe abortion in adolescents. *International Journal of Gynecology and Obstetrics*, 75, pp. 137–147.

Opie, I. and Opie, P. (1959) *The Lore and Language of School Children*. Oxford: Oxford University Press.

(eds.) (1992) *The Oxford Dictionary of Nursery Rhymes*. Oxford: Oxford University Press.

Oregon Resiliency Project (2003) *Self-Esteem in Children and Adolescents*. Portland: University of Oregon.

Ormond, C., Luszcz, M.A., Mann, L. and Beswick, G. (1991) A meta-cognitive analysis of decision-making in adolescence. *Journal of Adolescence*, 14, pp. 275–291.

Orr, D.P. and Langefeld, C.D. (2001) Factors associated with condom use by sexually active male adolescents at risk for sexually transmitted disease. *Pediatrics*, 91, pp. 873–879.

Oskamp, S. (1965) Overconfidence in case study judgements. *Journal of Consulting Psychology*, 29, pp. 261–265.

Otake, K. and Shimai, S. (2001) Adopting the stage model for smoking acquisition in Japanese adolescents. *Journal of Health Psychology*, 6, pp. 629–643.

Ozer, E.J. and Weinstein, R.S. (2004) Urban adolescents' exposure to community violence: the role of support, school safety, and social constraints in a school-based sample of boys and girls. *Journal of Clinical Child and Adolescent Psychology*, 33, pp. 463–476.

Ozolin, A.R. and Stenstrom, U. (2003) Validation of health locus of control patterns in Swedish adolescents. *Adolescence*, 38, pp. 651–657.

Palardy, N., Greening, L., Ott, J., Holderby, A. and Atchison, J. (1998) Adolescents' health attitudes and adherence to treatment for insulin-dependent diabetes mellitus. *Journal of Developmental and Behavioural Padiatrics*, 19, pp. 31–37.

Pallonen, U.E. (1998) Transtheoretical measures for adolescent and adult smokers: similarities and differences. *Preventive Medicine: An International Journal Devoted to Practice and Theory*, 27, A29–A38.

Palmqvist, R.A. and Martikainen, L.K. (2005) Changes in reasons given for adolescent smoking. *Substance Use and Misuse*, 40, pp. 645–656.

Parekh, S.A. (2007) Child consent and the law: an insight and discussion into the law relating to consent and competence. *Child: Care, Health and Development*, 33, pp. 78–82.

Pechmann, C., Levine, L., Loughlin, S. and Leslie, F. (2005) Impulsive and self-conscious: adolescents' vulnerability to advertising and promotion. *Journal of Public Policy and Marketing*, 24, pp. 202–221.

Pechmann, C., Zhao, G., Goldberg, M.E. and Reibling, E.T. (2003) What to convey in antismoking advertisements for adolescents: the use of protection motivation theory to identify effective message themes. *Journal of Marketing*, 67, pp. 1–18.

Peretti-Watel, P. (2006) Cognitive dissonance and risk denial: the case of cannabis use in adolescents. *Journal of Socio-Economics*, 35, pp. 1032–1049.

Petersen, A.C. and Leffert, N. (1995) Developmental issues influencing guidelines for adolescent health research: a review. *Journal of Adolescent Health*, 17, pp. 298–305.

Petty, R.E. and Cacioppo, J.T. (1986) *The Elaboration Likelihood Model of Persuasion*. New York: Academic Press.

Pfefferbaum, B., Stuber, J., Galea, S. and Fairbrother, G. (2006) Panic reactions to terrorist attacks and probable posttraumatic stress disorder in adolescents. *Journal of Traumatic Stress*, 19, pp. 217–228.

Phelan, J.C. and Link, B.G. (1999) Social contingencies in labelling theory. In A.V. Horwitz. and T.L. Scheid (eds.) *A Handbook for the Study of Mental Health* (pp. 139–149). New York: Cambridge University Press.

Phillips, G.C. (2004) Gender roles and sexism in adolescents: an examination of gender and race. *Dissertation Abstracts International: Section B: The Sciences and Engineering*, 64 (9–B).

Piaget, J. (1954) *The Construction of Reality in the Child* (trans. M. Cook). New York: Basic Books.

Piaget, J. and Inhelder, B. (1956) *The Child's Conception of Space*. London: Routledge and Kegan Paul.

Pimple, K.D. (2006) Science prediction rate would be good in gambling. *Nature*, 443, p. 632.

Piper, B. (2006) *Growing Pains*. London: Hodder and Stoughton.

Plous, S. (1993) Prisoner's dilemma or perceptual dilemma? *Journal of Peace Research*, 30, pp. 163–179.

Plummer, B.A., Velicer, W.F., Redding, C.A., Prochaska, J.O., Rossi, J.S., Pallonen, U.E. and Meier, K.S. (2001) Stage of change, decisional balance and temptations for smoking: measurement and validation in a large, school-based population of adolescents. *Addictive Behaviours*, 26, pp. 551–571.

Pogge, D.L., Borgaro, S.R., Horan, W.P., Stokes, J.M., Lord, J.J. and Harvey, P.D. (1996) Conduct disorder, impulsivity, and substance abuse in adolescents. *Biological Psychiatry*, 39, pp. 536–537.

Porcerelli, J.H., Thomas, S., Hibbard, S. and Cogan, R. (1998) Defence mechanisms development in children, adolescents, and late adolescents. *Journal of Personality Assessment*, 71, pp. 411–420.

Prochaska, J.O., DiClemente, C.C. and Norcross, J.C. (1992) In search of how people change. *American Psychologist*, 47, pp. 1102–1104.

Prochaska, J.O. and Velicer, W.F. (1997) The transtheoretical model of health behaviour change. *American Journal of Health Promotion*, 12, pp. 38–48.

Prochaska, J.O., Velicer, W.F., Rossi, J.S., Goldstein, M.G., Marcus, B.H., Rakowski, W., Fiore, C., Harlow, L.L., Redding, C.A., Rosenbloom, D. and Rossi, S.R. (1994) Stages of change and decisional balance for 12 problem behaviours. *Health Psychology*, 13, pp. 39–46.

Prosser, L.A., Hammitt, J.K. and Keren, R. (2007) Measuring health preferences for use in cost–utility and cost–benefit analysis of interventions in children: theoretical and methodological considerations. *PharmacoEconomics*, 25, pp. 713–726.

Pullman, H., Raudsepp, L. and Allik, J. (2006) Stability and change in adolescents' personality: a longitudinal study. *European Journal of Personality*, 20, pp. 447–459.

Rachlin, H. (1995) Self-control: beyond commitment. *Behavioural and Brain Sciences*, 18, pp. 109–159.

Radford, M.H.B., Mann, L. and Kalucy, R.S. (1986) Psychiatric disturbance and decision making. *Australian and New Zealand Journal of Psychiatry*, 20, pp. 10–217.

Reed, V. and Wittchen, H.U. (1998) DSM-IV panic attacks and panic disorder in a community sample of adolescents and young adults. *Journal of Psychiatric Research*, 32, pp. 335–345.

Renaud, S. and Guile, J.M. (2004) A neurobiological approach to temperamental traits associated with personality disorders. *Annales Medico Psychologiques*, 162, pp. 731–738.

Reyna, V.F. and Farley, F. (2006) Risk and rationality in adolescent decision-making. *Psychological Science*, 7, pp. 1–44.

Rippetoe, P.A. and Rogers, R.W. (1987) Effects of components of protection motivation theory on adaptive and maladaptive coping with a health threat. *Journal of Personality and Social Psychology*, 52, pp. 596–604.

Rise, J. (2004) Modifying adolescent health behaviours. *Current Opinion in Psychiatry*, 17, pp. 129–132.

Robbins, R.N. and Bryan, A. (2004) Relationships between future orientation, impulsive sensation seeking, and risk behaviour among adjudicated adolescents. *Journal of Adolescent Research*, 19, pp. 428–445.

Roberts, B.W., Caspi, A. and Moffitt, T.E. (2001) The kids are alright: growth and stability in personality development from adolescence to adulthood. *Journal of Personality and Social Psychology*, 81, pp. 670–683.

Rodham, K., Hawton, K. and Evans, E. (2004) Reasons for deliberate self-harm: comparison of self-poisoners and self-cutters in a community sample of adolescents. *Journal of the American Academy of Child and Adolescent Psychiatry*, 43, pp. 80–87.

Rogacheva, A., Laatikainen, T., Tossavainen, K., Vlasoff, T., Panteleev, V. and Vartiainen, E. (2007) Changes in cardiovascular risk factors among adolescents from 1995 to 2004 in the Republic of Karelia, Russia. *European Journal of Public Health*, 17, pp. 257–262.

Rogel, M.J., Zuehlke, M.E., Petersen, A.C., Tobin-Richards, M. and Shelton, M. (1980) Contraceptive behaviour in adolescence: a decision-making perspective. *Journal of Youth and Adolescence*, 9, pp. 491–506.

Rogers, R.W. (1975) A protection motivation theory of fear appeals and attitude change. *Journal of Psychology*, 91, pp. 93–114.

(1983) Cognitive and physiological processes in fear appeal and attitude change: a revised theory of protection motivation. In B.L. Cacioppo, L.L. Petty and D. Shapiro (eds.) *Social Psychophysiology: A Source Book*. London: The Guilford Press.

Rogers, R.W. and Mewborn, C.R. (1976) Fear appeals and attitude change: effects of a threat's noxiousness, probability of occurrence, and the efficacy of coping responses. *Journal of Personality and Social Psychology*, 34, pp. 54–61.

Rosen, N.O., Knauper, B. and Sammut, J. (2007) Do individual differences in intolerance of uncertainty affect health monitoring? *Psychology and Health*, 22, pp. 413–430.

Rosenberg, M. (1986) Self-concept from middle childhood through adolescence. In J. Suls and A.G. Greenwald (eds.) *Psychological Perspectives on the Self*, vol. 3 (pp. 107–135). Hillsdale, NJ: Lawrence Erlbaum.

Rosenstock, I.M. (1974) Historical origins of the Health Belief Model. *Health Education Monographs*, 2, pp. 328–335.

Rosenthal, S.L., Biro, F.M., Succop, P.A., Baker, J. and Stanberry, L.R. (1994) Reasons for condom utilization among high-risk adolescent girls. *Clinical Pediatrics*, 33, pp. 706–711.

Rossi, S.R., Greene, G.W., Rossi, J.S., Plummer, B.A., Benisovich, S.V., Keller, S., Velicer, W.F., Redding, C.A., Prochaska, J.O., Pallonen, U.E. and Meier, K.S. (2001) Validation of decisional balance and situational temptations measures for dietary fat reduction in a large school-based population of adolescents. *Eating Behaviours*, 2, pp. 1–18.

Roth, M. and Herzberg, P.Y. (2004) A validation and psychometric examination of the Arnett Inventory of Sensation Seeking (AISS) in German adolescents. *European Journal of Psychological Assessment*, 20, pp. 205–214.

Ruisel, I., Ruiselova, Z. and Prokopcakova, A. (1994) Subjective aspects of problem solving and decision making in the context of coping. *Studia Psychologica*, 36, pp. 77–89.

Ruiter, R.A.C., Verplanken, B., Cremer, D.D. and Kok, G. (2004) Danger and fear control in response to fear appeals: the role of need for cognition. *Basic and Applied Social Psychology*, 26, pp. 13–24.

Ruiter, R.A.C., Verplanken, B., Kok, G. and Werrij, M.Q. (2003) The role of coping appraisal in reactions to fear appeals: do we need threat information? *Journal of Health Psychology*, 8, pp. 465–474.

Ryan, R.M. and Connell, J.P. (1989) Perceived locus of causality and internalisation: examining reasons for acting in two domains. *Journal of Personality and Social Psychology*, 57, pp. 749–761.

Ryan, R.M. and Deci, E.L. (1989) Bridging the traditions of task/ego involvement and intrinsic/extrinsic motivation: a comment on Butler (1987). *Journal of Educational Psychology*, 81, pp. 265–268.

(2000) Intrinsic and extrinsic motivations: classic definitions and new directions. *Contemporary Educational Psychology*, 25, pp. 54–67.

Sak, U. (2004) A synthesis of research on psychological types of gifted adolescents. *Journal of Secondary Gifted Education*, 15, pp. 70–79.

Sakai, H. and Andow, K. (1980) Attribution of personal responsibility and dissonance reduction. *Japanese Psychological Research*, 22, pp. 32–41.

Santacroce, S.J. and Lee, Y.L. (2006) Uncertainty, posttraumatic stress, and health behaviour in young adult childhood cancer survivors. *Nursing Research*, 55, pp. 259–266.

Saqib, N.U. (2006) The effects of involvement, time, and vividness on consumers' value judgments: a test of prospect theory. *Dissertation Abstracts International: Section A: Humanities and Social Sciences*, 66 (10–A).

Saunders, D. (1989) *Type Differentiation Indicator Manual: A Scoring System for Form J of the Myers-Briggs Type Indicator*. Palo Alto, CA: Consulting Psychologists Press.

Scandell, D.J. and Wlazelek, B. (2002) A validation study of the AIDS Health Belief Scale. *Canadian Journal of Human Sexuality*, 11, pp. 41–49.

Schachter, S. and Singer, J.E. (1962) Cognitive, social and physiological determinants of emotional states. *Psychological Review*, 69, pp. 379–399.

Scheffels, J. and Lund, K.E. (2005) Occasional smoking in adolescence: constructing an identity of control. *Journal of Youth Studies*, 4, pp. 445–460.

Schensul, J.J. (1998–9) Learning about sexual meaning and decision-making from urban adolescents. *International Quarterly of Community Health Education*, 18, pp. 29–48.

Schinnerer, J.L. (2001) Influences on optimistic bias and risk-taking in adolescents and adults. *Dissertation Abstracts International: Section B: The Sciences and Engineering*, 62 (1–B).

Schmalz, D.L., Deane, G.D., Birch, L.L. and Davison, K.K. (2007) A longitudinal assessment of the links between physical activity and self-esteem in early adolescent non-Hispanic females. *Journal of Adolescent Health*, 41, pp. 559–565.

Schuman, S.H. and Polkowski, J. (1975) Drug and risk perceptions of ninth-grade students: sex differences and similarities. *Community Mental Health Journal*, 11, pp. 184–194.

Schwarzer, R. and Fuchs, R. (1996) Self-efficacy and health behaviours. In M. Conner and P. Norman (eds.) *Predicting Health Behaviour* (pp. 163–196). Buckingham: Open University Press.

Scott, R.L. (1996) The adolescent's decision to use a condom for the prevention of HIV/ AIDS and other STDs: an examination of gender and the cognitive determinants of decision making. *Dissertation Abstracts International: Section A: Humanities and Social Sciences*, 57 (3–A).

Seginer, R. and Somech, A. (2000) In the eyes of the beholder: how adolescents, teachers and school counsellors construct adolescent images. *Social Psychology of Education*, 4, pp. 139–157.

Serpell, L., Neiderman, M., Emanuelli, F., Howarth, E. and Lask, B. (2003) The use of the Pros and Cons of Anorexia Nervosa (P-CAN) scale with children and adolescents. *Journal of Psychosomatic Research*, 54, pp. 567–571.

Sexton, K.A. and Dugas, M.J. (2008) The Cognitive Avoidance Questionnaire: validation of the English translation. *Journal of Anxiety Disorders*, 22, pp. 355–370.

Shannon, C., Story, M., Fulkerson, J.A. and French, S.A. (2002) Factors in the school cafeteria influencing food choices by high school students. *Journal of School Health*, 72, pp. 229–234.

Shaw, R.J. (2001) Treatment adherence in adolescents: development and psycho-pathology. *Clinical Child Psychology and Psychiatry*, 6, pp. 137–150.

Shaw, S.M., Caldwell, L.L. and Kleiber, D.A. (1996) Boredom, stress and social control in the daily activities of adolescents. *Journal of Leisure Research*, 28, pp. 274–292.

Sheeran, P. and Abraham, C. (1996) The health belief model. In M. Conner and P. Norman (eds.) *Predicting Health Behaviour* (pp. 23–61). Buckingham: Open University Press.

Sheeran, P. and Orbell, S. (1999) Augmenting the theory of planned behavior: roles for anticipated regret and descriptive norms. *Journal of Applied Social Psychology*, 29, pp. 2007–2102.

Shoda, Y., Mischel, W. and Peake, P.K. (1990) Predicting adolescent cognitive and self regulatory competencies from preschool delay of gratification. *Developmental Psychology*, 26, pp. 976–986.

Shoveller, J.A., Lovato, C.Y., Young, R.A. and Moffat, B. (2003) Exploring the development of sun-tanning behaviour: a grounded theory study of adolescents' decision making experiences with becoming a sun tanner. *International Journal of Behavioural Medicine*, 10, pp. 299–314.

Siebert, A. (1996) *The Survivor Personality*. Berkeley, CA: Perigee Publishing.

Silk, J.S., Steinberg, L. and Morris, A.S. (2003) Adolescents' emotion regulation in daily life: links to depressive symptoms and problem behaviour. *Child Development*, 74, pp. 1869–1880.

Simons-Morton, M., Bruce, B.G., Hartos, J.L., Leaf, W.A. and Preusser, D.F. (2006) Increasing parent limits on novice young drivers: cognitive mediation of the effect of persuasive messages. *Journal of Adolescent Research*, 21, pp. 83–105.

Siqueira, L., Diab, M., Bodian, C. and Rolnitzky, L. (2000) Adolescents becoming smokers: the role of stress and coping methods. *Journal of Adolescent Health*, 27, pp. 399–408.

Skaret, E., Raadal, M., Berg, E. and Kvale, G. (1998) Dental anxiety among 18-yr-olds in Norway. *European Journal of Oral Sciences*, 106, pp. 835–843.

Smekal, V. (1975) Relationship between temperament and character traits in adolescents. *Psychologia a Patopsychologia Dietata*, 10, pp. 13–30.

Smith, H.P. (1998) Motivation for change in adolescent substance abuse patients. *Dissertation Abstracts International: Section B: The Sciences and Engineering*, 59 (1–B).

Smith, K., Shanteau, J. and Johnson, P. (eds.) (2004) *Psychological Investigations of Competence in Decision Making*. Cambridge: Cambridge University Press.

Smith, K. and Stutts, M. (2003) Effects of short-term cosmetic versus long-term health fear appeals in anti-smoking advertisements on the smoking behavior of adolescents. *Journal of Consumer Behavior*, 3, pp. 157–177.

Soetens, B. and Braet, C. (2007) Information processing of food cues in overweight and normal weight adolescents. *British Journal of Health Psychology*, 12, pp. 285–304.

Somers, C.L. and Surman, A. (2004) Adolescents' perceptions of reasons for postponing sexual intercourse. *American Secondary Education*, 33, pp. 26–42.

Sowell, R.L., Murdaugh, C.L., Addy, C.L., Moneyham, L. and Tavokoli, A. (2002) Factors influencing intent to get pregnant in HIV-infected women living in the southern USA. *AIDS Care*, 14, pp. 181–191.

Spear, H.J. and Kulbok, P.A. (2001) Adolescent health behaviours and related factors: a review. *Public Health Nursing*, 18, pp. 82–93.

Spencer, L., Adams, T.B., Malone, S., Roy, L. and Yost, E. (2006) Applying the transtheoretical model to exercise: a systematic and comprehensive review of the literature. *Health Promotion Practice*, 7, pp. 428–443.

Stauber, H.Y. (1995) Living on the edge: adolescents' perceptions of danger and invulnerability. *Dissertation Abstracts International: Section B: The Sciences and Engineering*, 55 (7–B).

Steadman, L. and Quine, L. (2004) Encouraging young males to perform testicular self-examination: a simple, but effective implementation intentions intervention. *British Journal of Health Psychology*, 9, pp. 479–487.

Steinacker, A. (2006) Externalities, prospect theory, and social construction: when will Government act, what will Government do? *Social Science Quarterly*, 87, pp. 459–476.

Steinberg, L. (2007) Risk taking in adolescence: new perspectives from brain and behavioural science. *Current Directions in Psychological Science*, 16, pp. 55–59.

Steinberg, L. and Scott, E. S. (2003) Less guilty by reason of adolescence: developmental immaturity, diminished responsibility, and the juvenile death penalty. *American Psychologist*, 58, pp. 1009–1018.

Steinberg, L. and Cauffman, E. (1996) Maturity of judgement in adolescence: psychosocial factors in adolescent decision-making. *Law and Human Behaviour*, 20, pp. 249–272.

Stellefson, M., Wang, Z. and Klein, W. (2006) Effects of cognitive dissonance on intentions to change diet and physical activity among college students. Poster accepted for presentation at the Texas AandM University Educational Research Exchange Symposium, College Station, TX.

Stepp, L. S. (2002) Generation hex: stereotypes hurt today's teens. *Washington Post*, 31 January.

Stewart, J. E., Strack, S. and Graves, P. (1999) Self-efficacy, outcome expectancy, dental health value, and dental plaque. *American Journal of Health Behaviour*, 23, pp. 303–310.

Stults, D. M. and Messe, L. A. (1995) Behavioural consistency: the impact of public versus private statements of intentions. *Journal of Social Psychology*, 125, pp. 277–278.

Sturges, J. W. and Rogers, R. W. (1996) Preventive health psychology from a developmental perspective: an extension of protection motivation theory. *Health Psychology*, 15, pp. 158–166.

Subratty, A. H., Imrit, S. and Jowaheer, V. (2002) A Web-based survey on adolescents' perceptions of food. *Nutrition and Food Science*, 32, pp. 210–213.

Sundberg, N. D., Rohila, P. K. and Tyler, L. E. (1970) Values of Indian and American adolescents. *Journal of Personality and Social Psychology*, 16, pp. 374–397.

Sung, Y. S. and Kim, W. S. (1987) Research on consumer information overload: a dynamic approach. *Korean Journal of Psychology*, 6, pp. 34–50.

Suppes, P. (1993) The transcendental character of determinism. *Midwest Studies in Philosophy*, 18, pp. 242–257.

Svenson, O. and Maule, A. (1993) *Time Pressure and Stress in Human Judgement and Decision Making*. New York: Plenum Press.

Svetlak, M. and Kukleta, M. (2006) Pros and cons of smoking evaluated in Czech adolescents. *Homeostasis in Health and Disease*, 44, pp. 89–92.

Tabachnick, B. G. and Fidell, L. S. (1996) *Using Multivariate Statistics*. New York: HarperCollins.

Tan, A. L., Kendis, R. J., Fine, J. T. and Porac, J. (1977) A short measure of Eriksonian ego identity. *Journal of Personality Assessment*, 41, pp. 279–284.

Tani, F. (2001) Structure of the sense of identity in adolescents: development of the Multidimensional Ego Identity Scale (MEIS). *Japanese Journal of Education Psychology*, 49, pp. 265–273.

Tanner, J. F., Hunt, J. B. and Eppright, D. R. (1991) The protection motivation model: a normative model of fear appeals. *Journal of Marketing*, 55, pp. 36–45.

Teare, J.F., Garrett, C.R., Coughlin, D.G. and Shanahan, D.L. (1995) America's children in crisis: adolescents' requests for support from a national telephone hotline. *Journal of Applied Developmental Psychology*, 16, pp. 21–33.

Teen Help (2000–2006) Archive [online]. Jelsoft Enterprises Ltd, available from http://helplink.teenhelp.org/archive.php (accessed December 2006).

Teens Living with Cancer (2002–2006) Stories [online]. Melissa's Living Legacy Foundation, Children's Oncology Group, available from www.teenslivingwithcancer.org/home.asp (accessed March 2007).

Tilgner, L., Wertheim, E.H. and Paxton, S.J. (2004) Effect of social desirability on adolescent girls' responses to an eating disorders prevention program. *International Journal of Eating Disorders*, 35, pp. 211–216.

Tilleczek, K.C. and Hine, D.W. (2006) The meaning of smoking as health and social risk in adolescence. *Journal of Adolescence*, 29, pp. 273–287.

Tolou-Shams, M., Payne, N., Houck, C., Pugatch, D., Beausoleil, N. and Brown, L.K. (2007) HIV testing among at-risk adolescents and young adults: a prospective analysis of a community sample. *Journal of Adolescent Health*, 41, pp. 586–593.

Trierweiler, V.A. (1996) Affective, attitudinal, and decision making variables that influence adolescents' risky sexual behaviour. *Dissertation Abstracts International: Section B: The Sciences and Engineering*, 56 (9–B).

Tuakli, N., Smith, M.A. and Heaton, C. (1990) Smoking in adolescence: methods for health education and smoking cessation: a MIRNET study. *Journal of Family Practice*, 31, pp. 369–374.

Tubman, J.G., Langer, L.M. and Calderon, D.M. (2001) Coerced sexual experiences among adolescent substance abusers: a potential pathway to increased vulnerability to HIV exposure. *Child and Adolescent Social Work Journal*, 18, pp. 281–303.

Tuinstra, J., van Sonderen, F.L.P., Groothoff, J.W., van den Heuvel, W.J.A. and Post, D. (2000) Reliability, validity, and structure of the adolescent decision making questionnaire among adolescents in the Netherlands. *Personality and Individual Differences*, 28, pp. 273–285.

Turner, L.R. and Mermelstein, R. (2004) Motivation and reasons to quit: predictive validity among adolescent smokers. *American Journal of Health Behaviour*, 28, pp. 542–550.

Turner, S.L. (2007) Preparing inner-city adolescents to transition into high school. *Professional School Counseling*, 10, pp. 245–252.

Turrell, S.L. (2005). Capacity to consent to treatment in adolescents with anorexia nervosa. *Dissertation Abstracts International: Section B: The Sciences and Engineering*, 65 (10–B).

Tversky, A. and Kahneman, D. (1974) Judgement under uncertainty. *Science*, 185, pp. 1124–1130.

Tyas, S.L. and Pederson, L.L. (1998) Psychosocial factors related to adolescent smoking: a critical review of the literature. *Tobacco Control*, 7, pp. 409–420.

Udry, E., Shelbourne, K.D. and Gray, T. (2003) Psychological readiness for anterior cruciate ligament surgery: describing and comparing the adolescent and adult experiences. *Journal of Athletic Training*, 38, pp. 167–171.

Umeh, K. (1998a) Coping styles as moderators of cognition–decision relations amongst adolescents. *Psychology and Health*, 13, pp. 987–1003.

(1998b) A conflict-theory approach to understanding adolescents' health behaviour. PhD thesis, University of Leicester.

(2002) Should health behaviour models incorporate maladaptive coping mechanisms? *Health Psychology Update*, 11, pp. 30–35.

(2003) Social cognitions and past behaviour as predictors of behavioural intentions related to cardiovascular health. *Journal of Applied Social Psychology*, 33, pp. 1417–1436.

(2004) Cognitive appraisals, maladaptive coping, and past behaviour in protection motivation. *Psychology and Health*, 19, pp. 719–735.

(2008) The theory of compliant detraction. Unpublished manuscript, Liverpool John Moores University.

Umeh, K. and Crabtree, L. (2006) Is fruit and vegetable intake in children a rationalistic choice? *British Food Journal*, 108, pp. 859–874.

Umeh, K. and Griffiths, M. (2001) Adolescent smoking: behavioural risk factors and health beliefs. *Education and Health*, 19, pp. 31–33.

Underwood, M.K. (1998) Competence in sexual decision-making in African American female adolescents: the role of peer relations and future plans. In A. Colby, J.B. James and D. Hart (eds.) *Competence and Character through Life* (pp. 57–88). Chicago: University of Chicago Press.

Ungar, M.T. (2000) The myth of peer pressure. *Adolescence*, 35, pp. 167–180.

Useem, M., Cook, J. and Sutton, L. (2005) Developing leaders for decision making under stress: Wildland Firefighters in the South Canyon Fire and its aftermath. *Academy of Management Learning and Education*, 4, pp. 461–485.

van Beurden, E., Zask, A., Brooks, L. and Dight, R. (2005) Heavy episodic drinking and sensation-seeking in adolescents as predictors of harmful driving and celebrating behaviours: implications for prevention. *Journal of Adolescent Health*, 37, pp. 37–43.

van der Pligt, J. (1994) Risk appraisal and health behaviour. In D.R. Rutter and L. Quine (eds.) *Social Psychology and Health: European Perspectives* (pp. 131–151). Aldershot: Avebury.

van der Velde, F.W., Hooykaas, C. and van der Pligt, J. (1992) Risk perception and behaviour: pessimism, realism and optimism about AIDS-related health behaviour. *Psychology and Health*, 6, pp. 23–38.

van der Velde, F.W. and van der Pligt, J. (1991). AIDS-related health behaviour: coping, protection, motivation, and previous behavior. *Journal of Behavioral Medicine*, 14, pp. 429–451.

van Empelen, P. and Kok, G. (2006) Condom use in steady and casual sexual relationships: planning, preparation and willingness to take risks among adolescents. *Psychology and Health*, 21, pp. 165–181.

van Inwagen, P. (1983) *An Essay on Free Will*. Oxford: Clarendon Press.

van Osch, S.M.C., van den Hout, W.B. and Stiggelbout, A.M. (2006) Exploring the reference point in prospect theory: gambles for length of life. *Medical Decision Making*, 26, pp. 338–346.

Vansteenkiste, M., Matos, L., Lens, W. and Soenens, B. (2007) Understanding the impact of intrinsic versus extrinsic goal framing on exercise performance. The conflicting role of task and ego involvement. *Psychology of Sports and Exercise*, 8, pp. 771–794.

Vansteenkiste, M., Simons, J., Soenens, B. and Lens, W. (2004) How to become a persevering exerciser: the importance of providing a clear, future goal in an autonomy-supportive way. *Journal of Sport and Exercise Psychology*, 26, pp. 232–249.

van Wel, F. and Knobbout, J. (1998) Adolescents and fear appeals. *International Journal of Adolescence and Youth*, 7, pp. 121–135.

Vega, W.A., Chen, K.W. and Williams, J. (2007) Smoking, drugs, and other behavioural health problems among multiethnic adolescents in the NHSDA. *Addictive Behaviours*, 32, pp. 1949–1956.

Vika, M., Raadal, M., Skaret, E. and Kvale, G. (2006) Dental and medical injections: prevalence of self-reported problems among 18-yr-old subjects in Norway. *European Journal of Oral Sciences*, 114, pp. 122–127.

Viney, W. (1990) The tempering effect of determinism in the legal system: a response to Rychlak and Rychlak. *New Ideas in Psychology*, 8, pp. 31–42.

Viney, W. and King, D.B. (2003) *History of Psychology: Ideas and Context* (third edition). Boston: Allyn and Bacon.

Voice of America News (2007) No need to freak out about some idioms, even in more formal contexts [online]. Voice of America News, available from www.voanews.com/specialenglish/archive/2007-09/2007-09-18-voa2.cfm> (accessed 3 March 2008).

Walker, D.M., Torres, P., Gutierrez, J.P., Flemming, K. and Bertozzi, S.M. (2004) Emergency contraception use is correlated with increased condom use among adolescents: results from Mexico. *Journal of Adolescent Health*, 35, pp. 329–334.

Walters, K.S. (2001) Emotional, behavioural, and interpersonal assessment of social phobia in adolescents. *Dissertation Abstracts International: Section B: The Sciences and Engineering*, 61 (7–B).

Wang, S.L., Charron-Prochownik, D., Sereika, S.M., Siminerio, L. and Kim, Y. (2006) Comparing three theories in predicting reproductive health behavioural intention in adolescent women with diabetes. *Paediatric Diabetes*, 7, pp. 108–115.

Washburn-Ormachea, J.M., Hillman, S.B. and Sawilowsky, S.S. (2004) Gender and gender-role orientation differences on adolescents' coping with peer stressors. *Journal of Youth and Adolescence*, 33, pp. 31–40.

Watson, M.C., Cleland, J., Inch, J., Bond, C.M. and Francis, J. (2007) Theory-based communication skills training for medicine counter assistants to improve consultations for non-prescription medicines. *Medical Education*, 41, pp. 450–459.

Weems, C.F. (2000) Anxiety sensitivity in children and the development of panic and anxiety in adolescents: a prospective study. *Dissertation Abstracts International: Section B: The Sciences and Engineering*, 60 (9–B).

Wegner, D.M. (1989). *White Bears and Other Unwanted Thoughts: Suppression, Obsession, and the Psychology of Mental Control*. London: The Guilford Press.

    (1994). Ironic processes of mental control. *Psychological Review*, 101, pp. 34–52.

Weinstein, N.D. (1993) Testing four competing theories of health-protective behavior. *Health Psychology*, 12, pp. 324–333.

Weir, M. (1984) *Goal-directed Behaviour*. Newark, NJ: Gordon and Breach.

Weiss, J.W., and Garbanati, J.A. (2006) Effects of acculturation and social norms on adolescent smoking among Asian-American subgroups. *Journal of Ethnicity in Substance Abuse*, 5, pp. 75–90.

Welch, N. (2006) The role of anticipatory affect in risky decision-making. *Dissertation Abstracts International: Section B: The Sciences and Engineering*, 66 (10–B).

Werch, C.E., Bian, H., Moore, M.J., Ames, S., DiClemente, C.C. and Weiler, R.M. (2007) Brief multiple behaviour interventions in a college student health care clinic. *Journal of Adolescent Health*, 41, pp. 577–585.

Westenberg, P.M., Drewes, M.J., Goedhart, A.W., Siebelink, B.M. and Treffers, P.D.A. (2004) A developmental analysis of self-reported fears in late childhood through mid adolescence: social-evaluative fears on the rise? *Journal of Child Psychology and Psychiatry*, 45, pp. 481–495.

Wetzel, N. and Schroger, E. (2007) Cognitive control of involuntary attention and distraction in children and adolescents. *Brain Research*, 1155, pp. 134–146.

Whalen, C.K., Henker, B., O'Neil, R., Hollingshead, J., Holman, A. and Moore, B. (1994) Optimism in children's judgements of health and environmental risks. *Health Psychology*, 13, pp. 319–325.

White, J.L., Moffitt, T.E., Caspi, A., Bartusch, D.J., Needles, D.J. and Stouthamer-Loeber, M. (1994) Measuring impulsivity and examining its relationship to delinquency. *Journal of Abnormal Psychology*, 103, pp. 192–205.

White, N., Augoustinos, M. and Taplin, J. (2007) Parental responsibility for the illicit acts of their children: effects of age, type and severity of offence. *Australian Journal of Psychology*, 59, pp. 43–50.

Whiteside, S.P. and Lynam, D.R. (2001) The Five-Factor Model and impulsivity: using a structural model of personality to understand impulsivity. *Personality and Individual Differences*, 30, pp. 669–689.

WHO (2000) *Health and Health Behaviour among Young People*. Copenhagen: World Health Organization.

Williams, W.I. (2006) Complex trauma: approaches to theory and treatment. *Journal of Loss and Trauma*, 11, pp. 321–335.

Wills, T.A., Isasi, C.R., Mendoza, D. and Ainette, M.G. (2007) Self-control constructs related to measures of dietary intake and physical activity in adolescents. *Journal of Adolescent Health*, 41, pp. 551–558.

Wilson, D.J., Lavelle, S. and Hood, R. (1990) Health knowledge and beliefs as predictors of intended condom use among Zimbabwean adolescents in probation/remand homes. *AIDS Care*, 2, pp. 267–274.

Wilson, D.K., Friend, R., Teasley, N., Green, S., Reaves, I.L. and Sica, D.A. (2002) Motivational versus social cognitive interventions for promoting fruit and vegetable intake and physical activity in African American adolescents. *Annals of Behavioural Medicine*, 24, pp. 310–319.

Wilson, D.K., Griffin, S., Saunders, R.P., Evans, A., Mixon, G., Wright, M., Beasley, A., Umstattd, M.R., Lattimore, D., Watts, A. and Freelove, J. (2006) Formative evaluation of a motivational intervention for increasing physical activity in underserved youth. *Evaluation and Program Planning*, 29, pp. 260–268.

Wilson, F. (1990) *Psychological Analysis and the Philosophy of John Stuart Mill*, Toronto: University of Toronto Press.

Wilson, G.S., Pritchard, M.E. and Revalee, B. (2005) Individual differences in adolescent health symptoms: the effects of gender and coping. *Journal of Adolescence*, 28, pp. 369–379.

Wilson, K.A. and Hayward, C. (2005) A prospective evaluation of agoraphobia and depression symptoms following panic attacks in a community sample of adolescents. *Journal of Anxiety Disorders*, 19, pp. 87–103.

—— (2006) Unique contributions of anxiety sensitivity to avoidance: a prospective study in adolescents. *Behaviour Research and Therapy*, 44, pp. 601–609.

Wiltshire, S., Amos, A., Haw, S. and McNeill, A. (2005) Image, context, and transition: smoking in mid-to-late adolescence. *Journal of Adolescence*, 28, pp. 603–617.

Windich, B.A., Sjoberg, I., Dale, J.C., Eshelman, D. and Guzzetta, C.E. (2007) Effects of distraction on pain, fear, and distress during venous port access and venipuncture in children and adolescents. *Journal of Pediatric Oncology Nursing*, 24, pp. 8–19.

Witte, K. and Allen, M. (2000) A meta-analysis of fear appeals: implications for effective public health campaigns. *Health Education and Behaviour*, 27, pp. 591–615.

Wong, K.F.E. and Kwong, J.Y.Y. (2005) Between-individual comparisons in performance evaluation: a perspective from prospect theory. *Journal of Applied Psychology*, 90, pp. 284–294.

Wood, S.L. and Lynch, J.G. (2002) Prior knowledge and complacency in new product learning. *Journal of Consumer Research*, 29, pp. 416–426.

Wu, C. and Shaffer, D.R. (1987) Susceptibility to persuasive appeals as a function of source credibility and prior experience with the attitude object. *Journal of Personality and Social Psychology*, 52, pp. 677–688.

Wulfert, E., Block, J.A., Santa Ana, E., Rodriguez, M.L. and Colsman, M. (2002) Delay of gratification: impulsive choices and problem behaviours in early and late adolescence. *Journal of Personality*, 70, pp. 533–552.

Wulfert, E., Safren, S.A., Brown, I. and Wan, C.K. (1999) Cognitive, behavioral, and personality correlates of HIV-positive persons' unsafe sexual behavior. *Journal of Applied Social Psychology*, 29, pp. 223–244.

Yeh, Y. (2006) Applicability of the transtheoretical model in weight management in an adolescent population in Taiwan. *Dissertation Abstracts International: Section B: The Sciences and Engineering*, 67 (2–B).

Young, R.McD., Conner, J.P., Ricciardelli, L.A. and Saunders, J.B. (2005) The role of alcohol expectancy and drinking refusal self-efficacy beliefs in university student drinking. *Alcohol and Alcoholism*, 41, pp. 70–75.

Youth Smoking Prevention (2005) *Peer Pressure and Smoking*. Richmond, VA: Phillip Morris USA, Youth Smoking Prevention.

Zanini, D.S., Forns, M. and Kirchner, T. (2005) Coping responses and problem appraisal in Spanish adolescents. *Perceptual and Motor Skills*, 100, pp. 153–166.

Zanna, M.P. (1982) *Consistency in Social Behaviour*. Hillsdale, NJ: Lawrence Erlbaum.

Zebracki, K. and Drotar, D. (2004) Outcome expectancy and self-efficacy in adolescent asthma self-management. *Children's Health Care*, 33, pp. 133–149.

Zubenko, W. and Capozzoli, J. (eds.) (2002) *Children and Disasters: A Practical Guide to Recovery*. London: Oxford University Press.

Zuckerman, M., Eysenck, S.B. and Eysenck, H.J. (1978) Sensation seeking in England and America: cross-cultural, age, and sex comparisons. *Journal of Consulting and Clinical Psychology*, 46, pp. 139–149.

Zuckerman, V.H. (1999) Social support and decision making in hospitalised adolescents. *Dissertation Abstracts International: Section B: The Sciences and Engineering*, 59 (9–B).

Zwaanswijk, M., Verhaak, P.F.M., Bensing, J.M., van der Ende, J. and Verhulst, F.C. (2003) Help seeking for emotional and behavioural problems in children and adolescents: a review of recent literature. *European Child and Adolescent Psychiatry*, 12, pp. 153–161.

Zwaanswijk, M., Verhaak, P.F.M, van der Ende, J., Bensing, J.M. and Verhulst, F.C. (2006) Change in children's emotional and behavioural problems over a one-year period: associations with parental problem recognition and service use. *European Child and Adolescent Psychiatry*, 15, pp. 127–131.

Zwane, I.T., Mngadi, P.T. and Nxumalo, M.P. (2004) Adolescents' views on decision making regarding risky sexual behaviour. *International Nursing Review*, 51, pp. 15–22.

Index

Locators for tables appear in **bold**
Locators for figures appear in *italics*

Academic Search Premier database 34
addiction 63; *see also* substance use
adolescent/s, decision making 26, 28,
    29–33; *see also* health behaviour
  avoidance 30
  childhood tactics 197–198, 209
  cognitive ability 221
  complacency 30
  conflict-theory 21
  decision making styles 39
  definitions 28–29
  emotion driven decision making 35
  feedback 86–88
  feeling grown-up 89
  free will 46–47
  importance 34–36, 38, 39
  literature 34
  panic 30, 233
  pregnancy 35
  rationality 6, 13, 17, 31, 35, **35**
  relevance of adult studies 37
  vigilance 30
Adolescent Decision Making Questionnaire
    (ADMQ) 26
advice seeking 97–99, 147–149
age differences; *see also* developmental
    psychology
  avoidance 197–198, 204–206, 209
  changeability 246, 253
  decision making 7
  fear 117–118
  health warnings 152
  impulsivity 234–235
  personality traits 246
  reality constraints 81
AIDS/HIV 76–77, 159, 166
  avoidance 206, 207–208
  complacency 230
  panic 226–227
  previous experience 252
  short/long-term effects 170, 234

alcohol use; *see also* substance use
  avoidance 190
  cognitive dissonance theory 128
  competence 177
  family of curves model 109
  intrinsic goals 90
  social anxiety 113
  thoughtlessness 215
allergy 126, 159, 188–189
Allport, Gordon 47
ambivalence, decision making 227–229, *228*
anchoring heuristic 9
anecdotal evidence xv
animals, fear of 97
anorexia 176, 207; *see also* dieting; eating disorders
antecedents, behavioural 20, 193–194, 232–234
anticipatory regret 124, 132–133, *133*, 142
antisocial behaviour 31
anxiety; *see also* fear
  consistency 141
  definitions 116
  disapproval 76
  goals 68, 75–77
  health 76–77, 97, 99, 100–101
  image/appearance 76
  panic 222
  sensitivity 115, 232, 233
  social anxiety 96, 99, *100*, 113
  thought substitution 188
  thought suppression 186–187
  worst case scenario comparisons 191
appearance *74*, 184, 205, 214–215, 223; *see also*
    image
appendicitis 206
approach/avoidance goals 69, 70
argument/discussion 151–152, 215–216
arousal seeking *see* sensation seeking
asking advice 97–99, 147–149
asthma 160–161, 173, 221, 250
Atkins diet 127
attachment 232

attention 86
attitude–behaviour correspondence (intention–
    behaviour correspondence) 123–125, *125*
attractiveness heuristic 9
availability heuristic 9
avoidance 7, 36, 38, 181–182, **185–186, 191,**
    195–196, 208–209
    adolescents 30
    age/gender differences 204–206, *205*, 209
    anorexia 207
    attitudes to 182–183
    behavioural consequences 200–201
    buck-passing **185–186**, 202, 204, 208
    childhood tactic 197–198, 209
    competence 198–200
    conflict-theory 19, 20, 21, 110, 194–195
    contextual issues 196, 206
    deadline pressures 20
    decision making 182
    distraction 184, **185–186**, 188–189
    effectiveness 206–208
    emotional discharge/expression **185–186**
    facets 184–186, **185–186**
    and fear 111, 112, 115
    health behaviour 209
    health behaviours susceptible 201–202
    health warnings 152
    measuring 26
    media spotlight 207
    multidimensionality/multifaceted nature 184, 209
    overcoming 253
    parental input 202–203
    person-relative-to-event perspective 195–196
    prevalence 192–193, *193*
    psychological antecedents 193–194
    purpose 183–184
    qualitative research methodology 192–193
    research spotlight 199
    stability over time 253
    thought substitution 184, **185–186**, 188
    thought suppression 184, **185–186**, 186–187, *187*
    threatening stimulus avoidance 184, **185–186,**
        189–190
    transforming mental images 184, **185–186**, 190
    wishful thinking **185–186**
    worst case scenario comparisons 190–192, **191**

behavioural antecedents 20, 193–194, 232–234
bias, decision making 7–8, 27; *see also* social
    desirability bias
bicycle riding 31
Blair Witch Project 95, 101
blood pressure medication 161
boredom susceptibility 218
boundary setting 57, 150, 160, 179
brain tumour 140–141
breast cancer 111, 151–152

buck-passing 20, 110; *see also* avoidance;
    parental input
    adolescents 30–31
    and avoidance **185–186**, 202, 204, 208
    consistency 120, 123, 139–140, 143
bulimia *see* anorexia; dieting; eating disorders
Bush, President George W. 55

cancer 55, 111, 151–152, 230, 234
cannabis use 190–191; *see also* substance use
cardiovascular disease 159, 161, 170, 230, 234
cartoon information presentation 151
causality 45–46; *see also* determinism
    avoidance 115
    chains of/first cause 48–49, 50
    fear 107
    free will 48–50
    knowledge/behavioural 61–62
    multiple 50
CDT *see* compliant detraction theory
certainty/uncertainty 14–16, 55, 62
chains of causality 48–49, 50
change/stability in decision making 18, 238–240,
        253–254; *see also* conflict-theory;
        consistency; transtheoretical model of
        behaviour change
    age/gender differences 246, 253
    developmental factors 247–248, 254
    facets 240–241
    genetic/environmental constraints 244–245, 247
    group behaviour 241–242, *242*
    identity 252–253, 254
    impulsivity 241
    individual behaviour 242–244, *244*
    labelling 249
    over time 240
    personality traits 242, 243–244
    predictability 245–246, 253
    previous experience 250–252, *251*, 254
    profiles 246–247
    relative differences 246
    resistance to change 251
    social learning 247
    stable/unstable traits 248–249
childhood tactics 197–198, 209
children/adolescents *see* adolescents
choice, research spotlight 57; *see also* decision making
cigarettes *see* smoking behaviour
clinical populations 35
coercion 130–132, 142
cognition, need for 151–152, 215–216
cognitive ability 44, 221
cognitive appraisals 24
cognitive avoidance *see* avoidance
Cognitive Avoidance Questionnaire 186
cognitive dissonance theory 121–123, *122, 123*,
    128–129

cognitive incentives 125–126
commitment, decision making process 4, 176
competence, decision making 144–145,
    178–179; *see also* risk–benefit evaluations
  avoidance 198–200
  behavioural consequences 175–177
  boundary setting 150
  commitment/implementation of decisions 176
  compliant detraction theory 161, 163–166, *166*, *167*
  confidence 169–170, 179
  contextual issues 171–173, 178
  control over circumstances 177
  definitions 145–146
  health behaviour 175–176, 179
  implementing decisions 173–175
  information seeking 147–149
  options/alternatives 149–150
  over-familiarity 157–159
  past experience 172, 177, 179
  previous experience 179
  problem recognition 146–147
  rationality 157
  research spotlight 158
  risk seeking/risk aversion 177–178
  stress 170–171, 179
  working out the best option 159–160
complacency, adolescents' 30, 230
  conflict-theory 19, 20
  measuring use 26
  and panic 230–232
compliant detraction theory (CDT) 160–161,
    162–164, *167*, 179
  asthma 160–161
  basic tenets 162
  competence at decision making 161, 163–166,
    166, *167*
  fear 167
  gender differences 167
  past experience 166
  real world situations 166–169
  reluctant compliance 161, *166*
  risk seeking/risk aversion 178
conditioning 141
condom use 44, 90, *168*, **191**, 206,
    207–208; *see also* AIDS/HIV; sexual
    behaviour
confidence 169–170, 179; *see also* self-confidence
conflicts of interest 194
conflict-theory 11, 17–18, *19*, 38, 110
  avoidance 19, 20, 21, 110, 194–195
  children/adolescents 21
  complacency 19, 20
  decision making styles 25
  limitations 21–22
  panic 19, 20, 21
  personality traits/situational
    factors 27

psychological antecedents 20
  real world applications 21
  research evidence 21–22
  smoking behaviour 110, 194–195
  vigilance 18–19, 20, 21
conscientiousness 124
consistency 120–121, *123*, 141–143; *see also*
    change/stability in decision making
  anticipatory regret 132–133, *133*, 142
  anxiety reduction 141
  buck-passing 120, 139–140, 143
  coercion 130–132, 142
  cognitive dissonance theory 121–123, *122*, *123*
  cognitive incentives 125–126
  convoluted information 127
  craving 121, 141, 142
  decision making strategy 122
  denial 120, 138, 139, 143
  detrimental behaviour 137, 142
  emotional incentives 128–129
  influence of past experience 129–130, *130*, 142
  information overload 127
  intention–behaviour correspondence
    123–125, *125*
  naivety/inexperience 129
  negative consequences 140–141
  public commitment/going public *133*,
    134–135, *135*, 143
  reducing inconsistency 138–140
  research spotlight 139
  social desirability bias 136–137,
    137, 142
contextual issues 27
  activity type 90
  avoidance 196, 206
  competence 171–173, 178
  family circumstances 196
  fundamental attribution error 8
  situational interpretation of fear 116
  social constraints on free will 60
contraception 153–155, 177; *see also* condom use;
    pregnancy; sexual behaviour
control over circumstances 177
coping styles 111, 116–117
cost–benefit *see* risk–benefit evaluations
criminal behaviour 54
cultural comparisons, free will 47, *48*, 55
curiosity 89

danger fears 72, 96, 114, 175
dangerous games 31
databases 34
deadline pressures 5, 10; *see also* decision making
    as event
  avoidance 20
  emergency decisions 169, 215, 220
  impulsivity 220–221

panic 214, 225, *226*
    sense of urgency 214–215
death fears 72, 96, 114, 175
decision implementation 4, 176
    competence 173–175
    social support 167, 172, 173, 174–175
decision making xiii–xiv
    and avoidance 182
    bias 7–8
    definitions 2–3, 38
    emotion driven 3, 13, 32, 35, **35**; *see also*
        conflict-theory
    as event 2, 4–5
    and fear 98–99, 112, 113, 116,
        117, 119
    heuristics 7, 8–10, *10*, 38, 160
    and impulsivity 223
    justifications 24
    multifaceted nature 3, 38
    and panic *232*
    perspectives 2
    planning 124
    process 2, 3–4, 38
    and reassurance 103
    sexual behaviour 34–35, 102
    short/long-term effects 170–171
    single-goal 89–91
    smoking behaviour *10*, 100–101, 103
    snap decisions 5
    social disapproval fears 99
    steps 145
    styles *see* decision making styles
    substance use 106
    triggers 176
Decision Making Questionnaire (DMQ) 26, 32,
        38, 157
    avoidance 183, 200, 202
    avoidance strategies 192
    impulsivity 234
decision making styles 25–26, *33*
    conflict-theory 25
    consistency 122
    goals 83, 92
    personality traits 27, 240–241
    preference 25, 32
decisional balance 11, 22–23, 24, 152–153,
        155–156, *156*; *see also* transtheoretical model
        of behaviour change
Decisional Balance Inventory 153
defensive avoidance *see* avoidance
defensive responses to fear 108–110, 119; *see also*
        avoidance; conflict-theory
definitions
    competence at decision making 145–146
    fear 116
    health behaviour 27–28, 38, 39
delayed gratification 219

delinquent behaviour 31
demographics *see* age differences; gender
        differences
denial 117, 120, 138, 139, 143, 197; *see also*
        avoidance
dental health 105, 108, 112
depression 200
descriptive models *see* conflict-theory
determinism 41–42, 64–65; *see also* causality;
        free will
    historical dominance 42–43
    personal responsibility 43–44, 47, 53
    philosophy of 47
    psychology 42
    scientific prediction 45–46, 47, 53, 58
detrimental behaviour *see* risk taking behaviour
developmental psychology 37–38, 247–248,
        254; *see also* age differences
diabetes 34, 35
dieting 31; *see also* eating behaviour; eating
        disorders; obesity
    Atkins diet 127
    avoidance 193
    cognitive incentives 126
    compliant detraction theory (CDT) *168*
    consistency 136–137
    convoluted information 127
    identification 82
    information overload 127
    information seeking 149
    panic 224
    previous experience 250
    public commitment/going public
        134–135
    risk–benefit evaluations 155
    single-goal decision making 91
    thought suppression 186–187
diminishing returns 109
disappointment 72
disapproval *see* social disapproval
discussion/argument 151–152, 215–216
disinhibition 218
distraction 184, **185–186**, 188–189
drive-reduction model 102–103, *102*, 107
drug use *see* substance use

eating behaviour; *see also* dieting; eating disorders
    buck-passing 140
    competence 177
    contextual issues 172–173
    eating disorders 98–99
    free will 44, 56
    freedom of choice 57
    gender differences 83, 84–85
    goal setting theory 71
    habit, role of 63–64
    health beliefs 52

eating behaviour (cont.)
  influence of past experience 129–130
  information seeking 150
  parental input 202–203
  personal responsibility 53–54
  previous experience 129–130, 242–243, *251*
  resistance to change 251
  short/long-term effects 171
eating disorders 98–99; *see also* dieting; eating
    behaviour
  anorexia 176, 207
  buck-passing 203; *see also* avoidance
  change/stability in decision making
    242–243, *251*
  impaired thinking 226
  panic 232
  sense of urgency 214
  worst case scenario comparisons **191**
economic constraints 51
effort heuristic 9
ego identity 252
ego/task involvement dichotomy 69, 92
emergency decisions 169, 214–215, 220; *see also*
    deadline pressures
emotion driven decision making 3, 13, 32, 35,
    35; *see also* conflict-theory
emotion driven heuristic 9
emotional expression **185–186**
emotional incentives 128–129
enjoyment seeking 89, 90
environmental constraints 244–245, 247; *see also*
    nature–nurture issue
exercise *see* physical activity 31
expected utility theory *see* subjective expected
    utility
experience *see* previous experience/prior
    knowledge; *see also* over-familiarity
extrinsic goals *see* intrinsic/extrinsic goals

facilitating forces 5
facilitating responses 109–110
FAE *see* fundamental attribution error
familiarity heuristic 9
family circumstances 196
family of curves model 109–110
fatalism 111
fear 94–95, **106**, 118–119; *see also* anxiety
  advice seeking 97–99
  age differences 117–118
  avoidance 111, 112, 115
  causality 107
  compliant detraction theory (CDT) 167
  cost–benefits 104–105
  decision making impact 98–99, 112, 113, 116,
    117, 119
  defensive responses 108–110, 119; *see also*
    conflict-theory

definitions 116
drive reduction model 102–103, *102,*
    103, 107
driving force 101–103, 104–105
freaking out 114–115
gender differences 117–118
goals 88–89, 91, 92
goal setting theory 105
initial reactions 97–99, *99*
managing 102, 116–117
mental rehearsal 101
multiple sources of 96–97, 118, 119
parallel response model 72
persistent 115–117
phobias 112–114, *113,* 119, 232; *see also* social
    phobia
potential outcome 104–105
pregnancy 117, 118
previous failure *106,* 107–108
reassurance 103, 114, 118, 119
and risk taking behaviour 105–107,
    106, **106**
short/long-term 99–101, *99*
significance of 95–96
situational interpretation 116
smoking behaviour 89, **106**
subjective expected utility (SEU) 119
teenage magazines, fear references 97
Fear Survey Schedule for Children-Revised
    (FSSC-R) 96
feedback
  children and adolescents 86–88
  and goal attainment 87
  goals *74,* 85–88, *88,* 91
  goal setting theory 85
  physical activity 86
  research spotlight 87
  sexual behaviour 85, 86
  single-goal decision making 91
  smoking behaviour 85
feeling-of-knowing 126, 157; *see also*
    over-familiarity
force field of decision making 5
framing 13–14, 178
freaking out 114–115, 223
free will 41, 43, 46–47, 49, 61; *see also* determinism
  adolescent health behaviour 46–47
  boundaries 57
  causality 48–50
  cognitive ability 44
  cultural comparisons 47, *48,* 55
  eating behaviour 44, 56
  empirical value 58–59
  exercising *49,* 55–58, *61*
  extreme position 54
  habit, role of 63–64
  health behaviour 64–65

health related scenarios 62–63
media spotlights 51, 55
number of options 57
personal responsibility 43–44, 53–55
risk taking behaviour *49*, 60–62
scientific prediction 50–53, 58–59
sexual behaviour 56, 57–58
smoking behaviour 47, 56
social constraints 60
substance use 43
witch-hunts 43
freedom of choice 40–41, 57, 64–65; *see also*
    determinism; free will
Freud, Sigmund 81, 103, 141, 197
fun seeking 89, 90
fundamental attribution error (FAE) 8, 43

gain–loss appraisals 22, 23–25
gang membership 175
gender differences *33*
    avoidance 204–206, *205*
    changeability 246, 253
    compliant detraction theory 167
    eating behaviour 83, 84–85
    fear 117–118
    goals 83–85, *85*
    impulsivity 234–235
    personality traits 246
    physical appearance 205
    pregnancy fears 205
    sexual behaviour 84
    smoking behaviour 84, 101
    substance use 118
gender stereotypes 235
genetic constraints 244–245, 247; *see also* nature–
    nurture issue
goals 67–68, 69–70, *70*, 91, 92
    anxiety 68, 75–77
    approach/avoidance goals 69, 70
    cosmetic issues/personal appearance 74–85, *74, 85*
    danger/death fears 175
    decision making styles 83, 92
    fear/danger themes 88–89, 91, 92
    feedback 74, 85–88, *88*, 91
    gender differences 83–85, *85*
    health behaviour 92
    health outcomes 82–83, 92
    intrinsic/extrinsic *see* intrinsic/extrinsic goals
    mastery/performance dichotomy 69
    multiple/conflicting 82–83, 89, 92
    peer pressure 75, 83
    perceived threat 72–75
    single-goal decision making 89–91
    task/ego involvement dichotomy 69, 92
goal setting theory 68–69, 70–72
    eating behaviour 71
    fear 105

feedback 85
goals 70–72, *70*, 92
parallel response model 71–72, 73
risk–benefit evaluations 156–157
smoking behaviour 68
goal theory 69–70, *70*, 92
group behaviour 241–242, *242*
gut instinct 9

habit, role of 63–64, 141
health anxiety 76–77, 97, 99, 100–101
health behaviour, adolescents 28, 31–33; *see also*
    alcohol use; eating behaviour; reckless
    driving; sexual behaviour; smoking behaviour;
    substance use
    avoidance 199, 201–202, 209
    competence 175–176, 179
    definitions 27–28, 38, 39
    fear/anxiety 62–63
    free will 64–65
    goals 78, 92
    impulsivity 236
    model limitations 11
    panic 224, 236
    role of uncertainty 55, 62
    World Health Organization categories 31
health belief model 4, 25, 36, 51–52
health compromising/damaging behaviour *see* risk
    taking behaviour
health education 221–222
health enhancing behaviour 28, 35, 38
health outcomes 82–83, 92
health psychology 36
health warnings 152
heart disease 159, 161, 170, 230, 234
heuristics 7, 8–10, *10*, 38, 160
HIV *see* AIDS/HIV
hobgoblin of little minds 137
homosexuality 43
hopelessness 111
horror movie genre 95–96
Hume, David 46

identification, intrinsic/extrinsic goals 81–82
identity 252–253, 254
illness behaviour 28
image 74–85, *74, 76, 85*, 128; *see also* physical
    appearance; self-image
immediate/remote threats *see* short/long-term
    effects
impulsive behaviour 117, 142, 211–212, *213*,
    236; *see also* panic
    age/gender differences 234–235
    behavioural consequences 219–220, *232*
    change/stability in decision making 241
    as clever strategy 220–221, 236
    convenience 221–222

impulsive behaviour (cont.)
  deadline pressures 220–221
  decision making 223
  dimensions 212–214, 236
  emergency decisions 215
  health behaviour 236
  immediate gratification 216–218
  instant gratification 211
  media spotlight 215, 235
  need for cognition 215–216
  overcoming 253
  sensation seeking 218–219, *219*
  sense of urgency 214–215
  stereotypes, teenage 212
  thoughtlessness 215–216
Impulsive Behaviour Scale 213–214, 234
incentives 125–126, 128–129, 130; *see also* coercion
inconsistency *see* consistency
indecision 227–229
inexperience 129, 130
infertility 55
information overload 127, 156, 227, 234
information seeking 148–149, *148*, 150; *see also*
    asking advice; Internet use; risk–benefit
    information
instant gratification 211, 216–218
intention–behaviour correspondence 123–125, *125*
interfering responses 109–110
Internet use 148–149, *148*, 179
interviews, in-depth 153–155
intrinsic/extrinsic goals 77–79, **78**, 92
  activity type 90
  health outcomes 83
  identification 81–82
  integration 82
  peer pressure 82
  physical activity 79, 80
  reality constraints on intrinsic goals 81
  reasons for health behaviours 78
  relative importance 79–81
  sexual behaviour 79
  smoking behaviour 79, 80
invulnerability perception 49–50
irrational fears (phobias) 112–114, *113*, 119,
    232; *see also* social phobia

Janis, Irving 17
jargon xiv–xv
Journal of Adolescent Health 42–43
Jung, Carl 47
justifications 24

kidney transplant 173, 174, 201, 239
knowledge, health behaviour 49, 60–62, 221–222,
    240; *see also* over-familiarity; previous
    experience/prior knowledge; risk taking
    behaviour

labelling theory 249
legal responsibility 195–196
Lewin, Kurt 5
libertarians 47; *see also* free will
life changing experiences 244
literature, decision making 34
logic driven decision making 3
long/short-term effects *see* short/long-term effects

magazines, teenage 97
mastery/performance goals 69
mathematical models xv, 17, 38; *see also* prospect
    theory; subjective expected utility
MBTI (Myers Briggs Type Indicator) 32
Mean Girls 45
media spotlights
  free will 51, 55
  ignoring signs of illness 207
  impulsivity 215, 235
  opportunity, role of 6
  panic 223
  power/status effects on free will 45
  teenage magazines, fear references 97
medical treatment; *see also* dental health
  accessing 52
  avoidance 201, 203, 206
  fears 96, 188–189
  free will 44
  previous experience 250
medication use/self-medication 31
mental deliberation 4
mental images, transforming 184, **185–186**, 190
mental rehearsal 101
methodology, research 153–155, 192–193
Mill, John Stuart 46, 48–50
mistakes, learning from *see* feedback
models
  decision making 11, 22–23; *see also* conflict-
    theory
  mathematical xv, 17, 38; *see also* prospect theory,
    subjective expected utility
  transtheoretical model of behaviour change 11,
    23–25, 38, *156*
Multidimensional Ego Identity Scale
    (MEIS) 252
music, playing loud 31
Myers Briggs Type Indicator (MBTI) 32

naivety 129, 130
natural disasters 195
nature–nurture issue 244–245, 246, 247
need for cognition 151–152, 215–216
nervous disposition 115

obesity 115, 182, 250; *see also* dieting; eating
    disorders
Oliver Twist 95

One-on-One 235
oral contraceptives 153–155; *see also* pregnancy;
    sexual behaviour
over-familiarity 157–159, 214

panic 211, 222–227, 236; *see also* impulsivity
  adolescents/children 30, 233
  ambivalence 227–229, *228*, 229
  anxiety 222
  consequences 229–232, *232*
  deadline pressures 214, 225, *226*
  decision making *232*
  impaired thinking 225–227
  information overload 234
  measuring use 26
  media spotlight 223
  phobias 232
  and physical activity 230, *231*
  pregnancy 229
  previous experience 232
  psychological precursors 232–234
  reasonableness *231*
  reassurance 234
  research spotlight *231*
  in response to traffic accident 223
parallel response model 71–72, *73*, 88
parental input 202–203; *see also* buck-passing
passive smoking 108
past experience
  competence 172, 177, 179
  compliant detraction theory (CDT) 166
  consistency 129–130, *130*, 142
  eating behaviour 129–130
peer pressure 8, 37
  goals 75, 82, 83
  impulsivity 235
  single-goal decision making 91
  smoking behaviour 41, 42, 48, 50
  social phobia 114
perceived threats 72–75
performance goals 69
personal appearance 74–85, *74*, *76*, *85*, 128
personal responsibility 195–196; *see also*
    buck-passing
  criminal behaviour 54
  determinism 43–44
  eating behaviour 53–54
  free will 43–44, 53–55
  risk taking behaviour 54
  sexual behaviour 53, 55
  smoking behaviour 54
personal satisfaction *see* intrinsic/extrinsic goals
personality traits
  age/gender differences 246
  changeability 242
  changes over time 243–244
  conflict-theory 27

decision making styles 27, 240–241
developmental factors 247–248
genetic/environmental constraints
    244–245, 247
need for cognition 152
panic 232
profiles 246–247
relative differences 246
stable/unstable 248–249, 254
person-relative-to-event perspectives 195–196
pessimism 110, 111
phobias 112–114, *113*, 119, 232; *see also* social
    phobia
physical activity 31, 115
  avoidance 200, 201–202, 208
  competence 163, 177
  feedback 86
  habit, role of 63–64
  intrinsic/extrinsic goals 79, 80
  panic 230, 231
  public commitment/going public 134–135
  reasons for health behaviours 78
  short/long-term effects 171
physical appearance *74*, 184, 205, 214–215,
    223; *see also* image
Piaget, Jean 6, 37
planning decisions 124
pleasure seeking 89, 90
popularity 253
power/status 45
prediction
  and changeability 245–246, 253
  determinism 45–46
  and free will 50–53, 58–59
  teenage pregnancy 46
  variables 52–53
pregnancy/pregnancy fears 171
  adolescents 35
  avoidance 193, *204*
  fear 117, 118
  freaking out 114
  gender differences 205
  panic 229
  person-relative-to-event perspective 195
  predicting 46
  thought substitution 188
previous experience/prior knowledge 159,
    250; *see also* over-familiarity
  AIDS/HIV 252
  allergy medication 126
  asthma 250
  changeability 250–252, *251*, 254
  and competence 179
  eating behaviour 129–130, 242–243,
    250, *251*
  and fear *106*, 107–108
  panic 232

previous experience/prior knowledge (cont.)
  sexual behaviour 250
  smoking behaviour *130*
  trauma 232
Prisoner's Dilemma 134
problem recognition 4, 146–147
procrastination 20, 110, 111, 193, *204*; *see also*
    avoidance
professional psychology 36–38
pros/cons *see* risk–benefit evaluations
prospect theory 11, 13, *16*, 38
  evaluation 14–16, *16*
  framing 13–14
  limitations 16–17
  research evidence 16
protection motivation theory 4, 36,
    104, 111
proverbial anomaly *see* risk taking behaviour
psychological antecedents 20, 193–194,
    232–234
psychological constructs, validity 26
psychology
  determinism 42
  professional 36–38
  social 36–37
psychopathology 169
PsycINFO database 34
public commitment/going public *133*, 134–135,
    135, 143
punishment fears 117

qualitative research methodology 153–155,
    192–193
quantitative research methodology 153
questionnaires 22, 52

rationalisation 110
rationality 5–6, *33*; *see also* reasonableness; risk
    taking behaviour
  adolescents 13, 17, 31, 35, **35**, 36
  competence at decision making 157
  developmental psychology 37–38
  real-world situations 6, 17
real-world applications 6, 17, 21, 166–169
reality constraints 81
reasonableness 158, *231*; *see also* rationality
reassurance 103, 104, 114, 118, 119, 234; *see also*
    transforming mental images
reckless driving 31, 121, 217, 218, 222, 239
regret, anticipatory 124, 132–133, *133*, 142
religious faith 111
reluctant compliance 161, *166*
remote threats *see* short/long-term effects
representativeness heuristic 9
reproductive behaviour *see* pregnancy; sexual
    behaviour
research methodology 153–155, 192–193

research spotlight
  avoidance 199
  competence 158, 199
  consistency 139
  decision making impact of fear 112
  feedback and goal attainment 87
  maximising choice 57
  Myers Briggs Type Indicator (MBTI) 32
  panic *231*
  reasonableness 158, *231*
  reassurance 104
resistance to change 251
responsibility
  legal 195–196
  personal *see* personal responsibility
  shifting *see* buck-passing
risk aversion 177–178
risk–benefit evaluations 150, 163; *see also*
    compliant detraction theory
  decisional balance 152–153, 155–156, *156*
  fear 104–105
  goal setting 156–157
  information, using 155–157
  need for cognition 151–152
  qualitative research 153–155
  sexual behaviour 150
risk taking behaviour 28, 38, 120, 123, 177–178
  competence 163–164
  consistency 137, 142
  and fear 105–107, *106*, **106**, 109; *see also* family
      of curves model
  and free will *49*, 60–62
  knowledge of risks 60–62, 221–222, 240
  and personal responsibility 54
road traffic accidents 223; *see also* reckless driving
Rogers, R. W. 111

scarcity heuristic 9
school, changing 248
scientific prediction *see* prediction
The Scream 215
self-efficacy 24
self-esteem 128
self-harming behaviour 200
self-image 249, 252–253
self-medication 31
sensation seeking
  dimensions 218
  health behaviour 218
  impulsivity 218–219, *219*
sense of urgency 214–215; *see also* deadline
    pressures
sensitivity, anxiety 115, 232, 233
SEU *see* subjective expected utility
sexual behaviour 8, 31, **35**
  adolescents 35
  anticipatory regret 133

avoidance 193, 208
behavioural consequences 175
coercion 131
cognitive incentives 126
competence 158, 165
compliant detraction theory 165–166,
    167–169, *168*
condom use 44, 90, *168*, **191**, 206, 207–208; *see*
    also AIDS/HIV
confidence 169
decision making 34–35, 102
feedback 85, 86
free will 56, 57–58
gender differences 84
health beliefs 52
impulsivity 221
intrinsic goals 90
intrinsic/extrinsic goals 79
labelling 249
media spotlight 235
panic 226–227
personal responsibility 53, 55
power/status effects on free will 45
previous experience 250
reality constraints on intrinsic goals 81
reasons for health behaviours **78**
risk–benefit evaluations 150
sensation seeking 218
sense of urgency 214
short/long-term effects 171
worst case scenario comparisons **191**
sexually transmitted diseases (STDs) 56, 193,
    214; *see also* AIDS/HIV
shopping 235
short/long-term effects 32
    AIDS/HIV 170, 234
    cancer 234
    decision making 170–171
    eating behaviour 171
    and fear 99–101, *99*
    heart disease 234
    instant gratification 217–218
    physical activity 171
    sexual behaviour 171
    smoking behaviour 171, 217–218
sick role behaviour 28
single-goal decision making 89–91
situational factors *see* contextual issues
smoking behaviour 6
    anticipatory regret 132
    avoidance 182, 196–197, 208
    coercion 131
    cognitive dissonance theory 128
    competence 165
    compliant detraction theory 163
    conflict-theory 110, 194–195
    consistency 124–125, 128, 136, 139

decision making *10*
denial 138
fear 89, 100–101, 103, **106**
feedback 85
free will 47, 56
gender differences 84, 101
goal setting 68
habit, role of 63–64
identification 81–82
immediate gratification 216–217
impulsivity 220
information seeking 149
intention–behaviour correspondence 123–125, *125*
intrinsic/extrinsic goals 79, 80
knowledge of risks 221–222
labelling 249
panic 227
parallel response model 71
peer pressure 41, 42, 48, 50
personal responsibility 54
predicting 50
prior behaviour adherence *130*
reasons for health behaviours **78**
reassurance 103, 104
sensation seeking 218
sense of urgency 214
short/long-term effects 171, 217–218
social constraints on free will 60
thoughtlessness 215
withdrawal symptoms 107
worst case scenario comparisons **191**
snap decisions 5; *see also* decision making as event
social anxiety 96, 99, *100*, 113
social desirability bias 7, 136–137, *137*, 142,
    192, 235
social disapproval 72, 76, 117
    decision making impact 99
    fears 96, 99, 100–101
social learning theory 108, 247
social phobia 113, 114
social psychology 36–37
social transition 248, 254
spots/pimples 114
stable/unstable personality traits 248–249, 254
Star Wars 249
status 45
STDs *see* sexually transmitted diseases
stereotypes, teenage 31, 236, 239–240,
    241–242
    competence 145–146, 147, 149, 155
    gender stereotypes 235
    impulsivity 212
stress
    avoidance 206
    competence 170–171, 179
    definitions 116
    distraction 189

stroke 159
subjective expected utility (SEU) 11–13, 14, 36, 38
    fear 119
    limitations 12–13
subjectivity 7–8, *33*
submissiveness 113
substance use 31, 35; *see also* alcohol use
    addiction/habit 63
    competence 177
    decision making impact of fear 106
    decision making styles 83
    free will 43
    gender differences 118
    intrinsic goals 90
    reality constraints 81
    reasons for health behaviours 78
    sensation seeking 218
    single-goal decision making 90
    social anxiety 113
    thoughtlessness 215
    treatment 147
    worst case scenario comparisons
        190–191
suicidal feelings 147, 175
sun tanning 35

task/ego involvement dichotomy 69, 92
TAT (Thematic Apperception Test) 30
teenage magazines 97
teenagers *see* adolescents
temptations 24
Thematic Apperception Test (TAT) 30
theory of planned behaviour 4, 124
theory of reasoned action 124
thinking/thought; *see also* need for cognition
    before acting 163
    impaired 225–227

substitution 184, **185–186**, 188
    suppression 184, **185–186**, 186–187, *187*
thoughtlessness 215–216
threatening stimulus avoidance 184, **185–186**,
    189–190
thrill seeking 218
time pressure *see* deadline pressures
transforming mental images 184,
    185–186, 190
transtheoretical model of behaviour change 11,
    23–25, 38, *156*
trauma 232
triggers
    avoidance 184, **185–186**, 189–190
    decision making 176
TV/video games 31

uncertainty 14–16, **16**, 55, 62
unconscious mind 141
unknown, fear of 96
UPPS Impulsive Behaviour Scale 213–214, 234
urgency, sense of 214; *see also* deadline pressures

vacillation 227–229, *228*, 229
validity
    psychological constructs 26
    questionnaires 52
video games 31
vigilance 18–19, 20, 21, 26, 30, 36

Western culture 47, *48*, 55
wishful thinking 111, **185–186**
witch-hunts 43
withdrawal symptoms, smoking 107
World Health Organization health behaviour
        categories 31, *33*
worst case scenario comparisons 190–192, **191**